# Eat
# Right
## For
# Your
# Baby

## Also by Dr. Peter J. D'Adamo with Catherine Whitney

# DR. PETER J. D'ADAMO

## WITH CATHERINE WHITNEY

MICHAEL JOSEPH
*an imprint of*
PENGUIN BOOKS

# Eat Right For Your Baby

**THE INDIVIDUALIZED
GUIDE TO FERTILITY AND
MAXIMUM HEALTH
DURING PREGNANCY,
NURSING AND
YOUR BABY'S FIRST YEAR**

MICHAEL JOSEPH

Published by the Penguin Group

Penguin Books Ltd, 80 Strand, London WC2R 0RL, England
Penguin Putnam Inc, 375 Hudson Street, New York, New York 10014, USA
Penguin Books Australia Ltd, 250 Camberwell Road, Camberwell, Victoria 3124, Australia
Penguin Books Canada Ltd, 10 Alcorn Avenue, Toronto, Ontario, Canada M4V 3B2
Penguin Books India (P) Ltd, 11 Community Centre,
Panchsheel Park, New Delhi – 110 017, India
Penguin Books (NZ) Ltd, Cnr Rosedale and Airborne Roads,
Albany, Auckland, New Zealand
Penguin Books (South Africa) (Pty) Ltd, 24 Sturdee Avenue,
Rosebank 2196, South Africa

Penguin Books Ltd, Registered Offices: 80 Strand, London WC2R 0RL, England

www.penguin.com

First published in the United States of America by G. P. Putnam's Sons 2003
First published in Great Britain by Michael Joseph 2003

1

Copyright © Hoop-A-Joop, LLC, 2003

The moral right of the authors has been asserted

Set in 9.5/13pt Caslon 540
Printed in Great Britain by Clays Ltd, St Ives plc

A CIP catalogue record for this book is available from the British Library

ISBN 0–718–14627–1

# ACKNOWLEDGEMENTS

I AM PARTICULARLY DELIGHTED to introduce *Eat Right 4 (for) Your Baby,* a book I have wanted to write since Martha and I gave birth to our first child almost twelve years ago. Today, Martha and I are the parents of two healthy daughters. I have discovered such a deep wellspring of joy in my spirited, happy children that I feel tremendous compassion for the couples who come to me with their myriad problems—couples who are striving to attain the same experiences that have become the cornerstones of my life. With this book I am able to offer the best that naturopathic and blood type science have to offer, to guide parents-to-be through the most significant journey of their lives.

This effort has been a collaborative process, and I want to express my deep thanks to the people who have been involved in its creation.

I am most grateful to Martha Mosko D'Adamo, not only my partner in life and in parenting but also my partner in bringing the valuable wisdom about blood type to the world. Martha daily provides love, support, insight, and inspiration to all of my endeavours.

Catherine Whitney, my writer, and her partner, Paul Krafin, are invaluable word masters, who have once again captured exactly the right tone in tackling this sensitive topic. Their agent, Jane Dystel, continues to provide advice and encouragement.

I would also like to acknowledge others who have made significant contributions to this book: my colleague Bronner Handwerger, N.D., whose research and clinical abilities helped make this book comprehensive and practical; my friend Cathy Rogers, N.D., a naturopath/midwife whose compassion and understanding of the emotional and medical concerns of pregnant women has added a wonderful element to this book; and my associate Heidi Merritt, who continues to make an important contribution to the work.

My literary agent and friend, Janis Vallely, always takes time to listen and advise. Her quiet guidance and personal support make the work possible.

# Acknowledgements

Amy Hertz, my editor at Riverhead/Putnam, has been the force behind the success of all the blood type books, and she continues to guide my work with dedication and skill.

As always, I am extremely grateful to the wonderful staffs at Riverhead Books and Putnam. They have been tireless and enthusiastic, and their efforts have made it possible to continue bringing this important work to the market.

PETER J. D'ADAMO, N.D.

# CONTENTS

## A Personal Word from Martha D'Adamo

BLOOD TYPE AND BABIES are two realities that have forever changed my life. Blood type came first, in 1985, when I met Peter D'Adamo. He transformed the way I viewed food and, in the process, transformed who I was as an individual. Babies arrived later—Claudia in 1991 and Emily in 1994.

When we decided to start our family, Peter and I had the same concerns every other young couple has—could we conceive, would our child be healthy, would we be good parents? As we looked forward to the future, we also looked back into our family histories for information that would be helpful.

Although our backgrounds were very different, neither of us had family histories of troubled pregnancies, births, or miscarriages. Further, we knew our blood types—I am Type O and Peter is Type A. This gave us important information about our genetic profiles, as well as a basis for establishing nutritional needs. What we didn't know was what we would actually experience. Every couple is unique, every pregnancy is different, and every baby is unlike any other baby that came before.

I was lucky that my mother was still alive during both my pregnancies. I pestered her with questions about her pregnancies unmercifully, until one day she said, "When I was having all my children, I went to the doctor, he told me to drink lots of fluids—it didn't matter what, just that it was fluid. He said when I started to have contractions, get to the hospital. I went to the hospital, they knocked me out, and when I woke up, I had a baby."

This was a stunning example of how things have changed so dramatically in the world of obstetrics. In the fifties, most obstetricians were men, and the system seemed to be set up to accommodate them rather than their pregnant patients. Women were rarely encouraged to ask questions about their pregnancies and about all the changes they were experiencing. Little or no nutritional guidance was provided. Nor was there much attention given to toxic behaviours like smoking or alcohol consumption—issues that are well understood today. Breast-feeding had become déclassé, as the development of formula was heralded as "better than mother can provide" and more convenient.

Today we live in a vastly different environment. Pregnancy, birth, and women's health in general are getting more attention than ever before. Maternity centres in major hospitals are "patient-centred" with birthing rooms, labour tubs, midwife consultants, doula referrals, childbirth educators, and in-house breast-feeding consultants. Nutritional support, stress reduction techniques, exercise programs, and a host of natural remedies for pregnancy-related conditions are widely available.

I was very fortunate with both my pregnancies, since Peter was there to serve as my loving and supportive husband as well as my in-house medical consultant. My midwives were open to incorporating naturopathic and blood type–related practices into my pregnancy and birth plans. For my first pregnancy, Peter helped me work out a nutritional plan to support each trimester, and he recommended an exercise and supplement program that enhanced the diet. We made refinements for the second pregnancy based on what we'd learned.

We didn't realize it at the time but Peter was actually creating the template for *Eat Right 4 (for) Your Baby*. What you will find as you read through the book are the dietary, exercise, and supplement guidelines that we used for both my pregnancies, adapted for the four blood types. refined to include the wisdom that came from our experiences.

I was also fortunate during my two pregnancies to have our good friend, Dr. Cathy Rogers, as my long-distance midwifery consultant. Cathy is a naturopath/midwife who organized the Seattle Midwifery School and has been a leader in the field of naturopathy for twenty-four years. Cathy was invaluable in guiding me through the physical preparation for birth, postpartum issues, and nursing. Every year as I celebrate Claudia's and Emily's birthdays, I recall the phone calls with Cathy, tracking the contractions, making suggestions to ease the discomfort of labour, her nursing suggestions, and her calm and gentle guidance as I made the shift into new motherhood. She was such a wonderful support for both of us that Peter and I decided to incorporate her wisdom into *Eat Right 4 (for) Your Baby*.

The journey to conception, pregnancy, birth, and motherhood is wondrous and mysterious. For some women it occurs without complications, and for others it is a challenging, frustrating, and a sometimes deeply disappointing experience. By utilizing the key concepts of blood type diet, we are able to strengthen our overall health and optimize our genetic individuality. Although this won't guarantee a trouble-free pregnancy, it will assist in the best of all possible outcomes—increased energy levels, appropriate weight gain during pregnancy and loss of the weight afterward, and an overall enhanced sense of well-being. As Peter often says, the blood type information is a way of zeroing in on the exact health and nutrition information that corresponds to your biological profile. Armed with this new information, you can make choices about your diet, exercise regimen, and general health that are based on the dynamic natural forces within your own body.

In *Eat Right 4 (for) Your Baby*, he custom-tailors this concept to address all the health and physical issues that are present during pregnancy, birth, postpartum, and the first months of your baby's life. By supporting these dietary recommendations with the most current naturopathic and midwifery advice, he has created a primer for women who are in all the various stages of the childbearing years and who are committed to having the best of all possible pregnancies and raising strong, healthy children.

Our children are the greatest gifts in our lives, and there's no better gift we can give them than a healthy start in life that celebrates and supports their individuality. The blood type diet is an invaluable tool in bringing them into the world, and it provides the legacy of optimum health and well-being as they grow and develop.

Peter and I have grown tremendously because of our children. They have brought joy, love, and an expansive quality into our lives that touches everything we do. *Eat Right 4 (for) Your Baby* represents not only good science and the evolution of the blood type diet, but also the "on the job" training we received as we became new parents. I hope as you read this book you will find the guidance, support, and wisdom that will assist you on your journey to becoming a parent.

MARTHA MOSKO D'ADAMO

# Blood Type and Fertility:
# A Vital Connection

EARLY IN MY PRACTICE AS A NATUROPATH, I discovered, almost by co-incidence, that when my female patients followed the correct diet for their blood type, fertility increased dramatically. Even women with long-standing fertility problems, including repeated miscarriages, were able to con-ceive and carry their babies to term.

It wasn't immediately apparent why this was so. Just a couple of decades ago, our overall understanding of genetics was still fairly limited. Like so many dis-coveries, observation predated the explanation. Today, we have the knowledge to explain what once appeared to be simply a happy phenomenon. I am now able to predict with some degree of accuracy which of my patients will have problems conceiving, and am able to offer blood type–specific guidelines that effectively over-come those problems. It has been one of the more gratifying aspects of my work.

## A Question of Compatibility

Rachel and Eric were typical of many couples who come to my clinic. I first met with them in July 1993, after they had tried for almost ten years to have a child. During that time, Rachel had become pregnant twelve times. But each hopeful beginning had ended in a devastating miscarriage within the first two months. For the last couple of years, Rachel and Eric had been treated by a physician who spe-cialized in reproductive health, and Rachel had become pregnant twice more. But again, both pregnancies had ended in miscarriage. At thirty-seven, Rachel was running out of time—and hope.

Rachel initially heard about me from a woman she'd met in her fertility specialist's waiting room. Even though she decided to go ahead and see me, she was clearly sceptical of the concept that making changes in her diet according to her blood type could enhance her fertility. "I don't even know my blood type," she admitted. "But I guess I have nothing to lose."

I began by blood typing Rachel and Eric and found that Rachel was Type O and Eric was Type A. The result wasn't surprising. Research has shown that many of the problems associated with fertility result from some form of blood type incompatibility, either between the mother and her foetus, or between the mother and the father.

Why would this occur? Each blood type is a chemical marker called an antigen. These blood type antigens can act like barriers against foreign intruders, such as bacteria, viruses, and parasites. When our immune system encounters a harmful foreign intruder, it creates antibodies against it. These antibodies serve as an early warning system. The next time the foreign intruder is encountered, it will be attacked and destroyed. The antibodies we make against other blood types are actually induced early in life by bacteria and sometimes by the first foods we eat.

Blood Type O carries anti-A and anti-B antibodies and rejects anything with an A-like or B-like antigen. Type A carries anti-B antibodies, and Type B carries anti-A antibodies. Only Type AB carries no anti-blood type antibodies, which is why Type AB individuals can receive blood transfusions from anybody.

## The Antigen-Antibody Dynamic

| IF YOU ARE . . . | YOU PRODUCE ANTIBODIES TO . . . |
| --- | --- |
| Type O | A and B |
| Type A | B |
| Type B | A |
| Type AB | None |

Several studies conducted over the past forty years have concluded that infertility and habitual miscarriage may be the result of antibodies in the woman's vaginal secretions reacting with blood type antigens in the man's sperm. In one of these studies, it was determined that the majority of miscarriages were of Type A or Type B foetuses, caused as the result of incompatibility with Type O mothers who produced anti-A and anti-B antibodies. What seems to be missing in many physicians' understanding of miscarriage is that these anti-blood type antibodies are often the result of provocations produced by eating the wrong foods for one's blood type. These foods act in many ways as a "bad blood transfusion," sensitizing the person against future exposure to foreign blood type antigens—including that of a spouse.

Since Rachel was Type O and Eric was Type A, there was a heightened chance that Eric's sperm could be rejected, although that didn't seem to be the case here, as Rachel was able to repeatedly conceive. More likely, the incompatibility was between Rachel and her foetus, which would occur if the foetus were Type A.

A Type O mother and a Type A father can produce either Type O or Type A offspring—although A is dominant over O. If Rachel's foetus was Type A, blood type incompatibility could not be ruled out as the cause of miscarriage.

The good news is that mixed–blood type parents can have healthy babies, even if they produce antibodies against each other's blood type antigens. How? By creating the properly balanced immune system and minimizing provocations that might compromise it.

Rachel began following the Type O diet, being especially careful to avoid foods that triggered an antigen-antibody reaction. Eric began following the Type A diet, which contributed not only to his overall health, but to the health of his semen. I suggested to Rachel that she follow the protocol for at least six months before trying to conceive.

Ten months after her first visit, Rachel became pregnant again. In her sixth month, she came to see me for a checkup. She looked wonderful. Her mood matched her looks.

"Everything seems to be going well, Doctor," Rachel beamed at me. "I feel good, Eric is ecstatic, and we're both taking it step by step. We've never gotten this far before, so we're just trying to relax and enjoy every second." It was clear that Rachel was thrilled, but she was also very nervous. Now, in addition to her previous miscarriages, she was worried about her age and the possibility of her foetus having Down's syndrome or some other developmental disorder. Her obstetrician recommended amniocentesis, which is common for women over age thirty-five. I advised against it, because the procedure carries a risk of miscarriage, there was not a family history of Down's syndrome, and their religious beliefs had convinced them that any child is a gift from God, so abortion was out of the question. After talking with Eric, Rachel decided to forego the amniocentesis. In January 1995, Rachel and Eric gave birth to a perfectly healthy baby girl they named Rebecca.

Even though Rebecca was blood Type A, Rachel had been able to create a welcome environment in her womb. Rachel and Eric assured me that they would continue to make the blood type diet a part of their lives—and a part of their daughter's life when she began eating solid food.

## Not for Women Only

Naftali is a blood Type O patient I "inherited" from my dad, who had been his physician since he was a boy in the years following World War II. Naftali had contracted a very high fever either from a viral or bacterial infection when he was young, which had apparently damaged the cells in the testicles responsible for manufacturing sperm. Naftali and his parents are Hasidic Jews originally from Eastern Europe, and the family had very limited medical care immediately after the Holocaust.

Fertility is a big issue in Naftali's community, and as the son of a renowned rabbi, he was expected to produce an heir. Consequently, this caused a lot of stress for him and his wife.

Pious Jews do not easily consent to semen analysis, since semen is viewed as a precious seed. However, when it comes to health, Judaism is a remarkably flexible religion, and after much consultation Naftali was allowed to have his semen analyzed.

Result: Naftali's semen had no sperm in it.

When I began working with him I could only promise to do my best. Naftali's wife had no fertility problems, but would be following the diet for her blood type, which was AB. I began Naftali on the basic Type O diet, plus a few herbal supplements, and he followed it assiduously. Six months later we again tested his semen.

Result: Semen showed one sperm cell, nonmotile (not able to move).

Well, anyone else might have been discouraged, but this man was relentless. If any individual could do the program perfectly, it was Naftali. "One cell!" he exclaimed. "It's working!"

Four months later Naftali came in with the good news that his wife was pregnant, and they have since had another child. I cannot tell you the final results of his sperm count; the rabbis have now decided that since his "seed" is viable, it cannot be tested anymore. Why tell you this story? Because you might think that following the blood type diet is only for females.

But this is not true. Fertility is a joint endeavour.

I'm not trying to give infertile couples unrealistic hopes. Obviously, blood type incompatibility is not the only cause of infertility. Nor does the blood type diet magically resolve all fertility problems. But it's just common sense to approach pregnancy in the optimum state of health. Following a dietary regimen that is geared precisely for your blood type seems an excellent choice for enhancing your system's response to the many stresses involved in bringing a child to full term. And there is no question in my mind that you can minimize the risk of incompatibility with the right diet.

## Why Diet Matters

So, what does diet have to do with fertility?

Simply put, there is a chemical reaction between your blood type antigen and the food you eat. That's because the proteins in foods have antigens as well, and these antigens are similar to the blood type antigens. If you eat food that contains a foreign antigen, your immune system will create anti–blood type antibodies to it, and it will be rejected by your system.

These antibody reactions can dramatically affect your health—weakening your immune system, increasing inflammation, disturbing your digestive processes, and upsetting your metabolic balance. They can also be a factor in infertility or miscarriage when a mother and father have opposing blood types or when a mother is carrying a foetus of an opposing blood type.

It stands to reason that the best way to minimize the chances of blood type incompatibility is to eat foods that are right for your blood type and avoid foods that trigger an antibody or antigen reaction. To this day my wife, Martha, credits her easy pregnancies and the delivery of two healthy daughters to the fact that she "lived in the land of the beneficials." That is, she ate the foods that were most beneficial for her blood type.

Ramona, Type B, is a case in point. Ramona was in her early thirties and about 50 pounds overweight. She had been unable to conceive after nearly six years of trying, and I was her last stop on the way to a fertility clinic. In addition to her weight problem, Ramona had problems with recurrent urinary tract infections and persistent allergies. Ramona's husband, Franklin, was Type A, and it appeared that an antibody reaction to his sperm was being exacerbated by Ramona's infections and allergies.

I have found that most of the problems Type Bs have with infections and allergies can be resolved with a change in diet. There is a direct connection between our digestive activity and our immune system. In fact, more than 50 percent of all immune function occurs in our digestive tracts.

Ramona's weight was an impediment to fertility as well. Obesity can disrupt a woman's menstrual cycle, change her hormonal balance, and interfere with fertility. Most of the overweight women I've treated in my practice have histories of menstrual irregularity.

In addition to her excess weight, Ramona's dieting history was a factor. She admitted that during the past ten years she had frequently tried to lose weight by going on extremely low-calorie diets. That was a significant piece of information.

When you go on a very low-calorie diet, you are telling your body not to get pregnant. Nature is very smart. It has endowed us with automatic signals designed to guarantee the survival of our species. One of these is related to nutrition. In times of famine, women's reproductive abilities shut down—nature's way of preventing the growth of a population during a period when mothers do not have the fat stores to nurture more children. Modern women who follow starvation diets are inadvertently triggering that protective signal.

Ramona's challenge was to lose weight in a gradual, healthy way, while also improving her immune function by avoiding foods that made her more vulnerable to allergies and infections. Numerous studies of blood Type B cells have conclusively demonstrated that specific foods caused haemolytic (blood cell–destroying) and allergic reactions—among them chicken, corn, lentils, peanuts, and buckwheat. Not surprisingly, chicken was a staple of Ramona's diet. I created a diet plan for her that would substitute beneficial foods for problem foods—for example, turkey and lean venison instead of chicken, rice instead of wheat, and abundant green vegetables instead of problematic beans. I also encouraged Ramona to begin including daily servings of low-fat dairy foods. Most Type Bs thrive on dairy, and cultured dairy foods such as yogurt and kefir are instrumental in the health of the intestines and the prevention of infections.

I also put Ramona on an exercise program specifically designed for Type B— a combination of moderate aerobic activity and calming exercises such as yoga. This combination has been shown to dramatically reduce stress and promote fitness for Type Bs. Chronic stress itself is a factor in obesity and also interferes with ovulation and fertility.

In my experience, when people follow the blood type diet, they lose weight naturally, without having to significantly lower their calorie levels, and this happened with Ramona. Within six months on the diet she had lost 35 pounds, her allergic symptoms had disappeared, and she had had no further problems with urinary tract infections. She continued on the program, and on the first-year anniversary she and her husband decided she was ready to try conceiving. This time Ramona got pregnant with relative ease. During her pregnancy we continued to adapt the Type B diet to her special needs, and she delivered a healthy baby boy.

Ramona likes to talk about her "miracle baby". I agree that life is a miracle, but I also believe that we have the power to help miracles happen by listening to the wisdom of our bodies.

## The Genetic Power of Blood Type

Blood type is the most powerful genetic connection you have with your ancestors and therefore plays a vital role in reproduction. Your blood type is the key to your body's entire immune system. Blood type determines and controls the influence of viruses, bacteria, infections, chemicals, stress, and any other invaders and conditions that might compromise your immune system.

Like the colour of your eyes or hair, your blood type is determined by two sets of genes—the inheritance you receive from your mother and father. It is from those genes commingling that your blood type is selected at the moment of your conception. Like genes, some blood types are dominant over others. In the cellular creation of a new human being, the A gene and B gene are dominant over O. If at conception the embryo is given an A gene from the mother and an O gene from the father, the infant's blood will be Type A, although it will continue to carry the father's O gene unexpressed in its DNA. When the infant grows up and passes these genes on to its offspring, half of the genes will be for Type A blood and half will be for Type O blood. Because A and B genes are equally strong, you are Type AB if you received an A gene from one parent, and a B gene from the other. Finally, because the O gene is recessive to all the others, you are Type O only if you receive an O gene from each parent.

It is quite possible for two Type A parents to conceive a child who is Type O. This occurs when the parents each have one A gene and one O gene, and both pass the O gene on to their offspring. In the same way, two brown-eyed parents can conceive a blue-eyed offspring if each carries within them the dormant recessive gene for blue eyes.

Both of my parents are Type A. I presume that I received an A from each parent (making me genotype AA) because my two daughters are both Type A. My wife Martha is Type O and can only have two Os, so it is certain that our daughters are genotypically *AO*.

| Blood Type Inheritance | |
| --- | --- |
| PARENTS' BLOOD TYPES | POSSIBLE BLOOD TYPES OF CHILDREN |
| Both A | A or O |
| Both B | B or O |
| Both AB | A, B, or AB |
| Both O | O |
| One A and one B | A, B, AB, or O |
| One A and one O | A or O |
| One A and one AB | A, B, or AB |
| One B and one O | B or O |
| One B and one AB | A, B, or AB |
| One AB and one O | A or B |

## The Rh Factor

When your blood is typed, you also learn whether you are "negative" or "positive". Many people don't realize that this is an additional blood type called the rhesus or Rh system, and it really has nothing to do with your ABO blood type. However, it has everything to do with reproduction. The Rh system is named for the rhesus monkey, a commonly employed laboratory animal in whose blood it was first discovered. For many years, it remained a mystery to doctors why some women who had normal first pregnancies developed complications in their second and subsequent pregnancies, which often resulted in miscarriage and even the death of the mother. In 1940, the mystery was solved by Dr. Karl Landsteiner, an Austrian-American scientist. Landsteiner discovered that these women were carrying different blood types than their babies, who took their blood types from their fathers. The babies were Rh-positive, which meant that they carried the Rh antigen on their blood cells. Their mothers were Rh-negative, which meant that this antigen was missing from their blood.

Unlike the ABO system, where the antibodies to other blood types develop from birth, Rh-negative women do not make an antibody to the Rh antigen unless they are first sensitized. This sensitization usually occurs when blood is exchanged between the mother and infant during birth, so the mother's immune system does not have enough time to react to the first baby. However, should a later conception result in yet another Rh-positive baby, the mother, now sensitized, will produce antibodies to the baby's blood type. The result is an attack on the baby's blood cells that can be devastating and potentially fatal. Complications include severe anaemia, haemorrhage, decline in the number of blood cells, and heart failure. Reactions to the Rh factor can only occur in Rh-negative women who conceive the children of Rh-positive fathers. If the mother and father are both Rh-negative, there is no problem. Rh-positive women, who comprise 85 percent of the population, have nothing to worry about.

Today we have a simple immunization given to Rh-negative women after the birth of their first child, which protects against the effects of this incompatibility. Rh immune globulin (Rho-GAM, GammulinRH) is routinely given to Rh-negative women after delivery—although if you are delivering in an underdeveloped country you'll want to make certain it is available.

Rh sensitization is not just an issue in full-term deliveries. Even if you have a miscarriage, ectopic pregnancy, or abortion, you will need to receive Rh immune globulin. Since there's a small chance that foetal blood can enter a woman's bloodstream during amniocentesis, it is recommended that Rh-negative women receive Rh immune globulin after this procedure.

## Eat Right for Your Baby

A successful pregnancy is a miraculous holistic event. The atmosphere that you create for this extraordinary happening is one that is formed long before you conceive. Pregnancy is an excellent example of body/mind integration, involving every physical and neurological function.

How can you use your knowledge about your blood type's role in nutrition and health to maximize your well-being before pregnancy, improve your condition during pregnancy, and give your baby the best start in life—from the moment he or she is conceived?

I have said many times that blood type science is about individuality, and perhaps no experience is as completely individual as pregnancy and childbirth. Chances are you will hear many stories from others during your pregnancy and receive more advice than you care to. Some of it will be contradictory. Some of it will not conform to your experience. Your blood type advisory is a touchstone that can offer you reliable individualized recommendations. All of these recommendations are safely within our current scientific and medical understanding of reproduction and childbirth. This book is not designed to replace that knowledge, but to enhance and personalize it.

In the following sections you will learn how to maximize your chances of enjoying a healthy, successful pregnancy by employing strategies that have been individually crafted for your blood type. Obviously, blood type is not the sole factor involved in a healthy pregnancy. So your plan is really a combination of the best naturopathic advice and the best blood type–factored advice.

Every so often I'll see a pregnant woman in my practice who is so obsessed with doing everything perfectly that she's a nervous wreck. She's convinced that if she makes one bad choice or eats one food that isn't right for her blood type, she'll jeopardize her baby's health.

Although it's wonderful to live in an era when we have so much knowledge about how to keep both mother and baby healthy during pregnancy, I always advise mothers-to-be (and dads-to-be, too) not to go overboard in monitoring their compliance with every detail of the blood type diet and other recommendations. Such rigidity is a big stress-inducer, and right now you need to be eliminating stress, not adding to it. For the most part, your body will let you know if you've gone astray.

Pregnancy can be a uniquely rich and satisfying period. Don't miss the opportunity to savour the totality of this experience.

# Your Pregnancy:
# A Naturopathic Primer

 THE FOLLOWING ADVICE APPLIES TO ALL BLOOD TYPES. In combination with your specific blood type guidelines, it constitutes the best of naturopathic wisdom.

## Get Started *Before* You're Pregnant

Your level of fitness at conception is a critical factor in the long course that will finally lead to birth. Consider: A microscopic foetus's heart, lungs, liver, kidneys, limbs, and nervous system are being formed before many women have even missed their period. This is the best reason to consider your state of health before you become pregnant.

If infertility is an issue, you and your partner should both evaluate the factors in your lifestyle and health history that may be contributory. For example:

Impediments to female fertility include:

- Pelvic inflammatory disease (PID), chlamydia, or any other sexually transmitted diseases
- History of menstrual irregularities
- Taking medications for allergies
- Use of tobacco or recreational drugs
- Excessive alcohol consumption
- Thyroid disease

Impediments to male fertility—especially sperm production—include:

- Use of tobacco, recreational drugs, and steroids
- Excessive consumption of alcohol
- Treatment of cancer with radiation or chemotherapy
- Exposure to radiation, chemicals, and toxins in the workplace
- Sexually transmitted diseases
- Use of saunas or hot tubs
- Wearing tight underwear

In your pre-pregnancy blood type advisory, you will find strategies for achieving the best condition possible. These strategies, which you should employ at least six months prior to pregnancy, emphasize individualized dietary guidelines for losing weight if you need to, controlling chronic conditions that may interfere with conception and pregnancy, and ridding your body of toxins. In addition, there are supplementary protocols, using vitamins, minerals, and herbs; and a blood type–specific exercise and stress-reduction plan.

All blood types should use the following pre-pregnancy checklist:

## Pre-pregnancy Checklist

In the months before you become pregnant, take care of these crucial matters.

### LAB TESTS
- Blood test to determine blood type and Rh status (both partners)
- Blood test to screen for thyroid activity, anaemia, and sexually transmitted diseases (both partners)
- Diabetes screening—especially if you've previously gained excessive weight in pregnancy or have given birth to a baby weighing more than 9 pounds
- Test for urinary indican levels and levels of serum albumin; high levels are indicators of toxicity.

### EXAMS
- Full physical exam
- Pap smear and gynaecological exam
- Dental checkup and the performance of any necessary dental work

### INFORMATION GATHERING
- Family and personal health history, including any genetic factors (both partners)

- Evaluation of weight and body composition
- Evaluation of all current medications and natural supplements you're using

## Detoxification Guidelines

Resolve to rid your body of any toxins that diminish your health, sap your strength, and heighten the risks for you and your baby. What exactly do I mean by toxins? These are the by-products of bacterial activity on unabsorbed foods that grow in your intestinal tract. In my conservative estimate, at least 50 percent of all the illnesses I treat involve some sort of toxicity. Hippocrates, the father of modern medicine, knew the elemental importance of what he advised physicians in the treatment of their patients: "First, cleanse the bowels."

Follow these guidelines to detoxify:

- *Eat only those foods that are recommended for your blood type.* When you eat foods on the "avoid" list, they are poorly digested and leave toxic by-products in your digestive tract.
- *Eat organic.* Chemicals, pollutants, and improper storage make foods harder to digest and leave toxins lingering in your digestive tract.
- *Eat natural.* Avoid artificial sweeteners, colours, and flavourings.
- *Eat fresh.* Limit your consumption of packaged, frozen, and canned foods.
- *Eat safe.* Avoid nitrates and nitrites—found in smoked, cured, and pickled foods. Avoid fish high in mercury—swordfish, tuna, shark (canned tuna is okay). Avoid fish that contain potentially harmful PCBs—mackerel, seabass, fresh-water fish. Avoid shellfish—shrimps, crab, lobster, clams, prawns, oysters. Forego raw fish and sushi during your pregnancy.
- *Avoid excessive use of fermented foods (cheese, beer, and yeast extracts) and canned and frozen foods.* These foods are particularly high in proteins that are destructive to the intestinal tract.
- *Stop smoking, drinking alcohol, and taking recreational drugs.* If you smoke, it's important to stop well before you become pregnant. You may already be aware that smoking during pregnancy can result in low birth weight and even birth defects. But smoking *before* pregnancy can have a lingering ill effect. Smoking impedes circulation and reduces your oxygen supply—making it much harder to deliver the necessary nutrients to your foetus. Studies show that smoking during pregnancy has been associated with low birth weight and even the development of ADD. Similarly, excessive alcohol consumption and the use of recreational drugs place you in a nutrient-deprived state—hardly a welcoming

environment for foetal growth. Lead and other heavy-metal exposures have also been linked to ADD.

- *Follow safe food preparation guidelines.*

  - Meat and fish: Take this added measure before cooking. Bring a pot of water to a boil. Turn off water and let meat or fish soak for 3 to 5 minutes. This will help remove any chemicals and kill bacteria. Then, be sure to cook the meat and fish thoroughly.
  - Use a vegetable/fruit wash to clean the skin and outer surface of fruits and vegetables before you slice into them.
  - Don't cook in copper, aluminium, or pewter pots. These metals can get into the food.

## A Word to Dad

During the vital pregnancy preparation stage, don't consider yourself a bystander. You're able to command a leading role in determining the health of your offspring. You, too, need to rigorously comply with your own blood type diet and work toward a maximum state of health and fitness. In particular, eliminate bad habits that can interfere with the quality of your sperm. There are extensive studies clearly indicating that smoking, inhaling secondhand smoke, and exposure to toxic chemicals can have a negative influence on your sperm count. Studies also show that infants born to alcohol-free fathers are healthier and have higher birth weights. Never underestimate the influence you have over the well-being of your future son or daughter. This is truly a combined effort in which you play a crucial role.

**TIPS FOR DAD**

1. Follow the diet appropriate for your blood type. Clinical experience has shown that following the blood type diet as a couple increases your overall chances for a healthy conception.
2. Drink a cup of green tea once or twice daily.
3. Take 250 milligrams of vitamin C daily, preferably from food sources, such as acerola cherry or rose hip.
4. Take a daily multivitamin (preferably blood type–specific) to assure adequate levels of certain nutrients necessary for sperm count and motility.
5. Consult your physician if you take prescription medications. Some can interfere with fertility.

## MALE FERTILITY-ENHANCING SUPPLEMENTS

VITAMIN C protects sperm from oxidative damage. Supplementing vitamin C improves the quality of sperm in smokers. When sperm stick together (a condition called agglutination), fertility is reduced. Vitamin C reduces sperm agglutination, increasing the fertility of men with this condition. Many doctors of natural medicine recommend 250 to 500 milligrams of vitamin C per day (preferably from acerola cherries or rose hips) for infertile men, particularly those diagnosed with sperm agglutination.

ZINC supplementation can raise testosterone levels and increase fertility if you have low semen zinc levels. The standard recommendation is 25 milligrams daily.

ARGININE is an amino acid found in many foods. It is needed to produce sperm. Most research shows that several months of arginine supplementation (1 to 2 grams daily) increases sperm count and quality and, therefore, fertility.

COENZYME $Q_{10}$ is a nutrient used by the body in the production of energy. While its exact role in the formation of sperm is unknown, there is evidence that as little as 10 milligrams per day (over a two-week period) will increase sperm count and motility.

VITAMIN E deficiency in animals leads to infertility. In a preliminary human trial, 100 to 200 international units of vitamin E given to each man and woman of infertile couples led to a significant increase in fertility. (Type Os may want to limit vitamin E intake, except from foods.)

VITAMIN $B_{12}$ is needed to maintain fertility. Vitamin $B_{12}$ injections have increased sperm counts in men with low numbers. These results have been duplicated in double-blind research. Men seeking $B_{12}$ injections should consult a nutritionally oriented physician.

CARNITINE is a substance made in the body and also found in supplements. It appears to be necessary for normal functioning of sperm cells. Supplementing with 250 milligrams to 1 gram per day for four months has helped normalize sperm in men with low sperm quality in several studies.

If you plan to implement any of these recommendations, be sure to talk them over with your physician.

## Your Pregnancy: The Three Trimesters

It is helpful to understand what you can basically expect from each trimester of your pregnancy, as a context for the recommendations made in your individual blood type section. Your nutrient and exercise needs change as your foetus grows. In addition, each trimester brings with it a number of common conditions. Through blood type recommendations, you will be able to control the severity of your symptoms.

## First Trimester Basics

The first trimester is the most critical time in your pregnancy. Although the foetus at the end of three months is less than 4 inches (10 cm) long and weighs less than 1 ounce (25 g), all of its functions have begun to form—major organs and nervous system, heartbeat, arms, fingers, legs, toes, hair, and buds for future teeth.

This is not a time to skimp on food or count calories. You're not quite eating for two people, but you do need extra nutrients for your growing foetus. The general recommendation is to eat about 300 extra calories a day. You'll need to gain 25 to 35 pounds (11.5 to 16 kg) during your pregnancy. This will allow you to nourish your foetus and store nutrients for breast-feeding. Expect to gain at least 3 to 4 pounds (1.4 to 1.8 kg) during the first trimester.

For many women, the first trimester is also the period when you experience the most profound changes. Although you may not appear pregnant, you'll certainly feel all of the differences.

### COMMON FIRST TRIMESTER CONDITIONS

MORNING SICKNESS AND NAUSEA. The nausea—"morning sickness"—that many women experience during the first trimester of pregnancy is the result of hormonal changes. Morning sickness (which isn't necessarily limited to mornings) may actually be a positive thing—though you may not feel particularly grateful. Some scientists believe that morning sickness evolved as a natural way of protecting women against foods that might contain dangerous microorganisms or parasites, or foods whose chemical compositions might prove harmful to a developing foetus, by expelling those foods. Also, increasing levels of the hormone beta-hcg have been linked to nausea. Since high levels of beta-hcg tend to protect against miscarriage, look on the bright side: Your morning sickness may well be an early sign that your pregnancy is off to a good start. Morning sickness usually disappears after the first trimester.

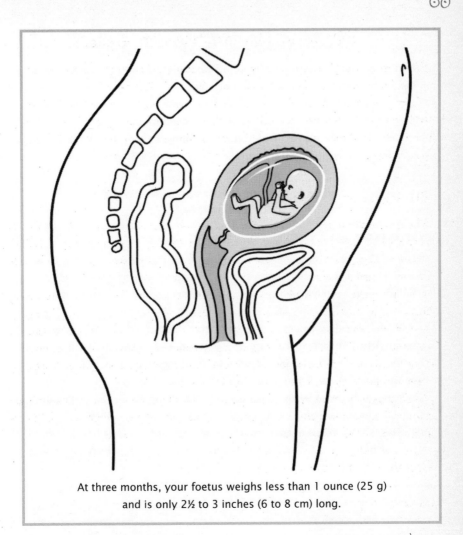

At three months, your foetus weighs less than 1 ounce (25 g)
and is only 2½ to 3 inches (6 to 8 cm) long.

MOOD SWINGS. Women are often surprised that they don't feel more buoyant at the start of pregnancy—especially when it is a long-awaited result. The stresses of the first trimester can produce many emotional ups and downs. Although you may be delighted that you're pregnant, the hormonal adjustments you're experiencing can make you feel anything but joyous. You may experience mood swings, fatigue and insomnia, anxiety about your ability to experience a successful pregnancy, and fear about what will happen.

CONSTIPATION. Constipation is a fact of life for most pregnant women. Hormonal changes are largely responsible, signaling food to move more slowly through your system as it nourishes your foetus.

FATIGUE. Your entire system is fully engaged in creating a healthy environment for your foetus—producing the placenta, a process that is completed at the end of the third month, as well as providing sufficient nutrients. Every organ is engaged in a vast reorganization. No wonder you're tired.

FOOD AVERSIONS AND CRAVINGS. The food cravings and aversions that many women experience during pregnancy are something of a mystery. While you may

## Advice from the Naturopath Midwife Cathy Rogers, N.D.

### RELIEVING YOUR ANXIETY

It's normal to feel some ambivalence early in your pregnancy. In a way, it would be odd if you *weren't* ambivalent. You're inviting a perfect stranger into your body! Even when a pregnancy is planned, the physical reality of it can be a shock.

If you're feeling anxious, it's important to address the issues beneath your anxiety. Get specific. For example, you may have anxieties about being a mum. Or you may be feeling exposed to the world (pregnancy is a very visible "out there" state). If you have compulsivity about eating and body image, you may worry about what is happening to the shape of your body. Remind yourself that you are growing a new life within. Breathe—and allow it.

This is a good time to connect with your mate—who may be having some anxieties of his own. Talk about what you want as parents. Solidify as a family unit.

#### Anti-Anxiety Soak

This bath, taken at neutral (tepid) temperature calms the nervous system. Neutral means body temperature, not hot.

*1 ounce (25 g) rose*
*1 ounce (25 g) lavender*

Mix the herbs together and tie them into a cotton scarf.

Place the scarf over the tub nozzle. Run hot water through the herbs until the tub is half full, then add cold water to bring it to the right temperature. As the water cools while you're soaking, add more warm water.

An alternative method is to mix 2 drops each of rose and lavender essential oils with a teaspoon of olive oil and pour it into the tub once the water has reached the right temperature.

crave what's good for you and be repelled by foods that are harmful, it doesn't always work that way. Your best strategy is to eat what's right for you and try to find replacements within your diet for the harmful foods you may crave.

## PRENATAL SUPPLEMENTS

Vitamins are very important to the developing foetus. However, you should be aware that overdoing supplements can cause grave problems in the baby, so consult your physician before taking *any* vitamins or supplements.

Virtually any of the commercial prenatal multivitamins will be effective. But many are made with synthetic components rather than the preferred whole food ingredients. Choose a blend of the B vitamins, along with antioxidants. Look for quality, not quantity. Not all formulations release the specified amount of nutrients on the label. When researchers at the University of Maryland tested nine prescription prenatal vitamin tablets to see whether the folate contained would dissolve, only three passed the muster. Two failed so miserably that they released less than 25 percent of the folate specified on the label. That means that if swallowed by someone, more than 75 percent of the folate in those pills could possibly travel right through the body with very little chance of being absorbed by the blood and transported to various tissues, including tissues belonging to the foetus. If possible, use powder-in-capsule versus compacted pills: Evidence suggests that dissolvability is a big problem with many prenatals. Encapsulated ingredients do not need to dissolve.

Your daily prenatal vitamin/mineral supplement probably doesn't give you enough calcium. Most of the daily prenatal formulas only contain about 200 to 300 milligrams of calcium—about 1,000 milligrams less than you and your baby need every day. So check the label on your bottle or talk to your doctor. You'll want to make sure that you are getting at least 1,200 milligrams of calcium every day from natural food sources and supplements.

If you wish to take a prenatal supplement specifically formulated for your blood type, see appendix B for information.

SPECIAL NOTE: DHA SUPPLEMENTATION: A natural nutrient for humans of all ages, DHA, an omega-3 long-chain polyunsaturated fatty acid, is one of the essential building blocks of human brain tissue. Found naturally in breast milk, DHA is also present in egg yolk and oily fish, such as salmon and sardines. What does having enough DHA mean for you and your baby? Whether you're a baby or an adult, DHA is important for signal transmission in the brain, eye, and nervous system. Your developing baby receives the DHA through the blood, via the placenta and umbilical cord. Seventy percent of the brain cells are formed before birth. These cells are mainly composed of essential fatty acids, with DHA being the most important because it gives great flexibility to the cell membranes. Flexibility is essential for fast and accurate message transfer in the brain. During pregnancy, the recommended intake of DHA is 300 milligrams per day, in food and supplements. Studies have shown that mothers' diets deficient in DHA are often linked with low head circumference, low placental weight, and low birth weight in their babies.

## Medications to Avoid During Pregnancy

Certain prescription and over-the-counter medications can potentially harm a growing foetus. Avoid these during your pregnancy.

| OTC PAINKILLERS | ACNE MEDICATIONS | ANTICONVULSANTS |
|---|---|---|
| Aspirin | Ro acutane | Diazepam |
| Acetaminophen | Retin-A | Clonazepam |
| Ibuprofen | And similar medications | Lorazepam |
| And similar medications | | And similar medications |
| **ANTIBIOTICS** | **TRANQUILIZERS** | **MAO INHIBITORS** |
| Tetracycline | Librium | Isocarboazid |
| Streptomycin | Valium | Phenelzine |
| And similar medications | And similar medications | And similar medications |

## Herbs to Avoid During Pregnancy

Herbs are medicine just like drugs and should be respected during pregnancy. Just as you would not take an unnecessary drug, avoid unnecessary herbs.

| | | |
|---|---|---|
| Aloe vera | Fenugreek | Poke root |
| Angelica | Feverfew | Rosemary |
| Arnica | Ginger | Rue |
| Black cohosh | Ginseng | Sage |
| Bladderwrack | Goldenseal | Senna |
| Bloodroot | Gugul | St. John's wort |
| Blue cohosh | Horsetail | Thuja |
| Celery seed | Indian tobacco | Turmeric root |
| Chaste berry | Iris | Uva ursi |
| Chichona | Licorice | Vervain |
| Cinnamon | Male fern | Wild carrot |
| Coltsfoot | Motherwort | Wild indigo |
| Comfrey | Nutmeg | Wormwood |
| Curcumin | Parsley | Yarrow |
| Ephedra | Pennyroyal | |

## EXERCISE GUIDELINES

There are tremendous benefits to maintaining your exercise program throughout your pregnancy. Regular exercise improves your condition and reduces the risk factors associated with pregnancy. It can also alleviate many of the uncomfortable side effects of early pregnancy, such as fatigue and morning sickness.

One of the most important functions of exercise is its ability to reduce stress and improve your mental condition. Pregnancy itself can be stressful. Throughout your pregnancy, you are also grappling with the effects this new reality will have on your relationship to the world. Your feelings, fears, and expectations about yourself, your family, and the impending arrival of your baby are important, too. To make matters a bit more complicated, your emotions can be affected by the dramatic hormonal changes you're experiencing. This is especially true during the first trimester.

Exercising three to four times a week, according to the blood type recommendations contained in chapters 3 to 6, will help you reduce stress, fight fatigue, and stabilize your emotions.

Exercise is good for your baby, too. Studies show that babies born to mums who exercise during pregnancy may benefit from better stress tolerance and advanced neurobehavioural maturity. These children are leaner at five years of age and have better early neurodevelopment. The new findings are added to the already-known benefits of exercise during pregnancy, including improved cardiovascular function, improved attitude and mood, easier and less complicated labour, quicker recovery, and improved fitness.

In addition to individual blood type guidelines, all blood types should bear in mind the following:

- All aerobic exercise is not of equal value. If your regular workout involves contact sports or in-line skating, I'd suggest you forego them during pregnancy, to avoid any potential injury to the abdominal area.
- Make your aerobic exercises the low-impact variety. If you are taking dance or movement classes, keep your feet on the floor. No jumping or bouncing. Or choose exercises such as cycling, swimming, or brisk walking that have little or no impact risks.
- Take extra time to warm up and properly stretch your muscles before exercising.
- Wear a good support bra to protect your breasts and limit discomfort, especially if they are feeling tender.
- Drink plenty of water throughout the workout.
- Don't exercise on an empty stomach. Eat a snack 30 minutes before exercising.

EXERCISE CAUTION. Though exercise in pregnancy is generally safe, mums-to-be embarking on an exercise program should be aware of warning signs. If any of these symptoms occur, stop exercising and contact your practitioner: sudden and severe abdominal pain; uterine contractions lasting 30 minutes once exercising stops; dizziness; and vaginal bleeding. Other signs to watch for are decreased foetal activity, visual disturbances, or numbness in any part of the body.

For some women, such as those with heart disease, blood clots, recent pulmonary embolism, or for those who have a "high-risk" pregnancy, exercise may not be recommended. In taking the complete medical history, your practitioner will determine if maternal conditions limit, or exclude, an exercise program.

## Second Trimester Basics

As you enter your second trimester, your pregnancy begins to show. The chance of miscarriage is substantially lessened, and you may begin to relax as some of the more uncomfortable symptoms—morning sickness, constipation, fatigue—begin to disappear.

During the second trimester you should gain about 1 pound (450 g) a week—for a total of 12 to 14 pounds (5.5 to 6 kg). You may experience a greater appetite, especially if you no longer suffer from nausea. Monitor your weight, and, if needed, increase your calorie intake by 100 to 300 calories a day.

Foetal growth is rapid during the second trimester, and you'll experience a number of physiological changes related to that growth. As your blood volume increases to pump more nutrients to your foetus, you may find yourself more susceptible to nosebleeds and bleeding gums due to extra pressure on these sensitive membranes. You'll also be more vulnerable to conditions that can be dangerous to the health of your foetus if they are not kept in check.

### COMMON SECOND TRIMESTER CONDITIONS

ALLERGIES. If you are susceptible to allergies, they may be exacerbated during this time by hyperimmunity—the increased vigilance of your immune system designed to protect your foetus.

BLEEDING GUMS/NOSEBLEEDS. High levels of reproductive hormones circulating in your body increase blood flow to the delicate mucous membranes of the nose and mouth. This can bring easy bleeding when you stress these areas—by brushing your teeth too vigorously or by blowing your nose too hard. If you have allergies, a runny nose can make the problem worse.

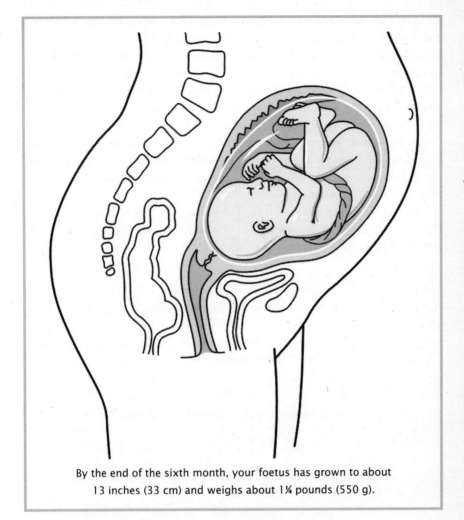

By the end of the sixth month, your foetus has grown to about
13 inches (33 cm) and weighs about 1¼ pounds (550 g).

BLOOD SUGAR IMBALANCE. Most pregnant women have more sugar (glucose) in their blood during the second trimester. This is normal, since your foetus requires more nourishment. However, elevated blood sugar can lead to a dangerous condition called gestational diabetes, which can cause premature birth and even birth defects.

HAEMORRHOIDS AND VARICOSE VEINS. These are inflammatory conditions. Haemorrhoids are actually varicose veins of the anus.

EXERCISE GUIDELINES
As your pregnancy progresses, the extra weight and its unwieldy distribution place stress on your joints and muscles, especially in the lower back and pelvis.

You might also have problems with circulation, causing leg cramps and dizziness. Adapt your exercise regimen accordingly. If you are still engaging in rigorous workouts, such as cycling or step exercises, this would be a good time to shift to less strenuous activities—and those that don't require careful balance. As your foetus has grown, your centre of gravity has shifted. You also may have less oxygen available, so reduce the pace of your routines, or stop altogether if you become breathless.

After the first trimester, avoid exercises that require lying flat on your back. The weight of your expanding uterus can compress major blood vessels and restrict circulation. Do your abdominal exercises in a standing position, and other floor exercises lying on your side.

Overheating during exercise can be dangerous. Keep your body temperature at a moderate level. An increase of more than one degree of body heat can be dangerous. If you're not sure, wear a monitor.

WHEN *not* TO EXERCISE

> You have pregnancy-induced high blood pressure
> You have asthma
> You experience bleeding during the second trimester
> You have a history of late miscarriage

## Do Your Pelvic Floor Exercises

Pelvic floor exercises should be a part of your daily routine, beginning in the second trimester. During the last months of pregnancy the growing foetus puts pressure on your bladder, which makes you feel the need to urinate frequently. Sometimes women limit their fluids when this happens, but it's absolutely essential that you keep your fluid intake high to stay hydrated. A better solution: pelvic floor exercises to strengthen the muscles around your urethra. Here's how: Contract the muscles in your vagina, urethra, and anus—as if you were trying to hold back urine. Hold for 5 to 7 seconds, then release. Repeat 10 to 20 times a day.

## Third Trimester Basics

The third trimester is dedicated to intensive foetal growth. Your foetus will gain fully half its weight during this period. In the final months there will be further essential lung and brain development. The food you eat during the final three months is directly utilized in increasing your baby's birth weight. The quality of the food you eat continues to be of primary importance.

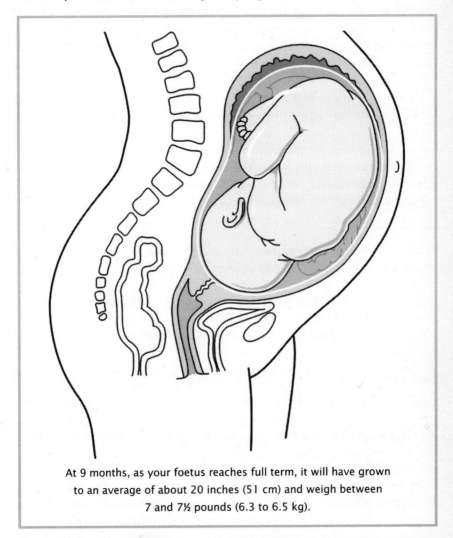

At 9 months, as your foetus reaches full term, it will have grown to an average of about 20 inches (51 cm) and weigh between 7 and 7½ pounds (6.3 to 6.5 kg).

As you approach the birth of your baby, typically after some forty weeks, it's normal to feel equal measures of excitement and apprehension. If this is your first pregnancy, you're entering the great unknown. You may find your thoughts filled with worries about whether your baby is all right, and dread about what you'll experience during labour.

If you've participated in childbirth classes and have a strong partnership with your doctor or midwife, some of that anxiety will be alleviated. And if you've adhered to your blood type plan, you can have some degree of confidence that you've done the best you can to assure a healthy baby.

The key now, as you prepare for labour, is to be as physically and mentally prepared as possible. Continue to gain about 1 pound (450 g) per week during the seventh and eighth months. Your weight may stabilize—and you may even drop a pound or two (up to 1 kg) during the ninth month.

## COMMON THIRD TRIMESTER CONDITIONS

LACK OF APPETITE. Many women find they have far less appetite later in pregnancy. One reason is the pressure of the growing foetus on your abdomen. There's simply less room for food. The best way to combat this is to eat something, even a small snack, every 3 to 4 hours. Don't drink water or juice with a meal. Liquid fills your stomach quickly, leaving less room for solid food.

CONSTIPATION. Constipation, which afflicts many women in the first trimester, often reappears in the final months of pregnancy.

OEDEMA. Sluggish metabolism, often triggered by eating the wrong foods for your blood type, leads to an accumulation of extracellular water, which, in turn, causes oedema. Mild swelling, especially in your legs and feet, is to be expected during pregnancy.

SHORTNESS OF BREATH/FATIGUE. By the third trimester, you'll be carrying a heavy and awkward load. The pressure of the expanding uterus on your respiratory system can cause shortness of breath even with mild exertion. Fatigue can also be caused by sleeplessness. Many women have trouble sleeping in the final months because they can't get comfortable.

INDIGESTION AND HEARTBURN. You may find that the pressure from your growing foetus constricts your digestive tract, forcing stomach contents back up through the oesophagus. You can minimize acid reflux or heartburn by eating small, regular meals, chewing food thoroughly, and eating slowly. Don't lie down for at least an hour after eating.

HIGH BLOOD PRESSURE. If your oedema is more serious, it could be a sign of preeclampsia. Eclampsia is a severe condition associated with elevated blood pressure. Even women who are not normally at risk for high blood pressure sometimes develop a pregnancy-induced hypertension. High blood pressure can restrict blood flow to the placenta and rob your foetus of oxygen and vital nutrients. If you have hypertension, you'll need to get more rest and even stay off your feet.

URINARY TRACT INFECTIONS. UTIs are very common during pregnancy. In the third trimester they are more serious because of the potential for developing a kidney infection. Kidney infections can provoke preterm labour.

EXERCISE GUIDELINES

Keep in mind that exercise is not only tolerated, it can prevent potentially serious complications, such as high blood pressure that can lead to preeclampsia. Exercise during pregnancy may also prevent some of the aches and pains associated with carrying extra weight and the changes in gait. However, pregnancy is such a different experience for each individual that, according to your own level of fitness and your needs at this time, it is best to approach your exercise program with great care and scrupulous attention to both form and function. Don't hesitate to adapt your daily workout according to your needs. It is common for women in the final months to feel short of breath, especially when exercising. Awkwardness, leg cramps, and pelvic aching can all hinder your ability to exercise as fully as you once did. Care should be taken to rise gradually from the floor to avoid dizziness.

## Advice from the Naturopath Midwife Cathy Rogers, N.D.

### PERINEAL MASSAGE

Your body is making lots of new hormones that enhance the relaxation and elasticity of your muscles. This elasticity allows your abdomen and pelvis to accommodate the rapidly growing foetus. You can use this to your benefit by beginning to stretch the vaginal opening to ease the delivery of your infant's head and minimize the need for an episiotomy.

Recline comfortably, either on your bed or the floor. Place a small amount of warm almond or olive oil on your thumb. Insert your thumb into the vaginal tract, and gradually apply light pressure downward toward your feet. Do this for a count of 10, then allow another count of 10 for relaxation. Repeat five to six times. Practise this stretching routine daily in the third trimester— and invite your partner to participate.

DADS TAKE NOTE: STRESS AND WEIGHT GAIN

As your wife's pregnancy progresses, be aware of your own stress triggers. A recent study showed that men gained an average of 3 to 4 pounds (1.3 to 1.8 kg) during their wives' pregnancies. First-time fathers tended to eat and drink too much in response to stress.

## Labour and Delivery Basics

I can assure you of one thing. No matter what your individual circumstances, good nutrition and regular exercise throughout your pregnancy will make your delivery far easier. Prepare for delivery the same way you would prepare for a strenuous athletic event.

- Pack more protein into your meals.
- Don't skimp on healthy complex carbohydrates, especially those found in vegetables and fruits, and blood type–friendly selections of grains and beans. These will increase your energy and balance your metabolism.
- Increase your consumption of vitamin C– and vitamin A–rich foods. These vitamins are essential for wound healing and tissue repair—especially for the genital and eliminative tissues, which will be so severely stressed during labour and delivery.
- Eat vitamin K–rich foods every day to improve circulation and blood-clotting factors.

## Prepare Yourself: Prelabour Guidelines

As you approach the birth of your baby, typically around forty weeks, it's normal to feel equal measures of excitement and apprehension. If this is your first pregnancy, you're entering the great unknown. You may find your thoughts filled with worries about whether your baby is all right and dread about what you'll experience during labour.

If you've participated in childbirth classes and have a strong partnership with your doctor or midwife, some of that anxiety will be alleviated. And if you've adhered to your blood type plan, you can have some degree of confidence that you've done the best you can to assure a healthy baby.

The key now, as you prepare for labour, is to be as physically and mentally prepared as possible.

Consider enlisting the services of a doula. *Doula* (pronounced DOO-la) is a Greek word that, roughly translated, means "an experienced woman who helps other women." Doulas are specially trained women who provide pregnant women with nonmedical emotional and physical assistance from late pregnancy through labour and delivery, and into the first weeks of a newborn's life. In the past, it was common for female friends and family members of a woman in labour to gather at the birth and offer assistance. Today, doulas offer a way for women to gain this support before, during, and after labour. Studies have shown that in hospitals with high cesarean rates, a doula's presence lowers the chances of a cesarean. Women have shorter labours and need less chemical intervention to speed birth or reduce pain. Women's satisfaction with their birth experiences, postpartum psychological state, success in breast-feeding, and interactions with their newborns are improved.

Doulas don't replace Dad. In fact, they make Dad's role more effective. With a doula present to relieve some of the stress and burden, dads take fewer breaks, remain closer to the mother, touch her more, and give her more support.

Most doulas have undergone special training. See appendix B for information on finding a doula in your area.

---

### 🐦 Advice from the Naturopath Midwife 🐦
### Cathy Rogers, N.D.

#### HOSPITAL OR HOME DELIVERY?

The setting of the birth is an important decision. Many hospitals today are labour-friendly, so you'll want to check out the hospitals in your area and visit their maternity floors.

When you're deciding between home or hospital birth, the important factors are: a practitioner you can communicate with and whom you trust, and a setting that offers a sense of safety. Some women need the medical environment to feel safe—and it *will* be necessary if you have a high-risk pregnancy. Other women feel safest in their own homes. They equate hospitals with being sick. Talk it over with your mate and your doctor/midwife, and do your research.

Whatever you decide, remember that a meaningful birth experience is less about *where* and more about how completely you involve yourself in the birth.

---

### THE STAGES OF LABOUR: WHAT TO EXPECT

The first stage of labour is called cervical dilation. It is the longest period, normally lasting several hours to a day. During this stage the cervix will fully dilate to 10 centimeters (4 inches).

In the second stage of labour, you will begin to voluntarily push the baby down the birth canal with contractions, which become very strong and can be painful. Each contraction lasts about 60 seconds. The contractions do, however, space out to about 2 to 3 minutes apart. The usual length of the second stage of labour for a first-time mother is about 2 hours. The second stage culminates in the birth of your baby.

The third stage comes after the birth and continues through the delivery of the placenta.

There is a fourth stage of labour, which is often ignored. The fourth stage begins after the birth of the baby and the delivery of the placenta, and lasts for about an hour. The fourth stage is a healing and mending time for the mother, and a time for her and her new child to begin to get acquainted. During this stage, the midwife or doctor will examine the placenta and the umbilical cord, look for episiotomy tears, and suture them and the episiotomy, if one was performed. The uterus will be firm or hard to the touch. This is the adjustment period to the stresses of labour. Many of the physiological changes that occurred in labour will stabilize within the first hour following the birth.

EASING YOUR LABOUR

The exertion of labour has sometimes been compared to running a marathon race. Your state of fitness and the steps you take to keep your energy levels high will play a major role in how well you do during labour. Realistically, you can probably expect to have a longer labour if it is your first child. Some women begin experiencing mild contractions one to two days before the birth. If you have followed your blood type diet and lifestyle guidelines throughout your pregnancy, you should be at a peak level of fitness. Here are some tips:

- In the weeks and especially days before delivery, get plenty of rest. If you experience sleep disturbances, institute a relaxing routine before bedtime, such as a warm bath and a light snack to raise your blood sugar.
- Keep your nutrition levels high. You'll need those extra nutrients for the job ahead.
- During the first stage of labour, when contractions begin and the dilation of your cervix occurs, stay as active as possible. Distract yourself by engaging in regular activities. Delay the time you have to give your full attention to the contractions. (Cathy Rogers suggests that you not consider yourself in "active" labour until you can't talk through a contraction.) Walk around as much as possible, as walking helps the cervix dilate.
- If you're using breathing exercises, start them when the contractions become intense enough that you have difficulty speaking.
- The first stage of labour can last many hours. Drink plenty of liquids and keep a light snack nearby. A strengthening broth of miso, vegetables, or chicken can be helpful in the early stages of labour. Ginger tea (okay now that you're in labour) can also help you avoid exhaustion.
- Be sure to discuss in advance with your doctor or midwife what the policy is about eating light foods or drinking liquids during labour.
- During the second stage of labour, when contractions are more intense and closer together, you'll be working harder to push the baby into the birth canal.

Try to change positions frequently—at least every 30 minutes. This will reduce the pressure and keep you more flexible.

### SAFE PAIN CONTROL

In my experience, most of the anxiety women experience prior to and during labour is related to fears that the pain will be too great to handle, or they won't be able to stay focused or in control. There are many artificial painkillers available in hospitals today. Some are analgesics, which carry some risk since they affect your baby as well. Others, such as the epidural, are regional blocks. Before you hand yourself over to a medicalized childbirth, I urge you to investigate the many non-medical pain-relief strategies that are available. Not only are they safe, they also allow you to be totally present for the birth experience.

### EIGHT NATURAL PAINKILLERS

1. *Relaxation techniques*. Visualization, meditation, and mild hypnosis can take the focus off your pain, relieve your anxiety, and make labour go a lot easier.
2. *Movement*. Changing position frequently enables the force of gravity to work with you, not against you. This decreases the feeling of pressure.
3. *Massage*. Prior to delivery, practise massage with your partner. In labour, light massage to your shoulders, scalp, legs, thighs, brow, face—wherever tension needs easing—can make you feel much better. Deeper massage can also be used at specific points. Counterpressure can be effective. This is pressure applied to areas of the body that are causing pain during labour.
4. *Hydrotherapy*. Water labour and birth can significantly increase your comfort and help you relax during labour. See box on page 36.
5. *Acupressure*. Acupressure is the stimulation of specific pressure points on the body to relieve pain. Refer to appendix B for additional resources.
6. *Acupuncture*. The insertion of tiny needles into nerve centres to block pain.
7. *Doula*. Studies show that doulas reduce a woman's need for pain medication by alleviating stress and the negative impact of high levels of stress hormones.
8. *Homeopathy*. The homeopathic remedy Gelsemium (in either the 6x or 30cc dilution or potency) can help to dilate the cervical opening. Homeopathic remedies are very gentle dilutions of a variety of plants, animals, and minerals. You can take two to three pellets of homeopathic Gelsemium under your tongue every 10 to 20 minutes.

## 🐦 Advice from the Naturopath Midwife 🐦
### Cathy Rogers, N.D.

### BIRTH POOLS AND SHOWERS

Waterbirth is gaining in popularity, for good reason. Contractions are less painful if you are in water. Water equalizes the pressure, relieving pain. It also allows you to change positions easily, which reduces the discomfort. Water puts you in a state of physiological relaxation.

Whether you are delivering at a hospital or at home, you can order a birth pool. There are a number of companies across the country that specialize in providing birth pools. You can order the pool in advance, call their service when you are in labour, and the pool will be delivered. It has a hard plastic shell wrapped around a soft foam interior. A sturdy reusable liner wraps the whole tub and a disposable liner wraps it a second time. A circular foam pad is used as a base. Most services include setup, support, cleaning, takedown, and removal of the pool.

You can also use your own pool or ask for a hospital room with a private pool. If it's not deep enough to cover your belly, cover your belly with a wash-cloth and continuously pour water over it.

If you only have access to a shower, sit on a towel-covered stool in the shower stall and direct the spray where it will help the most.

You can also use moist hot or cold compresses throughout labour—whichever is most comfortable. Use a washcloth and wring it well, then apply it to the brow, abdomen, lower back, or perineum. If you cover the hot wash-cloth with plastic, it will retain the heat longer.

In the next four chapters you will find individualized advice according to your blood type. Combined with this basic naturopathic wisdom, it will provide a complete plan for your healthy pregnancy.

# 3

# The Type O Pregnancy

THE HEALTHY TYPE O WOMAN IS LEAN, strong, metabolically efficient, and perfectly suited for childbearing. The fact that Type O remains the dominant blood type is a testament to its genetic hardiness. However, if you don't follow the diet and lifestyle guidelines for your blood type, conditions can develop that may compromise your health and your ability to pursue a successful pregnancy. There is good evidence that Type Os who consume too much wheat, simple carbohydrates, and sugar have problems regulating their blood sugar, which can be especially dangerous during pregnancy, potentially leading to gestational diabetes and preventing vital nutrients from reaching the foetus. Type O also has a tendency to suffer from hormonal and metabolic disorders, which are a major impediment to fertility. The Type O's hyperactive immune defences can lead to allergies, inflammation, chronic fatigue, and a number of other autoimmune disorders that can interfere with the ability to conceive. These disorders can also create problems during pregnancy.

Following the blood type diet provides an essential foundation, enabling you to optimize your health and prepare for an energetic and enjoyable pregnancy.

## The Type O Diet

The following food lists comprise the Type O Diet. Note that the values for certain foods change in preparation for pregnancy, during pregnancy, and/or while you are breast-feeding. I call these Chameleon Foods, and they are contained in the following table. Use this table for quick reference. Chameleon Foods are also marked with an asterisk (*) in the specific food lists.

## TYPE O CHAMELEON FOODS

Chameleons are foods whose values change before pregnancy, during pregnancy, and/or while breastfeeding.

| FOOD | PRE/POST PREGNANCY | PREGNANCY | FACTORS |
|---|---|---|---|
| **SEAFOOD** | | | |
| Bass | Beneficial | Avoid | Heightened risk of contamination |
| Carp | Neutral | Avoid | Heightened risk of contamination |
| Flounder | Neutral | Avoid | Heightened risk of contamination |
| Grouper | Neutral | Avoid | Heightened risk of contamination |
| Halibut | Beneficial | Avoid | High mercury content |
| Mackerel | Neutral | Avoid | Heightened risk of contamination |
| Mahimahi | Neutral | Avoid | Heightened risk of contamination |
| Shark | Neutral | Avoid | High mercury content |
| Swordfish | Beneficial | Avoid | High mercury content |
| Tilapia | Neutral | Avoid | Heightened risk of contamination |
| Tuna | Neutral | Avoid | High mercury content |
| Whitefish | Neutral | Avoid | Heightened risk of contamination |
| **DAIRY/EGGS** | | | |
| Egg/chicken | Neutral | Beneficial | Good source of DHA |
| **OIL** | | | |
| Borage | Neutral | Avoid | Uterine stimulant |
| Linseed (flaxseed) | Beneficial | Neutral | Limit intake; can be a uterine stimulant in large amounts.* |
| **NUTS/SEEDS** | | | |
| Flaxseed | Beneficial | Neutral | Limit intake; can be a uterine stimulant in large amounts. |
| **VEGETABLES** | | | |
| Parsley | Beneficial | Neutral | Limit intake; can be a uterine stimulant in large amounts. |
| **SPICES** | | | |
| Bladderwrack | Beneficial | Avoid | Potentially harmful to foetus |
| Cayenne Pepper | Beneficial | Neutral | May cause digestive difficulties |
| Chocolate | Neutral | Avoid | Contains caffeine |
| Fenugreek | Beneficial | Avoid | Uterine stimulant |

| FOOD | PRE/POST PREGNANCY | PREGNANCY | FACTORS |
|---|---|---|---|
| Ginger | Beneficial | Avoid | May cause miscarriage in large amounts |
| Licorice | Neutral | Avoid | Can influence oestrogen levels |
| Parsley | Beneficial | Neutral | Limit intake; can be a uterine stimulant in large amounts |
| Turmeric | Beneficial | Avoid | Uterine stimulant |
| **HERBAL TEAS** | | | |
| Catnip | Neutral | Avoid | Uterine stimulant |
| Chamomile | Neutral | Beneficial | A calmative and sleep aid |
| Dong quai | Neutral | Avoid | Can start uterine bleeding |
| Fenugreek | Beneficial | Avoid | Uterine stimulant |
| Ginger | Beneficial | Avoid | May cause miscarriage in large amounts. |
| Licorice | Neutral | Avoid | Can influence oestrogen levels |
| Raspberry leaf | Neutral | Beneficial | Supports the pregnancy |
| Vervain | Neutral | Avoid | Uterine stimulant |
| Yarrow | Neutral | Avoid | Uterine stimulant |
| **BEVERAGES** | | | |
| Tea, green | Neutral | Avoid | Contains caffeine; start weaning yourself before pregnancy, and avoid during pregnancy. |
| Wine, red | Neutral | Avoid | Alcohol should be completely avoided during pregnancy. |

## Meats and poultry

Eat only lean, organic meat and poultry of the highest grade available. If you are of African descent, emphasize lean red meats and game over fattier, more domestic choices like lamb or chicken. Avoid all pork and processed meat products, such as ham and bacon. They contain nitrites, which can be toxic for you and your foetus.

### HIGHLY BENEFICIAL

Beef      Mutton

Heart/Sweetbreads      Veal

Lamb      Venison

Liver (calf)

**NEUTRAL**

| | |
|---|---|
| Chicken | Ostrich |
| Duck | Partridge |
| Goat | Pheasant |
| Goose | Pigeon |
| Grouse | Rabbit |
| Guinea fowl | Turkey |

**AVOID**

| | |
|---|---|
| All commercially | Ham |
|    processed meats | Pork |
| Bacon | Quail |

## Seafood

Seafood, the second most concentrated animal protein, is well suited for Type O, but pregnant women must use special caution to avoid fish that may contain PCBs or that are otherwise potentially toxic. Check with your local health department about the safety of fish caught in local waters. In addition, avoid certain fish that are especially vulnerable to contamination by environmental pollutants, such as pesticides and PCBs. These include bass, grouper, mackerel, mahimahi, fresh salmon, tilapia, and whitefish. Also avoid fish that may contain a high level of mercury—halibut, swordfish, shark, and fresh tuna.

**HIGHLY BENEFICIAL**

| | |
|---|---|
| Bass* | Red snapper |
| Cod | Shad |
| Perch (all) | Sole (except Dover sole) |
| Pike | Sturgeon |
| Rainbow trout | |

---

Foods with different values than the standard Type O diet are indicated with an asterisk (*).

**NEUTRAL**

Anchovy

Beluga

Carp*

Chub

Clam

Crab

Caviar

Dover sole

Drum

Eel

Flounder*

Grouper*

Haddock

Hake

Herring (fresh)

Lobster

Monkfish

Mullet

Mussels

Orange roughy

Oysters

Porgy

Prawns

River trout

Sardine

Scallop

Sea trout

Shrimp

Smelt

Snail (*Helix pomatia*/
  escargot)

Whiting

**AVOID**

Abalone

Barracuda

Bass

Catfish

Caviar

Conch

Frog

Grouper

Halibut*

Herring (pickled)

Lox (smoked salmon)

Mackerel

Mahimahi*

Octopus

Pollack

Salmon

Shark*

Squid (calamari)

Swordfish*

Tilapia*

Tuna*

Whitefish*

Foods with different values than the standard Type O diet are indicated with an asterisk (*).

## Eggs and Dairy

Type Os should severely restrict the use of dairy products. Your system is not designed for their proper metabolism, and there are no highly beneficial foods in this group. Eggs are a good source of DHA, which is a beneficial nutrient for your health and the health of your developing foetus. Choose organic eggs only.

Since pregnant women need at least 1,200 milligrams of calcium daily, Type Os need to be sure to get plenty of calcium from nondairy sources. Calcium-enriched rice milk, almond milk, soy milk, and soy cheese are good alternatives, in addition to a calcium supplement.

**HIGHLY BENEFICIAL**
None

**NEUTRAL**

| | |
|---|---|
| Butter | Feta |
| Dairylea-style cheese | Ghee (clarified butter) |
| Egg (chicken)* | Goat's cheese |
| Egg (duck) | Mozzarella |

**AVOID**

| | |
|---|---|
| Blue cheese | Kefir |
| Brie | Milk (cow, goat) |
| Buttermilk | Monterey jack |
| Camembert | Muenster |
| Cheddar | Neufchâtel |
| Cottage cheese | Paneer |
| Cream cheese | Parmesan |
| Edam | Provolone |
| Egg (goose) | Quark cheese |
| Egg (quail) | Ricotta |
| Emmenthal | Sour cream |
| Gouda | String cheese |
| Gruyère | Swiss cheese |
| Ice cream | Whey |
| Jarlsberg | Yogurt (all varieties) |

Foods with different values than the standard Type O diet are indicated with an asterisk (*).

## Oils and Fats

When cooking, give preference to the healthful monounsaturated olive oil. Linseed (flaxseed) oil, normally beneficial for Type O, should be limited during pregnancy; in large amounts it may be a uterine stimulant. Borage oil should be avoided.

**HIGHLY BENEFICIAL**

| | |
|---|---|
| Linseed (flaxseed)* | Olive |

**NEUTRAL**

| | |
|---|---|
| Almond | Cod liver oil |
| Black currant seed | Sesame |
| Borage* | Vegetable |
| Canola | Walnut |

**AVOID**

| | |
|---|---|
| Castor | Peanut |
| Coconut | Safflower |
| Corn | Soy |
| Cottonseed | Sunflower |
| Evening primrose | Wheat germ |

## Nuts and Seeds

Nuts and seeds are normally a good source of supplemental vegetable protein for Type O. However, you may find them difficult to digest during pregnancy, especially if you have a very sensitive stomach. Occasional use of nut butters or purees may be more palatable. Again, limit your consumption of flaxseeds during pregnancy.

**HIGHLY BENEFICIAL**

| | |
|---|---|
| Flaxseed* | Walnut (black/English) |
| Pumpkin seed | |

**NEUTRAL**

| | |
|---|---|
| Almond | Macadamia |
| Almond butter | Pecan/butter |
| Almond cheese | Pignola (pine nut) |
| Almond milk | Safflower seed |
| Butternut | Sesame butter (tahini) |
| Filbert (hazelnut) | Sesame seed |
| Hickory | |

Food with different values than the standard Type O diet are indicated with an asterisk (*).

**AVOID**

| | |
|---|---|
| Beechnut | Peanut butter |
| Brazil nut | Pistachio |
| Cashew/butter | Poppy seed |
| Chestnut | Sunflower butter |
| Peanut | Sunflower seed |

## Beans and Legumes

Type Os of Asian ancestry utilize beans well because they are culturally accustomed to them. Even so, beans and legumes are not an important part of *any* Type O diet. They contain proteins that can interfere with other nutrients in your diet. Try to get most of your protein from animal foods instead. One exception is soy-based products, such as soy milk and soy cheese, which are a good source of calcium—extremely important during pregnancy, especially for dairy-free Type Os.

**HIGHLY BENEFICIAL**

| | |
|---|---|
| Aduki bean | Black-eyed pea |

**NEUTRAL**

| | |
|---|---|
| Black bean | Soy cheese |
| Broad bean | Soy flakes |
| Butter beans | Soy granules |
| Cannellini bean | Soy milk |
| Garbanzo bean (chickpea) | Soy, miso |
| Green bean | Soy, tempeh |
| Green pea | String bean |
| Mung bean (sprouts) | Tofu |
| Soybean | White bean |

**AVOID**

| | |
|---|---|
| Haricot beans | Pinto bean |
| Kidney bean | Tamarind bean |
| Lentil bean | |

## Grains, Breads, and Pasta

Type Os do not tolerate whole-wheat products at all, and you should eliminate them completely from your diet. They contain lectins or glutens that react both with your blood and your digestive tract and interfere with the proper absorption of beneficial foods.

Overall, Type O should limit the amount of grains in your diet.

**HIGHLY BENEFICIAL**
Manna bread

**NEUTRAL**

Amaranth
Artichoke pasta (pure)
Buckwheat/kasha
Gluten-free bread
Millet
Oat bran
Oat flour
Oatmeal
Quinoa
Rice bran
Rice bread
Rice cake

Rice (cream of)
Rice milk
Rice (puffed)
Rice (white, brown, basmati)
Rye bread (100%)
Soba noodles (100% buckwheat)
Soy flour bread
Spelt
Spelt flour products
Sprouted seed bread
Tapioca

**AVOID**

Barley
Cornflour
Cornflakes
Cornmeal
Couscous (cracked wheat)
Cream of wheat
English muffin
Gluten flour
Matzo
Popcorn
Pumpernickel

Seven-grain bread/cereal
Shredded wheat
Sorghum
Spinach pasta
Wheat (bran)
Wheat bread (sprouted commercial)
Wheat (germ)
Wheat (gluten flour products)
Wheat (refined unbleached)

Wheat (semolina flour
products)
Wheat (white flour products)

Wheat (whole-wheat
products)

## Vegetables

There are a tremendous number of vegetables available to Type Os, and they form a
critical component of your diet. You cannot, however, simply eat all vegetables indis-
criminately. Several classes of vegetables cause big problems for Type Os. For example, certain members of the Brassica family—cauliflower and mustard greens—can
inhibit thyroid function, which is already somewhat temperamental in Type Os.
Thyroid irregularity can interfere with ovulation and fertility and also present problems during pregnancy. Leafy green vegetables rich in vitamin K, like kale and collards, are very good for Type Os. This vitamin is critical for blood clotting. Type Os
have lower levels of certain clotting factors and need vitamin K to help blood clot
properly. This is particularly important as your delivery date approaches.

Alfalfa sprouts contain components that, by irritating the digestive tract, can
aggravate Type O hypersensitivity problems. The moulds in domestic and
shiitake mushrooms, as well as fermented olives, tend to trigger allergic reactions
in Type Os. The nightshade vegetables, like aubergine and potatoes, cause
arthritic conditions in Type Os, because their lectins cause immune reactions
against the tissues. Corn lectins may affect the sensitivity of your body to insulin
and can cause blood sugar imbalances—potentially dangerous during pregnancy.

Fennel and parsley should be minimized during pregnancy, as these are potential uterine stimulants. Also note that although onions and garlic are beneficial
for Type O, you may want to avoid or limit them while you're breast-feeding.
Some babies experience colic when mums eat these foods.

**HIGHLY BENEFICIAL**

| | |
|---|---|
| Artichoke (globe, Jerusalem) | Kohlrabi |
| Beet greens | Lettuce (Romaine/cos) |
| Broccoli | Okra |
| Collard greens | Onion (all) |
| Dandelion | Parsley* |
| Endive | Parsnip |
| Horseradish | Potato (sweet) |
| Kale | Pumpkin |
| Kelp | Seaweed |

---

Foods with different values than the standard Type O diet are indicated with an asterisk (*).

Spinach
Swiss chard

Turnip

**NEUTRAL**

Asparagus
Aubergine
Bamboo shoot
Beet
Bok choy
Brussels sprouts
Cabbage (Chinese, green,
   red, white)
Cabbage juice
Carrot
Celeriac
Celery
Chicory
Chilli pepper
Courgette
Endive
Fennel*
Garlic
Lettuce (bibb, Boston,
   butter, iceberg, mesclun)
Marrow
Mushroom (abalone, enoki,

maitake, oyster,
   portabello, straw)
Olive (Greek, green, Spanish)
Parsley*
Pea (green, pod, mangetout)
Pepper (green, yellow,
   jalapeño, pimento)
Radicchio
Radish, sprouts
Rappini (broccoli rabe)
Rocket
Sauerkraut vegetables
Shallot
Spring onion
Squash, (all types except
   pumpkin)
String bean
Swede
Tomato
Water chestnut
Watercress
Yam

**AVOID**

Alfalfa sprouts
Aloe
Avocado
Cauliflower
Corn
Cucumber

Leek
Mushroom (shiitake, open
   cup)
Olive (black)
Potato (purple, red, white,
   yellow)

## Fruits

Many wonderful fruits are available on the Type O diet. Fruits are not only an important source of fibre, vitamins, and minerals, but they can be an excellent alter-

---

Foods with different values than the standard Type O diet are indicated with an asterisk (*).

native to breads and pasta. If you eat a piece of fruit rather than a slice of bread, your system will be better served. Oranges and tangerines should be avoided due to their high acid content and tendency to increase intestinal toxicity. Most berries are okay, but stay away from blackberries, which contain a lectin that aggravates Type O digestion. Unless noted separately, all values of the whole fruits apply to their juices as well.

**HIGHLY BENEFICIAL**

| | |
|---|---|
| Banana | Guava |
| Blueberry | Mango |
| Cherry (all) | Pineapple juice |
| Cherry juice (black) | Plum (all types) |
| Fig (fresh, dried) | Prune |

**NEUTRAL**

| | |
|---|---|
| Apple/cider | Nectarine |
| Apricot | Papaya |
| Cranberry | Peach |
| Currants (black, red) | Pear |
| Date | Persimmon |
| Dewberry | Pineapple |
| Elderberry (dark blue, purple) | Pomegranate |
| Gooseberry | Prickly pear |
| Grape (all types) | Quince |
| Grapefruit | Raisin |
| Kumquat | Raspberry |
| Lemon | Sago palm |
| Lime | Spanish melon |
| Loganberry | Star fruit (carambola) |
| Mulberry | Strawberry |
| | Watermelon |

**AVOID**

| | |
|---|---|
| Asian pear | Kiwi |
| Blackberry | Orange |
| Cantaloupe | Plantain |
| Coconut/milk | Tangerine |
| Honeydew melon | |

## Spices

Spices can be either helpful or dangerous, and this is especially true during pregnancy. A number of spices are uterine stimulants and should be avoided during pregnancy, especially if you have a high-risk pregnancy or a history of miscarriage. Ginger can be an excellent remedy for digestive ailments. However, it can cause miscarriage in high amounts, so limit its use to pre- and post-pregnancy. Bladderwrack, normally beneficial for Type O, should also be avoided during pregnancy. However, you may consume seaweed in food form. Chocolate contains caffeine and should be avoided. Type Os should also limit the consumption of sugars.

Certain spices, normally used in tiny amounts for cooking, should be minimized during pregnancy, including cinnamon, marjoram, nutmeg, oregano, parsley, rosemary, sage, and thyme.

If you have problems with heartburn, nausea, or morning sickness, which occur mostly in the first trimester, you may find it helpful to eliminate strong spices such as curry and horseradish. However, if you don't have digestive problems, go ahead and use these spices.

**HIGHLY BENEFICIAL**

| | |
|---|---|
| Bladderwrack* | Fenugreek* |
| Carob | Ginger* |
| Cayenne pepper* | Horseradish |
| Curry | Parsley* |
| Dulse | Turmeric* |

**NEUTRAL**

| | |
|---|---|
| Agar | Chilli powder |
| Allspice | Chive |
| Almond extract | Chocolate* |
| Anise | Cinnamon |
| Apple pectin | Clove |
| Arrowroot | Coriander |
| Barley malt | Cream of tartar |
| Basil | Cumin |
| Bay leaf | Dill |
| Bergamot | Garlic |
| Blackstrap molasses | Gelatine, plain |
| Caraway | Honey |
| Cardamon | Licorice |
| Chervil | Maple syrup |

Foods with different values than the standard Type O diet are indicated with an asterisk (*).

| | |
|---|---|
| Marjoram | Soy sauce |
| Miso | Spearmint |
| Molasses | Stevia |
| Mustard (dry) | Sucanat |
| Nutmeg | Sugar (brown, white) |
| Oregano | Tamari (wheat-free) |
| Paprika | Tamarind |
| Peppermint | Tapioca |
| Rice syrup | Tarragon |
| Rosemary | Thyme |
| Saffron | Vanilla |
| Sage | Vinegar (apple cider) |
| Savory | Wintergreen |
| Sea salt | Yeast (baker's, brewer's) |

**AVOID**

| | |
|---|---|
| Acacia (gum arabic) | Guarana |
| Algae (blue-green) | Juniper |
| Aspartame | Licorice* |
| Capers | Mace |
| Carrageenan | Maltodextrin |
| Cinnamon* | MSG |
| Cornflour | Nutmeg* |
| Corn syrup | Pepper (black ground, |
| Dextrose | white ground) |
| Fructose | Vinegar (except apple cider) |
| Guar gum | |

## Condiments

There are no highly beneficial condiments for Type Os. If you must have mustard, mayonnaise, or salad dressing on your foods, use them in moderation and stick to the low-fat, low-sugar varieties. Another option is to make your own from acceptable ingredients. Although Type Os can have tomatoes occasionally, avoid ketchup, as it also contains ingredients like vinegar and corn syrup. All pickled foods are indigestible for Type Os. Replace these condiments with healthier seasonings like olive oil, lemon juice, and garlic. There are a number of recipes in appendix A for healthy, delicious dressings.

---

Foods with different values than the standard Type O diet are indicated with an asterisk (*).

**HIGHLY BENEFICIAL**

None

**NEUTRAL**

Apple butter

Jam (from acceptable
   fruits)

Jelly (from acceptable fruits)

Mustard (prepared,
   vinegar-free)

Salad dressing (low-fat, from
   acceptable ingredients)

**AVOID**

Ketchup

Mayonnaise

Pickle relish

Pickles (all types)

Worcestershire sauce

## Herbal Teas

Herbal teas can deliver strong doses of herbs, and for this reason many are not advised for pregnant women. However, certain teas are particularly beneficial, especially late in pregnancy. Raspberry leaf is rich in vitamins and nourishes the uterus; it should only be used during the last 4 weeks of pregnancy. Chamomile is excellent as a calming tea and sleep aid. Dandelion tea aids digestion. Rose hip tea is a good source of vitamin C. Slippery elm tea is an excellent remedy for intestinal problems.

**HIGHLY BENEFICIAL**

Chickweed

Dandelion

Fenugreek*

Ginger*

Hops

Linden

Mulberry

Peppermint

Rose hip

Sarsaparilla

Slippery elm

**NEUTRAL**

Catnip*

Chamomile*

Dong quai*

Elder

Ginseng

Hawthorn

Horehound

Licorice root*

Mullein

Raspberry leaf*

Skullcap

Spearmint

Valerian

Vervain*

White birch

White oak bark

Yarrow*

Foods with different values than the standard Type O diet are indicated with an asterisk (*).

**AVOID**

| | |
|---|---|
| Alfalfa | Red clover |
| Aloe | Rhubarb |
| Burdock | Senna |
| Coltsfoot | Shepherd's purse |
| Corn silk | St. John's wort |
| Echinacea | Strawberry leaf |
| Gentian | Yellow dock |
| Goldenseal | |

## Miscellaneous Beverages

Start eliminating caffeine and alcohol three to six months before pregnancy and continue until you are no longer breast-feeding. The common caffeine withdrawal symptoms—headache, fatigue, and irritability—won't occur if you wean yourself gradually.

**HIGHLY BENEFICIAL**

Sparkling water
Tea, green*

**NEUTRAL**

Wine, red*

**AVOID**

| | |
|---|---|
| Beer | Tea (black regular and |
| Coffee (regular and decaf) | decaf) |
| Spirits | Wine, white |
| Soda (all types) | |

## Before You Get Pregnant

The best guarantee for a healthy pregnancy is to be in top condition before you get pregnant. Start getting ready at least six months before you conceive.

---

Foods with different values than the standard Type O diet are indicated with an asterisk (*).

## Pre-pregnancy Diet Strategies

### Get Serious About the Type O Diet

Check the Type O Chameleon Foods in the table on page 38. Some of these show different values for the pre-pregnancy period.

Begin to increase your compliance to the Type O diet at least six months prior to attempting to conceive. The most efficient approach is to add to the number of Type O beneficial foods you consume. These beneficial foods exert a powerful medicinal influence on your system, creating the optimal atmosphere for conception. At the same time, make an effort to eliminate foods in the avoid category.

### Control Your Weight

If you are overweight, take steps to reduce to a healthy weight before you get pregnant. Type Os utilize animal protein quite efficiently, but gain weight when too many grains, breads, legumes, and beans are eaten. The worst offenders are the lectins, glutens, and gliandins found in wheat germ and whole-wheat products. It is unfortunate that wheat is ubiquitous in almost all cereal and grain products. The vast majority of Type Os report weight loss and a gradual decrease in water retention solely by eliminating wheat from their diets.

Type Os have a special susceptibility to metabolic disorders which can be a factor in both obesity and infertility.

#### TYPE O HEALTHY WEIGHT-LOSS GUIDELINES

1. Eat a high-protein diet, emphasizing organic, chemical-free meats.
2. Minimize carbohydrates found in grains, beans, and legumes, except those allowed for Type O.
3. Include sources of essential fatty acids, especially omega-3 oils found in fish.
4. Eat plenty of fresh vegetables and fruit to provide proper natural fibre. This will aid in the eliminative process.
5. Avoid stimulants found in alcohol, caffeine, and refined sugars.
6. Eliminate sweet fizzy drinks, even diet ones.
7. Engage in rigorous aerobic exercise several times a week.

## Type O

| THESE FOODS PROMOTE WEIGHT LOSS | THESE FOODS PROMOTE WEIGHT GAIN |
|---|---|
| Lean, organic red meat | Wheat gluten |
| Seafood | Dairy foods |
| Kelp (seaweed) | Corn |
| Kale, spinach, broccoli | Haricot beans |
| Pineapple | Kidney beans |
|  | Lentils |
|  | Cabbage |
|  | Potatoes |

## Regulate Thyroid Activity

In my clinical experience, Type Os tend to have "tippy" thyroids. That is, they have problems with both overactive and underactive thyroids. Both hyperthyroidism and hypothyroidism can interfere with fertility and upset your metabolic balance. If you have the following symptoms, have your thyroid levels tested.

| HYPOTHYROIDISM | HYPERTHYROIDISM |
|---|---|
| Hair loss | Unexplained weight loss |
| Dry skin | Heavy sweating |
| Fluid retention | Palpitations |
| Cold intolerance | Frequent bowel movements |
| Constipation | Bulging eyeballs |
| Fatigue | Goitre |
| Unexplained weight gain | |

To regulate your thyroid activity, follow the Type O diet and adhere to the following protocol for a period of four weeks.

**TYPE O METABOLIC ENHANCEMENT PROTOCOL**
(Use *before* pregnancy only.)

- Dandelion (*Taraxacum officinale*). 250 mg, 1 capsule, twice daily.
- Gum Guggul (guggulsterones of types E and Z), 1 capsule, once or twice daily.
- Selenium. 50–75 mcg daily.

- Lectin-blocking formula specific for Type O. 2 capsules with meals.
- Green tea. 1 to 3 cups daily.
- Diet. Increase consumption of sea vegetables, such as seaweed.

## Incorporate Detoxifiers into Your Diet

Toxins are the by-products of bacterial activity on unabsorbed foods that grow in your intestinal tract. Most often these toxins are the result of eating foods that are poorly digested by your blood type—including foods that are overly processed and chemically treated.

**SIGNS OF TOXICITY IN TYPE O**
- Water retention
- Difficulty losing weight
- Inflammation and joint pain
- Bad breath
- Bowel problems—cramping, flatulence, and constipation
- Fatigue; mental hyperactivity

To aid in detoxification before pregnancy, follow this protocol for one week.

**TYPE O DETOXIFICATION PROTOCOL**
(Do not use during pregnancy)

- Standardized Chinese garlic extract (*Allium sativum*). 400 mg, 1 capsule, twice daily.
- Prune powder or boiled prunes. 1 tablespoon before bed with a large glass of water.
- Saunas and steam treatments as appropriate for your physical health and constitution.
- Probiotic supplement (friendly bacteria). Twice daily, preferably blood type specific.
- Larch arabinogalactan (soluble fibre supplement). 1 tablespoon mixed with water or juice, twice daily.

Detoxifying foods that are especially effective for Type O include soy products, such as miso, soy sauce, and tempeh. These do not replace meat for Type O. You still need plenty of lean, organic meat protein. However, the cultured soy foods are excellent supplements for intestinal health. Be sure to choose wheat-free varieties.

## Pre-pregnancy Supplement Guidelines

| VITAMINS | MINERALS | HERBS |
|---|---|---|
| Vitamin B complex—daily, with: 400–600 mcg folic acid, 500 mcg vitamin B$_{12}$ | Calcium citrate—1,000 mg daily | Horsetail (equisetum)—250 mg daily as a source of trace minerals and the mineral silica. |
| Vitamin C from rose hip or acerola cherry—250 mg daily | | Dandelion—250-mg capsule daily; also use fresh in salads or as tea |
| Vitamin K—food sources only | | Green tea—1 to 3 cups daily *before* pregnancy |
| | | Licorice (DGL) 150-mg capsule or chewable tablet as needed |

The Type O diet offers abundant quantities of important nutrients, such as protein and iron. It's important to get as many nutrients as possible from fresh foods, and only use supplements to fill in the minor blanks in your diet. In addition to vitamins, minerals, protein, carbohydrates, and fats, many grains, beans, vegetables, and fruits are excellent sources of fibre, which is necessary for proper digestion. In addition, fresh vegetables are an important source of phytochemicals, the substances in foods that strengthen the immune system and help prevent cancer and heart disease.

### VITAMINS

VITAMIN B. I have found that Type Os often benefit from a high-potency vitamin B complex, which seems to have an energizing effect on metabolism. If you take a B supplement, be sure to choose one that is free of fillers or binders. Avoid any formula that contains yeast or wheat germ. Make sure that your supplement provides at least 400 to 600 micrograms of folic acid and 500 micrograms of vitamin B$_{12}$ (methylcobalamin form is best) at the standard dose.

VITAMIN K. Type Os have lower levels of several blood-clotting factors, which make you "thin-blooded" and can cause bleeding problems. You definitely want to boost your clotting factors as much as possible before pregnancy. However, vitamin K is generally not advisable in supplement form. Instead, take supplemental vitamin C (250 milligrams daily, preferably from food sources, such as acerola cherry or rose hips), and incorporate vitamin K–rich foods into your diet. These include liver, egg yolks, and green leafy vegetables, such as spinach, kale, and Swiss chard.

MINERALS

CALCIUM. Type Os should always include a calcium supplement, since your diet does not include dairy foods, which are the best sources of this mineral. It is especially important now, since pregnancy is a very calcium-intensive condition. A mother's calcium stores are constantly being depleted to furnish the foetus with nourishment for the growth of bone and tissue.

SILICA. The most commonly known benefit of silica is its role in preventing osteoporosis and restoring bone density by assisting the utilization of calcium within the bones. It also improves the strength of hair and nails by stimulating the production of keratin and collagen. Horsetail (equisetum) grass is one of the best sources of natural silica, with high bio-availability. Silica is available in most health-food stores. A typical dose is 250 to 500 milligrams daily.

HERBS

DANDELION (*Taraxacum officinale*). Very effective for mild water retention. It can be used in salads, as a tea, or in capsule form. Take one 250-milligram capsule daily.

GREEN TEA (*Camellia sinensis*). Regular consumption of green tea appears to enhance chances of conception. Drink one to three cups daily, before pregnancy only.

LICORICE (DGL). DGL licorice can be used to control heartburn. Do not use "whole-herb" forms of licorice: They can encourage water retention. Use DGL licorice before pregnancy only—a 150-milligram capsule or chewable tablet as needed.

## Improve Your Emotional Health

Your emotional well-being—especially your ability to adapt to stress—is every bit as important to your overall health as the physical. Indeed, the two are inextricably linked.

Studies show that Type Os are susceptible to an imbalance of the stress hormones called catecholamines. One effect of this imbalance is a marked tendency toward so-called "type A behaviour", which is known to be much more common in Type Os than in the other blood types. People who exhibit type A behaviour have an intense, competitive desire for achievement; an exaggerated sense of urgency;

are afraid of the passage of time; are always in a hurry; and display frequent aggression or hostility toward others. These people often try to do two or more things at once and believe that the only way to get something done right is to do it themselves. They're often fast talking, fast thinking, and abrupt. They are typically too busy to notice the things around them, like the colour of the wallpaper in the dining room, or to be interested in things of beauty such as art, music, or sunsets.

Not surprisingly, I've found that Type Os who exhibit these characteristics have an especially difficult time getting pregnant. When they do get pregnant, they are likely to be plagued with sleep disturbances, digestive problems and severe mood swings.

It is crucial that you take steps to regulate your stress levels before you become pregnant. The key to Type O stress regulation is the Type O diet combined with intense aerobic exercise. In addition, you can benefit from adaptogens, which help regulate your stress response. The most effective is *Rhodiola rosea*, which literally helps your body stay in the adaptive stage of stress—a relatively safe place that prevents stress from causing a physiological breakdown.

In addition, Type Os generally need an ample supply of B vitamins to balance stress hormones. Of particular importance are $B_1$ (50 milligrams once daily), pantethine (500 milligrams once daily), and $B_6$ (50-milligram capsule once daily). (Dosages suitable *before* pregnancy only.)

A SPECIAL NOTE FOR TYPE OS WHO ARE PREPARING FOR PREGNANCY. There is a powerful, synergistic relationship between the release of the neurochemical dopamine and feelings of satisfaction. Type Os are more prone to dopamine imbalances than are the other blood types. In conditions of stress, when dopamine levels plummet, you may feel drawn to substitute "rewards" to boost that sensation. Cigarette smoking, alcohol, caffeine, and recreational drug use can all result from that compulsion. These substances must be avoided during your pregnancy, so if you have a tendency to turn to any of them when you're anxious, bored, or fatigued, now is the time to begin finding effective alternatives to stress reduction.

## Pre-pregnancy Exercise Guidelines

For Type O, stress regulation and overall fitness depend on engaging in brisk regular exercise that taxes the cardiovascular and muscular/skeletal systems. More than any other blood type, Type O relies on physical exercise to maintain health and emotional balance. Below is a list of exercises that are recommended for Type O. Choose from among these exercises for a minimum regimen of 45 minutes, three to four times a week. Later, I'll give you the appropriate adjustments for each trimester of pregnancy.

| EXERCISE | DURATION | FREQUENCY |
|---|---|---|
| Aerobics | 40–50 minutes | 3–4 × week |
| Weight training | 25–35 minutes | 3–4 × week |
| Running | 40–45 minutes | 3–4 × week |
| Calisthenics | 30–45 minutes | 3 × week |
| Treadmill | 30 minutes | 3 × week |
| Kick boxing | 30–45 minutes | 3 × week |
| Cycling | 30 minutes | 3 × week |
| Contact sports | 60 minutes | 2–3 × week |
| In-line/roller skating | 30 minutes | 2–3 × week |

# Your Pregnancy:
# Type O Three-Trimester Plan

## Diet Strategies

### First Trimester

## Choose Type O Beneficial Foods

Continue your compliance with the Type O diet, paying special attention to the Type O Chameleon Foods in the table on page 38. These are foods whose normal values are different during pregnancy. If you are new to the Type O diet, your most important first steps are inclusion of high-quality protein found in lean, organic meat and the avoidance of wheat and dairy foods.

The first trimester is such a critical time that you should emphasize your highly beneficial foods whenever possible. These foods act as medicine for Type O. While many foods are good choices of important nutrients, your power foods offer an extra benefit. For example:

- Choose lean, organic beef over chicken.
- Choose greens—collard, dandelion, kale, Swiss chard, or spinach—over asparagus, mushrooms, or squash.
- Choose olive oil over vegetable oil.
- Choose blueberries, plums, and pineapple over apples and grapefruit.

## Emphasize Pregnancy Power Foods

There are some nutrients that have special importance. These include protein, calcium, folic acid, and iron.

| Blood Type O Pregnancy Power Foods | | | |
|---|---|---|---|
| **PROTEIN** | **CALCIUM** | **IRON** | **FOLIC ACID** |
| Lean, organic beef | Canned sardines (with bones) | Lean, organic beef | Liver, kidney, muscle meats |
| Beef liver | Canned salmon (with bones) | Heart | Fish |
| Lean, organic venison | Calcium-enriched rice or almond milk | Sweetbreads | Dark green leafy vegetables |
| | Soy milk* | | |
| | Seaweed | | |
| | Broccoli | | |
| | Spinach | | |

## Minimize Digestive Discomfort

Type O has naturally high levels of stomach acid, which can add to the digestive discomfort common in the first trimester of pregnancy. If you keep your stomach acid levels in check, you'll experience far less heartburn, nausea, and "morning sickness".

### HEARTBURN

- Eat frequent, small meals.
- Eat slowly and chew thoroughly.
- Bend at the knees, not at the waist.
- Avoid acid-stimulating foods, such as oranges, tangerines, and strawberries.
- Avoid coffee, chocolate, mints, and black tea, all of which can provoke heartburn.
- Avoid sugars and sweets.
- Avoid wheat and dairy.
- Don't lie down directly after meals.
- Supplement with slippery elm bark or drink slippery elm tea. Slippery elm promotes the health of the membranes of the stomach, intestine, and urinary tract. Slippery elm bark is also soothing to intestinal tissue and encourages the growth of good bacteria. (See Supplement Guidelines, page 89.)
- Keep your head and upper body elevated while sleeping.
- Avoid eating while lying down.

- Use this simple reflexology technique for heartburn and nausea: Place your fingers above the navel in the midline. Press at 10-second intervals. Stimulating this point should bring substantial relief.

> **NOTE:** Before taking any medications, such as antacids, talk with your doctor. Not all medications, no matter how benign they may appear to be, are safe during pregnancy.

## CONSTIPATION
- Get plenty of exercise.
- Drink lots of water.
- Include dietary sources of inulin, a form of soluble fibre found in over 30,000 plants such as cabbage, endive, onion, and asparagus. Inulin helps increase stool volume and intestinal motility.
- Take a daily probiotic supplement to keep your intestines healthy. (See Supplement Guidelines, page 89).
- Get plenty of fibre from fresh fruits and vegetables.

## MORNING SICKNESS
- Adhere to the blood type diet.
- Drink plenty of water and nonacidic juices (no caffeine—it dehydrates).
- Eat frequent, small meals throughout the day.
- Do not mix fluids with meals.
- Dry carbohydrates are usually well tolerated. Eat a rice cake with almond or walnut butter before bed.
- Exercise to reduce stress, which can promote nausea.
- Avoid the sight and smell of offensive foods.
- Avoid being around smokers.
- Wear an acupressure wrist band, used by travellers to prevent motion sickness.
- There is some evidence that vitamin $B_6$ minimizes nausea. Foods rich in vitamin $B_6$ include fish and bananas.

> **SPECIAL NOTE:** Two herbal remedies for high stomach acid normally recommended for Type O should not be used during pregnancy. They can increase the risk of miscarriage. They are: ginger rhizome and DGL licorice.

## Balance Your Moods

Mood swings are common in the first months of pregnancy, triggered by the many hormonal changes that are occurring, as well as the extra stress that comes with a major life change. The hyperintensity characteristic of many Type Os won't serve you well during this time. Here are some suggestions for maintaining your emotional balance:

- Find a support group or friend you can share your anxieties with. The typically extroverted Type O releases stress by engaging in a supportive conversation.
- Keep a journal detailing what you are experiencing.
- Break up your workday with physical activity, especially if your job is sedentary. You'll feel more energized, and exercise serves as a natural mood elevator.
- Plan ahead to have foods on hand for a quick energy snack when you're feeling tired or moody. Mood changes can be triggered by a decrease in blood sugar.
- Type Os who suffer from mood swings should always supplement with extra folic acid, along with other B-complex vitamins. Folic acid has the additional benefit of being essential for foetal development. (See Supplement Guidelines, page 89).

## Handle Your Cravings and Aversions

I've seen many Type O pregnant women who've developed a strong aversion to red meat during the first trimester. Since red meat is the best source of high-quality protein for Type O, this aversion isn't necessarily based on healthy instincts. I encourage these women to incorporate very small amounts of red meat into vegetable and rice dishes, and make sure to trim all visible fat—similar to Chinese-style cooking. Sometimes the real aversion is to the fat, rather than to the meat itself.

If you crave foods that are not beneficial for your blood type, find healthy blood type–friendly substitutes. For example:

| WHEN YOU CRAVE . . . | EAT . . . |
| --- | --- |
| Sugar | Raisins or a plum; any suitable fruit |
| Salty foods | Nori (seaweed) snack; miso soup |
| Ice cream | Frozen fruit ice or sorbet; soy- or rice-based ice cream |

| Fatty foods | A banana or walnuts |
| Creamy foods | Vegetable puree—sweet |
| | potato, onion, pumpkin, or |
| | turnip; fruit smoothie |

## First Trimester Menu Plans

The following menus offer a guide to healthy eating during the first trimester of your pregnancy. They are designed to offer well-balanced, delicious meals that include the primary values critical for Type O:

- They emphasize lean meats, fish, and fresh fruits and vegetables.
- They provide an extra boost of calcium and protein with Type O–specific smoothies and energy bars.
- They provide many foods to help overcome first trimester problems, such as constipation, fatigue, and morning sickness.
- They break the daily diet into six meals/snacks a day—aiding digestion and reducing fatigue by avoiding an empty stomach.

The menus are flexible and can be mixed and reorganized according to your personal needs. I have purposely not included portion sizes for most dishes, since caloric needs vary depending on your height and weight. However, try to eat about 300 calories a day more than normal during the first trimester.

Although beverages are listed with some meals, I suggest you drink them half an hour before or after eating. Liquids consumed with solid foods dilute the digestive juices. Don't forget to keep drinking water throughout the day.

### A NOTE ABOUT CERTAIN FOODS

- The following menus avoid wheat and limit most other grains. However, there are occasional allowances for sprouted seed bread and spelt bread. They can be found in health-food stores and some supermarkets. A recipe for homemade spelt bread appears in the recipe section on page 381.
- The Type O Bar is a specially formulated blood type–specific product. The Super Baby Smoothie also utilizes a blood type–specific protein powder, *Proteus ABO*. They are included only as an option. If you prefer, you can substitute other listed snacks and drinks or a beneficial fruit. You can find out more about these products in appendix B.

## Menus

### DAY 1

**BREAKFAST**
One-Egg Omelette with fresh spinach
  and feta
Glass of Calcium-enriched rice milk
Pineapple slices
Red raspberry tea

**MID-MORNING SNACK**
Sassy Smoothie*

**LUNCH**
Mozzarella, tomato, and basil on
  spelt bread
Mixed green salad

**MID-AFTERNOON SNACK**
Type O Bar

**DINNER**
Pan-Fried Liver and Onions*
Baked sweet potato
Steamed broccoli

**EVENING SNACK**
Super Baby Smoothie*

### DAY 2

**BREAKFAST**
Spelt flakes with raisins and soy milk
Mixed berries
Slippery elm tea

**MID-MORNING SNACK**
Type O Bar

**LUNCH**
Farmer's Vegetable Soup*
Mesclun Salad*

**MID-AFTERNOON SNACK**
Type O Trail Mix-1*
Almond milk

**DINNER**
Grilled Lamb Chops*
Wild rice
Braised leeks

**EVENING SNACK**
Super Baby Smoothie*

## DAY 3

**BREAKFAST**
Spinach Frittata*
Fruit Salad
Slippery elm tea

**MID-MORNING SNACK**
Apricot Silken Tofu Shake*

**LUNCH**
"Watch Dog Salad"*
Sprouted seed bread with almond
    butter

**MID-AFTERNOON SNACK**
Toasted Tamari Pumpkin Seeds*
Glass of calcium-enriched rice milk

**DINNER**
Sesame Chicken*
Green Bean Salad with Walnuts and
    Goat's Cheese*
Beneficial vegetable

**EVENING SNACK**
Sliced banana with soy milk
Chamomile tea

## DAY 4

**BREAKFAST**
Fruit Silken Tofu Scramble*
Pineapple juice
Spelt toast

**MID-MORNING SNACK**
Type O Bar

**LUNCH**
Salmon with Wakame Seaweed*
Cuban Black Bean Soup*

**MID-AFTERNOON SNACK**
Type O Trail Mix-2*

**DINNER**
Great Meatloaf*
Pureed sweet potato
Braised Collards*

**EVENING SNACK**
Super Baby Smoothie*

## DAY 5

**BREAKFAST**
Date-Prune Smoothie*
Poached eggs
Rose hip tea

**MID-MORNING SNACK**
Type O Bar

**LUNCH**
Leftover meatloaf sandwich on spelt
    bread, with Romaine lettuce and
    tomato

**MID-AFTERNOON SNACK**
Sliced apple with walnuts and raisins

**DINNER**
Grilled filet of beef
Steamed spinach
Faro Pilaf*

**EVENING SNACK**
Tofu Banana Pudding*
Chamomile tea

## DAY 6

**BREAKFAST**
2 scrambled eggs
½ grapefruit
Spelt toast
Slippery elm tea

**MID-MORNING SNACK**
Banana-Papaya Smoothie*

**LUNCH**
Mushroom Barley Soup with Spinach*
Mesclun Salad*

**MID-AFTERNOON SNACK**
Type O Bar
Pineapple Seltzer*

**DINNER**
Baked red snapper
Steamed Artichoke*
Wild Rice Salad*

**EVENING SNACK**
Super Baby Smoothie*

## DAY 7

**BREAKFAST**
Wheat-Free Waffles*
Mixed berries
Rose hip tea

**MID-MORNING SNACK**
High-Energy Protein Shake*

**LUNCH**
Sardine Salad*
Ryvita crackers
Apple slices

**MID-AFTERNOON SNACK**
Rice cakes with prune butter

**DINNER**
Pasta with Rappini*
Glazed Turnips and Onions*
Beneficial vegetable

**EVENING SNACK**
Super Baby Smoothie*

## DAY 8

**BREAKFAST**
Vegetable Frittata*
Sprouted seed toast with almond
    butter

**MID-MORNING SNACK**
Banana Yogurt Drink*

**LUNCH**
Aduki Bean and Pumpkin Soup*
Spinach Salad*

**MID-AFTERNOON SNACK**
Beneficial fruit

**DINNER**
Grilled filet of beef
Griddled Portabello Mushrooms*
2 Beneficial vegetables

**EVENING SNACK**
Super Baby Smoothie*

## DAY 9

**BREAKFAST**
Poached egg on toasted sprouted
  seed bread
Pineapple juice
Rose hip tea

**MID-MORNING SNACK**
Type O Bar

**LUNCH**
Leftover sliced beef on bed of Romaine
Vegetable crudité
Apple slices

**MID-AFTERNOON SNACK**
Type O Trail Mix-1*

**DINNER**
Sesame Chicken*
Brown Rice Pilaf* with carrots and
  onions

**EVENING SNACK**
Super Baby Smoothie*

## DAY 10

**BREAKFAST**
Heidi's Early Morning Shake*
Sprouted seed toast with almond
  butter

**MID-MORNING SNACK**
Type O Bar

**LUNCH**
Grilled Chicken Salad* on a bed of
  Romaine
Plums
Rice cakes

**MID-AFTERNOON SNACK**
Raisins and chopped walnuts
Glass of soy or rice milk

**DINNER**
Prawn Kebabs*
Stir-fried leeks
Artichoke and Sweet Onion Tart*

**EVENING SNACK**
Super Baby Smoothie*

## DAY 11

**BREAKFAST**
Spelt flakes with fresh berries and soy
  milk
Soft-boiled egg
Slippery elm tea

**MID-MORNING SNACK**
Pineapple-Apricot Silken Smoothie*

**LUNCH**
Carrot-Tofu Soup with Dill*
Mesclun Salad*

**MID-AFTERNOON SNACK**
Beneficial fruit

**DINNER**
Pan-Fried Liver and Onions*
Braised Swiss chard
Wild rice

**EVENING SNACK**
Super Baby Smoothie*

## DAY 12

**BREAKFAST**
Tropical Salad*
Sprouted seed toast with cherry
   preserves
Vegetable juice
Slippery elm tea

**MID-MORNING SNACK**
Type O Bar

**LUNCH**
Black-Eyed Peas with Leeks*
Carrot-Raisin Salad*

**MID-AFTERNOON SNACK**
Type O Trail Mix-2*

**DINNER**
Cellophane Noodles with Grilled
   Sirloin and Green Vegetables*
Beneficial vegetable

**EVENING SNACK**
Super Baby Smoothie*

## DAY 13

**BREAKFAST**
Leftover sirloin and eggs
Spelt toast
Red raspberry tea

**MID-MORNING SNACK**
Super Baby Smoothie*

**LUNCH**
Super Broccoli Salad*
Sliced chicken on a bed of Romaine

**MID-AFTERNOON SNACK**
Type O Bar

**DINNER**
Baked red snapper
Glazed Turnips and Onions*
Steamed asparagus

**EVENING SNACK**
Sliced banana with soy milk
Chamomile tea

## DAY 14

**BREAKFAST**
Banana Spelt Muffin*
Poached egg
Mixed fruit
Slippery elm tea

**MID-MORNING SNACK**
Rice cakes with apple butter

**LUNCH**
Speltberry and Basmati Rice Pilaf*
Green salad

**MID-AFTERNOON SNACK**
Type O Trail Mix-1*

**DINNER**
Grilled Loin of Lamb Chops*
Sautéed greens
Romaine-feta salad

**EVENING SNACK**
Super Baby Smoothie*

---

* You can find recipes for asterisk-marked items in appendix A.

## Second Trimester

### Adjust to an Increased Appetite

Foetal growth is rapid during the second trimester, and you may experience a greater appetite, especially if you no longer suffer from the nausea that may have plagued you during the first three months. Use your extra calories to maximum benefit.

**EMPHASIS FOR EXTRA CALORIES**
- High-quality protein—lean red meat, fish
- Calcium-rich foods—sardines, unboned canned salmon, calcium-enriched rice milk, almond milk, soy milk
- Vitamin C–rich foods—dark green leafy vegetables, plums, pineapple, bananas

### Keep Your Blood Sugar in Check

For Type O, blood sugar irregularities are usually the result of carbohydrate intolerance—especially if you're eating too many grains, beans, and potatoes. While some increase in blood sugar is normal during pregnancy, be aware that severely elevated blood sugar leads to a dangerous condition called gestational diabetes, which can cause premature birth and even birth defects. The following symptoms should alert you to blood sugar imbalances:

Sweating
Palpitations
Extreme hunger
Restlessness
Anxiety
Dizziness and light-headedness

To restore a proper balance:

- Increase the protein and decrease the carbohydrates in your diet.
- Eliminate refined sugars and starches.
- Eat fibre-rich foods every day.
- Never skip meals. Preferably, eat six small meals a day.

### Reduce Allergic Reactions

Type Os have a greater susceptibility to respiratory and food allergies than the other blood types—and pregnancy can make your allergies worse. Follow the Type O diet to rid your intestinal tract of lectins, which can exacerbate allergic tendencies. In addition:

- *Drink stinging nettle leaf as a tea.* This herb tends to promote a more balanced immune system and can be helpful to allergy sufferers. Drink one to two cups per day.
- *At the first sign of allergies, take a teaspoon of rose hip concentrate,* and continue every 30 minutes as needed. Or drink a strong tea made from rose hips one to three times a day.
- *Eliminate the allergen.* Reduce your exposure to allergens by removing dust-collecting furniture, carpets, and draperies; using plastic covers over mattresses and pillows; wet-mopping and dusting frequently; reducing the humidity level; and installing a high-efficiency air filter.
- *Avoid black pepper.* Specifically, commercially ground black pepper can provoke allergies. When the protective outer covering of the peppercorn is broken, several species of moulds can settle on the soft inner pepper parts. All Type Os should avoid black pepper, but it's especially crucial if you have a history of allergies, especially to mould.

## Minimize Problems with Varicose Veins and Haemorrhoids

Varicose veins and haemorrhoids are inflammatory conditions very common to pregnant women. (Haemorrhoids are basically varicose veins on the anus.) Type Os are particularly inclined toward inflammatory conditions.

- Avoid wheat and dairy foods, which trigger inflammatory conditions in Type Os.
- Avoid nightshade plants, which exacerbate inflammatory conditions. These include tomatoes, white potatoes, peppers, and aubergines.
- Increase your intake of safe deep-ocean fish to add helpful fish oils.

NATURAL REMEDY FOR HAEMORRHOIDS: This cold compress can be quite soothing. Pour witch hazel on an absorbent minipad and freeze. Apply to the area.

## Prevent Candida Infections

In general, Type Os are more inclined to candida hypersensitivity than other blood types. During pregnancy, many women find that they have more problems with vaginal candida, commonly called yeast infections. The best way to prevent these infections is to improve your overall bowel health. Here are some recommendations in addition to the Type O diet:

- Increase your consumption of olive oil by using it whenever possible in cooking and making dressings.

- Cut back on sugary foods.
- Take a probiotic supplement every day—preferably blood type–specific.

## Improve Your Blood-Clotting Ability

Studies show that Type Os have lower levels of certain blood-clotting factors, giving you "thin" blood. This can be a problem during the second trimester. The effort of pumping extra blood to the placenta can strain the blood vessels, causing nosebleeds and bleeding gums. Incorporate plenty of vitamin K– and vitamin C–rich foods into your diet to minimize this tendency.

One side effect of the extra blood volume experienced during pregnancy is inflammation of the mucous membranes. For Type Os, this can increase the tendency for gum problems.

NATURAL REMEDY FOR SORE OR BLEEDING GUMS: Dissolve two 400-microgram tablets of folic acid in 1 to 2 ounces of water and swish around in your mouth, coating the gums, then swallow. Do this once a day.

## Second Trimester Menu Plans

The following menus offer a guide to healthy eating during the second trimester of your pregnancy. They include some adjustments from the first trimester, taking into account the special emphasis on this period in your pregnancy.

- The menu suggestions place an even greater emphasis on lean meats, fish, and fresh fruits and vegetables—all foods that help regulate blood sugar.
- They include more calories than the first trimester menus, to accommodate the growing nutritional needs of your foetus.
- They provide an extra boost of calcium and protein with Type O–specific smoothies and energy bars.
- They provide additional foods that will help to overcome second trimester problems, such as haemorrhoids, varicose veins, bleeding gums, and allergic sensitivities.

The menus are flexible and can be mixed and reorganized according to your personal needs. I have purposely not included portion sizes for most dishes, since caloric needs vary depending upon your height and weight. However, these menus do offer more foods than the first trimester—and you should try to increase your intake by 100 to 300 calories per day.

NOTE: Although beverages are listed with some meals, I suggest you drink them half an hour before or after eating. Liquids consumed with solid foods dilute the digestive juices. Don't forget to keep drinking water throughout the day.

## Menus

### DAY 1

**BREAKFAST**
Silken Scramble* with fruit
Sprouted seed toast
Fresh vegetable juice
Stinging nettle leaf tea

**MID-MORNING SNACK**
2 plums
Glass of soy-rice milk

**LUNCH**
Salmon with Wakame Seaweed*

Rice cakes
Mixed fruit

**MID-AFTERNOON SNACK**
Type O Bar*

**DINNER**
Roast Chicken with Garlic and Herbs*
Glazed Turnips and Onions*
Brown Rice Pilaf*

**EVENING SNACK**
Super Baby Smoothie*

### DAY 2

**BREAKFAST**
Spinach and Feta Omelette
Poached fruit
Grapefruit juice
Rose hip tea

**MID-MORNING SNACK**
Pineapple-Apricot Silken Smoothie*

**LUNCH**
Mushroom Barley Soup with Spinach*
Caesar Salad*

**MID-AFTERNOON SNACK**
Beneficial fruit

**DINNER**
Fried Monkfish*
Griddled Pepper Medley*
Wild and Basmati Rice Pilaf*

**EVENING SNACK**
Baked Apple*
Glass of calcium-enriched almond
    milk

### DAY 3

**BREAKFAST**
Wheat-Free Waffles*
Cherry preserves
Banana
Grape juice
Rose hip tea

**MID-MORNING SNACK**
Type O Bar

**LUNCH**
Grilled Chicken Salad*

Rye crackers
Mixed greens

**MID-AFTERNOON SNACK**
Type O Trail Mix-2*

**DINNER**
Pan-Fried Liver and Onions*
Steamed broccoli
Pureed sweet potato*

**EVENING SNACK**
Super Baby Smoothie*

## DAY 4

**BREAKFAST**
Scrambled eggs
Poached Fruit*
Sprouted seed toast
Chamonile tea

**MID-MORNING SNACK**
Sassy Smoothie*

**LUNCH**
Grilled lean ground beef burger with
    melted goat's cheese, lettuce,
    tomato, and onion
Mixed green salad

**MID-AFTERNOON SNACK**
Type O Bar

**DINNER**
Grilled Salmon with Lemongrass*
Black-Eyed Peas with Leeks*
Steamed spinach

**EVENING SNACK**
Super Baby Smoothie*

## DAY 5

**BREAKFAST**
Heidi's Early Morning Shake*
Spelt toast with almond butter

**MID-MORNING SNACK**
Type O Bar

**LUNCH**
Jerusalem Artichoke Soup*
Super Broccoli Salad*
Rice cakes

**MID-AFTERNOON SNACK**
Super Baby Smoothie*

**DINNER**
Grilled beef filet
Brown rice
Carrots and Parsnips with Garlic
    and Coriander*

**EVENING SNACK**
Tofu Banana Pudding*
Glass of calcium-enriched rice milk

## DAY 6

**BREAKFAST**
Poached eggs on toasted spelt bread
Fresh pineapple slices
Slippery elm tea

**MID-MORNING SNACK**
Date-Prune Smoothie*

**LUNCH**
Spicy Stir-Fried Tofu with Apricots and
    Almonds*
Miso Soup*

**MID-AFTERNOON SNACK**
Type O Bar

**DINNER**
Beef Stew with Green Beans and
    Carrots*
Romaine salad with Olive Oil and
    Lemon Dressing*

**EVENING SNACK**
Baked Apple*
Glass of calcium-enriched rice milk

## DAY 7

**BREAKFAST**
Silken Scramble with Sautéed Pears*
Sprouted seed toast
Rose hip tea

**MID-MORNING SNACK**
Type O Bar

**LUNCH**
Farmer's Vegetable Soup*
Mesclun Salad*

**MID-AFTERNOON SNACK**
Sassy Smoothie*

**DINNER**
Grilled Loin of Lamb Chop*
Steamed Artichoke*
Pureed root vegetables*

**EVENING SNACK**
Super Baby Smoothie*

## DAY 8

**BREAKFAST**
Pumpkin Spelt Muffin*
Stewed plums
Soft-boiled egg
Pineapple juice

**MID-MORNING SNACK**
Type O Bar

**LUNCH**
Sardine Salad*
Rice cakes
Apple slices

**MID-AFTERNOON SNACK**
Super Baby Smoothie*

**DINNER**
Steamed Whole Red Snapper*
Grilled Sweet Potato Salad*
Steamed broccoli

**EVENING SNACK**
Tofu Banana Pudding*
Chamomile tea

## DAY 9

**BREAKFAST**
Tofu Carob Protein Drink*
Mixed berries
Chamomile tea

**MID-MORNING SNACK**
Type O Bar

**LUNCH**
Spinach Salad*
Spelt pitta
Apple

**MID-AFTERNOON SNACK**
Super Baby Smoothie*

**DINNER**
Pan-Fried Liver and Onions*
Vegetable Fritters*
2 Beneficial vegetables

**EVENING SNACK**
Fresh Fig Salad*
Glass of calcium-enriched
    almond milk

## DAY 10

**BREAKFAST**
Steak and eggs
Vegetable juice
Rose hip tea

**MID-MORNING SNACK**
Silken Smoothie*

**LUNCH**
Black-Eyed Peas and Barley Salad*
Mixed steamed vegetables

**MID-AFTERNOON SNACK**
Type O Bar

**DINNER**
Turkey Burgers*
Mixed green salad

**EVENING SNACK**
Super Baby Smoothie*

## DAY 11

**BREAKFAST**
Heidi's Early Morning Shake*
Banana spelt muffin

**MID-MORNING SNACK**
Sliced pear with walnuts and raisins
Sparkling cranberry drink

**LUNCH**
Salmon with Wakame Seaweed*
Rice cakes
Vegetable consommé

**MID-AFTERNOON SNACK**
Banana Yogurt Drink*

**DINNER**
Chicken Breasts with Artichoke
    Hearts*
Griddled Pepper Medley*
Baked Apple*

**EVENING SNACK**
Type O Bar

## DAY 12

**BREAKFAST**
Tropical Salad*
Slice of sprouted seed toast with
    blackberry preserves

**MID-MORNING SNACK**
Banana-Papaya Smoothie*

**LUNCH**
Grilled Chicken Salad* on spelt bread
Spinach Salad*

**MID-AFTERNOON SNACK**
Type O Bar

**DINNER**
Beef Stew with Green Beans and
    Carrots*
Baked sweet potato
Beneficial vegetable

**EVENING SNACK**
Super Baby Smoothie*

## DAY 13

**BREAKFAST**
Courgette-Carrot Omelette
Sautéed Pears
Rose hip tea

**MID-MORNING SNACK**
High-Energy Protein Shake*

**LUNCH**
Cuban Black Bean Soup*
Mixed green salad with Olive Oil and
    Lemon Dressing*

**MID-AFTERNOON SNACK**
Type O Bar

**DINNER**
Old-Fashioned Yankee Pot Roast*
Pureed root vegetables
Braised Collards*

**EVENING SNACK**
Spelt bread with apple butter
Glass of calcium-enriched rice milk

## DAY 14

**BREAKFAST**
Wheat-Free Waffles* with blackberry
  preserves
Fresh Fig Salad*
Slippery elm tea

**MID-MORNING SNACK**
Sassy Smoothie*

**LUNCH**
Mushroom Barley Soup with Spinach*
Green Bean Salad with Walnuts and
  Goat's Cheese*

**MID-AFTERNOON SNACK**
Type O Bar

**DINNER**
Baked Chicken with Plum Barbecue
  Sauce*
Vegetable stir fry
Basmati rice

**EVENING SNACK**
Tofu Banana Pudding*
Glass of soy-rice milk

## Third Trimester

## Reduce Swelling and Oedema

Some water retention can be expected toward the end of your pregnancy, the result of an oestrogen spike prior to the delivery of your baby. Type Os are particularly susceptible to the swelling and puffiness of oedema. If you have an
inflammatory condition, it will increase your discomfort.

Here are some suggestions for reducing oedema:

- Avoid Type O–reactive lectins, especially grains, in your diet.
- Elevate your legs when sitting or lying down.
- Drink six to eight 8-ounce (225 ml) glasses of water during the day.
- Wear comfortable clothing and avoid tight pantyhose. Support
  stockings may offer relief.
- Cut back on high-sodium foods; many processed foods are loaded with
  sodium.
- Make sure your shoes fit properly.
- Drink one to three cups of dandelion tea every day if you are
  experiencing mild water
  retention.
- Ask your partner to gently
  massage the area from
  your ankles to your thighs,
  with a very light touch.

> **WARNING**
> Do not use a diuretic to rid your body
> of excess water. Diuretics can cause
> dehydration and nutrient deficiency.

* You can find recipes for asterisk-marked items in appendix A.

## Control Your Blood Pressure

Blood Type O is more susceptible than the other blood types to toxaemia—also known as preeclampsia or pregnancy-induced hypertension. Left unchecked this can be an extremely dangerous condition.

Type O's risk factors for toxaemia include:

- Inadequate hydration
- Carbohydrate intolerance
- Calcium deficiency
- Food allergies

Maintaining your blood type diet is especially critical during this time—especially the avoidance of foods that trigger allergies or raise your blood sugar. Drink plenty of water throughout the day. Get plenty of calcium in your diet and include a calcium supplement. (See Supplement Guidelines, page 89).

NATURAL BLOOD PRESSURE REDUCTION TONIC: One excellent method for enabling healthy blood pressure is to juice several stalks of celery, taking 6 to 8 ounces (150–225 ml) as fresh juice daily.

## Third Trimester Menu Plans

During the third trimester you may feel full after eating very little. Smaller meals, eaten at regular intervals of 3 to 4 hours, may be required to get all the nutrients you need. The following menus offer a guide to healthy eating during the third trimester. They include some adjustments to account for the special emphasis of this period in your pregnancy.

- They place even greater emphasis on lean meats, fish, and fresh fruits and vegetables—all foods that help maintain metabolic balance.
- They provide an extra boost of calcium and protein with Type O–specific smoothies and energy bars. This will help you prepare for the rigours of labour and delivery.
- Vitamin A– and C–rich foods are abundant, also in preparation for delivery.

The menus are flexible and can be mixed and reorganized according to your personal needs. I have purposely not included portion sizes for most dishes, since caloric needs vary depending upon your height and weight. You may need to divide up the meals and snacks further if you don't think you can finish them at one sitting. However, it's vital that you maintain your overall caloric level.

Note that although beverages are listed with some meals, I suggest you drink them half an hour before or after eating. Liquids consumed with solid foods dilute the digestive juices and fill you up faster. Don't forget to keep drinking water throughout the day.

## Menus

### DAY 1

**BREAKFAST**
Omelette* with Fresh Spinach and
    Feta
Mixed berries
Vegetable juice
Raspberry leaf tea

**MID-MORNING SNACK**
Banana-Papaya Smoothie*

**LUNCH**
Jerusalem Artichoke Soup*
Carrot Raisin Salad*

**MID-AFTERNOON SNACK**
Type O Bar

**DINNER**
Cellophane Noodles with Grilled
    Sirloin and Green Vegetables*
Basmati rice
Beneficial vegetable

**EVENING SNACK**
Super Baby Smoothie*

### DAY 2

**BREAKFAST**
Heidi's Early Morning Shake*
Banana Plum Bread*

**MID-MORNING SNACK**
Poached Fruit*
Glass of soy-rice milk

**LUNCH**
Salmon Salad* on a bed of greens
Speltberry and Rice Salad*

**MID-AFTERNOON SNACK**
Type O Bar
Dandelion leaf tea

**DINNER**
Roast Turkey*
Braised Collards*
Brown Rice Pilaf with Carrots
    and Onions*

**EVENING SNACK**
Rice Pudding with Soy Milk*
Mint Tea

## DAY 3

**BREAKFAST**
Poached egg
Slice of sprouted seed toast with
    black cherry preserves
Mixed berries
Raspberry leaf tea

**MID-MORNING SNACK**
Type O Bar

**LUNCH**
Turkey Soup*
Super Broccoli Salad*
Crackers

**MID-AFTERNOON SNACK**
Type O Trail Mix-2*

**DINNER**
Grilled Salmon with Lemongrass*
Carrots and Parsnips with Garlic
    and Coriander*
Millet Couscous*

**EVENING SNACK**
Super Baby Smoothie*

## DAY 4

**BREAKFAST**
Scrambled eggs
Sprouted seed toast with almond
    butter
Sliced pear
Glass of soy-rice milk
Rose hip tea

**MID-MORNING SNACK**
Cherry-Peach Smoothie*

**LUNCH**
Grilled goat's cheese on sprouted seed
    bread
Mesclun Salad*

**MID-AFTERNOON SNACK**
Type O Bar

**DINNER**
Flank Steak*
Pureed root vegetables
Steamed asparagus

**EVENING SNACK**
Cranberry Biscotti*
Super Baby Smoothie*

## DAY 5

**BREAKFAST**
Amaranth Pancakes*
Blackberry preserves
Mixed fruit salad
Dandelion tea

**MID-MORNING SNACK**
Type O Bar

**LUNCH**
Sliced cold flank steak on a bed of
  Romaine
Mixed Roots Soup*

**MID-AFTERNOON SNACK**
Rice cakes with apple/prune butter
Sparkling cranberry drink

**DINNER**
Green Leafy Pasta*
Chicory salad

**EVENING SNACK**
Super Baby Smoothie*

## DAY 6

**BREAKFAST**
Spinach Frittata*
Spelt toast
Pineapple slices
Rose hip tea

**MID-MORNING SNACK**
Sassy Smoothie*

**LUNCH**
Grilled Chicken Salad*
Slice of spelt bread

**MID-AFTERNOON SNACK**
Sliced apple, raisins, and walnuts

**DINNER**
Braised Veal Shanks*
Glazed Turnips and Onions*
Steamed broccoli

**EVENING SNACK**
Super Baby Smoothie*

## DAY 7

**BREAKFAST**
Wheat-Free Waffles* with blueberry
    preserves
Pineapple slices
Soy-rice milk

**MID-MORNING SNACK**
Type O Bar

**LUNCH**
Waldorf Salad*
Tomato, mozzarella, and basil on
    spelt bread

**MID-AFTERNOON SNACK**
Super Baby Smoothie*

**DINNER**
Baked Chicken with Plum Barbecue
    Sauce*
Basmati rice
Steamed broccoli

**EVENING SNACK**
Pineapple sorbet
Chamomile tea

## DAY 8

**BREAKFAST**
Brown Rice–Spelt Pancakes* with
    maple syrup
Mixed fruit
Slippery elm tea

**MID-MORNING SNACK**
Type O Bar

**LUNCH**
White Bean and Wilted Greens Soup*
Mixed Mushroom Salad*

**MID-AFTERNOON SNACK**
Super Baby Smoothie*

**DINNER**
Steamed Whole Red Snapper*
Steamed broccoli
Grilled Sweet Potato Salad*

**EVENING SNACK**
Spelt bread with apple butter
Glass of calcium-enriched rice milk

## DAY 9

**BREAKFAST**
Heidi's Early Morning Shake*
Scrambled eggs
Plums

**MID-MORNING SNACK**
Type O Bar

**LUNCH**
Grilled lean ground beef burger with
    melted goat's cheese and raw
    spinach leaves
Spelt bread
Mixed green salad

**MID-AFTERNOON SNACK**
Toasted Tamari Pumpkin Seeds*
Carrot juice

**DINNER**
Sesame Chicken*
Braised Collards*
Griddled Pepper Medley*

**EVENING SNACK**
Super Baby Smoothie*

## DAY 10

**BREAKFAST**
Banana Walnut Bread*
Stewed apricots
Pineapple juice
Slippery elm tea

**MID-MORNING SNACK**
High-Energy Protein Shake*

**LUNCH**
Sardine Salad*
Mushroom Barley Soup with Spinach*
Crackers

**MID-AFTERNOON SNACK**
Beneficial fruit

**DINNER**
Grilled sirloin steak
Steamed Artichoke*
Wild rice

**EVENING SNACK**
Walnut Cookies*
Glass of soy or rice milk

## DAY 11

**BREAKFAST**
Poached eggs
Sprouted seed toast with almond
    butter
Stewed prunes
Rose hip tea

**MID-MORNING SNACK**
Silken Smoothie*

**LUNCH**
Grilled Chicken Salad* on spelt bread
    with lettuce and tomatoes

**MID-AFTERNOON SNACK**
Type O Bar

**DINNER**
Grilled Loin of Lamb Chops*
Green beans
Sweet Potato Pancakes*

**EVENING SNACK**
Super Baby Smoothie*

## DAY 12

**BREAKFAST**
Scrambled eggs
Slice of spelt toast with black cherry
    preserves
Pineapple juice
Rose hip tea

**MID-MORNING SNACK**
Type O Bar

**LUNCH**
Black-Eyed Peas and Barley Salad*
Mixed steamed vegetables

**MID-AFTERNOON SNACK**
Cherry-Peach Smoothie*

**DINNER**
Tempeh Kebabs*
Wild rice
2 Beneficial vegetables

**EVENING SNACK**
Super Baby Smoothie*

## DAY 13

**BREAKFAST**
Spelt flakes with raisins and soy milk
Mixed berries
Pineapple juice
Type O Tea

**MID-MORNING SNACK**
Banana Yogurt Drink*

**LUNCH**
Mozzarella, tomato, and sprouts on
   spelt bread
Mixed green salad

**MID-AFTERNOON SNACK**
Type O Bar

**DINNER**
Pan-Fried Liver and Onions*
Grilled mixed vegetables
Black-Eyed Peas with Leeks*

**EVENING SNACK**
Apple slices with walnuts and goat's
   cheese
Chamomile tea

## DAY 14

**BREAKFAST**
Courgette-Carrot Omelette
Sautéed Pears*
Rose hip tea

**MID-MORNING SNACK**
Tofu Carob Protein Drink*

**LUNCH**
Spinach Salad*
Grilled peppers and goat's cheese on
   spelt toast

**MID-AFTERNOON SNACK**
Beneficial fruit

**DINNER**
Old-Fashioned Yankee Pot Roast*
Pureed root vegetables
Braised Collards*

**EVENING SNACK**
Super Baby Smoothie*

# Exercise Guidelines

## First Trimester

### Maintenance for Healthy Type Os

If you are healthy and do not have a history of miscarriages, there is no reason why you cannot continue your regular exercise program during the first trimester. Type

---

* You can find recipes for asterisk-marked items in appendix A.

Os thrive on aerobic exercise. However, if your exercise of choice includes rollerblading, contact sports, or skating, I strongly suggest that you replace it with a safer routine—such as running, brisk walking, low-impact aerobics, or swimming. Be sure to wear a good support bra and drink plenty of water throughout your exercise period.

Pregnancy is not the time to *begin* an exercise program. Ideally, you've already been engaged in a pre-pregnancy conditioning program, or, better still, have been following the Type O exercise guidelines for some time.

Choose from among the following Type O exercises for a minimum regimen of 45 minutes, three to four times a week.

| EXERCISE | DURATION | FREQUENCY |
|---|---|---|
| Aerobics (low-impact) | 40–50 minutes | 3–4 × week |
| Weight training | 25–35 minutes | 3–4 × week |
| Running | 40–45 minutes | 3–4 × week |
| Calisthenics | 30–45 minutes | 3 × week |
| Treadmill | 30 minutes | 3 × week |
| Cycling | 30 minutes | 3 × week |
| Swimming | 30 minutes | 3 × week |
| Tennis (doubles) | 45–50 minutes | 1–2 × week |
| Brisk walking | 45 minutes | 3–4 × week |

CAUTIONS FOR HIGH-RISK PREGNANCIES

Consult with your doctor before continuing your exercise regimen if you are in a high-risk pregnancy. Most doctors will discourage exercise if you:

- Have a history of miscarriages, or have had even one miscarriage, if it is recent.
- Have a history of recurrent pelvic or abdominal infections.
- Have an incompetent cervix. This condition causes the cervix to open early, usually in the second trimester, leading to miscarriage.
- Have had toxaemia in a previous pregnancy.
- Have a history of premature deliveries.
- Have or have had a serious medical condition, such as cancer, heart disease, asthma, or kidney disease.

## Second Trimester

### Adaptations for Advancing Pregnancy

Your normal exercise regimen should change somewhat as you approach your sixth month. Replace any strenuous exercise with more controlled, less strenuous variations—for example, brisk walking instead of running. The following are second trimester guidelines:

- Spend more time on your warm-up and cool-down to fully warm and stretch your muscles. This will minimize the muscle cramps that are common as your pregnancy progresses.
- Look for opportunities to incorporate fitness into your daily routine. If feasible, walk to work instead of driving. Take the stairs instead of the elevator.
- You can continue to do a weight workout, but use extreme caution. Your centre of gravity has shifted, and you may feel awkward. Lighter weights may be the answer. Experiment to find the right balance. Consistency is more important than the amount of weight you use.
- Swimming is an excellent exercise for the second and third trimesters. It places minimum stress on your joints and heart rate. You may even want to replace your regular aerobics class with a water aerobics class.
- If you haven't already started your pelvic floor exercises (see page 28), do so now.

Choose from among the following Type O exercises for a minimum regimen of 45 minutes, three to four times a week.

| EXERCISE | DURATION | FREQUENCY |
| --- | --- | --- |
| Aerobics (low impact) | 40–50 minutes | 3–4 × week |
| Weight training (light free weights) | 25–35 minutes | 3–4 × week |
| Calisthenics | 30–45 minutes | 3 × week |
| Treadmill | 30 minutes | 3 × week |
| Cycling (recumbent bike) | 30 minutes | 3 × week |
| Swimming | 30 minutes | 3 × week |
| Tennis (doubles) | 45–50 minutes | 1–2 × week |
| Brisk walking | 45 minutes | 3–4 × week |
| Pelvic floor exercises | 2 minutes | 10–20 × daily |

PREGNANCY-SAFE EXERCISE SUBSTITUTIONS

| INSTEAD OF . . . | TRY . . . |
|---|---|
| Bicycling | exercise bike (recumbent) |
| Running | brisk walking/treadmill |
| Aerobics | water aerobics |
| Weight machines | free weights (5 to 10 pounds—2.25 to 4.5 kg)) |

# Third Trimester

## Adaptations for Late Pregnancy

Exercise is essential during the third trimester. It can help keep your blood pressure in check, combat fatigue, regulate your blood sugar, and reduce the effects of stress. It can also keep you limber and reduce some of the aches and pains you're probably experiencing. However, even if you have been exercising vigorously for years, you need to pay close attention to the signs that you may be pushing yourself too hard. If you feel light-headed or crampy during your workout routine, stop exercising. Avoid any exercises that place pressure on your abdominal area. Lie on your side for floor exercises. This position also helps your circulation and will decrease your blood pressure.

Type Os can benefit in the final months of pregnancy by replacing one or two of your weekly aerobic exercises with a prenatal yoga class. Also, begin your daily perineal massage to tone the vaginal canal (page 31).

An excellent third trimester exercise regimen for Type O would be the following.

THREE TIMES A WEEK, CHOOSE ONE:

| EXERCISE | DURATION |
|---|---|
| Water aerobics | 40–50 minutes |
| Treadmill | 30 minutes |
| Cycling (recumbent bike) | 30 minutes |
| Swimming | 30 minutes |
| Brisk walking | 45 minutes |

TWO TIMES A WEEK, CHOOSE ONE:

| EXERCISE | DURATION |
| --- | --- |
| Light yoga | 40–50 minutes |
| Stretching and relaxation | 30 minutes |
| Labour preparation class | 40–50 minutes |

DAILY, PERFORM BOTH:

| EXERCISE | DURATION |
| --- | --- |
| Pelvic floor exercises | 2 minutes, 10–20 times. |
| Perineal massage | 5 minutes, 1–2 times |

# Supplement Guidelines

## First Trimester

## Vitamins/Minerals

Take a standard prenatal vitamin supplement, choosing one made from whole food, not synthetic ingredients. Powder-in-capsule forms dissolve most efficiently. If you would like to use a prenatal supplement specifically formulated for Type O, see appendix B for information. The following nutrient breakdown is the optimal formula for Type O:

| PRENATAL SUPPLEMENT—TYPE O | |
| --- | --- |
| Vitamin A (100% as natural beta-carotene from *Dunaliella salina*) | 6,000 iu |
| Vitamin C (100% from acerola berry, *Malpighia puncifolia*) | 75 mg |
| Vitamin D (Cholecalciferol) | 100 iu |
| Vitamin K (Phytonadione) | 35 mcg |
| Thiamin (from Thiamin HCl) | 15 mg |
| Riboflavin | 20 mg |
| Niacin and Niacinamide (vitamin $B_3$) | 5 mg |
| Vitamin $B_6$ (from Pyridoxine HCl) | 15 mg |
| Folic Acid | 800 mcg |

| PRENATAL SUPPLEMENT—TYPE O | |
|---|---|
| Vitamin B$_{12}$ (Methylcobalamin) | 15 mcg |
| Biotin | 600 mcg |
| Pantothenic Acid (from D-Calcium Pantothenate) | 10 mg |
| Calcium (seaweed base, derived from *Lithothamnium corralliodes* and *Lithothamnium calcareum*) | 300 mg |
| Iron (Ferrous Succinate) | 18 mg |
| Iodine (Potassium Iodide) | 150 mcg |
| Magnesium (Citrate and Oxide) | 100 mg |
| Zinc (Picolinate) | 20 mg |
| Selenium (L-Selenomethionine) | 20 mcg |
| Copper (Gluconate) | 1 mg |

## Herbal Remedies

| HERB | FUNCTION | FORM AND DOSAGE |
|---|---|---|
| Chamomile | Calms; relieves heartburn | As tea, 1 to 2 cups daily; or add 2 to 4 drops of essential oil to bath |
| Horsetail | Contains silica, which supports healthy bones, skin, hair, and nails | 250-mg capsule daily |
| Peppermint | Calms; relieves indigestion | As tea, 2 to 3 cups daily, after meals |
| Slippery elm bark | Relieves heartburn | 250-mg capsule, twice daily; or as tea, 2 cups daily |

## Nutritional Supplements

| NUTRITIONAL SUPPLEMENT | FUNCTION | FORM AND DOSAGE |
|---|---|---|
| Larch arabinogalactan | Relieves constipation | Soluble fibre supplement; 1 tablespoon mixed with water or juice, twice daily |
| Probiotic | For intestinal health | 2 capsules, twice daily* |
| DHA | Provides essential nutrients for foetal development | 300-mg capsule daily |

* See appendix B for information on blood type–specific probiotics.

NOTE: Type O pregnant women should avoid the flu vaccine—especially if your baby's father is Type A or Type AB. The flu vaccine will boost the presence of anti-A antibodies in your system, which can attack your foetus.

## Second Trimester

### Vitamins/Minerals

Continue to take your prenatal supplement, preferably one formulated for Type O.

### Herbal Remedies

| HERB | FUNCTION | FORM AND DOSAGE |
|---|---|---|
| Bilberry | Relieves haemorrhoids and varicose veins | 25 mg, 2 capsules daily |
| Chamomile | Calms; relieves heartburn; relieves haemorrhoids and varicose veins | As tea, 1 to 2 cups daily; or add 2 to 4 drops of essential oil to bath |
| Horsetail | Contains silica, which supports healthy bones, skin, hair, and nails | 250-mg capsule daily |
| Peppermint | Calms; relieves indigestion | As tea, 2 to 3 cups daily, after meals |
| Rose hip | Treatment for varicose veins, bleeding gums, allergies | 1 tablespoon concentrate every 30 minutes for allergy attack; as tea, 2 to 3 cups daily |
| Stinging nettle leaf | Allergy relief | As tea, 2 cups daily for symptoms |
| Witch hazel | Treatment for haemorrhoids | Use topically as needed |

### Nutritional Supplements

| NUTRITIONAL SUPPLEMENT | FUNCTION | FORM AND DOSAGE |
|---|---|---|
| Larch arabinogalactan | Relieves constipation | Soluble fibre supplement: 1 tablespoon mixed with water or juice, twice daily |

| NUTRITIONAL SUPPLEMENT | FUNCTION | FORM AND DOSAGE |
|---|---|---|
| Probiotic | For intestinal health; prevention of candida infection | 2 capsules, twice daily* |
| DHA | Provides essential nutrients for foetal development | 300-mg capsule daily |

## Third Trimester

## Vitamins/Minerals

Continue to take your prenatal supplement, preferably one formulated for Type O.

### Herbal Remedies

| HERB | FUNCTION | FORM AND DOSAGE |
|---|---|---|
| Dandelion leaf/root | Lowers blood pressure; decreases oedema | As tea, 2 cups daily; or 250-mg capsule, twice daily |
| Nettles | Rich in vitamin K, promotes blood clotting | As tea, 2 cups daily; or 250-mg capsule, twice daily |
| Raspberry leaf (last 4 weeks) | Softens the cervix in preparation for birth; stimulates milk production | As tea, 2 cups daily; as tincture, 15 to 20 drops daily |
| Squaw vine | Prepares uterus for birth | As tincture, 10 drops in warm water, twice daily |

### Nutritional Supplements

| NUTRITIONAL SUPPLEMENT | FUNCTION | FORM AND DOSAGE |
|---|---|---|
| Larch arabinogalactan | Relieves constipation | Soluble fibre supplement: 1 tablespoon mixed with water or juice, twice daily |
| Probiotic | For intestinal health | 2 capsules, twice daily* |
| DHA | Provides essential nutrients for foetal development | 300-mg capsule daily |

* See appendix B for information on blood type–specific probiotics.

## Labour and Delivery

In addition to the general guidelines for labour and delivery (page 32), you have some specific Type O needs.

### Type O Blood-Building Needs

Type O has a limited amount of certain blood-clotting factors, making you more vulnerable in circumstances where surgical procedures are required. To guard against excessive bleeding in the event that a cesarean or other surgical procedure might be required, increase your blood-clotting factors. Follow these guidelines in the final weeks of pregnancy:

- Vitamin K is essential to blood clotting. Eat lots of leafy green vegetables, especially kale, spinach, and collard greens. Rye, oats, and nettle tea are also good sources of vitamin K.
- Make sure to include fish oils in your diet. They promote clotting factors.
- Avoid using aspirin, which has blood-thinning properties.
- Eat natto: Natto is a cultured soy product from Japan made by fermenting boiled soy beans with *Bacillus natto*. It is similar to miso. Natto has substantial fibrinolytic activity—that is, the ability of factors in the blood to break down or dissolve clots.

### Type O Energy Needs

In normal circumstances, Type Os maintain energy through diet and exercise. This can apply during labour, too. The first stage of labour can last many hours. Drink plenty of liquids and keep a light protein snack nearby. Stay hydrated. Be sure to discuss in advance with your doctor or midwife what the policy is about eating light foods or drinking liquids during labour.

Move around as much as possible during the early stages of labour. This will increase your energy and flexibility for the final stages.

### Type O Emotional Needs

Type O does best in situations where you have a sense of control. That's a big challenge during labour, when it's easy to feel as if something is occurring that is well beyond your control. Visualization is helpful here. Focus on yourself bringing your baby to birth—controlling the pace and intensity of the process with your breathing.

Type Os can benefit from having a doula to assist in labour, since you feel stronger and more emotionally stable when you are working with others to achieve a common purpose. (See page 32 for a discussion of the role of a doula.)

Anxiety is enhanced by fear of the unknown. Arrange in advance for your doctor, nurse, midwife, and other providers to keep you informed about the process and apprised of any problems or complications. Well before your delivery date, establish a partnership with your birth team.

See page 35 for natural childbirth painkillers.

# The Type A Pregnancy

## 4

A HEALTHY TYPE A WOMAN IS LEAN AND FIT, with a well-regulated metabolism and a strong immune system. However, when you don't follow the diet and lifestyle guidelines for your blood type, conditions can develop that may compromise your health and ability to pursue a successful pregnancy. Type A is particularly susceptible to stress-related health problems, such as colds and flu, high blood pressure, heart conditions, and even cancer. Stress has a weakening effect on body systems and hormonal activity and can also be an impediment to fertility. Gestational hypertension and diabetes are always potential risk factors for the Type A woman, and these tendencies can be countered by foods and supplements that maximize the most efficient use of your body's own healing mechanisms.

The adaptations that produced blood Type A were based on the need to fully utilize nutrients from plant sources. For this reason, Type A has difficulty digesting and metabolizing animal protein and fat. High-quality protein can be provided by increased consumption of legumes, fish, and small amounts of lean, organic poultry.

Following the blood type diet is an essential foundation, enabling you to optimize your health and prepare for an energetic and enjoyable pregnancy.

## The Type A Diet

The following food lists comprise the Type A diet. Note that the values for certain foods change in preparation for pregnancy, during pregnancy, and/or while you are breast-feeding. I call these Chameleon Foods, and they are included in the following table. Use this table for quick reference. Specific Chameleon Foods are also marked with an asterisk (*).

## Type A Chameleon Foods

Chameleons are foods whose values change before pregnancy, during pregnancy, and/or while breast-feeding.

| FOOD | PRE-/POST-PREGNANCY | PREGNANCY | FACTORS |
|---|---|---|---|
| **SEAFOOD** | | | |
| Bass | Neutral | Avoid | Heightened risk of contamination |
| Carp | Beneficial | Avoid | Heightened risk of contamination |
| Mahimahi | Neutral | Avoid | Heightened risk of contamination |
| Salmon | Beneficial | Neutral | Some risk of contamination |
| Shark | Neutral | Avoid | High mercury content |
| Swordfish | Neutral | Avoid | High mercury content |
| Tilapia | Neutral | Avoid | Heightened risk of contamination |
| Tuna | Neutral | Avoid | High mercury content |
| Whitefish | Beneficial | Avoid | Heightened risk of contamination |
| **DAIRY/EGGS** | | | |
| Egg/chicken | Neutral | Beneficial | Good source of DHA |
| **OIL** | | | |
| Linseed (flaxseed) | Beneficial | Neutral | Limit intake; can be a uterine stimulant in large amounts* |
| Borage | Neutral | Avoid | Uterine stimulant |
| **NUTS/SEEDS** | | | |
| Flaxseed | Beneficial | Neutral | Limit intake; can be a uterine stimulant in large amounts |
| **VEGETABLES** | | | |
| Aloe | Beneficial | Avoid | Uterine stimulant |
| Parsley | Beneficial | Neutral | Limit intake; can be a uterine stimulant in large amounts |
| **SPICES** | | | |
| Chocolate | Neutral | Avoid | Contains caffeine |
| Fenugreek | Beneficial | Avoid | Uterine stimulant |
| Ginger | Beneficial | Avoid | May cause miscarriage in large amounts |
| Licorice | Neutral | Avoid | Can influence oestrogen levels |
| Parsley | Beneficial | Neutral | Limit intake; can be a uterine stimulant in large amounts |
| Turmeric | Beneficial | Avoid | Uterine stimulant |

| FOOD | PRE-/POST-PREGNANCY | PREGNANCY | FACTORS |
|------|---------------------|-----------|---------|
| **HERBAL TEAS** | | | |
| Aloe | Beneficial | Avoid | Uterine stimulant |
| Dong quai | Neutral | Avoid | Can start uterine bleeding |
| Fenugreek | Beneficial | Avoid | Uterine stimulant |
| Ginger | Beneficial | Avoid | May cause miscarriage in large amounts |
| Goldenseal | Neutral | Avoid | Potentially harmful to foetus |
| Licorice | Neutral | Avoid | Can influence oestrogen levels |
| Parsley | Beneficial | Neutral | Limit intake; can be a uterine stimulant in large amounts |
| Raspberry leaf | Neutral | Beneficial | Supports late pregnancy |
| St. John's wort | Beneficial | Avoid | Can influence oestrogen levels |
| Yarrow | Neutral | Avoid | Uterine stimulant |
| **BEVERAGES** | | | |
| Coffee, regular | Beneficial | Avoid | Contains caffeine |
| Tea, green | Beneficial | Avoid | Contains caffeine; start weaning yourself before pregnancy, and avoid during pregnancy |
| Wine, red | Beneficial | Avoid | Alcohol should be completely avoided during pregnancy |
| Wine, white | Neutral | Avoid | Alcohol should be completely avoided during pregnancy |

## Meats and Poultry

To receive the greatest benefits, Type As should eliminate all meats from your diet. While neutral meats like chicken or turkey are acceptable, to maximize your pregnancy fitness, you should limit them to occasional consumption. Be sure to choose organic meats. Stay away from processed meat products like ham, frankfurters, and cold cuts. They contain nitrates, which are toxic for you and your foetus.

**HIGHLY BENEFICIAL**
None

**NEUTRAL**

| | |
|---|---|
| Chicken | Ostrich |
| Grouse | Pigeon |
| Guinea fowl | Turkey |

**AVOID**

| | |
|---|---|
| All commercially processed meats | Liver |
| Bacon | Mutton |
| Beef | Partridge |
| Duck | Pheasant |
| Goose | Pork |
| Ham | Quail |
| Heart | Rabbit |
| Lamb | Veal |
| | Venison |

## Seafood

Seafood is an excellent source of protein for Type As, but pregnant women must use special caution to avoid fish that may contain PCBs or that are otherwise potentially toxic. Check with your local health department about the safety of fish caught in local waters. In addition, avoid certain fish that are especially vulnerable to contamination by environmental pollutants, such as pesticides and PCBs. These include bass, grouper, mackerel, mahimahi, fresh salmon, tilapia, and whitefish. Also avoid fish that may contain a high level of mercury—halibut, swordfish, shark, and fresh tuna.

**HIGHLY BENEFICIAL**

| | |
|---|---|
| Carp* | Sardine |
| Cod | Sea trout |
| Monkfish | Silver perch |
| Pollack | Snail |
| Red snapper | Whitefish* |
| Rainbow trout | Whiting |
| Salmon* | Yellow perch |

**NEUTRAL**

| | |
|---|---|
| Abalone | Bass* |

---

Food with different values than the standard Type A diet are indicated with an asterisk (*).

Cusk

Drum

Halfmoon fish

Mahimahi*

Mullet

Ocean perch

Orange roughy

Pike

River trout

Salmon roe

Shark*

Smelt

Snapper

Sturgeon

Swordfish*

Tilapia*

Tuna*

White Perch

**AVOID**

Anchovy

Barracuda

Beluga

Bluegill bass

Catfish

Caviar

Clam

Conch

Crab

Crayfish

Dover sole

Eel

Flounder

Frog

Grouper

Haddock

Hake

Halibut

Harvest fish

Herring (fresh)

Herring (pickled)

Lobster

Lox

Mackerel

Molluscs

Mussels

Octopus

Oyster

Prawns

Scallop

Shad

Shrimp

Sole

Squid (calamari)

## Eggs and Dairy

Type As can tolerate small amounts of fermented dairy products, but you should avoid anything made with whole milk, and also limit egg consumption to occasional organically grown eggs.

Food with different values than the standard Type A diet are indicated with an asterisk (*).

Your Type A choices should be yogurt, kefir, nonfat sour cream, and cultured dairy products. Raw goat's milk is a good substitute for whole milk.

If you are a Type A allergy sufferer or are experiencing respiratory problems, be aware that dairy products greatly increase the amount of mucus you secrete. Type As normally produce more mucus than the other blood types, but an over-abundance of mucus means a greater risk of infection and respiratory problems. This is another good reason to limit your intake of dairy foods.

**HIGHLY BENEFICIAL**
None

**NEUTRAL**

| | |
|---|---|
| Dairylea-style cheese | Goat's milk |
| Egg, chicken* | Kefir |
| Egg, duck | Mozzarella |
| Egg, goose | Paneer |
| Egg, quail | Ricotta |
| Feta | Sour cream |
| Ghee (clarified butter) | Yogurt |
| Goat's cheese | |

**AVOID**

| | |
|---|---|
| Blue cheese | Ice cream |
| Brie | Jarlsberg |
| Butter | Milk (skimmed, 1%, 2%, whole) |
| Buttermilk | |
| Camembert | Monterey jack |
| Cheddar | Muenster |
| Cottage cheese | Neufchâtel |
| Cream cheese | Parmesan |
| Edam | Provolone |
| Emmenthal | String cheese |
| Gouda | Swiss |
| Gruyère | |

Food with different values than the standard Type A diet are indicated with an asterisk (*).

## Oils and Fats

When cooking, give preference to the healthful monounsaturated olive oil. Linseed (flaxseed) oil, normally beneficial for Type A, should be limited during pregnancy; in large quantities, it can be a uterine stimulant. Borage oil should be eliminated.

### HIGHLY BENEFICIAL

| | |
|---|---|
| Black currant seed | Olive |
| Linseed (flaxseed)* | Walnut |

### NEUTRAL

| | |
|---|---|
| Almond | Sesame |
| Borage* | Soy |
| Cod liver | Sunflower |
| Evening primrose | Vegetable |
| Safflower | Wheat germ |

### AVOID

| | |
|---|---|
| Castor | Cottonseed |
| Coconut | Peanut |
| Corn | |

## Nuts and Seeds

Since Type As eat very little animal protein, nuts and seeds supply an important protein component to your diet. If you have gallbladder problems or are suffering from pregnancy-related digestive problems limit yourself to small amounts of nut butters instead of whole nuts. Again, limit flaxseeds during pregnancy.

### HIGHLY BENEFICIAL

| | |
|---|---|
| Flaxseed* | Pumpkin seed |
| Peanut | Walnut |
| Peanut butter | |

### NEUTRAL

| | |
|---|---|
| Almond | Beechnut |
| Almond butter | Butternut |
| Almond cheese | Chestnut |
| Almond milk | Filbert (Hazelnut) |

Food with different values than the standard Type A diet are indicated with an asterisk (*).

Hickory nut                          Safflower
Macadamia nut                        Sesame butter (tahini)
Pecan                                Sesame seed
Pignola (pine nut)                   Sunflower butter
Poppy seed                           Sunflower seed

**AVOID**
Brazil nut                           Pistachio
Cashew

## Beans and Legumes

Type As thrive on the vegetable proteins found in beans and legumes. Many beans and legumes provide a nutritious source of protein. Be aware, however, that not *all* beans and legumes are good for you. Some, like kidney, butter, haricot, and garbanzo, can contain a lectin that produces a decrease in insulin production. This can be a factor in both obesity and diabetes—and during pregnancy can place you at risk of gestational diabetes.

Soy beans and their products—tofu, tempeh, soy milk, soy cheese—are highly recommended as Type A diet staples. Many supermarkets now carry these products, and they are available in health-food stores.

**HIGHLY BENEFICIAL**
Aduki bean                           Soybean
Black bean                           Soy cheese
Black-eyed pea                       Soy milk
Broad bean                           Soy, miso
Green bean                           Tempeh
Lentil bean                          Tofu
Pinto bean

**NEUTRAL**
Broad bean                           String bean
Cannellini bean                      Sugarsnap bean
Green pea                            White bean
Mung bean

**AVOID**
Butter bean                          Kidney bean
Garbanzo bean (chickpea)             Tamarind bean
Haricot bean

## Grains, Pastas, and Cereals

Type As generally do well on most cereals and grains, as long as you select the more concentrated whole grains instead of instant and processed cereals. If you have a pronounced mucus condition caused by asthma, or frequent respiratory infections, limit your wheat consumption, as wheat causes mucus production. You'll have to experiment for yourself to determine how much wheat you can eat.

**HIGHLY BENEFICIAL**

Amaranth
Artichoke pasta
Buckwheat
Manna bread
Oat bread
Oat flour
Rice
Rice bran

Rice cake
Rice flour
Rice milk
Rice (puffed)
Rye flour
Soba noodles
Sprouted seed bread

**NEUTRAL**

Barley
Cornflakes
Cornmeal
Corn muffin
Couscous
Cream of rice
Fin crisp
Gluten flour
Ideal flat bread
Kamut
Millet
Oat bran
Oatmeal
Popcorn

Quinoa
Rye bread
Sorghum
Spelt
Tapioca
Wheat (gluten flour products)
Wheat (refined, unbleached)
Wheat (semolina flour
  products)
Wheat (white flour products)
Wheat bread (sprouted/
  commercial)
Wheat (whole-wheat
  products)

**AVOID**

Cream of wheat

English muffin

Matzo                     Wheat germ
Wheat bran                Shredded wheat

## Vegetables

Vegetables are vital to the Type A diet, providing minerals, enzymes, and antioxidants. Eat your vegetables in as natural a state as possible (raw or steamed) to preserve their full benefits.

Most vegetables are available to Type As, but there are a few caveats: Peppers aggravate the delicate Type A stomach, as do the moulds in fermented olives. Potatoes, sweet potatoes, yams, and cabbage contain proteins that may interfere with the proper absorption of essential nutrients. Avoid tomatoes, as their lectins have a negative effect on the Type A digestive tract. Broccoli is highly recommended for its antioxidant benefits. Antioxidants strengthen the immune system and prevent abnormal cell division. Other vegetables that are excellent for Type As are carrots, collard greens, kale, pumpkin, and spinach. Yellow onions are very good immune boosters, too. They contain a substance called quercetin, which is a powerful antioxidant.

Aloe, normally beneficial for Type A, should be avoided during pregnancy, as it is a uterine stimulant. Limit parsley and fennel. Also note that although onions and garlic are beneficial for Type A, you may want to avoid or limit them while you're breast-feeding. Some babies experience colic when mums eat these foods.

**HIGHLY BENEFICIAL**

| | |
|---|---|
| Alfalfa sprouts | Leek |
| Aloe (plant, juice)* | Lettuce (Romaine) |
| Artichoke (domestic, globe, Jerusalem) | Mushroom (maitake, open cup) |
| Beet greens | Okra |
| Broccoli | Onion (green, red, Spanish, yellow) |
| Carrot/carrot juice | |
| Celery/celery juice | Parsley |
| Collard greens | Parsnip |
| Endive | Pumpkin |
| Garlic | Rappini (broccoli rabe) |
| Horseradish | Spinach |
| Kale | Swiss chard |
| Kohlrabi | Turnip |

Food with different values than the standard Type A diet are indicated with an asterisk (*).

**NEUTRAL**

Asparagus
Asparagus pea
Avocado
Bamboo shoot
Beet/beet greens juice
Bok choy
Brussels sprouts
Cabbage juice
Caraway
Cauliflower
Celeriac
Chervil
Chicory
Coriander
Corn
Courgette
Cucumber
Fennel
Lettuce (bibb, Boston,
    butter, iceberg, mesclun)
Mangetout
Mung bean sprouts

Mushroom (abalone, enoki,
    portabello, straw, tree oyster)
Mustard greens
Olive, green
Oyster plant
Pea, green
Pea, pod
Pickles (in brine)
Pimento
Radicchio
Radish
Radish sprouts
Rocket
Seaweed
Shallot
Spring onion
Squash (all types)
String bean
Swede
Water chestnut
Watercress

**AVOID**

Aubergine
Cabbage (not juice)
    (Chinese, red, white)
Juniper
Mushroom, shiitake
Olive (black, Greek, Spanish)
Peppers (all types)
Pickles (in vinegar)

Potato (all types)
Rhubarb
Sauerkraut
Sweet potato
Tomato
Yam
Yucca

## Fruits

Type As should eat fruits at least three times a day. Most fruits are allowable, although you should try to emphasize the more alkaline fruits, such as berries and melons, which can help to balance the acid-forming grains. Type As don't do well on tropical fruits like mangoes, oranges, and papaya. Grapefruit is closely related to oranges, but it has positive effects on the Type A stomach. Pineapple is an excellent digestive for Type As. Lemons are also excellent for Type As, helping to aid digestion and clear mucus from the system. Unless noted separately, all values of the whole fruit apply to the juice as well.

### HIGHLY BENEFICIAL

| | |
|---|---|
| Apricot | Grapefruit |
| Blackberry | Lemon |
| Blueberry | Lime |
| Boysenberry | Pineapple |
| Cherry (all types) | Plum (all types) |
| Cherry juice (black) | Prune |
| Fig (fresh or dried) | |

### NEUTRAL

| | |
|---|---|
| Apple | Nectarine |
| Apple cider | Peach |
| Asian pear | Pear |
| Cranberry juice | Persimmon |
| Currant (black and red) | Pomegranate |
| Date | Prickly pear |
| Dewberry | Quince |
| Elderberry (dark blue, purple) | Raisin |
| Gooseberry | Raspberry |
| Grape (all types) | Sago palm |
| Guava | Spanish melon |
| Kiwi | Star fruit (carambola) |
| Kumquat | Strawberry |
| Loganberry | Watermelon |
| Musk melon | |

**AVOID**

| | |
|---|---|
| Banana | Orange |
| Coconut | Papaya |
| Honeydew melon | Plantain |
| Mango | Tangerine |

## Spices

Spices can be either helpful or dangerous, and this is especially true during pregnancy. A number of spices are uterine stimulants and should be avoided—especially if you have a high-risk pregnancy or a history of miscarriage. Ginger can be an excellent remedy for digestive ailments. However, it can cause miscarriage in high amounts, so limit its use to pre- and post-pregnancy. Chocolate contains caffeine and should also be avoided. Type As should also limit the consumption of sugars.

Certain spices, normally used in small amounts for cooking, should be used sparingly during pregnancy. These include cinnamon, marjoram, nutmeg, oregano, parsley, rosemary, sage, and thyme.

If you have problems with heartburn, nausea, or morning sickness, which occur mostly in the first trimester, you may find it helpful to eliminate strong spices such as curry and horseradish. However, if you don't experience digestive problems, go ahead and use them.

**HIGHLY BENEFICIAL**

| | |
|---|---|
| Barley malt | Horseradish |
| Blackstrap molasses | Parsley* |
| Fenugreek* | Soy sauce |
| Garlic | Tamari |
| Ginger* | Turmeric* |

**NEUTRAL**

| | |
|---|---|
| Agar | Caraway |
| Allspice | Cardamon |
| Almond extract | Carob |
| Anise | Chervil |
| Arrowroot | Chive |
| Basil | Chocolate* |
| Bay leaf | Cinnamon |
| Bergamot | Clove |
| Brown rice syrup | Coriander |

---

Food with different values than the standard Type A diet are indicated with an asterisk (*).

Cornflour

Corn syrup

Cream of tartar

Cumin

Curry

Dextrose

Dill

Dulse

Fructose

Guarana

Honey

Licorice root*

Mace

Maple syrup

Marjoram

Mint (all kinds)

Mustard (dry)

Nutmeg

Oregano

Paprika

Peppermint

Rice syrup

Rosemary

Saffron

Sage

Savory

Sea salt

Spearmint

Stevia

Sugar (brown, white)

Tamarind

Tapioca

Tarragon

Thyme

Vanilla

Yeast (baker's and brewer's)

**AVOID**

Aspartame

Capers

Carrageenan

Chilli powder

Gelatine (plain)

Guar gum

Gum arabic

MSG

Pepper (all types)

Sucanat

Vinegar (all types)

Wintergreen

## Condiments

You can eat small quantities of jam and low-fat salad dressing if it's made without vinegar. Vinegar-pickled foods have been linked to stomach cancer in people with low levels of stomach acid. Eliminate ketchup from your diet. Type As react badly to tomato and vinegar.

**HIGHLY BENEFICIAL**

Mustard (prepared, no wheat or vinegar)

---

Food with different values than the standard Type A diet are indicated with an asterisk (*).

**NEUTRAL**

Jam (from acceptable fruits)
Jelly (from acceptable fruits)

Salad dressing (low-fat, from
    acceptable ingredients)

**AVOID**

Ketchup
Mayonnaise
Pickles (all types)
Pickle relish

Vinegar-pickled vegetables
    and fruit
Worcestershire sauce

## Herbal Teas

Herbal teas can deliver strong doses of herbs, and for this reason many are not advised for pregnant women. However, certain teas are particularly beneficial, especially late in pregnancy. Raspberry leaf is rich in vitamins and nourishes the uterus in late pregnancy. Chamomile is excellent as a calming tea and sleep aid. Dandelion tea aids digestion. Rose hip tea is a good source of vitamin C. Slippery elm tea is an excellent remedy for intestinal problems.

**HIGHLY BENEFICIAL**

Alfalfa
Aloe*
Ashwagandha
Burdock
Chamomile
Dandelion
Echinacea
Fenugreek*
Gentian
Ginger*
Gingko biloba

Ginseng, siberian
Hawthorn
Holy basil
Milk thistle
Parsley*
Rose hip
Slippery elm
St. John's wort*
Stone root
Valerian

**NEUTRAL**

Chickweed
Coltsfoot
Dong quai*
Elderberry
Goldenseal*
Hops

Horehound
Licorice root*
Linden
Mulberry
Mullein
Peppermint

---

Food with different values than the standard Type A diet are indicated with an asterisk (*).

| | |
|---|---|
| Raspberry leaf* | Spearmint |
| Sage | Strawberry leaf |
| Sarsaparilla | Thyme |
| Senna | White birch |
| Shepherd's purse | White oak bark |
| Skullcap | Yarrow |

**AVOID**

| | |
|---|---|
| Catnip | Red clover |
| Cayenne | Rhubarb |
| Chaparral | Sassafras |
| Comfrey | Yellow dock |
| Corn silk | |

## Miscellaneous Beverages

Start eliminating caffeine and alcohol three to six months before pregnancy, and continue until you are no longer breast-feeding. The common caffeine withdrawal symptoms—headache, fatigue, and irritability—won't occur if you wean yourself gradually.

**HIGHLY BENEFICIAL**

| | |
|---|---|
| Coffee, decaf | Tea, green* |
| Coffee, regular* | Wine, red* |

**NEUTRAL**

Wine, white*

**AVOID**

| | |
|---|---|
| Beer | Spirits, all distilled |
| Soda, all types | Tea, black (regular and decaf) |
| Sparkling water | |

## Before You Get Pregnant

The best guarantee for a healthy pregnancy is to be in top condition before you get pregnant. Start getting ready at least six months before you conceive.

---

Food with different values than the standard Type A diet are indicated with an asterisk (*).

## Pre-pregnancy Diet Strategies

### Get Serious About the Type A Diet

Begin to increase your compliance to the Type A diet at least six months before you attempt to conceive. The most efficient approach is to add to the number of Type A beneficial foods you consume. These foods exert a powerful medicinal influence on your system, creating the optimal atmosphere for conception. Simultaneously, make an effort to eliminate those foods that are "avoids" for Type A.

Check the Type A Chameleon Foods in the chart on page 96. Some of these show different values for the pre-pregnancy period.

### Control Your Weight

The most effective way for Type A to control weight gain is to reduce your intake of animal protein. Poorly digested by Type A, animal protein has the effect of slowing down your metabolism and promoting water retention and increased body fat.

**TYPE A HEALTHY WEIGHT-LOSS GUIDELINES**
1. Eat a low-fat, largely plant-based diet.
2. Avoid red meats and non-cultured dairy.
3. Derive your primary protein from soy-based foods, fresh seafoods, and beans.
4. Limit grains, especially wheat, if you have a weight problem.
5. Eat plenty of fibre derived from fresh fruits and vegetables.
6. Reduce your stress levels. High stress hormones contribute to weight gain.
7. Engage in regular moderate exercise, with an emphasis on stress-reducing exercises, such as Hatha yoga and T'ai chi.

## Type A

| THESE FOODS PROMOTE WEIGHT LOSS | THESE FOODS PROMOTE WEIGHT GAIN |
| --- | --- |
| Cultured soy foods | Meat |
| Olive and flaxseed oil | Dairy foods (uncultured) |
| Green vegetables | Wheat (in overabundance) |
| Pineapple | |

## Incorporate Detoxifiers into Your Diet

Toxins are the by-products of bacterial activity on unabsorbed foods that grow in your intestinal tract. Most often these toxins are the result of eating foods that are poorly digested by your blood type—including foods that are overly processed and chemically treated.

**SIGNS OF TOXICITY IN TYPE A**
- Skin problems, such as acne, eczema, and psoriasis
- Headaches
- Mental agitation
- Bad breath
- Low blood sugar
- Odoriferous stools
- Blurred vision

To aid in detoxification before pregnancy, follow this protocol for one week:

**TYPE A DETOXIFICATION PROTOCOL**
(Do not use during pregnancy)

- Milk thistle (*Silymarin*). 250 mg daily.
- Dandelion (*Taraxacum officinale*). One 250-mg capsule, twice daily.
- Fig powder or dried figs. One tablespoon fig powder or three figs before bed with an 8-ounce (225 ml) glass of water.
- Dry skin brushing. See page 171.

Detoxifying foods that are especially effective for Type A include cultured dairy foods, such as yogurt and kefir, and soy products, such as miso, natto, okara, soy sauce, and tempeh.

## Pre-pregnancy Supplement Guidelines

| VITAMINS | MINERALS | HERBS |
|---|---|---|
| Vitamin B complex—daily, with: 400–600 mcg folic acid 500 mcg vitamin $B_{12}$ | Calcium citrate—1,000 mg daily | Chamomile—1 to 3 cups daily |
| Vitamin C from rose hip or acerola cherry—500 mg daily | Iron—45–60 mg daily | Dandelion—250-mg capsule, daily: also use fresh in salads or as tea |

| VITAMINS | MINERALS | HERBS |
|----------|----------|-------|
| Vitamin E—400 iu daily | Zinc—15–25 mg daily | Green tea—1 to 3 cups daily *before* pregnancy |
| | | Holy basil—50 mg twice daily |

The Type A diet offers abundant quantities of important nutrients. It's vital to get as many nutrients as possible from fresh foods, and only use supplements to fill in the minor blanks in your diet. In addition to vitamins, minerals, protein, carbohydrates, and fats, many grains, beans, vegetables, and fruits are excellent sources of fibre, which is necessary for proper digestion. Also, fresh vegetables are an important source of phytochemicals, the substances in foods that strengthen the immune system and help prevent cancer and heart disease.

## VITAMINS

VITAMIN B. Type As may need extra amounts of $B_1$, $B_5$, and $B_6$ to have an optimal stress response. $B_{12}$ is vital if you are strictly a vegetarian Type A. Vitamins $B_1$ and $B_6$ help improve the cortisol function of the adrenal gland (an area of stress-related weakness for Type As) and simultaneously normalize the rhythmic activity of the gland. Stress in virtually all forms places extra demands on your $B_5$ status, increasing overreaction and exhaustion in the face of stress. I advise all Type As to take a well-rounded vitamin B supplement. Be sure it provides at least 400 to 600 micrograms of folic acid.

VITAMIN C. Vitamin C in amounts greater than 500 milligrams per day provides a buffer against high levels of the stress hormone cortisol. Look for food-derived vitamin C preparations, such as those found from rose hip or acerola cherry.

VITAMIN E. A daily supplement of no more than 400 international units will help enhance the immune system and cardiac health for Type A.

## MINERALS

IRON. The Type A diet is naturally low in iron, which is found in the greatest abundance in red meats. If you take an iron supplement, I recommend Floradix, a liquid iron and herb supplement, found in most health-food stores. Floradix is well assimilated by Type As.

ZINC. About 15 to 25 milligrams per day of supplemental zinc can reduce cortisol and offer protection against infection. Be aware that in high doses zinc can be dangerous. Do not exceed 50 milligrams per day.

HERBS

CHAMOMILE. This is an effective antistress remedy.

DANDELION (*Taraxacum officinale*). It is very effective for mild water retention. It can be used in salads or as a tea. Dandelion is also a good source of potassium.

GREEN TEA (*Camellia sinensis*). Regular consumption of green tea appears to enhance chances of conception.

HOLY BASIL. Holy basil is another excellent antistress remedy.

## Improve Your Emotional Health

Your emotional well-being—especially your ability to adapt to stress—is every bit as important to your overall health as your physical well-being. Indeed, the two are inextricably linked. As a Type A, you are particularly sensitive to an overreaction to stress, due to your naturally high levels of the stress hormone cortisol. High cortisol levels are implicated in a wide range of health conditions, including insulin resistance, metabolic imbalances, heart disease, chronic fatigue, and susceptibility to infections.

It is crucial that you take steps to regulate your stress levels before you become pregnant. Here are some suggestions:

- Reduce stress in your environment. The following factors are known to increase cortisol levels and mental exhaustion for Type A individuals. Be aware of them and limit your exposure.

| | |
|---|---|
| Crowds of people | Smoking |
| Long telephone calls | Too much sugar and starch |
| Cold or hot weather conditions | Strong smells or perfumes |
| | Too much exercise |
| Coffee (more than 1 cup) | Financial concerns |
| High-carbohydrate breakfast | Anxiety for others |
| Strong chemicals | Lack of sleep |
| Overwork | Dieting (low calories) |
| Unproductive meetings | Violent movies |
| Negative emotions | Loud noise |
| Sunbathing | Arguments |

- If you are being treated for an anxiety disorder, ask your doctor about taking a melatonin supplement. People with high anxiety often have low levels of melatonin.

Some of my Type A patients who have had difficulty sleeping through the night because of anxiety have benefited from the installation of a small, diochromatic green light. You can find it on the Internet or from a theatre lighting supplier.

If you are experiencing anxiety or sleep deprivation, I also recommend a technique called alternate nostril breathing. Left nostril breathing generates a more relaxing effect. Right nostril breathing generates a more energized effect. Switching back and forth tends to balance your nervous system. Holding your right nostril closed, breathe slowly through the left nostril to the count of 10. Switch nostrils and repeat. Perform the exercise five times.

## Pre-pregnancy Exercise Guidelines

### MAINTENANCE FOR HEALTHY TYPE As

For Type A, stress regulation and overall fitness depend on engaging in regular exercise, with an emphasis on calming exercises such as Hatha yoga and T'ai chi, as well as light aerobic exercise such as walking.

Hatha yoga has become increasingly popular in Western countries as a method for coping with stress, and in my experience it is an excellent form of exercise for Type As.

T'ai chi, a martial art that is basically a form of moving meditation, has also been studied for its antistress effects. T'ai chi helps reduce stress, lowers blood pressure, and improves mood.

Walking or brisk walking is the ideal aerobic exercise for Type A, especially when you walk outdoors in a quiet, natural setting. Walking promotes the type of stress-balancing effect you need, along with cardiovascular, immune, and other health benefits.

The following comprises the ideal exercise regimen for Type A:

### THREE TO FOUR TIMES A WEEK, CHOOSE ONE:

| EXERCISE | DURATION |
|---|---|
| Hatha yoga | 40–50 minutes |
| T'ai chi | 40–50 minutes |

TWO TO THREE TIMES A WEEK, CHOOSE ONE:

| EXERCISE | DURATION |
| --- | --- |
| Aerobics (low-impact) | 40–50 minutes |
| Treadmill | 30 minutes |
| Weight training (5–10 lb (2.25–4.5 kg) free weights) | 15 minutes |
| Cycling (recumbent bike) | 30 minutes |
| Swimming | 30 minutes |
| Brisk walking | 45 minutes |
| Pilates | 40–50 minutes |

## Your Pregnancy: Type A Three-Trimester Plan

## Diet Strategies

### First Trimester

## Choose Type A Beneficial Foods

Continue your compliance with the Type A diet, paying special attention to the Type A Chameleon Foods in the table on page 96. These are foods whose normal values are different during pregnancy. If you are new to the Type A diet, your most important first steps are the replacement of animal proteins with soy and other high-quality vegetable proteins, and the elimination of dairy products, except for cultured dairy foods such as yogurt and kefir.

The first trimester is such a critical time that you should emphasize highly beneficial foods whenever possible. These foods act as medicine for Type A. While many foods are good choices of important nutrients, your power foods offer an extra benefit. For example:

Choose tofu over chicken.
Choose soy cheese and soy milk over beans and bean sprouts.
Choose walnuts over almonds.
Choose oat flour over wheat flour.
Choose artichokes and fennel over asparagus and Brussels sprouts.
Choose blackberries and blueberries over apples and melons.

## Emphasize Pregnancy Power Foods

There are some nutrients that have special importance. These include protein, calcium, iron, and folic acid.

| Blood Type A Pregnancy Power Foods | | | |
|---|---|---|---|
| **PROTEIN** | **CALCIUM** | **IRON** | **FOLIC ACID** |
| Cultured soy (miso, natto, okara, soy sauce, tempeh) Fish (cod, mackerel, red snapper, salmon) | Yogurt, kefir, soy milk Canned sardines (with bones) Canned salmon (with bones) | Whole grains Beans (aduki, black, black-eyed peas) Figs Blackstrap molasses | Whole grains Fish Dark green leafy vegetables Lentil beans Sunflower seeds |

A special note for vegetarians: You may be concerned about getting enough protein in your diet to meet the increased needs of your pregnancy. Be sure to consume a varied diet and eat adequate amounts of soy protein. If you use rice- and soy-based protein supplements, avoid those containing added sugar.

## Enhance Digestive Enzymes

Type As have low levels of stomach acid, which can contribute to digestive problems common early in pregnancy. By improving digestive efficiency, you'll experience far less heartburn, nausea, and "morning sickness".

- Avoid meat, which requires high levels of digestive enzymes to consume.
- Use a plant-derived enzyme formula, such as bromelain. Heartburn can be a persistent problem in the first trimester of the Type A pregnancy. Enzymes help break down foods and help transport nutrients across the intestinal walls for your body to use. (See Supplement Guidelines, page 148.)
- Avoid carbonated beverages, such as mineral water and soda. The carbonation decreases gastrin production, which decreases stomach acidity and makes it difficult to properly digest food. Type A is also at greater risk of developing coeliac disease, a digestive condition linked to wheat. If you have digestive distress, it's best to avoid wheat.
- Morning sickness results from excessive liver activity, a condition that Type A has a tendency toward. Vitamin $B_6$ is a good remedy because it impacts the metabolic cycle directly. (See Supplement Guidelines, page 148).

## Fight Fatigue and Mood Swings

It is common to feel especially fatigued during the first trimester of pregnancy, as your body adapts to the tremendous changes taking place. Elevated stress hormones also contribute to fatigue and mood swings. Try to establish a regular sleep schedule and adhere to it as closely as possible. When you have a normal sleep-wake rhythm, it reduces cortisol levels. During the day, schedule at least two breaks of 20 minutes each for complete relaxation. Combat sleep disturbances with regular exercise and a relaxing pre-bedtime routine. A light snack before bedtime will help raise your blood sugar levels and improve sleep.

A contributing factor to Type A fatigue—especially if you are on a vegetarian diet—is the increased susceptibility to iron-deficiency anaemia. Ask your doctor about taking an iron supplement and increase your consumption of foods high in folic acid, vitamin C, iron, selenium, and zinc. These include coldwater fish (salmon, mackerel, herring, and sardines), eggs, green beans, tahini, beets, spinach, kelp, green vegetables, parsley, lettuce, prunes, currants, peaches, and mulberries.

**BEST TYPE A IRON SOURCES**
Seaweed
Brewer's yeast
Molasses
Prunes
Raisins
Mushrooms
Chard
Spinach
Nuts and seeds

## Handle Your Cravings and Aversions

If you crave foods that are not beneficial for your blood type, find healthy blood type–friendly substitutes. For example:

| WHEN YOU CRAVE . . . | EAT . . . |
| --- | --- |
| Sugar | Fresh berries; pineapple slices |
| Salty foods | Miso soup; soy sauce |
| Ice cream | Frozen yogurt; soy- or rice-based ice cream |
| Fatty foods | Peanut butter; almond butter on spelt or sprouted seed bread |
| Creamy foods | Soy shakes; soy and fruit smoothies |

## First Trimester Menu Plans

The following menus offer a guide to healthy eating during the first trimester of your pregnancy. They are designed to offer well-balanced, delicious meals that include the primary values critical for Type A:

- They emphasize a variety of delicious soy-food preparations, fish, pasta and beneficial beans, fresh fruits, and vegetables.
- They provide an extra boost of calcium and protein with Type A–specific smoothies and energy bars.
- They provide many foods to help overcome first trimester problems, such as constipation, fatigue, and morning sickness.
- They break the daily diet into six meals/snacks a day—aiding digestion and reducing fatigue by avoiding an empty stomach.

The menus are flexible and can be mixed and reorganized according to your personal needs. I have purposely not included portion sizes for most dishes, since caloric needs vary depending on your height and weight. However, try to eat about 300 calories a day more than normal during the first trimester.

Although beverages are listed with some meals, I suggest you drink them half an hour before or after eating. Liquids consumed with solid foods dilute the digestive juices. Don't forget to keep drinking water throughout the day.

A NOTE ABOUT CERTAIN FOODS.
- The Type A Bar is a specially formulated, blood type–specific product. The Super Baby Smoothie also utilizes a blood type–specific protein powder, *Proteus ABO*. They are included only as an option. If you prefer, you can substitute other listed snacks and drinks or a beneficial fruit.

## Menus

### DAY 1

**BREAKFAST**
Silken Scramble with Fresh Spinach
    and Feta*
Spelt toast
Pineapple juice
Rose hip tea

**MID-MORNING SNACK**
Super Baby Smoothie*

**LUNCH**
Artichoke and Sweet Onion Tart*
Mixed green salad

**MID-AFTERNOON SNACK**
Beneficial fruit

**DINNER**
Steamed Whole Red Snapper*
Basmati rice
Steamed broccoli

**EVENING SNACK**
Fresh Fig Salad*
Chamomile tea

### DAY 2

**BREAKFAST**
Spelt flakes with raisins and soy milk
Sprouted seed toast
Mixed berries
Slippery elm tea

**MID-MORNING SNACK**
Type A Bar

**LUNCH**
Farmer's Vegetable Soup*
Mesclun Salad*

**MID-AFTERNOON SNACK**
Type A Trail Mix-1*

**DINNER**
Tofu-Sesame Fry*
Faro Pilaf*
Braised leeks

**EVENING SNACK**
Super Baby Smoothie*

## DAY 3

**BREAKFAST**
Millet-Spelt-Soy Pancakes* with
blueberry syrup
2 plums
Slippery elm tea

**MID-MORNING SNACK**
Silken Smoothie*

**LUNCH**
Grilled soy cheese on sprouted seed
bread
Apple

**MID-AFTERNOON SNACK**
Super Baby Smoothie*

**DINNER**
Baked chicken breast
Brown rice
Green Bean Salad with Walnuts and
Goat's Cheese*

**EVENING SNACK**
Sliced strawberries with soy milk
Chamomile tea

## DAY 4

**BREAKFAST**
Silken Scramble*
Pumpkin Almond Bread*
Pineapple juice
Rose hip tea

**MID-MORNING SNACK**
Type A Bar

**LUNCH**
Salmon with Wakame Seaweed*
Cuban Black Bean Soup*

**MID-AFTERNOON SNACK**
Oatmeal Cookies*

**DINNER**
Spicy Stir-Fried Tofu with Apricots and
Almonds*
Braised shiitake mushrooms
Braised greens with garlic
Raw Enzyme Relish*

**EVENING SNACK**
Super Baby Smoothie*

## DAY 5

**BREAKFAST**
Scrambled eggs
Rice cakes with almond butter and
    cherry preserves
Grapefruit juice
Rose hip tea

**MID-MORNING SNACK**
Type A Bar

**LUNCH**
Turkey sandwich on spelt bread with
    Romaine lettuce and mustard

**MID-AFTERNOON SNACK**
Peanut butter on manna bread

**DINNER**
Quinoa Tortillas with Pureed Pinto
    Beans*
Steamed spinach
Braised escarole

**EVENING SNACK**
Tofu Pumpkin Pudding*
Chamomile tea

## DAY 6

**BREAKFAST**
Silken Scramble*
Mixed berries
Slippery elm tea

**MID-MORNING SNACK**
Sliced apple with walnuts and raisins

**LUNCH**
Mushroom Barley Soup with Spinach*
Mesclun Salad*

**MID-AFTERNOON SNACK**
Beneficial fruit

**DINNER**
Fried Monkfish*
Steamed Artichoke*
Apple and Onion Confit*

**EVENING SNACK**
Super Baby Smoothie*

## DAY 7

**BREAKFAST**
Wheat-Free Waffles*
Mixed berries
Rose hip tea

**MID-MORNING SNACK**
High-Energy Protein Shake*

**LUNCH**
Sardine Salad*
Ryvita crackers
Mixed green salad

**MID-AFTERNOON SNACK**
Type A Trail Mix-2*

**DINNER**
Quinoa Pasta with Rappini
2 Beneficial vegetables

**EVENING SNACK**
Super Baby Smoothie*

## DAY 8

**BREAKFAST**
Kasha with brown sugar and soy milk
Grapefruit juice
Rose hip tea

**MID-MORNING SNACK**
Pineapple Protein Shake*

**LUNCH**
Aduki Bean and Pumpkin Soup*
Spinach Salad*

**MID-AFTERNOON SNACK**
Type A Bar

**DINNER**
Grilled Salmon Steak*
Griddled Portabello Mushrooms*
Steamed Artichoke*
Raw Enzyme Relish*

**EVENING SNACK**
Rice Pudding with Soy Milk*
Chamomile tea

## DAY 9

**BREAKFAST**
Poached egg on toasted sprouted
    seed bread
Pineapple juice
Rose hip tea

**MID-MORNING SNACK**
Type A Bar

**LUNCH**
Leftover salmon on a bed of Romaine
Miso soup*
Spelt bread

**MID-AFTERNOON SNACK**
Type A Trail Mix-1*

**DINNER**
Teriyaki Tofu Steak*
Brown Rice Pilaf* with carrots and
    onions
Beneficial vegetable

**EVENING SNACK**
Super Baby Smoothie*

## DAY 10

**BREAKFAST**
Pumpkin Almond Bread*
½ grapefruit
Vegetable juice
Rose hip tea

**MID-MORNING SNACK**
Super Baby Smoothie*

**LUNCH**
Grilled Chicken Salad* on bed of
    Romaine
Simple Fish Soup*

**MID-AFTERNOON SNACK**
Raisins and chopped walnuts
Glass of soy-rice milk

**DINNER**
Fried Monkfish*
Wild rice
Steamed broccoli

**EVENING SNACK**
Type A Bar

## DAY 11

**BREAKFAST**
Spelt flakes with fresh berries and soy
    milk
Sprouted seed bread with almond
    butter
Slippery elm tea

**MID-MORNING SNACK**
Pineapple-Apricot Silken Smoothie*

**LUNCH**
Jerusalem Artichoke Soup*
Mesclun Salad*

**MID-AFTERNOON SNACK**
Type A Bar

**DINNER**
Spicy Stir-fried Tofu with Apricots
    and Almonds*
Braised Swiss chard
Wild rice

**EVENING SNACK**
Super Baby Smoothie*

## DAY 12

**BREAKFAST**
Poached egg
Tropical Salad*
Sprouted seed toast with cherry
  preserves
Slippery elm tea

**MID-MORNING SNACK**
Type A Bar

**LUNCH**
Black-Eyed Peas with Leeks*
Carrot-Raisin Salad*

**MID-AFTERNOON SNACK**
Type A Trail Mix-2*

**DINNER**
Game hen roasted with onions and
  parsnips
Green vegetables

**EVENING SNACK**
Super Baby Smoothie*

## DAY 13

**BREAKFAST**
Blueberry Buckwheat Muffin*
Fresh pineapple
Rose hip tea

**MID-MORNING SNACK**
Super Baby Smoothie*

**LUNCH**
Super Broccoli Salad*
Sliced chicken on a bed of Romaine

**MID-AFTERNOON SNACK**
Beneficial fruit

**DINNER**
Steamed Whole Red Snapper*
Glazed Turnips and Onions*
Steamed asparagus
Raw Enzyme Relish*

**EVENING SNACK**
Sliced strawberries with soy milk
Mint tea

## DAY 14

**BREAKFAST**
Brown Rice–Spelt Pancakes*
Mixed fruit
Slippery elm tea

**MID-MORNING SNACK**
Super Baby Smoothie*

**LUNCH**
Carrot-Tofu Soup with Dill*
Mesclun Salad*

**MID-AFTERNOON SNACK**
Type A Trail Mix-1*

**DINNER**
Butternut Squash and Tofu with
    Mixed Vegetables*
Spinach Salad*

**EVENING SNACK**
Rice cakes with apple butter
Chamomile tea

## Second Trimester

### Adjust to an Increased Appetite

Foetal growth is rapid during the second trimester, and you may experience a greater appetite, especially if you no longer suffer from the nausea that may have plagued you during the first three months. Use your extra calories to maximum benefit.

**EMPHASIS FOR EXTRA CALORIES**
- High-quality protein—soy, fish, beans
- Calcium-rich foods—sardines, canned salmon with bones, soy milk
- Vitamin C–rich foods—dark green leafy vegetables, plums, pineapple

### Keep Your Blood Sugar in Check

Type A's susceptibility to blood sugar irregularities can be increased by elevated stress levels and high cholesterol, especially if your diet includes too much animal protein and fat. Gestational diabetes, a dangerous condition late in pregnancy, can place you and your baby in serious jeopardy. The following symptoms should alert you to blood sugar imbalances:

Sweating
Palpitations
Extreme hunger
Restlessness

---

* You can find recipes for asterisk-marked items in appendix A.

Anxiety
Dizziness and light-headedness

To restore a proper balance:

- Reduce the amount of fat in your diet.
- Eliminate refined sugars and starches.
- Eat fibre-rich foods every day.
- Never skip meals. Preferably, eat six small meals a day.
- Reduce your stress levels. There is a direct connection between high cortisol and blood sugar irregularities.

## Build Your Immunity

Type A often struggles with compromised immune function, which can make you more vulnerable to colds and flu. Your overall immune health is critical to your ability to carry a foetus to term, since your immune system is suppressed during pregnancy to accept the foetus. If you have a history of miscarriages, immune health should be your top priority. Many dietary factors have been linked to immune function. Failure to eat breakfast, irregular eating habits, low vegetable intake, inadequate protein, excessive wheat intake, and high-fat diets (especially those with excessive amounts of polyunsaturated fatty acids) have all been associated with lowered immune function.

Deficiencies in a range of nutrients can result in decreased immune function, so keep your nutrient levels high. In particular, selenium, zinc, vitamin C, beta-carotene, vitamin A, vitamin E, and vitamin D deficiencies should be addressed.

Check the nutrient chart below to be sure your diet contains plenty of these nutrient-rich foods.

| SELENIUM | ZINC | VITAMIN C | BETA-CAROTENE |
|---|---|---|---|
| Whole grains | Turkey | Citrus fruit | Dark green |
| Seafood | Dried beans | Strawberries | vegetables |
| | and peas | Brussels sprouts | Carrots |
| | | Dark green | Pumpkin |
| | | vegetables | Peaches |

| VITAMIN A | VITAMIN E | VITAMIN D |
|---|---|---|
| Chicken liver | Spinach | Fatty fish |
| Eggs | Safflower oil | Egg yolk |

## Eliminate Excess Mucus Production

Type A has a tendency to suffer from excessive mucus production, which can cause a stuffy nose, respiratory problems, and ear infections. I recommend that all Type As begin the day with a glass of room temperature water mixed with the juice of a quarter to half a lemon. This will reduce mucus production. Two to three cups of stinging nettle tea every day can also minimize mucus.

If you have problems with mucus, you should also avoid dairy products, which are known to increase mucus.

## Second Trimester Menu Plans

The following menus offer a guide to healthy eating during the second trimester of your pregnancy. They include some adjustments from the first trimester, taking into account the special emphasis on this period in your pregnancy.

- The menu suggestions place an even greater emphasis on soy, fish, grains, and fresh fruits and vegetables—all foods that help regulate Type A blood sugar.
- They include more calories than the first trimester menus, to accommodate the growing nutritional needs of your foetus.
- They provide an extra boost of calcium and protein with Type A–specific smoothies and energy bars.
- They provide additional foods that will help to overcome second-trimester problems, such as haemorrhoids, varicose veins, and mucus production.

The menus are flexible and can be mixed and reorganized according to your personal needs. I have purposely not included portion sizes for most dishes, since caloric needs vary depending upon your height and weight. However, these menus do offer more foods than the first trimester—and you should try to increase your intake by 100 to 300 calories per day.

Note that although beverages are listed with some meals, I suggest you drink them half an hour before or after eating. Liquids consumed with solid foods dilute the digestive juices. Don't forget to keep drinking water throughout the day.

## Menus

### DAY 1

**BREAKFAST**
Fruit Silken Scramble*
Sprouted seed toast
Fresh vegetable juice
Rose hip tea

**MID-MORNING SNACK**
Peanut butter on manna bread

**LUNCH**
Salmon Salad* on a bed of Romaine
    lettuce
Rice cakes
Raisins and walnuts

**MID-AFTERNOON SNACK**
Type A Trail Mix-1*

**DINNER**
Sesame Chicken*
Glazed Turnips and Onions*
Brown Rice Pilaf*

**EVENING SNACK**
Super Baby Smoothie*

### DAY 2

**BREAKFAST**
Silken Scramble* with brown rice and
    vegetables
Date-Prune Smoothie*
Rose hip tea

**MID-MORNING SNACK**
Pineapple Yogurt Drink*

**LUNCH**
Cold Buckwheat Noodles with Peanut
    Sauce*
Mixed steamed vegetables

**MID-AFTERNOON SNACK**
Type A Bar

**DINNER**
Grilled Salmon Steaks*, marinated in
    Tamari Dipping Sauce*
Kasha*
Stewed okra and onion

**EVENING SNACK**
Baked Apple*
Glass of soy-rice milk

## DAY 3

**BREAKFAST**
Wheat-Free Waffles*
Cherry preserves
Fresh blueberries
Slippery elm tea

**MID-MORNING SNACK**
Type A Bar

**LUNCH**
Grape Ice*
Tofu, avocado, alfalfa sprouts, on
    spelt bread
Sweet Onion Vinaigrette*

**MID-AFTERNOON SNACK**
Super Baby Smoothie*

**DINNER**
Tofu Vegetable Stir-Fry*
Steamed broccoli
Wild rice

**EVENING SNACK**
Peanut Butter Cookies*
Chamomile tea

## DAY 4

**BREAKFAST**
Scrambled eggs
Poached Fruit*
Rose hip tea

**MID-MORNING SNACK**
Sassy Smoothie*

**LUNCH**
Peanut butter and blueberry jam on
    soy-flour bread
Glass of goat's milk
2 apricots

**MID-AFTERNOON SNACK**
Beneficial fruit

**DINNER**
Tofu and Black Bean Chilli*
2 Beneficial vegetables

**EVENING SNACK**
Super Baby Smoothie*

## DAY 5

**BREAKFAST**
Amaranth Pancakes* with maple syrup
Fresh blueberries

**MID-MORNING SNACK**
Type A Bar

**LUNCH**
Jerusalem Artichoke Soup*
Super Broccoli Salad*

**MID-AFTERNOON SNACK**
Type A Trail Mix-1*

**DINNER**
Grilled rainbow trout
Basmati rice
Carrots and Parsnips with Garlic
    and Coriander*

**EVENING SNACK**
Chocolate soy pudding (available in
    health-food stores)
Chamomile tea

## DAY 6

**BREAKFAST**
Poached egg
Blueberry Muffin*
Fresh pineapple slices
Slippery elm tea

**MID-MORNING SNACK**
Date-Prune Smoothie*

**LUNCH**
Grilled mozzarella and courgette
    sandwich
Miso Soup*

**MID-AFTERNOON SNACK**
Raisin Peanut Balls*

**DINNER**
Green Leafy Pasta*
Romaine salad with Olive Oil and
    Lemon Dressing*

**EVENING SNACK**
Super Baby Smoothie*

## DAY 7

**BREAKFAST**
Silken Scramble*
Sautéed Pears*
Slippery elm tea

**MID-MORNING SNACK**
Type A Bar

**LUNCH**
Lentil Soup*
Mesclun Salad*

**MID-AFTERNOON SNACK**
Pineapple-Apricot Silken Smoothie*

**DINNER**
Peter's Escargot*
Faro Pilaf*
Steamed artichoke
Pureed root vegetables

**EVENING SNACK**
Rice cakes with apple butter
Mint tea

## DAY 8

**BREAKFAST**
Spelt flakes with soy milk
Stewed plums
Pineapple juice
Rose hip tea

**MID-MORNING SNACK**
Type A Bar

**LUNCH**
Sardine Salad*
Rice cakes
Apple slices

**MID-AFTERNOON SNACK**
Super Baby Smoothie*

**DINNER**
Kung Pao Tofu and Chicken*
Braised dandelion greens
    with garlic
Steamed broccoli

**EVENING SNACK**
Frozen yogurt
Chamomile tea

## DAY 9

**BREAKFAST**
Tofu Carob Protein Drink*
Mixed berries
Slippery elm tea

**MID-MORNING SNACK**
Type A Bar

**LUNCH**
Greek Salad*
Salmon Salad* on a bed of Romaine
  lettuce

**MID-AFTERNOON SNACK**
Carrot-Cucumber-Apple Smoothie*

**DINNER**
Sautéed Monkfish*
Millet Couscous*
Steamed broccoli and carrots

**EVENING SNACK**
Super Baby Smoothie*

## DAY 10

**BREAKFAST**
Fresh blueberries and yogurt
Sprouted seed toast
Vegetable juice
Rose hip tea

**MID-MORNING SNACK**
Super Baby Smoothie*

**LUNCH**
Black-Eyed Peas and Barley Salad*
Mixed steamed vegetables

**MID-AFTERNOON SNACK**
Type A Bar

**DINNER**
Tasty Tofu-Pumpkin Stir-Fry*
Brown rice
Green beans

**EVENING SNACK**
Rice cakes with almond butter
Grapes

## DAY 11

**BREAKFAST**
Pineapple Yogurt Drink*
Sprouted seed toast with almond
    butter

**MID-MORNING SNACK**
Super Baby Smoothie*

**LUNCH**
Tofu Vegetable Stir-Fry*
Rice crackers

**MID-AFTERNOON SNACK**
Peanut Butter Cookies*

**DINNER**
Turkey Cutlets*
Black-Eyed Peas, Okra, and Leek
    Melange*
Baked Apple*

**EVENING SNACK**
Type A Bar

## DAY 12

**BREAKFAST**
Tropical Salad*
Sprouted seed toast with blackberry
    preserves
Vegetable juice
Type A Tea

**MID-MORNING SNACK**
Silken Smoothie* with peaches and
    mixed berries

**LUNCH**
Grilled Chicken Salad* on spelt bread
Spinach Salad*

**MID-AFTERNOON SNACK**
Type A Bar

**DINNER**
Butternut Squash and Tofu with
    Mixed Vegetables*
Braised greens

**EVENING SNACK**
Poached Fruit*
Glass of soy-rice milk
Mint tea

## DAY 13

**BREAKFAST**
Courgette-carrot omelette
Sautéed Pears*
Spelt toast

**MID-MORNING SNACK**
High-Energy Protein Shake*

**LUNCH**
Aduki Bean and Pumpkin Soup*
Mixed green salad with Olive Oil and
    Lemon Dressing*

**MID-AFTERNOON SNACK**
Type A Bar

**DINNER**
Roast Turkey*
Pureed root vegetables
Braised Collards*

**EVENING SNACK**
Super Baby Smoothie*

## DAY 14

**BREAKFAST**
Wheat-Free Pancakes* with blackberry
   preserves
Pineapple juice
Slippery elm tea

**MID-MORNING SNACK**
Cherry-Peach Smoothie*

**LUNCH**
Miso Soup*
Green Bean Salad with Walnuts and
   Goat's Cheese*
Rice cakes

**MID-AFTERNOON SNACK**
Type A Bar

**DINNER**
Pan-Fried Grouper with Peanut Sauce*
Steamed broccoli
Wild rice

**EVENING SNACK**
Chocolate soy pudding (available at
   health-food stores)
Glass of soy-rice milk
Mint tea

## Third Trimester

### Increase Healthy Blood Flow

Pregnancy places extra stress on your blood vessels as your blood volume increases to support your foetus. Type A has naturally "thicker" blood, making you more susceptible to pulmonary embolisms and clots. To keep your blood flowing efficiently:

- Drink a glass of water with the juice of one quarter to one half a fresh lemon every morning upon rising.
- Get serious about reducing stress. There is good evidence that Type As react to stress by increasing the viscosity (thickness) of your blood. Deep breathing, long walks, and stretching are all wonderful.

### Control Your Blood Pressure

Type As need to be particularly careful to keep blood pressure under control during pregnancy. Preeclampsia, or pregnancy-induced hypertension, is a very serious condition that afflicts some women in the late stages of pregnancy.

   Maintaining your blood type diet is essential.

---

* You can find recipes for asterisk-marked items in appendix A.

NATURAL BLOOD PRESSURE REDUCTION TONIC. One excellent method for ensuring healthy blood pressure is to juice several stalks of celery, taking 6 to 8 ounces (200 to 225 ml) as fresh juice daily.

## Fight Fatigue and Stress

Many women experience great fatigue toward the end of pregnancy, which is perfectly understandable. For Type As, fatigue is often the result of a buildup of stress, sleep disruptions, and digestive problems—all of which cause a weakening of your immune system. Your focus as you prepare for delivery is to strengthen your immune system.

- Don't undereat or skip meals. Use appropriate blood type snacks between meals if you get hungry.
- If you haven't already, cut down on your work hours during the final months of pregnancy.
- Get extra sleep. Try to add an extra hour or two to your nightly sleep. If possible, take a restorative 30-minute nap during the afternoon. If you have trouble falling asleep because of discomfort, a body pillow might be helpful. A neutral (body temperature) bath with a little lavender oil is a good remedy for insomnia.

## Third Trimester Menu Plans

During the third trimester you may feel full after eating very little. Smaller meals, eaten at 3- or 4-hour intervals, may be required to get all the nutrients you need. The following menus offer a guide to healthy eating during the third trimester of your pregnancy. They include some adjustments to account for the special emphasis of this period in your pregnancy.

- They place even greater emphasis on soy foods, fish, and fresh fruits and vegetables—all foods that help maintain metabolic balance.
- They provide an extra boost of calcium and protein with Type A–specific smoothies and energy bars. This will help you prepare for the rigours of labour and delivery.
- Vitamin A– and C–rich foods are abundant, also in preparation for delivery.

The menus are flexible and can be mixed and reorganized according to your personal needs. I have purposely not included portion sizes for most dishes, since caloric needs vary depending upon your height and weight. You may need to divide up the meals and snacks further if you don't think you can finish them at one sitting. However, it's vital that you maintain your overall caloric level.

Note that although beverages are listed with some meals, I suggest you drink them half an hour before or after eating. Liquids consumed with solid foods dilute the digestive juices and fill you up faster. Don't forget to keep drinking water throughout the day.

## Menus

### DAY 1

**BREAKFAST**
Silken Scramble* with spinach and
    feta
Spelt toast
Mixed fruit
Raspberry leaf tea

**MID-MORNING SNACK**
Glass of soy-rice milk
Manna bread with peanut butter

**LUNCH**
Jerusalem Artichoke Soup*
Carrot-Raisin Salad*
Crackers

**MID-AFTERNOON SNACK**
Type A Bar

**DINNER**
Tasty Tofu-Pumpkin Stir-Fry*
Basmati rice
2 Beneficial vegetables

**EVENING SNACK**
Super Baby Smoothie*

### DAY 2

**BREAKFAST**
Spelt flakes with raisins and soy milk
½ grapefruit
Sprouted seed toast with soy spread
Rose hip tea

**MID-MORNING SNACK**
Poached Fruit*
Glass of soy-rice milk

**LUNCH**
Salmon Salad* on a bed of greens
2 slices spelt or sprouted seed bread
Tofu, avocado, and sprouts on spelt
    bread

**MID-AFTERNOON SNACK**
Type A Bar
Chamomile tea

**DINNER**
Sesame Chicken*
Brown Rice Pilaf* with carrots and
    onions
Raw Enzyme Relish*

**EVENING SNACK**
Super Baby Smoothie*

## DAY 3

**BREAKFAST**
Oatmeal with soy milk
Sprouted seed toast with black cherry
    preserves
Mixed berries
Raspberry leaf tea

**MID-MORNING SNACK**
Type A Bar

**LUNCH**
Lentil Soup*
Super Broccoli Salad*

**MID-AFTERNOON SNACK**
Type A Trail Mix-2*

**DINNER**
Grilled Salmon with Lemongrass*
Carrots and Parsnips with Garlic
    and Coriander*
Black-Eyed Peas with Leeks*

**EVENING SNACK**
Fresh sliced peaches, nectarines,
    figs, and plums
or
Super Baby Smoothie*

## DAY 4

**BREAKFAST**
Scrambled eggs
Sliced pear
Manna toast
Glass of soy-rice milk
Raspberry leaf tea

**MID-MORNING SNACK**
Cherry-Peach Smoothie*

**LUNCH**
Vegetable Fritters*
Mesclun Salad*

**MID-AFTERNOON SNACK**
Beneficial fruit

**DINNER**
Spicy Stir-Fried Tofu with Apricots and
    Almonds
Pureed root vegetables
Steamed asparagus

**EVENING SNACK**
Super Baby Smoothie*

## DAY 5

**BREAKFAST**
Amaranth Pancakes*
Blackberry preserves
Mixed fruit salad
Rose hip tea

**MID-MORNING SNACK**
Type A Bar

**LUNCH**
Sardines on a bed of Romaine lettuce
Mixed Roots Soup*
Crackers

**MID-AFTERNOON SNACK**
Super Baby Smoothie*

**DINNER**
Green Leafy Pasta*
Chicory salad
Beneficial vegetable

**EVENING SNACK**
Tofu-Pumpkin Pudding*
Glass of soy milk

## DAY 6

**BREAKFAST**
Spinach Frittata*
Pineapple slices
Raspberry leaf tea

**MID-MORNING SNACK**
Silken Smoothie*

**LUNCH**
Grilled Chicken Salad*
2 slices of spelt bread

**MID-AFTERNOON SNACK**
Raisin Peanut Balls*

**DINNER**
Tofu Vegetable Stir-Fry*
Steamed broccoli
Raw Enzyme Relish*

**EVENING SNACK**
Poached Fruit*
Type A Tea

## DAY 7

**BREAKFAST**
Poached egg
Spelt flakes with soy-rice milk
Mixed berries
Rose hip tea

**MID-MORNING SNACK**
Type A Bar

**LUNCH**
Waldorf Salad*
Spelt bread with peanut butter and
   jam

**MID-AFTERNOON SNACK**
Rye cracker with prune butter
Chamomile-mint tea

**DINNER**
Grilled Salmon Steak, Marinated in
   Tamari Dipping Sauce*
Brown rice
Mixed green salad with Seaweed
   Dressing*

**EVENING SNACK**
Super Baby Smoothie*

## DAY 8

**BREAKFAST**
Amaranth Pancakes* with maple
   syrup
Mixed fruit
Slippery elm tea

**MID-MORNING SNACK**
Type A Bar

**LUNCH**
White Bean and Wilted Greens Soup*
Mixed green salad
Crackers

**MID-AFTERNOON SNACK**
Rice cakes with prune butter

**DINNER**
Steamed Whole Red Snapper*
Steamed broccoli
Brown Rice Pilaf*

**EVENING SNACK**
Super Baby Smoothie*

## DAY 9

**BREAKFAST**
Silken Scramble
Sautéed Pears*
Sprouted seed toast
Pineapple juice

**MID-MORNING SNACK**
Type A Bar
Slippery elm tea

**LUNCH**
Grilled ground turkey burger with
    melted goat cheese and raw
    spinach leaves
Spelt or wheat toast

**MID-AFTERNOON SNACK**
Toasted Tamari Pumpkin Seeds*
Carrot juice

**DINNER**
Pasta with Rappini*
Mixed steamed vegetables

**EVENING SNACK**
Peanut Butter Cookies*
Glass of soy-rice milk

## DAY 10

**BREAKFAST**
Wheat-Free Waffles*
Berry preserves
Stewed apricots
Vegetable juice
Slippery elm tea

**MID-MORNING SNACK**
Pineapple-Apricot Silken Smoothie*

**LUNCH**
Sardine Salad*
Farmer's Vegetable Soup*
Crackers

**MID-AFTERNOON SNACK**
Type A Bar

**DINNER**
Sesame Chicken*
Steamed Artichoke*
Black-Eyed Peas with Leeks*

**EVENING SNACK**
Super Baby Smoothie*

## DAY 11

**BREAKFAST**
Scrambled eggs
Stewed prunes
Manna toast with peanut butter
Raspberry leaf tea

**MID-MORNING SNACK**
Heidi's Early Morning Shake

**LUNCH**
Grilled Chicken Salad* on spelt bread
Mixed green salad
Slippery elm tea

**MID-AFTERNOON SNACK**
Type A Trail Mix-1*

**DINNER**
Grilled Wild Rice Tempeh*
Broccoli rabe
Turkey Soup*

**EVENING SNACK**
Walnut Cookies*
Glass of soy-rice milk

## DAY 12

**BREAKFAST**
Silken Scramble*
Sprouted seed toast with blueberry
    preserves
Raspberry leaf tea

**MID-MORNING SNACK**
Type A Bar

**LUNCH**
Black-Eyed Peas and Barley Salad*
Mixed steamed vegetables

**MID-AFTERNOON SNACK**
Raisins and chopped walnuts
Glass of soy-rice milk

**DINNER**
Tofu Vegetable Stir-Fry*
Basmati rice

**EVENING SNACK**
Super Baby Smoothie*

## DAY 13

**BREAKFAST**
Poached egg
Blueberry Muffin*
Mixed fruit
Rose hip tea

**MID-MORNING SNACK**
Rye cracker with prune butter
Pineapple-Apricot Silken Smoothie*

**LUNCH**
Farmer's Vegetable Soup*
Mesclun Salad*

**MID-AFTERNOON SNACK**
Type A Bar

**DINNER**
Peanut Chicken*
Brown rice
Steamed broccoli

**EVENING SNACK**
Super Baby Smoothie*

## DAY 14

**BREAKFAST**
Spelt flakes with mixed fruit and soy-
    rice milk
Sprouted seed toast
Raspberry leaf tea

**MID-MORNING SNACK**
Tofu Carob Protein Shake*

**LUNCH**
Greek Salad*
Rye cracker
Apple
Lemon chamomile tea

**MID-AFTERNOON SNACK**
Super Baby Smoothie*

**DINNER**
Grilled Salmon Steak*
Brown rice
Sesame Broccoli*

**EVENING SNACK**
Type A Bar
Valerian-chamomile tea

## Exercise Guidelines

### First Trimester

### Maintenance for Healthy Type As

Since Type A is particularly susceptible to high levels of stress hormones causing anxiety and mood swings, it is particularly important that you employ stress-reducing strategies during this period. The best way for Type A to accomplish that is to continue a program of regular aerobic exercise, incorporated with meditative and stretching exercises, such as Hatha yoga and T'ai chi.

Do not begin an exercise program during your pregnancy. Hopefully, you've already been engaged in a pre-pregnancy conditioning program, or, better still, have been following the Type A exercise guidelines for some time. The following comprises the ideal exercise regimen for Type A, which is safe for healthy Type As during the first trimester:

THREE TO FOUR TIMES A WEEK, CHOOSE ONE:

| EXERCISE | DURATION |
|---|---|
| Hatha yoga | 40–50 minutes |
| T'ai chi | 40–50 minutes |

* You can find recipes for asterisk-marked items in appendix A.

TWO TO THREE TIMES A WEEK, CHOOSE ONE:

| EXERCISE | DURATION |
|---|---|
| Aerobics (low-impact) | 40–50 minutes |
| Treadmill | 30 minutes |
| Weight training (5–10 lb (2.25–4.5 kg) free weights) | 15 minutes |
| Cycling | 30 minutes |
| Swimming | 30 minutes |
| Brisk walking | 45 minutes |

TYPE A NOTE: A healthy lifestyle that includes exercise, adequate rest, and good nutrition can help to reduce the impact of anxiety attacks. Rhythmic aerobic and yoga exercise programs lasting for more than fifteen weeks have been found to help reduce anxiety. Strength, or resistance, training does not seem to help anxiety, although it is not to be discouraged, as it has many positive benefits.

CAUTIONS FOR HIGH-RISK PREGNANCIES

Consult with your doctor before continuing your exercise regimen if you are in a high-risk pregnancy. Most doctors will discourage exercise if you:

- Have a history of miscarriages, or have had even one miscarriage, if it is recent.
- Have a history of recurrent pelvic or abdominal infections.
- Have an incompetent cervix. This condition causes the cervix to open early, usually in the second trimester, leading to miscarriage.
- Have had toxaemia in a previous pregnancy.
- Have a history of premature deliveries.
- Have or have had a serious medical condition, such as cancer, heart disease, asthma, or kidney disease.

## Second Trimester

## Adaptations for Advancing Pregnancy

Continue your regular program of exercise during the second trimester, with an additional emphasis on gentle stretching and calming exercises.

- Join a yoga class specifically designed for pregnant women.
- Spend more time on your warm-up and cool-down to fully warm and stretch your muscles. This will minimize the muscle cramps that are common as your pregnancy progresses.

- Look for opportunities to incorporate fitness into your daily routine. If feasible, walk to work instead of driving. Take the stairs instead of the elevator.
- Limit your weight workouts to very light weights—no more than 10 pounds (4.5 kg). Your centre of gravity has shifted, and you may feel awkward. Lighter weights may be the answer. Experiment to find the right balance. Consistency is more important than the amount of weight you use.
- Swimming is an excellent exercise for the second and third trimesters. It places minimum stress on your joints and heart rate. A water aerobics class is an ideal substitution for more strenuous aerobics.
- If you haven't already started your pelvic floor exercises (see page 28), do so now.

The following comprises a good mix for your second trimester.

THREE TO FOUR TIMES A WEEK, CHOOSE ONE:

| EXERCISE | DURATION |
|----------|----------|
| Hatha yoga | 40–50 minutes |
| T'ai chi | 40–50 minutes |

ONE TO THREE TIMES A WEEK, CHOOSE ONE:

| EXERCISE | DURATION |
|----------|----------|
| Water aerobics | 40 minutes |
| Treadmill | 30 minutes |
| Weight training (5–10 lb (2.25–4.5 kg) free weights) | 15 minutes |
| Cycling (recumbent bike) | 30 minutes |
| Swimming | 30 minutes |
| Brisk walking | 30–45 minutes |

DAILY:

| EXERCISE | DURATION |
|----------|----------|
| Pelvic floor exercises | 2 minutes, 10 to 20 times |

PREGNANCY-SAFE EXERCISE SUBSTITUTIONS

| INSTEAD OF . . . | TRY . . . |
| --- | --- |
| Bicycling | Exercise bike (recumbent) |
| Running | Brisk walking/treadmill/ stair climbing |
| Aerobics | Water aerobics |

## Third Trimester

### Adaptations for Late Pregnancy

Your focus during the final months of pregnancy should be on stress reduction. Not only is this a particularly stressful time, but Type A has a heightened tendency to produce excess cortisol in response to even minor stress. These calming exercises can help:

MEDITATION. Calming yourself through the process of meditation is a wonderful way to reduce your stress level. Quieting the mind will help you eliminate stress-causing thoughts and help you to approach your day in a more positive and efficient manner.

MEDITATION EXERCISE
- Choose a quiet place.
- Sit in a comfortable chair.
- Close your eyes.
- Relax your muscles.
- Become aware of your breathing.
- Choose a pleasant word or visual image that you can hear and see in your imagination. Think of this word or image every time you exhale, for about 15 minutes each day. If you have an intrusive thought or feeling during your meditation, return to the repetition of your relaxing word or image.

DEEP BREATHING. Many of us breathe too fast for the conditions in which we find ourselves; that is, we hyperventilate. This fast, shallow breathing expels carbon dioxide too quickly and can have damaging effects on physical and emotional health. However, when our breathing is deep (using not only the respiratory muscles of the chest but also the belly, lower rib cage, and lower back) it slows the breathing. This slower, deeper breathing, combined with the rhythmical pumping of the diaphragm, abdomen, and belly, helps turn on our parasympathetic nervous system—our "relaxation response". Such breathing helps to harmonize our nervous system and reduce the amount of stress in our lives. And this, of course, has a positive impact on our overall health.

## Breathing Exercise

The art of deep breathing is rather simple. Begin by lying on your back in a quiet room. Place your fingers below your rib cage and feel your abdomen rise and fall while you breathe. It should rise up as you breathe in and fall as you breathe out. Now try a deep breath, always keeping the same pattern. Breathe in through your nose and out through your mouth. Inhale for a count of 4 and exhale for a count of 4 with a slight pause in the middle.

Begin daily perineal massage to tone the vaginal canal (page 31). An excellent third trimester exercise regimen for Type A would be the following.

THREE TO FIVE TIMES A WEEK, CHOOSE ONE:

| EXERCISE | DURATION |
| --- | --- |
| Light yoga | 40–50 minutes |
| Stretching, relaxation, breathing | 30 minutes |
| Meditation | 30–40 minutes |
| Labour preparation class | 40–50 minutes |

ONE TO THREE TIMES A WEEK, CHOOSE ONE:

| EXERCISE | DURATION |
| --- | --- |
| Water aerobics | 40 minutes |
| Cycling (recumbent bike) | 30 minutes |
| Swimming | 30 minutes |
| Brisk walking | 30–45 minutes |

DAILY, PERFORM BOTH:

| EXERCISE | DURATION |
| --- | --- |
| Pelvic floor exercises | 2 minutes, 10–20 times |
| Perineal massage | 5 minutes, 1–2 times |

# Supplement Guidelines

## First Trimester

### Vitamins/Minerals

Take a standard prenatal vitamin supplement, choosing one made from whole food, not synthetic ingredients. Powder-in-capsule forms dissolve most efficiently. If you would like to use a prenatal supplement specifically formulated for Type A, see appendix B for information about "Healthy Start ABO." The following nutrient breakdown is the optimal formula for Type A.

| PRENATAL SUPPLEMENT TYPE A | |
| --- | --- |
| Vitamin A (100% as natural beta-carotene from *Dunaliella salina*) | 2,500 iu |
| Vitamin C (100% from acerola berry, *Malpighia puncifolia* | 75 mg |
| Vitamin D (cholecalciferol | 125 iu |
| Vitamin E (natural d alpha-tocopheryl succinate) | 75 iu |
| Vitamin K (phytonadione) | 25 mcg |
| Thiamin (from thiamin HCl) | 7.5 mg |
| Riboflavin | 10 mg |
| Niacin and niacinamide (vitamin $B_3$) | 10 mg |
| Vitamin $B_6$ (from pyridoxine HCl) | 10 mg |
| Folic acid | 800 mcg |
| Vitamin $B_{12}$ (methylcobalamin) | 10 mcg |
| Biotin | 600 mcg |
| Pantothenic acid (from D-calcium pantothenate) | 20 mg |
| Calcium (seaweed base, derived from *Lithothamnium corralliodes* and *Lithothamnium calcareum*) | 300 mg |
| Iron (ferrous succinate) | 25 mg |
| Iodine (potassium iodide) | 100 mcg |
| Zinc (picolinate) | 25 mg |
| Selenium (L-selenomethionine) | 30 mcg |
| Copper (gluconate) | 1 mg |

## Herbal Remedies

| HERB | FUNCTION | FORM AND DOSAGE |
|---|---|---|
| Chamomile | Calms; relieves heartburn | As tea, 1 to 2 cups daily; or add 2–4 drops of essential oil to bath |
| Peppermint | Calms; relieves indigestion | As tea, 2 to 3 cups daily, after meals |
| Slippery elm bark | Relieves heartburn | 250-mg capsule, twice daily; or as tea, 2 cups daily |
| Stinging nettle leaf | Rich in iron | As tea, 2 cups daily |

## Nutritional Supplements

| NUTRITIONAL SUPPLEMENT | FUNCTION | FORM AND DOSAGE |
|---|---|---|
| Digestive enzymes | Aid digestion | Bromelain, 500-mg capsule before meals |
| Larch arabinogalactan | Relieves constipation | Soluble fibre supplement: 1 tablespoon mixed with water or juice, once daily |
| Probiotic | For intestinal health | 2 capsules, twice daily* |
| DHA | Provides essential nutrients for foetal development | 300-mg capsule daily |

* See appendix B for information on blood type–specific probiotics.

## Second Trimester

### Vitamins/Minerals

Continue to take your prenatal supplement, preferably one formulated for Type A.

## Herbal Remedies

| HERB | FUNCTION | FORM AND DOSAGE |
|------|----------|-----------------|
| Bilberry | Relieves haemorrhoids and varicose veins | 25-mg capsule, twice daily |
| Chamomile | Calms; relieves heartburn; relieves haemorrhoids and varicose veins | As tea, 1 to 2 cups daily; or add 2–4 drops of essential oil to bath |
| Horsetail | Contains silica, which supports healthy bones, skin, hair, and nails | 250-mg capsule daily |
| Peppermint | Calms; relieves indigestion | As tea, 2 to 3 cups daily, after meals |
| Rose hip | Treatment for varicose veins, bleeding gums, allergies | 1 tablespoon concentrate every 30 minutes for allergy attack; as tea, 2 to 3 cups daily |
| Stinging nettle leaf | Allergy relief | As tea, 2 cups daily for symptoms |
| Witch hazel | Treatment for haemorrhoids | Use topically as needed |

## Nutritional Supplements

| NUTRITIONAL SUPPLEMENT | FUNCTION | FORM AND DOSAGE |
|------------------------|----------|-----------------|
| Larch arabinogalactan | Relieves constipation | Soluble fibre supplement: 1 tablespoon mixed with water or juice, twice daily |
| Probiotic | For intestinal health | 2 capsules, twice daily* |
| DHA | Provides essential nutrients for foetal development | 300-mg capsule daily |

* See appendix B for information on blood type–specific probiotics.

## Third Trimester

### Vitamins/Minerals

Continue to take your prenatal supplement, preferably one formulated for Type A.

| Herbal Remedies | | |
|---|---|---|
| **HERB** | **FUNCTION** | **FORM AND DOSAGE** |
| Dandelion leaf/root | Lowers blood pressure; decreases oedema | As tea, 2 cups daily; or 250-mg capsule, twice daily |
| Raspberry leaf (last 4 weeks) | Softens the cervix in preparation for birth; stimulates milk production | As tea, 2 cups daily; as tincture, 15–20 drops daily |
| Squaw vine | Prepares uterus for birth | As tincture, 10 drops in warm water, twice daily |

| Nutritional Supplements | | |
|---|---|---|
| **NUTRITIONAL SUPPLEMENT** | **FUNCTION** | **FORM AND DOSAGE** |
| Larch arabinogalactan | Relieves constipation | Soluble fibre supplement: 1 tablespoon mixed with water or juice, twice daily |
| Probiotic | For intestinal health | 2 capsules, twice daily* |
| DHA | Provides essential nutrients for foetal development | 300-mg capsule daily |

* See appendix B for information on blood type–specific probiotics.

## Labour and Delivery

In addition to the general guidelines for labour and delivery (page 32), you have some specific Type A needs.

### Type A Energy Needs

Begin several weeks before your delivery date to prepare yourself for the stress of labour and delivery. Try to get more sleep than usual and eat plenty of nutrient-rich foods. Type As have a tendency to let stress levels build, and you don't want to reach the point of labour with all of your energy resources depleted.

The first stage of labour can last many hours. Drink plenty of liquids and eat a small amount of nourishing food—a vegetable broth, soy milk, or yogurt. Stay hydrated. Be sure to discuss in advance with your doctor or midwife what the policy is about eating light foods or drinking liquids during labour.

## Type A Emotional Needs

Type As are extremely sensitive to environmental factors. Try to arrange for your labour room to be in a quiet area; use soothing music if that helps.

Your partner and coach can help you here by encouraging you to focus on your rhythmic breathing and offering encouragement and support. Relaxation techniques can be essential during this period. Some facilities allow women to shower or relax in a warm tub. You might also find it helpful to practise a form of visualization or meditation.

### Creative Visualization

This exercise helps to reduce stress by imagining a very calm and relaxing scene in your mind. Some people picture themselves at the beach, feeling the warmth of the sun and the sound of the waves crashing on the shore. Others think of being in the mountains, with eagles soaring overhead, as they breathe in the cool clean air. Others imagine being a leaf floating on the water. The goal is to replace negative, stressful thoughts with more relaxing ones. As your mind relaxes, so does your body.

See page 35 for natural childbirth painkillers.

# 5

# The Type B Pregnancy

A HEALTHY TYPE B WOMAN IS PHYSICALLY FIT and mentally focused. Type B carries the genetic potential for great adaptability and the ability to thrive in changeable conditions. This can give you a substantial advantage during pregnancy. However, to fully realize these benefits, you must adhere to the blood type diet. Type Bs are susceptible to the effects of high stress, such as chronic viral and bacterial infections. Stress has a weakening effect on body systems and hormonal activity and can also be an impediment to fertility. Your digestive tract tends to be sensitive to the protein lectins in certain foods. Dietary lectins can induce inflammation, cause water retention, and influence the control of your blood sugar.

Following the blood type diet is an essential foundation, enabling you to optimize your health and prepare for an energetic and enjoyable pregnancy.

## The Type B Diet

The following food lists comprise the Type B diet. Note that the values for certain foods change in preparation for pregnancy, during pregnancy, and/or while you are breast-feeding. I call these Chameleon Foods, and they are contained in the following table. Use this table for quick reference. Chameleon Foods are also marked with an asterisk (*) in the specific food lists.

## Type B Chameleon Foods

Chameleons are foods whose values change before pregnancy, during pregnancy, and/or while breast-feeding.

| FOOD | PRE-/POST-PREGNANCY | PREGNANCY | FACTORS |
|---|---|---|---|
| **SEAFOOD** | | | |
| Bass | Neutral | Avoid | Heightened risk of contamination |
| Carp | Neutral | Avoid | Heightened risk of contamination |
| Catfish | Neutral | Avoid | Heightened risk of contamination |
| Flounder | Beneficial | Avoid | Heightened risk of contamination |
| Grouper | Beneficial | Avoid | Heightened risk of contamination |
| Halibut | Beneficial | Avoid | High mercury content |
| Mackerel | Neutral | Avoid | Heightened risk of contamination |
| Mahimahi | Beneficial | Avoid | Heightened risk of contamination |
| Salmon | Beneficial | Neutral | Some risk of contamination |
| Shark | Neutral | Avoid | High mercury content |
| Swordfish | Neutral | Avoid | High mercury content |
| Tilapia | Neutral | Avoid | Heightened risk of contamination |
| Tuna | Neutral | Avoid | High mercury content |
| Whitefish | Neutral | Avoid | Heightened risk of contamination |
| **DAIRY/EGGS** | | | |
| Egg/chicken | Neutral | Beneficial | Good source of DHA |
| **SPICES** | | | |
| Cayenne pepper | Neutral | Neutral | May cause digestive difficulties |
| Chocolate | Neutral | Avoid | Contains caffeine |
| Ginger | Beneficial | Avoid | May cause miscarriage in large amounts |
| Parsley | Beneficial | Neutral | Limit intake; can be a uterine stimulant in large amounts |
| Turmeric | Neutral | Avoid | Uterine stimulant |
| **HERBAL TEAS** | | | |
| Catnip | Neutral | Avoid | Uterine stimulant |
| Chamomile | Neutral | Beneficial | A calmative and sleep aid |
| Dandelion | Neutral | Beneficial | Aids digestion |
| Dong quai | Neutral | Avoid | Can start uterine bleeding |
| Ginger | Beneficial | Avoid | May cause miscarriage in large amounts |
| Goldenseal | Neutral | Avoid | Potentially harmful to foetus |
| Licorice | Beneficial | Avoid | Can influence oestrogen levels |

| FOOD | PRE-/POST-PREGNANCY | PREGNANCY | FACTORS |
|---|---|---|---|
| Parsley | Beneficial | Neutral | Limit intake; can be a uterine stimulant in large amounts |
| Sage | Beneficial | Neutral | Limit intake; can be a uterine stimulant in large amounts |
| St. John's wort | Neutral | Avoid | Can be harmful to foetus |
| Vervain | Neutral | Avoid | Uterine stimulant |
| Yarrow | Neutral | Avoid | Uterine stimulant |
| **BEVERAGES** | | | |
| Beer | Neutral | Avoid | Alcohol should be completely avoided during pregnancy |
| Coffee, regular | Neutral | Avoid | Contains caffeine |
| Tea, black regular | Neutral | Avoid | Contains caffeine |
| Tea, green | Neutral | Avoid | Contains caffeine; start weaning yourself before pregnancy, and avoid during pregnancy |
| Wine, red | Neutral | Avoid | Alcohol should be completely avoided during pregnancy |
| Wine, white | Neutral | Avoid | Alcohol should be completely avoided during pregnancy |

## Meats and Poultry

Eat only lean, organic meat of the highest grade available. If you are fatigued or suffer from immune deficiencies, you should eat a red meat such as lamb, mutton, or rabbit several times a week, in preference to beef or turkey.

Avoid chicken altogether. Chicken contains a blood Type B agglutinating protein in its muscle tissue. If you're accustomed to eating more poultry than red meat, you can eat other poultry, such as turkey.

**HIGHLY BENEFICIAL**

Goat
Lamb
Mutton
Rabbit
Venison

**NEUTRAL**

Beef
Liver

Ostrich            Turkey
Pheasant           Veal

**AVOID**

All commercially       Guinea fowl
    processed meats    Ham
Bacon                  Heart
Chicken                Partridge
Duck                   Pigeon
Goose                  Pork
Grouse                 Quail

## Seafood

Seafood is an excellent source of protein for Type B, but pregnant women must use special caution to avoid fish that may contain PCBs or that are otherwise potentially toxic. Check with your local health department about the safety of fish caught in local waters. In addition, avoid certain fish that are especially vulnerable to contamination by environmental pollutants, such as pesticides and PCBs. These include bass, flounder, grouper, halibut, mackerel, mahimahi, fresh salmon, tilapia, and whitefish. Also avoid fish that may contain a high level of mercury—halibut, swordfish, shark, and fresh tuna.

Avoid all shellfish—crab, lobster, shrimps, mussels, etc.

**HIGHLY BENEFICIAL**

Caviar (sturgeon)      Monkfish
Cod                    Ocean perch
Flounder*              Pike
Grouper*               Salmon*
Haddock                Sardine
Hake                   Shad
Halibut*               Sole
Mackerel               Sturgeon
Mahimahi*

Food with different values than the standard Type B diet are indicated with an asterisk (*).

**NEUTRAL**

| | |
|---|---|
| Abalone | Red snapper |
| Bass* | Rainbow trout |
| Bullhead | Scallop |
| Carp* | Shark* |
| Catfish* | Smelt |
| Chub | Snapper |
| Dover sole | Sole |
| Herring (fresh, kippers, pickled) | Squid (calamari) |
| | Swordfish* |
| Lox | Tilapia* |
| Mullet | Tuna* |
| Orange roughy | Whitefish* |
| Perch (silver, white, yellow) | Whiting |

**AVOID**

| | |
|---|---|
| Anchovy | Lox |
| Barracuda | Mussels |
| Beluga | Octopus |
| Clam | Oysters |
| Conch | Pollack |
| Crab | Prawns |
| Crayfish | Shrimps |
| Eel | Snail |
| Frog | Turtle |
| Lobster | |

## Eggs and Dairy

Type B is the only blood type that can fully enjoy a variety of dairy foods. If you are of Asian descent, you may initially have a problem adapting to dairy foods—

---

Food with different values than the standard Type B diet are indicated with an asterisk (*).

not because your system is resistant to them, but because your *culture* has typically been resistant. See page 168 for advice on introducing unfamiliar foods.

Eggs can be consumed in moderation. They are a good source of DHA, which is a beneficial nutrient for your health and the health of your developing foetus. Choose organic eggs only.

**HIGHLY BENEFICIAL**

| | |
|---|---|
| Cottage cheese | Mozzarella |
| Dairylea-style cheese | Paneer |
| Feta | Ricotta |
| Goat's cheese | Milk (cow) |
| Goat's milk | Yogurt |
| Kefir | |

**NEUTRAL**

| | |
|---|---|
| Brie | Gruyère |
| Butter | Jarlsberg |
| Buttermilk | Monterey jack |
| Camembert | Muenster |
| Cheddar | Neufchâtel |
| Cream cheese | Parmesan |
| Edam | Provolone |
| Egg, chicken* | Quark |
| Emmenthal | Sour cream (low, nonfat) |
| Ghee (clarified butter) | Swiss |
| Gouda | Whey |

**AVOID**

| | |
|---|---|
| Blue cheese | Egg, quail |
| Egg, duck | Ice cream |
| Egg, goose | String cheese |

## Oils and Fats

When cooking, give preference to the healthful monounsaturated olive oil. Linseed (flaxseed) oil is neutral for Type B, but limit its use during pregnancy.

---

Food with different values than the standard Type B diet are indicated with an asterisk (*).

**HIGHLY BENEFICIAL**
  Olive

**NEUTRAL**
  Almond                Linseed (flaxseed)
  Black currant seed    Walnut
  Cod liver             Wheat germ
  Evening primrose

**AVOID**
  Borage        Safflower
  Castor        Sesame
  Coconut       Soy
  Corn          Sunflower
  Cottonseed    Vegetable
  Peanut

## Nuts and Seeds

Most nuts and seeds are not advised for Type Bs. Peanuts, sesame seeds, and sunflower seeds, among others, contain lectins that can cause inflammation and upset the digestive tract.

**HIGHLY BENEFICIAL**
  Walnut (black)

**NEUTRAL**
  Almond          Flaxseed
  Almond butter   Hickory
  Beechnut        Macadamia
  Brazil          Pecan
  Butternut       Walnut (English)
  Chestnut

**AVOID**
  Cashew              Poppy seed
  Filbert (hazelnut)  Pumpkin seed
  Peanut              Sesame butter (tahini)
  Peanut butter       Sesame seed
  Pignola (pine nut)  Sunflower butter
  Pistachio           Sunflower seed

## Beans and Legumes

Type Bs can eat some beans and legumes, but many beans, such as lentils, garbanzos, pintos, and black-eyed peas, contain lectins that can cause inflammation and upset the digestive tract. Generally, Type B Asians tolerate beans and legumes better than other Type Bs because they are culturally accustomed to them.

**HIGHLY BENEFICIAL**

| | |
|---|---|
| Butter bean | Kidney bean |
| Haricot bean | |

**NEUTRAL**

| | |
|---|---|
| Broad bean | Soybean |
| Cannellini bean | String bean |
| Green bean | Tamarind bean |
| Green pea | White bean |
| Snap bean | |

**AVOID**

| | |
|---|---|
| Aduki bean | Pinto bean |
| Black bean | Soy cheese |
| Black-eyed pea | Soy flakes |
| Garbanzo bean (chickpea) | Soy granules |
| Lentil | Soy milk |
| Mung bean/sprouts | Soy (miso, tempeh, tofu) |

## Grains, Breads, and Pasta

I've encountered some Type Bs who can tolerate wheat products, but overall, they are more like Type O in their intolerance. Type Bs should also avoid rye, which is a common allergen in your system.

I would advise that you moderate your intake of breads, pasta, and rice. You won't need much of these nutrients if you're consuming the meat, seafood, and dairy products advised.

**HIGHLY BENEFICIAL**

| | |
|---|---|
| Millet | Oatmeal |
| Oat bran | Rice bran |

Rice cake
Rice milk
Rice (puffed)

Spelt (whole)
Sprouted seed bread

### NEUTRAL

Barley
Cream of rice
Gluten-free bread
Granola
100% sprouted seed bread
Quinoa
Rice (white, brown, basmati)
Rice bread
Rice flour

Soy flour bread
Spelt flour products
Spinach pasta
Wheat (refined, unbleached)
Wheat (semolina flour
   products)
Wheat (white flour products)
Wheat bread, sprouted

### AVOID

Amaranth
Artichoke pasta (pure)
Barley
Buckwheat/kasha
Corn (white, yellow, blue)
Cornflakes
Cornmeal
Couscous (cracked wheat)
Cream of wheat
Gluten flour
Grits
Kamut
Rice (wild)
Rye

Rye bread (100%)
Rye flour
Seven-grain bread/cereal
Shredded wheat
Soba noodles
   (100% buckwheat)
Sorghum
Tapioca
Wheat bran
Wheat germ
Wheat (gluten flour products)
Wheat (whole-wheat
   products)

## Vegetables

There are many high-quality, nutritious vegetables available for Type Bs. Take full advantage of them with three to five servings a day. There is only a handful of vegetables that Type Bs should avoid, but take these guidelines to heart. Corn is filled with lectins that negatively affect your blood and digestion. Radishes and artichokes are also bad for Type B digestion. Tomatoes should be eliminated by Type Bs. Also avoid olives, as their moulds can trigger allergic reactions.

Fennel and parsley should be limited during pregnancy, as these are uterine stimulants in large amounts. Also note that although onions and garlic are allowed for Type B, you may want to avoid or limit them while you're breast-feeding. Some babies experience colic when mums eat these foods.

**HIGHLY BENEFICIAL**

Aubergine  
Beets  
Beet greens  
Broccoli  
Brussels sprouts  
Cabbage (all types)  
Carrot  
Cauliflower  

Collard greens  
Kale  
Mushroom (shiitake)  
Mustard greens  
Parsnip  
Peppers (all types)  
Potato (sweet)  
Yam  

**NEUTRAL**

Alfalfa sprouts  
Asparagus  
Asparagus pea  
Bamboo shoots  
Bok choy  
Caraway  
Carrot juice  
Celeriac  
Celery  
Chervil  
Chicory  
Chilli peppers  
Coriander  
Courgette  
Cucumber  
Dandelion  
Dill  
Endive  
Fennel*  
Garlic  

Horseradish  
Kelp  
Kohlrabi  
Leek  
Lettuce (all types)  
Mangetout  
Marrow  
Mushroom (abalone, open cup, enoki, maitake, oyster, portabello)  
Okra  
Onion (all types)  
Oyster plant  
Pea (green, pod)  
Pickle (in brine or vinegar)  
Pimento  
Potato (all white-fleshed types)  
Radicchio  
Rappini (broccoli rabe)  

---

Food with different values than the standard Type B diet are indicated with an asterisk (*).

Rocket
Sauerkraut
Seaweed
Shallot
Spinach
Spring onion
Squash (all types,
    except pumpkin)

String bean
Swede
Swiss chard
Taro
Turnip
Water chestnut
Watercress
Yucca

**AVOID**

Artichoke (domestic, globe,
    Jerusalem)
Avocado
Corn
Olive (all types)

Pumpkin
Radish
Rhubarb
Sprouts (mung bean, radish)
Tomato

## Fruits

There are very few fruits a Type B must avoid and a wide range of beneficial fruits to choose from. Pineapple is an especially good digestive for Type Bs. Bromelain, an enzyme in the pineapple, helps you to more easily digest your food. On the whole, you can choose your fruits liberally from the following lists.

Unless noted separately, all values of the whole fruits apply to their juices as well.

**HIGHLY BENEFICIAL**

Banana
Cranberry
Grape (all types)
Papaya

Pineapple
Plum (all types)
Watermelon

**NEUTRAL**

Apple/cider
Apricot
Asian pear
Blackberry
Blueberry
Boysenberry
Cherry (all types)
Currant (black, red)

Date (fresh, dried)
Dewberry
Elderberry
Fig (fresh, dried)
Gooseberry
Grapefruit
Guava
Honeydew melon

Kiwi

Kumquat

Lemon

Lime

Loganberry

Mango

Mulberry

Nectarine

Orange

Peach

Pear

Plantain

Prune

Quince

Raisin

Raspberry

Sago plum

Strawberry

Tangerine

**AVOID**

Coconut/milk

Persimmon

Pomegranate

Prickly pear

Star fruit (carambola)

## Spices

Spices can be either helpful or dangerous, and this is especially true during pregnancy. A number of spices are uterine stimulants and should be avoided—especially if you have a high-risk pregnancy or a history of miscarriage. Ginger can be an excellent remedy for digestive ailments. However, it can cause miscarriage in high amounts. Chocolate contains caffeine and should also be avoided. Type Bs should also limit their consumption of sugars.

Certain spices, normally used in small amounts for cooking, should be minimized during pregnancy. These include marjoram, nutmeg, oregano, parsley, rosemary, sage, and thyme.

If you have problems with heartburn, nausea, or morning sickness, which occur mostly in the first trimester, you may find it helpful to eliminate strong spices such as curry and horseradish. However, if you have no digestive problems, go ahead and use these spices.

**HIGHLY BENEFICIAL**

Cayenne pepper*

Curry

Ginger*

Horseradish

Molasses (blackstrap)

Parsley*

**NEUTRAL**

Agar
Anise
Apple pectin
Arrowroot
Basil
Bay leaf
Bergamot
Caper
Caraway
Cardamom
Carob
Chervil
Chilli powder
Chive
Chocolate*
Clove
Coriander
Cream of tartar
Cumin
Dill
Dulse
Fructose
Garlic
Honey
Kelp
Mace

Maple syrup
Marjoram
Molasses
Mustard (dry)
Nutmeg
Oregano
Paprika
Pepper (peppercorn,
    red flakes)
Peppermint
Rice syrup
Rosemary
Saffron
Sage
Savory
Sea salt
Spearmint
Sugar (white, brown)
Tamarind
Tarragon
Thyme
Turmeric*
Vanilla
Vinegar (all types)
Wintergreen
Yeast (baker's, brewer's)

**AVOID**

Allspice
Almond extract
Aspartame
Barley malt
Carrageenan
Cinnamon
Cornflour

Corn syrup
Gelatine (plain)
Guarana
Gums (acacia, arabic)
Juniper
Maltodextrin
Miso

Food with different values than the standard Type B diet are indicated with an asterisk (*).

| | |
|---|---|
| MSG | Stevia |
| Pepper (black, white) | Sucanat |
| Soy sauce | Tapioca |

## Condiments

There are no highly beneficial condiments for Type Bs. If you must have mustard, mayonnaise, or salad dressing on your foods, use them in moderation and stick to the low-fat, low-sugar varieties. Another option is to make your own from okay ingredients. My recommendation is that you try to wean yourself from condiments or replace them with healthier seasonings like olive oil, lemon juice, and garlic. There are a number of recipes in appendix A for healthy, delicious dressings.

**HIGHLY BENEFICIAL**
None

**NEUTRAL**

| | |
|---|---|
| Jam (from acceptable fruits) | Pickles (all types) |
| Jelly (from acceptable fruits) | Pickle relish |
| Mayonnaise | Salad dressing (from |
| Mustard | acceptable ingredients) |

**AVOID**

| | |
|---|---|
| Ketchup | Worcestershire sauce |

## Herbal Teas

Herbal teas can deliver strong doses of herbs, and for this reason many are not advised for pregnant women. However, certain teas are particularly beneficial, especially late in pregnancy. Raspberry leaf is rich in vitamins and nourishes the uterus in late pregnancy. Chamomile is excellent as a calming tea and sleep aid. Dandelion tea aids digestion. Rose hip tea is a good source of vitamin C. Slippery elm tea is an excellent remedy for intestinal problems.

**HIGHLY BENEFICIAL**

Ginger*

Ginseng*

Licorice root*

Parsley*

Peppermint

Raspberry leaf

Rose hip

Sage*

**NEUTRAL**

Alfalfa

Burdock

Chamomile*

Catnip*

Chickweed

Dandelion*

Dong quai*

Echinacea

Elder

Goldenseal*

Hawthorn

Horehound

Mulberry

Rosemary

Sarsaparilla

Slippery elm

Spearmint

St. John's wort*

Strawberry leaf

Thyme

Valerian

Vervain*

White birch

White oak bark

Yarrow*

Yellow dock

**AVOID**

Aloe

Coltsfoot

Corn silk

Fenugreek

Gentian

Hops

Linden

Mullein

Red clover

Rhubarb

Senna

Shepherd's purse

Skullcap

## Miscellaneous Beverages

Start eliminating caffeine and alcohol three to six months before pregnancy, and continue until you are no longer breast-feeding. The common caffeine withdrawal symptoms—headache, fatigue, and irritability—won't occur if you wean yourself gradually. Consumption of alcohol during pregnancy can cause miscarriage, birth defects, and foetal alcohol syndrome.

---

Food with different values than the standard Type B diet are indicated with an asterisk (*).

**HIGHLY BENEFICIAL**
Tea, green*

**NEUTRAL**

| | |
|---|---|
| Beer* | Tea, black decaf |
| Coffee, decaf | Wine, red* |
| Coffee, regular* | Wine, white* |
| Tea, black regular* | |

**AVOID**

| | |
|---|---|
| Fizzy drinks (all types) | Spirits |
| Seltzer water | |

## Before You Get Pregnant

The best guarantee for a healthy pregnancy is to be in top condition before you get pregnant. Start getting ready at least six months before you conceive.

## Pre-pregnancy Diet Strategies

### Get Serious About the Type B Diet

Begin to increase your compliance with the Type B diet at least six months prior to attempting to conceive. The most efficient approach is to add to the number of Type B super foods you consume. These beneficial foods exert a powerful medicinal influence on your system, creating the optimal atmosphere for conception. At the same time, make an effort to eliminate those foods that are obviously detrimental to Type B. Check the Type B Chameleon Foods in the table on page 154. Some of these foods show different values for the pre-pregnancy period.

### Introduce Yourself Gradually to Unfamiliar Foods

Many new subscribers to the Type B diet are not accustomed to eating dairy foods. In fact, a high percentage of people of Asian ancestry are Type B, and these cultures emphasize soy over dairy—especially that derived from cows. These intolerances are not classic food intolerances but, rather, deeply ingrained cultural values. If you are not used to dairy foods, you will need to proceed more slowly in

---

Food with different values than the standard Type B diet are indicated with an asterisk (*).

adapting to the Type B diet. The same holds true for Type Bs who have been vegetarians and are introducing red meat.

- Introduce dairy foods gradually, after you have been on the Type B diet for
  several weeks. Begin with cultured dairy products, such as yogurt and kefir,
  which are more easily tolerated than fresh dairy products. Be sure to choose
  hormone-free, organic dairy foods.
- Take a digestive enzyme with your main meal until you adapt to eating meat
  and dairy. Bromelain, an enzyme found in pineapple, is available in supplemental form.
- Keep in mind that some Type Bs can have problems with milk that are not related to blood type, such as lactose intolerance. In these cases, you will have to
  navigate through the diet with that knowledge guiding your final choices.

## Control Your Weight

If you are overweight prior to becoming pregnant, it's important to gain control of
your weight before you conceive. Overweight women are at increased risk for
elevated blood pressure, diabetes, joint aches and pains, and muscle spasms during pregnancy.

### TYPE B HEALTHY WEIGHT-LOSS GUIDELINES

1. Eliminate foods that slow your metabolism—in particular, chicken,
   corn, buckwheat, peanuts, and lentils.
2. Derive your primary proteins from highly beneficial meats, seafood,
   and dairy.
3. Limit grains, especially those that impair your metabolism, such as
   wheat.
4. Make sure you are ingesting plenty of fibre derived from fresh fruits
   and vegetables.
5. Engage in a regular exercise program. Type B does very well with a
   combination of cardiovascular, weight training, deep breathing, and
   meditation. Walking, easy running, hiking, swimming, and cycling can
   all provide potent metabolic boosts for the Type B woman.

## Type B

| THESE FOODS PROMOTE WEIGHT LOSS | THESE FOODS PROMOTE WEIGHT GAIN |
|---|---|
| Low-fat and cultured dairy foods | Chicken |
| Lean, organic venison | Corn |
| Green vegetables | Peanuts |
| | Buckwheat |
| | Wheat |

## Incorporate Detoxifiers into Your Diet

Toxins are the by-products of bacterial activity on unabsorbed foods that grow in your intestinal tract. Most often these toxins are the result of eating foods that are poorly digested by your blood type—including foods that are overly processed and chemically treated.

### SIGNS OF TOXICITY IN TYPE B
- Diminished sex drive
- Circulation problems
- Sensitivity to light
- Bad breath
- Feelings of fullness in lower intestine
- Cystic breasts

To aid in detoxification before pregnancy, follow this protocol for one week.

### TYPE B DETOXIFICATION PROTOCOL
(Do not use during pregnancy)

- Flaxseed (*Linum usitatissimum*). Take 1 tablespoon added to 8 ounces of water; allow to soak overnight and drink in morning.
- L-glutathione. Take a 100-mg capsule, twice daily.
- Epsom salt bath. Take a shower first, then start with a very clean tub; fill the tub with the hottest water you can stand. Begin with 1½ ounces (40 g) of Epsom salts, work up gradually to 1½ pounds (675 g), and soak as long as half an hour. If you experience light-headedness, drain the tub and hold a cold cloth on your brow until you feel steady enough to leave the tub.
- Probiotic supplement (friendly bacteria). Take twice daily (preferably blood type specific).

- Larch arabinogalactan (soluble fibre supplement). Take 1 tablespoon mixed with water or juice, twice daily.
- Dry skin brushing. Do this once a day.

## About Dry Skin Brushing

Dry skin brushing is a method of daily hygiene that has many benefits and has been around for a long time. The skin is a major organ of the body that functions as protection and as a means of elimination. Daily skin brushing will:

- Remove dried, dead cells that block the pores of the skin, allowing the skin to breathe easier and increasing its ability to protect and eliminate the waste products of metabolism.
- Increase circulation of the blood and lymph vessels that lie close to the surface just under the skin. The blood, fluid, and its contents are returned to the heart for redistribution and/or elimination.
- Increase the nutrients to the skin. By clearing out stagnant materials, there is an increased oxygen/carbon dioxide exchange, and other nutrients, vitamins, minerals, enzymes, etc., are also brought to the area.
- Remove waste products of cellular metabolism through the blood vessels and sweating.
- Decrease the workload on the rest of the body in regard to circulation and elimination.
- Warm the skin.

### PROCEDURE

Skin brushing should be done with a natural or nylon bristle body brush before the bath or shower. It is suggested that the brushing be done toward the heart; start with the lower limbs, arms, and back, and then the front of the body, using a moderate pressure with short strokes upward and inward. If you have a soft complexion brush, the face can be done as well using more circular motions. Strokes should bring a slight pink colour or slight tingling sensation to the skin—never bruising, scraping, bleeding, or pain. One time through for each body area is sufficient.

### AVOID SKIN BRUSHING IF:

- You have delicate skin.
- You have easily damaged skin.
- You have an open wound.
- You have known malignancies of the skin or lymph system.

## Pre-pregnancy Supplement Guidelines

| VITAMINS | MINERALS | HERBS |
|---|---|---|
| Vitamin B complex, daily, with: 400–600 mcg folic acid 500 mcg vitamin B$_{12}$ | Magnesium citrate— 500 mg, once daily | Bromelain—500-mg capsule before meals |
| Vitamin C from rose hip or acerola cherry— 250 mg daily | | Dandelion—250-mg capsule daily; also use fresh in salads or as tea |
| | | Green tea—1 to 3 cups daily *before* pregnancy |
| | | Licorice (DGL)—150-mg capsule or chewable tablet as needed |

The Type B diet is extremely well balanced and offers abundant quantities of important nutrients. It's important to get as many nutrients as possible from fresh foods and only use supplements to address minor additional needs. In addition to vitamins, minerals, protein, carbohydrates, and fats, many grains, beans, vegetables, and fruits are excellent sources of fibre, which is necessary for proper digestion. In addition, fresh vegetables are an important source of phytochemicals, the substances in foods that strengthen the immune system and help prevent cancer and heart disease.

## MINERALS

MAGNESIUM. While Type B gets a substantial amount of calcium from dairy foods, you can risk magnesium/calcium imbalance. Magnesium is essential to the metabolism of calcium and aids in the proper metabolism of foods. A supplement of 500 milligrams may be necessary if you experience the symptoms of sluggish metabolism. Magnesium can occasionally cause a loosening of the stool. If you notice this, just cut back until it disappears.

## HERBS

BROMELAIN (Pineapple enzyme). Aids digestion.

DANDELION (*Taraxacum officinale*). This is very effective for mild water retention. It can be used in salads or as a tea. It is also a good source of potassium.

GREEN TEA (*Camellia sinensis*). Regular consumption of green tea appears to enhance chances of conception. (Do not use during pregnancy.)

LICORICE (DGL). Many Type B women complain about stomach acidity (heartburn). This common form of licorice is very helpful. Do not use "whole herb" forms of licorice: They can encourage water retention. (Do not use during pregnancy.)

## Improve Your Emotional Health

Your emotional well-being—especially your ability to adapt to stress—is every bit as important to your overall health as is your physical well-being. Indeed, the two are inextricably linked. Studies show that when Type B is in "balance" emotionally and physically, you are able to block stress, anxiety, and depression, using your powerful gift for relaxation and visualization. I have always noted these qualities in my Type B patients, and current research supports my observations.

Out of balance, Type B can suffer from the effects of high cortisol (a stress hormone manufactured by the adrenal gland), and a susceptibility to viral infections, chronic fatigue, mental fogginess, and autoimmune diseases. Your focus in achieving emotional balance needs to be on balancing your cortisol levels and increasing your mental acuity.

Type Bs have a remarkable ability to reduce stress through meditation and visualization. Of all the meditation techniques, transcendental meditation (TM) has been the most thoroughly studied for its antistress effects. Evidence indicates that cortisol decreases during meditation, especially for long-term practitioners, and remains somewhat lower after meditation.

## Pre-pregnancy Exercise Guidelines

For Type B, stress regulation and overall fitness is achieved with a balance of moderate aerobic activity and mentally soothing exercise. Below is a list of exercises that are recommended for Type Bs. Choose from among these exercises for a minimum regimen of 45 minutes, three to four times a week. Later, I'll give you the appropriate adjustments for each trimester of pregnancy.

| EXERCISE | DURATION | FREQUENCY |
|---|---|---|
| Tennis | 45–60 minutes | 2–3 × week |
| Martial arts | 30–60 minutes | 3 × week |
| Cycling | 45–60 minutes | 3 × week |
| Hiking | 30–60 minutes | 3 × week |
| Golf (no cart!) | 60–90 minutes | 2 × week |

# Your Pregnancy:
# Type B Three-Trimester Plan

## Diet Strategies

### First Trimester

## Choose Type B Beneficial Foods

Continue your compliance with the Type B diet, paying special atttention to the Type B Chameleon Foods in the table on page 154. These are foods whose normal values are different during pregnancy. If you are new to the Type B diet, your most important first steps are inclusion of high-quality protein found in lean, organic meat and the avoidance of chicken, buckwheat, and corn.

The first trimester is such a critical time that you should emphasize your beneficial foods whenever possible. These foods act as medicine for Type B. While many foods are good choices for important nutrients, your beneficial foods offer an extra benefit. For example:

> Choose lamb over beef.
> Choose goat's cheese over cheddar.
> Choose yogurt over cow's milk.
> Choose broccoli and greens over carrots and mushrooms.
> Choose bananas over apples.

## Emphasize Pregnancy Power Foods

There are some nutrients that have special importance. These include protein, calcium, iron, and folic acid.

| Blood Type B Pregnancy Power Foods | | | |
|---|---|---|---|
| PROTEIN | CALCIUM | IRON | FOLIC ACID |
| Lean, organic lamb | Low-fat dairy | Lean, organic | Liver, kidney, |
| Beef liver | foods, including | mutton | muscle meats |
| Lean, organic | cultured dairy | | Fish |
| venison | Canned sardines | | Dark green leafy |
| | (with bones) | | vegetables |

## Minimize Digestive Discomfort

Type B normally doesn't have many digestive problems, as long as you are eating right for your blood type. However, the first trimester of pregnancy brings some digestive challenges. In addition to following your diet, here are some ways to minimize common digestive complaints.

### HEARTBURN
- Eat frequent small meals—five to six a day instead of three.
- Eat slowly and chew thoroughly.
- Bend at the knees, not at the waist, when picking up objects.
- Avoid acid-stimulating foods, such as oranges, tangerines, and strawberries.
- Avoid coffee, chocolate, mints, and black tea, all of which can provoke heartburn.
- Avoid sugars and sweets.
- Don't lie down directly after meals.

### CONSTIPATION
- Get plenty of exercise.
- Drink lots of water between meals.
- Include dietary sources of inulin, a form of soluble fibre found in over 30,000 plants, such as cabbage, endive, onion, and asparagus. Inulin helps increase stool volume and intestinal motility.
- Take a daily probiotic supplement to keep your intestines healthy. (See appendix B for blood type–specific probiotics.)
- Get plenty of fibre from fresh fruits and vegetables.

### MORNING SICKNESS
- Adhere to the blood type diet.
- Drink plenty of water and nonacidic juices (no caffeine—it dehydrates).

- Eat small, frequent meals throughout the day.
- Do not mix fluids with meals. Drink 30 minutes before or after.
- Dry carbohydrates are usually well tolerated (such as spelt, rice, millet, oat breads or crackers, brown rice).
- Exercise to reduce stress, which can promote nausea.
- Avoid the sight and smell of offensive foods.
- Avoid second-hand smoke.
- Wear an acupressure wristband, used by travellers to prevent motion sickness.
- There is some evidence that vitamin $B_6$ minimizes nausea. Foods rich in vitamin $B_6$ include fish and bananas.

## Fight Fatigue and Mood Swings

It is common for women to feel especially fatigued during the first trimester of pregnancy, as your body adapts to the tremendous changes that are taking place. That is one reason it's so important for you to be in optimal condition before you get pregnant. A Type B who is run down and stressed out is extremely vulnerable to exhaustion, depression, and inertia.

You need to get at least 1 to 2 hours of additional sleep every night. Establish a regular sleep schedule and adhere to it as closely as possible. During the day, schedule at least two breaks of 20 minutes each for complete relaxation. Combat sleep disturbances with regular exercise and a relaxing pre-bedtime routine. A neutral bath (room temperature) with lavender oil prior to bedtime will help you sleep. (See page 22.)

Type Bs may also benefit from the daily consumption of what I call the Membrane Fluidizer Cocktail, which improves the health of your immune and nervous systems:

## MEMBRANE FLUIDIZER COCKTAIL

*1 tablespoon flaxseed oil*
*1 tablespoon high-quality lecithin granules*
*6 to 8 ounces (175–225 ml) fruit juice*

Shake well and drink.

## Handle Your Cravings and Aversions

If you crave foods that are not beneficial for your blood type, find healthy blood type–friendly substitutes. For example:

| WHEN YOU CRAVE . . . | EAT . . . |
|---|---|
| Sugar | Raisins or a plum; any suitable fruit |
| Salty foods | Nori (seaweed) snack; peppers; celery |
| Ice cream | Frozen yogurt; fruit sorbet |
| Fatty foods | A banana or walnuts |
| Creamy foods | Yogurt; vegetable puree— sweet potato, onion, parsnip, or carrot; a fruit smoothie |

## First Trimester Menu Plans

The following menus offer a guide to healthy eating during the first trimester of your pregnancy. They are designed to offer well-balanced, delicious meals that include the primary values critical for Type B:

- They emphasize lean meats, fish, dairy, and fresh fruits and vegetables.
- They provide an extra boost of protein and vital nutrients with Type B–specific smoothies and energy bars.
- They provide many foods to help overcome first trimester problems, such as constipation, fatigue, and morning sickness.
- They break the daily diet into six meals/snacks a day—aiding digestion and reducing fatigue by avoiding an empty stomach.

The menus are flexible and can be mixed and reorganized according to your personal needs. I have purposely not included portion sizes for most dishes, since caloric needs vary depending on your height and weight. However, try to eat about 300 calories a day more than normal during the first trimester.

Although beverages are listed with some meals, I suggest you drink them half an hour before or after eating. Liquids consumed with solid foods dilute the digestive juices. Don't forget to keep drinking water throughout the day.

### A NOTE ABOUT CERTAIN FOODS

- The following menus avoid wheat and limit most other grains. However, there are occasional allowances for sprouted seed bread and spelt bread. They can be found in health-food stores and some supermarkets. A recipe for homemade spelt bread appears in the recipe section in appendix A.

- The Type B Bar is a specially formulated blood type–specific product. The Super Baby Smoothie also utilizes a blood type–specific protein powder, *Proteus ABO*. They are included only as an option. If you prefer, you can substitute other listed snacks and drinks, or a beneficial fruit.

## Menus

### DAY 1

**BREAKFAST**
One-Egg Omelette* with fresh spinach and feta
1 slice of sprouted seed toast with apple butter
Papaya juice
Slippery elm tea

**MID-MORNING SNACK**
Apricot-Yogurt Drink*

**LUNCH**
Caesar Salad*
Cream of Butter Bean Soup*

**MID-AFTERNOON SNACK**
Type B Bar

**DINNER**
Pan-Fried Liver and Onions*
Baked sweet potato
Steamed broccoli

**EVENING SNACK**
Walnut Cookies*
Chamomile tea

### DAY 2

**BREAKFAST**
Poached egg
Spelt flakes with raisins and cow's milk
Mixed berries
Slippery elm tea

**MID-MORNING SNACK**
Type B Bar

**LUNCH**
Farmer's Vegetable Soup*
Mesclun Salad*

**MID-AFTERNOON SNACK**
Type B Trail Mix-1*

**DINNER**
Grilled Lamb Chops*
Wild rice
Braised leeks

**EVENING SNACK**
Super Baby Smoothie*

## DAY 3

**BREAKFAST**
Spinach Frittata*
2 plums
Manna toast
Slippery elm tea

**MID-MORNING SNACK**
Apricot Yogurt Drink*

**LUNCH**
Grilled Goat's Cheddar on Spelt Bread*
Spinach Salad*

**MID-AFTERNOON SNACK**
Toasted Tamari Pumpkin Seeds*

**DINNER**
Grilled Salmon Steak*
Steamed Brussels sprouts with butter,
    lemon, and parsley*
Green Bean Salad with Walnuts and
    Goat's Cheese*

**EVENING SNACK**
Sliced banana with cow's milk
Chamomile tea

## DAY 4

**BREAKFAST**
Omelette* with feta cheese
    and chopped parsley
Pineapple juice
Rose hip tea

**MID-MORNING SNACK**
Type B Bar

**LUNCH**
Smoked Mackerel Salad*
Rice cakes*

**MID-AFTERNOON SNACK**
Super Baby Smoothie*

**DINNER**
Braised Rabbit*
Pureed sweet potato
Braised greens with garlic

**EVENING SNACK**
Poached Fruit*
Chamomile tea

## DAY 5

**BREAKFAST**
Rice cereal with milk and berries
Spelt toast
Rose Water Lassi*
Rose hip tea

**MID-MORNING SNACK**
Type B Bar

**LUNCH**
Turkey sandwich on spelt bread with
    Romaine lettuce and mustard or
    chutney
Mixed green salad

**MID-AFTERNOON SNACK**
Super Baby Smoothie*

**DINNER**
Fried Monkfish*
Steamed spinach
Griddled Pepper Medley*

**EVENING SNACK**
Tofu Banana Pudding*
Glass of milk

## DAY 6

**BREAKFAST**
2 scrambled eggs
Manna toast with butter
½ grapefruit

**MID-MORNING SNACK**
Banana Plum Bread*

**LUNCH**
Cream of Butter Bean Soup*
Mesclun Salad*

**MID-AFTERNOON SNACK**
Beneficial fruit

**DINNER**
Fettucine with Grilled Lamb Sausages
    and Vegetables*
Mixed green salad

**EVENING SNACK**
Rice Pudding*
Chamomile tea

## DAY 7

**BREAKFAST**
Poached egg
Cottage cheese with fresh pineapple
and papaya
Slice of spelt bread with grape jelly
Rose hip tea

**MID-MORNING SNACK**
High-Energy Protein Shake*

**LUNCH**
Sardine Salad*
Ryvita crackers
Turkey Soup*

**MID-AFTERNOON SNACK**
Rice cakes with prune butter

**DINNER**
Pasta with Rappini*
2 Beneficial vegetables

**EVENING SNACK**
Super Baby Smoothie*

## DAY 8

**BREAKFAST**
Courgette and Mushroom Frittata*
Spelt toast
Cranberry juice
Slippery elm tea

**MID-MORNING SNACK**
Glass of kefir
Banana Walnut Muffin*
Grapes

**LUNCH**
White Bean and Wilted Greens Soup*
Mesclun Salad*

**MID-AFTERNOON SNACK**
Type B Bar

**DINNER**
Grilled Lamb Chops*
Griddled Portabello Mushrooms*
Steamed broccoli

**EVENING SNACK**
Walnut Cookies*
Mint tea

## DAY 9

**BREAKFAST**
Poached egg on toasted sprouted
    seed bread
Fresh figs with goat's cheese
Pineapple juice
Rose hip tea

**MID-MORNING SNACK**
Type B Bar

**LUNCH**
Grilled peppers and goat's cheese on
    spelt toast
Mixed green salad

**MID-AFTERNOON SNACK**
Type B Trail Mix-1*

**DINNER**
Roast Turkey*
Brown Rice Pilaf* with carrots and
    onions
Braised greens with garlic

**EVENING SNACK**
Super Baby Smoothie*

## DAY 10

**BREAKFAST**
High-Protein Energy Shake*
Banana Walnut Bread*

**MID-MORNING SNACK**
Slice of spelt bread with apple butter
Rose hip tea

**LUNCH**
Fresh Cherries and Yogurt Soup*
Rice cakes with almond butter
2 plums

**MID-AFTERNOON SNACK**
Raisins and chopped walnuts
Glass of cow's milk

**DINNER**
Fried Monkfish*
Mashed potatoes with butter
Tossed salad with olive oil and
    balsamic vinegar
Mineral water

**EVENING SNACK**
Super Baby Smoothie*

## DAY 11

**BREAKFAST**
Spelt flakes with fresh berries and
   cow's milk
Sprouted seed toast with melted
   cheese
Slippery elm tea

**MID-MORNING SNACK**
Banana Yogurt Drink*

**LUNCH**
Mushroom Barley Soup with Spinach*
Mesclun Salad*

**MID-AFTERNOON SNACK**
Beneficial fruit

**DINNER**
Pan-Fried Liver and Onions*
Braised Swiss chard
Wild rice

**EVENING SNACK**
Super Baby Smoothie*

## DAY 12

**BREAKFAST**
Tropical Salad*
Sprouted seed toast with cherry
   preserves
Rose hip tea

**MID-MORNING SNACK**
Type B Bar

**LUNCH**
Turkey Soup*
Carrot Raisin Salad*
Crackers

**MID-AFTERNOON SNACK**
Type B Trail Mix-2*

**DINNER**
Stuffed Cannelloni Shells with Pesto*
Braised Collards*
Mixed green salad

**EVENING SNACK**
Super Baby Smoothie*

## DAY 13

**BREAKFAST**
Scrambled eggs
Sprouted seed bread with plum
    preserves
Rose hip tea

**MID-MORNING SNACK**
Super Baby Smoothie*

**LUNCH**
Super Broccoli Salad*
Grilled goat's cheese sandwich on
    spelt bread

**MID-AFTERNOON SNACK**
Type B Bar

**DINNER**
Steamed Whole Red Snapper*
Braised Collards*
Steamed asparagus

**EVENING SNACK**
Sliced banana with cow's milk
Mint tea

## DAY 14

**BREAKFAST**
Banana Plum Bread*
Mixed fruit
Slippery elm tea

**MID-MORNING SNACK**
Rice cakes with apple butter

**LUNCH**
Simple Fish Soup*
Cole Slaw*
Mixed green salad

**MID-AFTERNOON SNACK**
Type B Trail Mix-1*

**DINNER**
Grilled Loin of Lamb Chops*
Sautéed greens
Romaine-feta salad

**EVENING SNACK**
Super Baby Smoothie*

## Second Trimester

### Adjust to an Increased Appetite

Foetal growth is rapid during the second trimester, and you may experience a greater appetite, especially if you no longer suffer from nausea or "morning sickness". Use your extra calories to maximum benefit.

---

* You can find recipes for asterisk-marked items in appendix A.

**EMPHASIS FOR EXTRA CALORIES**

- High-quality protein—organic lean red meat, fish, low-fat dairy
- Calcium-rich foods—organic cow's milk, goat's milk, yogurt, sardines
- Vitamin C–rich foods—dark green leafy vegetables, plums, pineapple, bananas

## Keep Your Blood Sugar in Check

For Type B, blood sugar irregularities are usually the result of carbohydrate intolerance—especially if you're eating too many grains, beans, and potatoes. While some increase in blood sugar is normal during pregnancy, be aware that severely elevated blood sugar leads to a dangerous condition called gestational diabetes, which can cause premature birth and even birth defects. The following symptoms should alert you to blood sugar imbalances:

Fatigue
Extreme hunger
Dry skin
Anxiety
Dizziness and light-headedness

To restore a proper balance:

- Increase the protein and decrease the carbohydrates in your diet.
- Eliminate refined sugars and starches.
- Eat fibre-rich foods every day.
- Never skip meals, especially breakfast. Preferably, eat six small meals a day.

## Avoid Urinary Tract Infections

Many women are susceptible to urinary tract infections (UTIs) during the second trimester. As a Type B, you need to be aware of this tendency, because Type Bs typically have an extremely high risk factor for UTIs. In addition to following the Type B diet, you can guard against UTIs with the following:

- Eat cranberries and blueberries—effective UTI fighters.
- Eat plenty of cultured dairy foods, such as yogurt and kefir.
- Urinate frequently to avoid a buildup of urine in the bladder.
- Continue taking your probiotic supplement. It will help keep the colon flora, vaginal flora, and urinary tract healthy.

## Help Your Body Resist Infection

Type Bs have the weakest defence of all the blood types against the most common influenza viruses. Since your immune system is suppressed during pregnancy, you need to be particularly alert. I highly recommend that you take regular doses of elderberry extract—1 teaspoon once or twice daily during the flu season. Elderberry has been used by herbalists for centuries, and it has been shown to inhibit replication of all strains of influenza virus. Don't exceed the recommended dosage, since it can make you slightly nauseated. You can also build your immune system with the following strategies:

- *Reduce stress.* There is ample evidence of a connection between stress and lowered immunity. Get away from the computer and the bill paying, at least for 30 minutes every day, to get a few moments of fresh air and sunshine. Try to go for a quick walk during lunch. Practise deep breathing while you walk.
- *Adopt good dietary habits.* Failure to eat breakfast, irregular eating habits, low vegetable intake, inadequate protein, excessive wheat intake, and high-fat diets (especially those with excessive amounts of polyunsaturated fatty acids) have all been associated with lowered immune function.
- *Eat exotic mushrooms.* Shiitake, maitake, and reishi mushrooms are very effective in supporting long-term antiviral resistance.

## Control Food Intolerance

Blood Type B can be intolerant to many common foods. Note that research shows that upward of 55 percent of our immune function is located in the digestive system. Avoid foods that trigger allergies for Type B:

> Coconut/milk
> Persimmon
> Avocado
> Artichoke
> Corn
> Olive
> Tomato
> Black bean
> Chickpea
> Lentil
> Soy bean/milk/tofu
> Peanut

Wheat germ
Whole wheat

## Second Trimester Menu Plans

The following menus offer a guide to healthy eating during the second trimester of your pregnancy. They include some adjustments from the first trimester, taking into account the special emphasis on this period in your pregnancy.

- The menu suggestions place an even greater emphasis on lean meats, fish, dairy, and fresh fruits and vegetables—all foods that help regulate blood sugar.
- They include more calories than the first trimester menus, to accommodate the growing nutritional needs of your foetus.
- They provide an extra boost of protein and vital nutrients with Type B–specific smoothies and energy bars.
- They provide additional foods that will help to overcome second trimester problems, such as haemorrhoids, varicose veins, bleeding gums, and allergic sensitivities. The menus are flexible and can be mixed and reorganized according to your personal needs. I have purposely not included portion sizes for most dishes, since caloric needs vary depending upon your height and weight. However, these menus do offer more foods than the first trimester—and you should try to increase your intake by 100 to 300 calories per day.

Note that although beverages are listed with some meals, I suggest you drink them half an hour before or after eating. Liquids consumed with solid foods dilute the digestive juices. Don't forget to keep drinking water throughout the day.

## Menus

### DAY 1

**BREAKFAST**
Oatmeal with raisins, warm milk,
    and maple syrup
Poached Fruit*
Cranberry juice
Slippery elm tea

**MID-MORNING SNACK**
Super Baby Smoothie*

**LUNCH**
Mackerel Salad* on a bed of Romaine
    lettuce
Rice cakes
Fruit salad

**MID-AFTERNOON SNACK**
Type B Trail Mix-1*

**DINNER**
Grilled cod
Tossed green salad with Balsamic
    Mustard Vinaigrette*
Brown Rice Pilaf*

**EVENING SNACK**
Sliced apple and walnuts
Chamomile tea

### DAY 2

**BREAKFAST**
Scrambled eggs
Spelt flakes with raisins and cow's
    milk
Prune Whip*
Rose hip tea

**MID-MORNING SNACK**
Pineapple Yogurt Drink*

**LUNCH**
Mushroom Barley Soup with Spinach*
Mixed green salad
Crackers

**MID-AFTERNOON SNACK**
Type B Bar

**DINNER**
Braised Rabbit*
Mixed Mushroom Salad*
Griddled Pepper Medley*

**EVENING SNACK**
Super Baby Smoothie*

## DAY 3

**BREAKFAST**
Wheat-Free Waffles*
Cherry preserves
Banana
Vegetable juice
Rose hip tea

**MID-MORNING SNACK**
Type B Bar

**LUNCH**
Grilled peppers and goat's cheddar on
    sprouted seed bread
Carrot and celery sticks
Grape Ice*

**MID-AFTERNOON SNACK**
Type B Trail Mix-2*

**DINNER**
Pan-Fried Liver and Onions*
Steamed broccoli
Pureed sweet potato

**EVENING SNACK**
Super Baby Smoothie*

## DAY 4

**BREAKFAST**
Omelette*
Spelt toast
Poached Fruit*
Rose hip tea

**MID-MORNING SNACK**
Mango-Lime Smoothie*

**LUNCH**
Grilled lean ground beef burger with
    lettuce and onion
Sprouted seed bread
Mixed green salad

**MID-AFTERNOON SNACK**
Type B Bar

**DINNER**
Grilled sole
Butter beans with goat's cheese and
    scallions
Steamed spinach

**EVENING SNACK**
Super Baby Smoothie*

## DAY 5

**BREAKFAST**
Pineapple Yogurt Drink*
Spinach Frittata*

**MID-MORNING SNACK**
Type B Bar

**LUNCH**
Sardines and lettuce on spelt bread
Super Broccoli Salad*
Mixed fruit

**MID-AFTERNOON SNACK**
Type B Trail Mix-1*

**DINNER**
Roast Turkey*
Brown rice
Carrots and Parsnips with Garlic
    and Coriander*

**EVENING SNACK**
Banana Pudding*
Chamomile tea

## DAY 6

**BREAKFAST**
Poached eggs on toasted spelt bread
Fresh pineapple slices
Slippery elm tea

**MID-MORNING SNACK**
Date-Prune Smoothie*

**LUNCH**
Spinach Salad*
Fresh mozzarella and sautéed
    courgette on spelt bread

**MID-AFTERNOON SNACK**
Beneficial fruit

**DINNER**
Green Leafy Pasta*
Romaine salad with Olive Oil and
    Lemon Dressing*

**EVENING SNACK**
Super Baby Smoothie*

## DAY 7

**BREAKFAST**
Cream of rice with dried cherries and
   milk
Manna toast
Fresh pineapple
Rose hip tea

**MID-MORNING SNACK**
Type B Bar

**LUNCH**
Farmer's Vegetable Soup*
Mesclun Salad*

**MID-AFTERNOON SNACK**
Strawberry-Banana Smoothie*

**DINNER**
Grilled Lamb Chops*
Braised leeks
Pureed root vegetables

**EVENING SNACK**
Rice cakes with apple butter
Mint tea

## DAY 8

**BREAKFAST**
Banana Plum Bread*
Stewed plums
Pineapple juice
Slippery elm tea

**MID-MORNING SNACK**
Type B Bar

**LUNCH**
Grilled cheese sandwich
   on spelt bread
Apple slices

**MID-AFTERNOON SNACK**
Super Baby Smoothie*

**DINNER**
Steamed Whole Red Snapper*
Grilled Sweet Potato Salad*
Steamed broccoli

**EVENING SNACK**
Banana Pudding*
Chamomile tea

## DAY 9

**BREAKFAST**
Scrambled eggs
Sprouted seed toast with cherry
    preserves
Mixed berries
Raspberry leaf tea

**MID-MORNING SNACK**
Type B Bar

**LUNCH**
Greek Salad*
Spelt pitta
Figs with goat's cheese and walnuts

**MID-AFTERNOON SNACK**
Type B Trail Mix-2*

**DINNER**
Pan-Fried Liver and Onions*
Vegetable Fritters*
Sautéed greens in olive oil

**EVENING SNACK**
Super Baby Smoothie*

## DAY 10

**BREAKFAST**
Scrambled eggs
Sautéed Bananas* with ricotta
Papaya juice
Slippery elm tea

**MID-MORNING SNACK**
Banana Yogurt Drink*

**LUNCH**
Simple Fish Soup*
Mesclun Salad*

**MID-AFTERNOON SNACK**
Type B Bar

**DINNER**
Turkey Cutlets*
Brown rice
Steamed broccoli

**EVENING SNACK**
Super Baby Smoothie*

## DAY 11

**BREAKFAST**
Apricot Yogurt Drink*
Brown Rice–Spelt Pancakes*
Berry preserves

**MID-MORNING SNACK**
Sliced pear with walnuts and raisins

**LUNCH**
Salmon with Wakame Seaweed*
Rice cakes
Vegetable consommé

**MID-AFTERNOON SNACK**
Super Baby Smoothie*

**DINNER**
Steamed Whole Red Snapper*
Brown Rice Pilaf*
Steamed broccoli

**EVENING SNACK**
Type B Bar

## DAY 12

**BREAKFAST**
Tropical Salad*
Sprouted seed toast with blackberry
    preserves

**MID-MORNING SNACK**
Cottage cheese and fresh fruit
Peppermint tea

**LUNCH**
Sardine Salad* on spelt bread
Spinach Salad*

**MID-AFTERNOON SNACK**
Type B Bar

**DINNER**
Beef Stew with Green Beans and
    Carrots*
Braised greens

**EVENING SNACK**
Super Baby Smoothie*

## DAY 13

**BREAKFAST**
One-Egg Omelette* with grated
  carrots
Sautéed Pears*
Rose hip tea

**MID-MORNING SNACK**
High-Energy Protein Shake*

**LUNCH**
Butter Beans with Goat's Cheese and
  Spring Onions*
Mixed green salad with Olive Oil and
  Lemon Dressing*

**MID-AFTERNOON SNACK**
Type B Bar

**DINNER**
Fried Monkfish*
Faro Pilaf*
Braised Collards*

**EVENING SNACK**
Spelt bread with apple butter
Mint tea

## DAY 14

**BREAKFAST**
Wheat-Free Pancakes* with plum
  preserves
Mixed berries
Slippery elm tea

**MID-MORNING SNACK**
Super Baby Smoothie*

**LUNCH**
Cucumber-Yogurt Soup*
Green Bean Salad with Walnuts and
  Goat's Cheese*

**MID-AFTERNOON SNACK**
Beneficial fruit

**DINNER**
Griddled Curried Leg of Lamb*
Mixed vegetable stir-fry
Basmati rice

**EVENING SNACK**
Banana Pudding*
Glass of milk

## Third Trimester

### Reduce Swelling and Oedema

Some water retention can be expected toward the end of your pregnancy, the result of an oestrogen spike prior to the delivery of your baby. Type Bs will experience oedema as the result of a sluggish metabolism.

---

* You can find recipes for asterisk-marked items in appendix A.

**SIGNS OF SLUGGISH METABOLISM**
- Fatigue
- Dry skin
- Cold hands and feet
- Light-headedness
- Constipation and water retention
- Depression

**AVOID REACTIVE LECTINS IN THESE FOODS**
- Chicken
- Buckwheat
- Corn
- Lentil beans
- Peanuts

Here are some additional suggestions for reducing oedema:

- Elevate your legs when sitting or lying down.
- Drink six to eight 8-ounce (225-ml) glasses of water during the day.
- Wear comfortable clothing and avoid tight pantyhose. Support stockings may offer relief.
- Cut back on high-sodium foods; many processed foods are loaded with sodium.
- Make sure your shoes fit properly.
- Drink 1 to 3 cups of dandelion tea every day for mild water retention.
- Ask your partner to gently massage the area from your ankles to your thighs with a very light touch.

> **WARNING:** Only use a diuretic on the advice of your doctor. Diuretics can cause dehydration and nutrient deficiency.

## Control Your Blood Pressure

Pregnancy-induced hypertension, also known as toxaemia or preeclampsia, can be extremely dangerous and can lead to miscarriage. Fortunately, Type Bs appear to have a special ability to control blood pressure using relaxation and visualization. This is something I have observed in my own practice. Take advantage of this ability to keep your blood pressure under control at this critical time. (See the visualization exercise on page 152.)

NATURAL BLOOD PRESSURE REDUCTION TONIC. One excellent method for ensuring healthy blood pressure is to juice several stalks of celery, taking 6 to 8 ounces (175–225 ml) as fresh juice daily.

## Ward Off Infections

Continue to make immune system health a top priority in the third trimester. Many bacterial infections attack Type Bs with special force. There's a reason. Many common bacteria-producing infections are B-like in nature, and you don't produce antibodies against them.

A particular risk for Type Bs that also has grave implications for your offspring is streptococcal disease. This disease occurs more often in Type Bs than other blood types, resulting in strep throat, or more serious illnesses such as bacter-aemia and heart valve malformation and damage.

Follow the standard Type B guidelines for building your immune system. In addition, you need to take preventive measures to avoid food-borne bacterial infections, such as *E. coli*, which favours Type B:

- Never serve hamburger or other foods containing minced beef that is rare or raw. When properly cooked, the inside of ground beef should be brown rather than pink, with an internal temperature of 160 degrees, and the juices should run clear.
- Do not eat raw sprouts.
- Hands, utensils, and food-contact surfaces must be washed with warm, soapy water between contact with raw meat and foods that have already been cooked or foods that will be served raw.

## Third Trimester Menu Plans

During the third trimester you may feel full after eating very little. Smaller meals, eaten at regular intervals of 3 to 4 hours, may be required to get all the nutrients you need. The following menus offer a guide to healthy eating during the third trimester of your pregnancy. They include some adjustments to account for the special emphasis of this period in your pregnancy.

- They place even greater emphasis on lean meats, fish, dairy, and fresh fruits and vegetables—all foods that help maintain metabolic balance.
- They provide an extra boost of protein and vital nutrients with Type B–specific smoothies and energy bars. This will help you prepare for the rigours of labour and delivery.
- Vitamin A– and C–rich foods are abundant, also in preparation for delivery.

The menus are flexible and can be mixed and reorganized according to your personal needs. I have purposely not included portion sizes for most dishes, since caloric needs vary depending upon your height and weight. You may need to divide up the meals and snacks further if you don't think you can finish them at one sitting. However, it's vital that you maintain your overall caloric level.

Note that although beverages are listed with some meals, I suggest you drink them half an hour before or after eating. Liquids consumed with solid foods dilute the digestive juices and fill you up faster. Don't forget to keep drinking water throughout the day.

## DAY 1

**BREAKFAST**
Omelette* with fresh spinach and feta
1 slice of manna toast with plum
    preserves
Grapes

**MID-MORNING SNACK**
Banana Yogurt Drink*

**LUNCH**
Farmer's Vegetable Soup*
Carrot Raisin Salad*
Crackers

**MID-AFTERNOON SNACK**
Type B Bar
Rose hip tea

**DINNER**
Pan-Fried Liver and Onions*
Baked sweet potato
Steamed broccoli

**EVENING SNACK**
Super Baby Smoothie*

## DAY 2

**BREAKFAST**
Oatmeal with raisins, maple syrup,
    and milk
Fresh pineapple
Slippery elm tea

**MID-MORNING SNACK**
Super Baby Smoothie*

**LUNCH**
Mackerel Salad* on a bed of greens
Rice cakes
Mixed fruit

**MID-AFTERNOON SNACK**
Type B Bar
Raspberry leaf tea

**DINNER**
Roast Turkey*
Brown Rice Pilaf* with carrots and
    onions
Brussels sprouts

**EVENING SNACK**
Banana Pudding*
Chamomile tea

## DAY 3

**BREAKFAST**
Sprouted seed toast with black cherry
  preserves
Yogurt with mixed berries
Raspberry leaf tea

**MID-MORNING SNACK**
Type B Bar

**LUNCH**
Turkey Soup*
Super Broccoli Salad*

**MID-AFTERNOON SNACK**
Type B Trail Mix-2*

**DINNER**
Fried Monkfish*
Carrots and Parsnips with Garlic
  and Coriander*
Millet Tabbouleh*

**EVENING SNACK**
Super Baby Smoothie*

## DAY 4

**BREAKFAST**
Scrambled eggs
Brown rice bread with plum preserves
Glass of milk
Rose hip tea

**MID-MORNING SNACK**
Cherry-Peach Smoothie*

**LUNCH**
Grilled aubergine and feta on spelt
  bread
Mesclun Salad*

**MID-AFTERNOON SNACK**
Type B Bar
Peppermint tea

**DINNER**
Flank Steak*
Pureed root vegetables
Steamed broccoli

**EVENING SNACK**
Cranberry Biscotti*
Glass of milk

## DAY 5

**BREAKFAST**
Brown Rice–Spelt Pancakes*
    with maple syrup
Grapes
Vegetable juice

**MID-MORNING SNACK**
Type B Bar

**LUNCH**
Sliced cold flank steak on a bed of
    Romaine lettuce
Mixed Roots Soup*

**MID-AFTERNOON SNACK**
Super Baby Smoothie*

**DINNER**
Green Leafy Pasta*
Chicory salad

**EVENING SNACK**
Banana Pudding*
Type B Tea

## DAY 6

**BREAKFAST**
Spinach Frittata*
Manna toast
Pineapple slices
Rose hip tea

**MID-MORNING SNACK**
Banana Yogurt Drink*

**LUNCH**
Sardines
Rice cakes
Cucumber Yogurt Soup*

**MID-AFTERNOON SNACK**
Sliced apple, raisins, and walnuts

**DINNER**
Griddled Curried Leg of Lamb*
Steamed broccoli
Wild rice

**EVENING SNACK**
Super Baby Smoothie*

## DAY 7

**BREAKFAST**
Spelt flakes with mixed fruit and milk
Banana Plum Bread*

**MID-MORNING SNACK**
Type B Bar

**LUNCH**
Waldorf Salad*
Toasted cheese sandwich
    on spelt bread

**MID-AFTERNOON SNACK**
Super Baby Smoothie*

**DINNER**
Fried Monkfish*
Brown rice
Mixed green salad

**EVENING SNACK**
Lemon sorbet with pineapple chunks
Rose hip tea

## DAY 8

**BREAKFAST**
Brown Rice–Spelt Pancakes*
    with maple syrup
Stewed prunes

**MID-MORNING SNACK**
Type B Bar

**LUNCH**
White Bean and Wilted Greens Soup*
Mixed green salad with Seaweed
    Dressing*

**MID-AFTERNOON SNACK**
Rice cakes with plum preserves

**DINNER**
Fettuccine with Grilled Lamb Sausages
    and Vegetables*
Mixed green salad

**EVENING SNACK**
Banana Yogurt Drink*
Type B Bar

## DAY 9

**BREAKFAST**
Poached egg on toasted sprouted
   seed bread
Poached Fruit*
Pineapple juice
Rose hip tea

**MID-MORNING SNACK**
Type B Bar

**LUNCH**
Cole Slaw*
Grilled lean ground beef burger with
   melted goat's cheese and raw
   spinach leaves
Spelt bread

**MID-AFTERNOON SNACK**
Toasted Tamari Pumpkin Seeds*
Carrot juice

**DINNER**
Grilled Salmon Steak*
Steamed broccoli
Brown rice

**EVENING SNACK**
Super Baby Smoothie*

## DAY 10

**BREAKFAST**
Banana Walnut Bread*
Stewed prunes
Red raspberry leaf tea

**MID-MORNING SNACK**
Banana Yogurt Drink*

**LUNCH**
Grilled Peppers on Rye Crackers with
   Chèvre*
Spinach Salad*

**MID-AFTERNOON SNACK**
Type B Bar

**DINNER**
Grilled sirloin steak with shiitake
   mushrooms
Baked sweet potato
Braised Collards*

**EVENING SNACK**
Super Baby Smoothie*

## DAY 11

**BREAKFAST**
Spelt flakes with sliced banana and
    cow's milk
Manna toast with butter
2 plums
Rose hip tea

**MID-MORNING SNACK**
Banana Yogurt Drink*

**LUNCH**
Sliced turkey on spelt bread
Mixed green salad

**MID-AFTERNOON SNACK**
Type B Bar

**DINNER**
Grilled Loin of Lamb Chops*
2 Beneficial vegetables
Apple and Onion Confit*

**EVENING SNACK**
Super Baby Smoothie*

## DAY 12

**BREAKFAST**
Scrambled eggs
Sprouted seed toast with grape jam
Pineapple slices
Chamomile tea

**MID-MORNING SNACK**
Type B Bar

**LUNCH**
Butter Beans with Goat's Cheese and
    Spring Onions*
Mixed steamed vegetables

**MID-AFTERNOON SNACK**
Rice cakes with plum preserves
Grapes

**DINNER**
Indian Lamb Stew with Spinach*
Basmati rice
Beneficial vegetable

**EVENING SNACK**
Super Baby Smoothie*

## DAY 13

**BREAKFAST**
Poached egg
Tropical Salad*
Sprouted seed toast with plum
    preserves
Rose hip tea

**MID-MORNING SNACK**
Banana Yogurt Drink*

**LUNCH**
Turkey Soup*
Mesclun Salad*

**MID-AFTERNOON SNACK**
Beneficial fruit

**DINNER**
Pan-Fried Liver and Onions*
Brown rice
Broccoli

**EVENING SNACK**
Super Baby Smoothie*

## DAY 14

**BREAKFAST**
Spelt flakes with mixed fruit and cow's
    milk
Manna toast
Raspberry leaf tea

**MID-MORNING SNACK**
Strawberry-Banana Smoothie*

**LUNCH**
Greek Salad*
Speltberry and Rice Salad*
Lemon-chamomile tea

**MID-AFTERNOON SNACK**
Raisins and walnuts
Super Baby Smoothie*

**DINNER**
Steamed Whole Red Snapper*
Brown rice
Steamed asparagus

**EVENING SNACK**
Type B Bar
Chamomile tea

## Exercise Guidelines

### First Trimester

## Maintenance for Healthy Type Bs

Since Type B is particularly susceptible to high levels of stress hormones causing
anxiety and mood swings, you can benefit by continuing to incorporate relaxation
and meditation exercises into your daily routine.

---

* You can find recipes for asterisk-marked items in appendix A.

Type Bs usually do best with moderate aerobic exercise, so this is not the time to engage in contact sports or in-line skating. I'd suggest you forego them during pregnancy, to avoid any potential injury to the abdominal area.

Choose from among the following Type B exercises for a minimum regimen of 45 minutes, three to four times a week.

| EXERCISE | DURATION |
|---|---|
| Tennis | 45–60 minutes |
| Martial arts | 30–60 minutes |
| Cycling | 45–60 minutes |
| Hiking | 30–60 minutes |
| Treadmill | 30–40 minutes |
| Golf (no cart) | 60 minutes |
| Swimming | 30–45 minutes |

CAUTIONS FOR HIGH-RISK PREGNANCIES

Consult with your doctor before continuing your exercise regimen if you are in a high-risk pregnancy. Most doctors will discourage exercise if you:

- Have a history of miscarriages, or have had even one miscarriage, if it is recent.
- Have a history of recurrent pelvic or abdominal infections.
- Have an incompetent cervix. This condition causes the cervix to open early, usually in the second trimester, leading to miscarriage.
- Have had toxaemia in a previous pregnancy.
- Have a history of premature deliveries.
- Have or have had a serious medical condition, such as cancer, heart disease, asthma, or kidney disease.

## Second Trimester

## Adaptations for Advancing Pregnancy

As your pregnancy progresses, you'll need to shift the emphasis of your exercise regimen. Discontinue exercises that require speed and balance—such as tennis, biking, and martial arts (with the exception of T'ai chi). Swimming is a very good exercise at this point in your pregnancy. Supplement your aerobic activity with a prenatal yoga class.

An ideal second trimester regimen for Type B includes the following.

THREE TIMES A WEEK, CHOOSE ONE:

| EXERCISE | DURATION |
|---|---|
| Water aerobics | 40–50 minutes |
| Treadmill | 30 minutes |
| Cycling (recumbent bike) | 30 minutes |
| Swimming | 30 minutes |
| Brisk walking | 45 minutes |

TWO TIMES A WEEK, CHOOSE ONE:

| EXERCISE | DURATION |
|---|---|
| Light yoga | 40–50 minutes |
| T'ai chi | 30 minutes |
| Labour preparation class | 40–50 minutes |

DAILY:

| EXERCISE | DURATION |
|---|---|
| Pelvic floor exercises | 2 minutes, 10–20 times |

- Spend more time on your warm-up and cool-down to fully warm and stretch your muscles. This will minimize the muscle cramps that are common as your pregnancy progresses.
- Look for opportunities to incorporate fitness into your daily routine. If feasible, walk to work instead of driving. Take the stairs instead of the elevator.
- Swimming is an excellent exercise for the second and third trimesters. It places minimum stress on your joints and heart rate. You may even want to replace your regular aerobics class with a water aerobics class.
- If you haven't already started your pelvic floor exercises (see page 28), do so now.

PREGNANCY-SAFE EXERCISE SUBSTITUTIONS

| INSTEAD OF ... | TRY ... |
|---|---|
| Bicycling | Exercise bike (recumbent) |
| Tennis | Brisk walking/treadmill |
| Aerobics | Water aerobics |

# Third Trimester

## Adaptations for Late Pregnancy

Your focus during the final months of pregnancy should be on stress reduction. Not only is this a particularly stressful time, but Type B has a heightened tendency to produce excess cortisol in response to even minor stress.

Avoid any exercises that place pressure on your abdominal area. Lie on your side for floor exercises. This position also helps your circulation and will decrease your blood pressure.

Type Bs can benefit in the final months of pregnancy by replacing one of your weekly aerobic exercises with a relaxation exercise. Also begin your daily perineal massage to tone the vaginal canal (page 31).

An excellent third trimester exercise regimen for Type B would be the following.

TWO TIMES A WEEK, CHOOSE ONE:

| EXERCISE | DURATION |
|---|---|
| Water aerobics | 40–50 minutes |
| Treadmill | 30 minutes |
| Cycling (recumbent bike) | 30 minutes |
| Swimming | 30 minutes |
| Brisk walking | 45 minutes |

THREE TIMES A WEEK, CHOOSE ONE:

| EXERCISE | DURATION |
|---|---|
| Light yoga | 40–50 minutes |
| Meditation | 30 minutes |
| Labour preparation class | 40–50 minutes |

DAILY, PERFORM BOTH:

| EXERCISE | DURATION |
|---|---|
| Pelvic floor exercises | 2 minutes, 10–20 times |
| Perineal massage | 5 minutes, 1–2 times |

MEDITATION. Calming yourself through the process of meditation is a wonderful way to reduce your stress level. Quieting the mind will help you eliminate stress-causing thoughts and help you to approach your day in a more positive and efficient manner.

## Meditation Exercise

- Choose a quiet place.
- Sit in a comfortable chair.
- Close your eyes.
- Relax your muscles.
- Become aware of your breathing.
- Choose a pleasant word or visual image that you can hear and see in your imagination. Think of this word or image every time you exhale for about 15 minutes each day. If you have an intrusive thought or feeling during your meditation, return to the repetition of your relaxing word or image.

# Supplement Guidelines

## First Trimester

## Vitamins/Minerals

Take a standard prenatal vitamin supplement, choosing one made from whole food, not synthetic ingredients. Powder-in-capsule forms dissolve most efficiently. If you would like to use a prenatal supplement specifically formulated for Type B, see appendix B for information. The following nutrient breakdown is the optimal formula for Type B.

| PRENATAL SUPPLEMENT—TYPE B | |
| --- | --- |
| Vitamin A (100% as natural beta-carotene from *Dunaliella salina*) | 3,000 iu |
| Vitamin C (100 % from acerola berry, *Malpighia puncifolia*) | 75 mg |
| Vitamin D (*cholecalciferol*) | 75 iu |
| Vitamin E (natural d,alpha-tocopheryl succinate) | 150 iu |
| Vitamin K (phytonadione) | 15 mcg |
| Thiamin (from thiamin HCl) | 20 mg |
| Riboflavin | 20 mg |
| Niacin and niacinamide (vitamin $B_3$) | 15 mg |
| Vitamin $B_6$ (from pyridoxine HCl) | 10 mg |

| PRENATAL SUPPLEMENT—TYPE B | |
|---|---|
| Folic acid | 800 mcg |
| Vitamin B$_{12}$ (methylcobalamin) | 15 mcg |
| Biotin | 400 mcg |
| Pantothenic acid (from D-calcium pantothenate) | 10 mg |
| Calcium (seaweed base, derived from *Lithothamnium corralliodes* and *Lithothamnium calcareum*) | 300 mg |
| Iron (ferrous succinate) | 20 mg |
| Iodine (potassium iodide) | 75 mcg |
| Magnesium (citrate and oxide) | 100 mg |
| Zinc (picolinate) | 15 mg |
| Selenium (L-selenomethionine) | 20 mcg |
| Copper (gluconate) | 1 mg |
| Manganese (citrate) | 1 mg |

## Herbal Remedies

| HERB | FUNCTION | FORM AND DOSAGE |
|---|---|---|
| Chamomile | Calms; relieves heartburn | As tea, 1 to 2 cups daily; or add 2–4 drops of essential oil to bath |
| Horsetail | Contains silica, which supports healthy bones, skin, hair, and nails | 250-mg capsule daily |
| Peppermint | Calms; relieves indigestion | As tea, 2 to 3 cups daily, after meals |
| Slippery elm bark | Relieves heartburn | 250-mg capsule, twice daily; or as tea, 2 cups daily |

| Nutritional Supplements | | |
| --- | --- | --- |
| **NUTRITIONAL SUPPLEMENT** | **FUNCTION** | **FORM AND DOSAGE** |
| Larch arabinogalactan | Relieves constipation | Soluble fibre supplement: 1 tablespoon mixed with water or juice, twice daily |
| Probiotic | For intestinal health | 2 capsules, twice daily* |
| DHA | Provides essential nutrients for foetal development | 300-mg capsule daily |

\* See appendix B for information on blood type–specific probiotics.

## Second Trimester

### Vitamins/Minerals

Continue to take your prenatal supplement, preferably one formulated for Type B.

| Herbal Remedies | | |
| --- | --- | --- |
| **HERB** | **FUNCTION** | **FORM AND DOSAGE** |
| Bilberry | Relieves haemorrhoids and varicose veins | 25-mg capsule, twice daily |
| Chamomile | Calms; relieves heartburn; relieves haemorrhoids and varicose veins | As tea, 1 to 2 cups daily; or add 2 to 4 drops of essential oil to bath |
| Horsetail | Contains silica, which supports healthy bones, skin, hair, and nails | 250-mg capsule daily |
| Peppermint | Calms and relieves indigestion | As tea, 2 to 3 cups daily, after meals |
| Rose hips | Treatment for varicose veins, bleeding gums, allergies | One tablespoon concentrate every 30 minutes for allergy attack; as tea, 2 to 3 cups daily |
| Stinging nettle leaf | Allergy relief | As tea, 2 cups daily for symptoms |
| Witch hazel | Treatment for haemorrhoids | Use topically as needed |

## Nutritional Supplements

| NUTRITIONAL SUPPLEMENT | FUNCTION | FORM AND DOSAGE |
|---|---|---|
| Larch arabinogalactan | Relieves constipation | Soluble fibre supplement: 1 tablespoon mixed with water or juice, twice daily |
| Probiotic | For intestinal health; prevention of candida infection | 2 capsules, twice daily* |
| DHA | Provides essential nutrients for foetal development | 300-mg capsule daily |

\* See appendix B for information on blood type–specific probiotics.

## Third Trimester

### Vitamins/Minerals

Continue to take your prenatal supplement, preferably one formulated for Type B.

## Herbal Remedies

| HERB | FUNCTION | FORM AND DOSAGE |
|---|---|---|
| Dandelion leaf/root | Lowers blood pressure; decreases oedema | As tea, 2 cups daily; or 250-mg capsule, twice daily |
| Nettles | Rich in vitamin K, promotes blood clotting | As tea, 2 cups daily; or 250-mg capsule, twice daily |
| Raspberry leaf (last 4 weeks) | Softens the cervix in preparation for birth; stimulates milk production | As tea, 2 cups daily; as tincture, 15 to 20 drops daily |
| Squaw vine | Prepares uterus for birth | As tincture, 10 drops in warm water, twice daily |

| Nutritional Supplements | | |
|---|---|---|
| **NUTRITIONAL SUPPLEMENT** | **FUNCTION** | **FORM AND DOSAGE** |
| Larch arabinogalactan | Relieves constipation | Soluble fibre supplement: 1 tablespoon mixed with water or juice, twice daily. |
| Probiotic | For intestinal health; prevention of candida infection | 2 capsules, twice daily* |
| DHA | Provides essential nutrients for foetal development | 300-mg capsule daily |

\* See appendix B for information on blood type–specific probiotics.

## Labour and Delivery

In addition to the general guidelines for labour and delivery (page 32), you have some specific Type B needs.

### Labour Preparation

One of the best ways I have found for Type Bs to deal with stress is through organization. When a Type B individual has a clear plan of action, she is more relaxed and confident. This being the case, it makes sense for you to spend time in the days and weeks prior to delivery carefully preparing for the big event. Make a list of questions for your practitioner, pack your bag, create a contingency plan—everything that *can* be controlled.

### Type B Blood-Building Needs

To guard against excessive bleeding in the event that a cesarean or other surgical procedure might be required, increase your blood-clotting factors. Follow these guidelines in the final weeks of pregnancy:

- Vitamin K is essential to blood clotting. Eat lots of greens, especially kale, spinach, and collard greens, and supplement your diet with liquid chlorophyll.
- Avoid using aspirin, which has blood-thinning properties and can prolong your bleeding.

## Type B Energy Needs

Begin several weeks before your delivery date to prepare yourself for the stress of labour and delivery. Try to get more sleep than usual and eat plenty of nutrient-rich foods. Type Bs have a tendency to let stress levels build, and you don't want to reach the point of labour with all of your energy resources depleted.

The first stage of labour can last many hours. Drink plenty of liquids and keep a light protein snack nearby. Stay hydrated. Be sure to discuss in advance with your doctor or midwife what the policy is about eating light foods or drinking liquids during labour.

## Type B Emotional Needs

Type Bs tend to be extraordinarily gifted in their ability to reduce stress and relieve anxiety with mental exercises, such as meditation and visualization.

Breathing is a critical component of meditation. Not surprisingly, a technique called "alternate nostril breathing" is a powerful tool in managing your physiology. Left nostril breathing generates a more relaxing effect, or toning down, of sympathetic activity. Right nostril breathing generates an increase in parasympathetic activity. The alternate nostril breathing technique generates a relative balance between the sympathetic and parasympathetic nervous systems and is a tremendous antistress measure.

CREATIVE VISUALIZATION. This exercise also helps to reduce stress by imagining a very calm and relaxing scene in your mind. Some people picture themselves at the beach feeling the warmth of the sun and the sound of the waves crashing on the shore. Others think of being in the mountains, with eagles soaring overhead, as they breathe in the cool clean air. The goal is to replace negative, stressful thoughts with more relaxing ones. As your mind relaxes, so does your body.

See page 35 for natural childbirth painkillers.

# The Type AB Pregnancy

TYPE AB IS THE RAREST BLOOD TYPE, comprising less than 5 percent of the population. In some respects, you're more vulnerable to health problems, since your complex immune system shares some aspects of Type A and some aspects of Type B. Similarly, although your digestive profile is A-like, there is a shared Type B preference for meat. So, although Type AB needs a bit more animal protein than Type A, they typically do not do well with a diet centred around animal protein. Similarly, Type AB has difficulty metabolizing combinations of fat and protein, because of low levels of an important enzyme called intestinal alkaline phosphatase. Type ABs should abide by this simple rule of thumb: Most foods that should be avoided by Type A and Type B should also be avoided by Type AB.

Type AB's rather unique immune defences can hyperfunction, leading to allergies, inflammation, chronic fatigue, and a number of other autoimmune disorders that can sap your vitality and interfere with the ability to conceive. These disorders can also create problems during pregnancy.

Following the blood type diet is an essential foundation, enabling you to optimize your health and prepare for an energetic and enjoyable pregnancy.

## The Type AB Diet

The following food lists comprise the Type AB diet. Note that the values for certain foods change in preparation for pregnancy, during pregnancy, and/or while you are breast-feeding. I call these Chameleon Foods, and they are contained in the following table. Use this table for quick reference. Chameleon Foods are also marked with an asterisk (*) in the specific food lists.

## Type AB Chameleon Foods

Chameleons are foods whose values change before pregnancy, during pregnancy, and/or while breast-feeding.

| FOOD | PRE-/POST-PREGNANCY | PREGNANCY | FACTORS |
|---|---|---|---|
| **SEAFOOD** | | | |
| Carp | Neutral | Avoid | Heightened risk of contamination |
| Catfish | Neutral | Avoid | Heightened risk of contamination |
| Grouper | Beneficial | Avoid | Heightened risk of contamination |
| Halibut | Beneficial | Avoid | High mercury content |
| Mackerel | Neutral | Avoid | Heightened risk of contamination |
| Mahimahi | Beneficial | Avoid | Heightened risk of contamination |
| Salmon | Beneficial | Neutral | Some risk of contamination |
| Shark | Neutral | Avoid | High mercury content |
| Swordfish | Neutral | Avoid | High mercury content |
| Tilapia | Neutral | Avoid | Heightened risk of contamination |
| Tuna | Neutral | Avoid | High mercury content |
| Whitefish | Neutral | Avoid | Heightened risk of contamination |
| **OILS** | | | |
| Borage | Neutral | Avoid | Uterine stimulant |
| **BEAN/LEGUME** | | | |
| Soy cheese | Neutral | Beneficial | Good source of calcium/protein |
| Soy milk | Neutral | Beneficial | Good source of calcium/protein |
| **VEGETABLES** | | | |
| Parsley | Beneficial | Neutral | Limit intake; can be a uterine stimulant in large amounts |
| **SPICES** | | | |
| Chocolate | Neutral | Avoid | Contains caffeine |
| Ginger | Beneficial | Avoid | May cause miscarriage in large amounts |
| Licorice | Neutral | Avoid | Can influence oestrogen levels |
| Parsley | Beneficial | Neutral | Limit intake; can be a uterine stimulant in large amounts |
| Turmeric | Neutral | Avoid | Uterine stimulant |

| FOOD | PRE-/POST-PREGNANCY | PREGNANCY | FACTORS |
|---|---|---|---|
| **HERBAL TEAS** | | | |
| Catnip | Neutral | Avoid | Uterine stimulant |
| Dandelion | Neutral | Beneficial | Aids digestion |
| Dong quai | Neutral | Avoid | Can start uterine bleeding |
| Ginger | Beneficial | Avoid | May cause miscarriage in large amounts |
| Goldenseal | Neutral | Avoid | Potentially harmful to foetus |
| Licorice | Beneficial | Avoid | Can influence oestrogen levels |
| Parsley | Beneficial | Neutral | Limit intake; can be a uterine stimulant in large amounts |
| Raspberry leaf | Neutral | Beneficial | Supports late pregnancy |
| St. John's wort | Neutral | Avoid | Can be harmful to foetus |
| Vervain | Neutral | Avoid | Uterine stimulant |
| Yarrow | Neutral | Avoid | Uterine stimulant |
| **BEVERAGES** | | | |
| Beer | Neutral | Avoid | Alcohol should be completely avoided during pregnancy |
| Soda water | Neutral | Avoid | Can cause digestive problems |
| Tea, green | Beneficial | Avoid | Contains caffeine; start weaning yourself before pregnancy, and avoid during pregnancy |
| Wine, red | Beneficial | Avoid | Alcohol should be completely avoided during pregnancy |
| Wine, white | Neutral | Avoid | Alcohol should be completely avoided during pregnancy |

## Meats and Poultry.

Type ABs need to limit the amount of meat you eat, since you do not produce enough stomach acid to effectively digest too much animal protein. The key for you is portion size and frequency. Give preference to lamb, mutton, rabbit, and turkey over beef, and avoid chicken. Choose lean, organic cuts of meat.

**HIGHLY BENEFICIAL**

| | |
|---|---|
| Lamb | Rabbit |
| Mutton | Turkey |

**NEUTRAL**

| | |
|---|---|
| Liver | Pheasant |
| Ostrich | |

**AVOID**

| | |
|---|---|
| All commercially processed meats | Ham |
| | Heart/sweetbreads |
| Bacon | Horse |
| Beef | Partridge |
| Chicken | Pigeon |
| Duck | Pork |
| Goose | Quail |
| Grouse | Veal |
| Guinea fowl | Venison |

## Seafood

Seafood is an excellent source of protein for Type ABs, but pregnant women must use special caution to avoid fish that may contain PCBs or that are otherwise potentially toxic. Check with your local health department about the safety of fish caught in local waters. In addition, avoid certain fish that are especially vulnerable to contamination by environmental pollutants, such as pesticides and PCBs. These include bass, flounder, grouper, halibut, mackerel, mahimahi, fresh salmon, tilapia, and whitefish. Also avoid fish that may contain a high level of mercury—halibut, shark, swordfish, and tuna.

**HIGHLY BENEFICIAL**

Cod

Grouper*

Mackerel

Mahimahi*

Monkfish

Pike

Red snapper

Salmon

Sardine

Shad

Snail

Sturgeon

Tuna*

**NEUTRAL**

Abalone

Carp*

Catfish*

Caviar

Chub

Drum

Herring (fresh)

Mackerel*

Mullet

Mussels

Orange roughy

Perch (all types)

Pollack

Salmon* (preferably farm-
    raised or canned)

Scallop

Shark*

Smelt

Snapper

Squid (calamari)

Swordfish*

Tilapia*

Whitefish*

**AVOID**

Anchovy

Barracuda

Bass (all types)

Beluga

Clam

Conch

Crab

Crayfish

Eel

Flounder

Frog

Haddock

Hake

Halibut

Herring (pickled)

Lobster

Lox

Octopus

Oysters

Prawns

Salmon roe

Shrimps

Sole (all types)

Trout (all types)

Whiting

Food with different values than the standard Type AB diet are indicated with an asterisk (*).

## Eggs and Dairy

Type ABs benefit from dairy foods, especially cultured and soured products—yogurt, kefir, and sour cream—which are easily digested. If you have respiratory problems, sinus attacks, or ear infections, cut back on dairy foods. Eggs are a very good source of protein for Type ABs, and also contain DHA, which is highly beneficial for pregnant women.

### HIGHLY BENEFICIAL

| | |
|---|---|
| Cottage cheese | Kefir |
| Dairylea-style cheese | Mozzarella |
| Egg, chicken | Ricotta |
| Feta | Sour cream (low-fat) |
| Goat's cheese | Yogurt |
| Goat's milk | |

### NEUTRAL

| | |
|---|---|
| Cheddar | Jarlsberg |
| Cream cheese | Monterey jack |
| Edam | Muenster |
| Egg, goose | Neufchâtel |
| Egg, quail | Paneer |
| Emmenthal | Quark cheese |
| Ghee (clarified butter) | String cheese |
| Gouda | Swiss |
| Gruyère | Whey |

### AVOID

| | |
|---|---|
| Blue cheese | Egg, duck |
| Brie | Ice cream |
| Butter | Milk |
| Buttermilk | Parmesan |
| Camembert | Provolone |

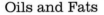

## Oils and Fats

When cooking, give preference to the healthful monounsaturated olive oil. Linseed (flaxseed) oil, neutral for Type AB, should be limited during pregnancy, and borage oil should be avoided.

**HIGHLY BENEFICIAL**

| | |
|---|---|
| Olive | Walnut |

**NEUTRAL**

| | |
|---|---|
| Almond | Linseed (flaxseed) |
| Black currant seed | Peanut |
| Borage* | Soy |
| Castor | Vegetable |
| Cod liver | Wheat germ |
| Evening primrose | |

**AVOID**

| | |
|---|---|
| Coconut | Safflower |
| Corn | Sesame |
| Cottonseed | Sunflower |

## Nuts and Seeds

Nuts and seeds present a mixed picture for Type ABs. Eat them in small amounts and with caution. Although they can be a good supplementary protein source, many seeds contain lectins that can induce immune reactions, making them a problem for Type ABs. Others, such as peanuts, are excellent immunity boosters.

**HIGHLY BENEFICIAL**

| | |
|---|---|
| Chestnut | Peanut butter |
| Peanut | Walnut |

---

Food with different values than the standard Type AB diet are indicated with an asterisk (*).

**NEUTRAL**

| | |
|---|---|
| Almond | Flaxseed (linseed) |
| Almond butter | Hickory |
| Almond cheese | Macadamia |
| Almond milk | Pecan/pecan butter |
| Beechnut | Pignola (pine nut) |
| Brazil nut | Pistachio |
| Cashew/cashew butter | Safflower seed |

**AVOID**

| | |
|---|---|
| Filbert (hazelnut) | Sesame seed |
| Poppy seed | Sesame butter (tahini) |
| Pumpkin seed | Sunflower seed/butter |

## Beans and Legumes

Beans and legumes are another mixed bag for Type ABs. Lentils are known to contain cancer-fighting antioxidants. On the other hand, kidney and butter beans can cause problems for Type ABs. Soy-based foods are highly beneficial for you during pregnancy, as they are excellent sources of calcium and protein.

**HIGHLY BENEFICIAL**

| | |
|---|---|
| Haricot bean | Pinto bean |
| Lentil (green) | Soybean |
| Miso | Soy (tempeh, tofu) |

**NEUTRAL**

| | |
|---|---|
| Cannellini bean | Soy cheese* |
| Green bean | Soy milk* |
| Green pea | String bean |
| Lentil (domestic, red) | Tamarind bean |
| Pea pod | White bean |
| Snap bean | |

---

Food with different values than the standard Type AB diet are indicated with an asterisk (*).

**AVOID**

| | |
|---|---|
| Aduki bean | Butter bean |
| Black bean | Garbanzo bean (chickpea) |
| Black-eyed pea | Kidney bean |
| Broad bean | Mung bean (sprouts) |

## Grains, Pastas, and Cereals

Generally, Type ABs do well on grains, but you need to limit your wheat consumption, especially if you have a pronounced mucous condition caused by asthma or frequent infections. Oatmeal, soy flakes, millet, farina, rice, and soy granules are good Type AB choices, as are manna and sprouted seed breads. Avoid buckwheat and corn.

**HIGHLY BENEFICIAL**

| | |
|---|---|
| Amaranth | Rice (puffed) |
| Millet | Rye bread (100%) |
| Oat bran | Rye crackers |
| Oat flour | Rye flour |
| Oatmeal | Ryvita |
| Rice bran | Soy flour bread |
| Rice bread | Spelt (whole) |
| Rice cake | Sprouted seed bread |
| Rice (white, brown, basmati, wild) | Wheat bread (sprouted) |

**NEUTRAL**

| | |
|---|---|
| Barley | Spelt bread |
| Couscous (cracked wheat) | Spinach pasta |
| Cream of rice | Wheat bran |
| Cream of wheat | Wheat bran muffin |
| Gluten flour | Wheat (gluten flour products) |
| Quinoa | Wheat (white flour products) |
| Semolina pasta | Wheat (whole-wheat products) |
| Seven-grain bread/cereal | Wheat germ |
| Shredded wheat | |

**AVOID**

| | |
|---|---|
| Artichoke pasta (pure) | Popcorn |
| Buckwheat/kasha | Soba noodles (100% |
| Corn (white, yellow, blue) | buckwheat) |
| Cornbread or muffin | Sorghum |
| Cornflakes | Tapioca |
| Cornmeal | Wheat (refined, unbleached) |

## Vegetables

Most vegetables are available to Type ABs, and they are an excellent source of vitamins, minerals, and phytochemicals. Fennel and parsley, normally good for Type AB, should be minimized during pregnancy, as these are uterine stimulants. Also note that although onions and garlic are acceptable for Type AB, you may want to avoid or limit them while you're breast-feeding. Some babies experience colic when mums eat these foods.

**HIGHLY BENEFICIAL**

| | |
|---|---|
| Alfalfa sprouts | Cucumber |
| Aubergine | Garlic |
| Beet | Kale |
| Beet greens | Mushroom (maitake) |
| Broccoli | Mustard greens |
| Cabbage juice | Parsley* |
| Carrot juice | Parsnip |
| Cauliflower | Sweet potato |
| Celery/juice | Yam |
| Collard greens | |

**NEUTRAL**

| | |
|---|---|
| Asparagus | Coriander |
| Bamboo shoot | Courgette |
| Bok choy | Cucumber juice |
| Brussels sprouts | Endive |
| Cabbage (all types) | Fennel* |
| Carrot | Horseradish |
| Celeriac | Kohlrabi |
| Chicory | Leek |

Food with different values than the standard Type AB diet are indicated with an asterisk (*).

Lettuce (all types)
Mangetout
Mushroom (open cup, portabello, tree, oyster, enoki)
Okra
Olive (Greek, green, Spanish)
Onion (all types)
Pea (green, pod)
Pimento
Potato (red, white)
Pumpkin
Radicchio
Rappini (broccoli rabe)
Rocket

Sauerkraut
Seaweed
Shallot
Spinach/juice
Spring onion
Squash (all types)
String bean
Swede
Swiss chard
Tomato/juice
Turnip
Water chestnut
Watercress
Yucca

**AVOID**

Aloe (tea, juice, leaves)
Artichoke (domestic, globe, Jerusalem)
Avocado
Corn
Mushroom (shiitake, abalone)

Olive, black
Peppers (all types)
Pickles (all types)
Radish (red)
Sprouts (mung, radish)

## Fruits

Type ABs should emphasize the more alkaline fruits, such as grapes, plums, and berries. Avoid oranges, which are a stomach irritant for Type ABs and also interfere with the absorption of important minerals. Lemons are excellent for Type ABs, helping to aid digestion and clear mucus from the system.

The banana lectin interferes with Type AB digestion. I recommend substituting other high-potassium fruits such as apricots, figs, and certain melons.

**HIGHLY BENEFICIAL**

Cherry
Cranberry/juice
Fig (fresh, dried)
Gooseberry
Grape (all types)
Grapefruit

Kiwi
Lemon/juice
Pineapple
Plum
Watermelon

**NEUTRAL**

| | |
|---|---|
| Apple/cider/juice | Mulberry |
| Apricot/juice | Mush melon |
| Blackberry/juice | Nectarine/juice |
| Blueberry | Papaya |
| Boysenberry | Peach |
| Cantaloupe | Pear/juice |
| Currants (black, red) | Pineapple juice |
| Date (all types) | Plantain |
| Elderberry (dark blue, purple) | Prune/juice |
| Grapefruit juice | Raisin |
| Honeydew | Raspberry |
| Kumquat | Strawberry |
| Lime/juice | Tangerine/juice |

**AVOID**

| | |
|---|---|
| Banana | Orange |
| Bitter melon | Persimmon |
| Coconut | Pomegranate |
| Dewberry | Prickly pear |
| Guava/juice | Quince |
| Loganberry | Sago palm |
| Mango/juice | Star fruit (carambola) |

## Spices

Spices can be either helpful or dangerous, and this is especially true during pregnancy. A number of spices are uterine stimulants and should be avoided—especially if you have a high-risk pregnancy or a history of miscarriage. Ginger can be an excellent remedy for digestive ailments. However, it can cause miscarriage in excessive amounts. Chocolate contains caffeine and should also be avoided. Type ABs should also limit the consumption of sugars.

Certain spices, normally used in small amounts for cooking, should be minimized during pregnancy. These include cinnamon, marjoram, nutmeg, oregano, parsley, rosemary, sage, and thyme.

If you have problems with heartburn, nausea, or morning sickness, which occur mostly in the first trimester, you may find it helpful to eliminate strong spices such as curry and horseradish. However, if you don't suffer digestive problems, go ahead and use these spices.

## HIGHLY BENEFICIAL

Curry
Garlic
Ginger*

Horseradish
Parsley*

## NEUTRAL

Agar
Apple pectin
Arrowroot
Basil
Bay leaf
Bergamot
Caper
Caraway
Cardamom
Carob
Chervil
Chilli powder
Chive
Chocolate*
Cinnamon
Clove
Coriander
Cream of tartar
Cumin
Dill
Dulse
Honey
Juniper
Kelp
Licorice root*
Mace
Maple syrup

Marjoram
Molasses
Mustard (dry)
Nutmeg
Oregano
Paprika
Peppermint
Rice syrup
Rosemary
Saffron
Sage
Savory
Sea salt
Senna
Soy sauce
Spearmint
Stevia
Sugar
Tamari
Tamarind
Tarragon
Thyme
Turmeric*
Vanilla
Wintergreen
Yeast (baker's, brewer's)

## AVOID

Allspice
Almond extract
Anise
Aspartame
Barley malt

Carrageenan
Cornflour
Corn syrup
Dextrose
Fructose

Food with different values than the standard Type AB diet are indicated with an asterisk (*).

Gelatine, plain           Sucanat
Guarana                   Tapioca
Gum (arabic, acacia)      Vinegar (all types)
Maltodextrin

## Condiments

Avoid all pickled condiments, due to a susceptibility to stomach cancer. Also avoid ketchup, which contains vinegar, and Worcestershire sauce.

**HIGHLY BENEFICIAL**
None

**NEUTRAL**
Jam (from acceptable fruits)      Mustard
Jelly (from acceptable fruits)    Salad dressing (from
Mayonnaise                            acceptable ingredients)

**AVOID**
Ketchup                   Pickle relish
Pickles (all types)       Worcestershire sauce

## Herbal Teas

Herbal teas can deliver strong doses of herbs, and for this reason many are not advised for pregnant women. However, certain teas are particularly beneficial, especially late in pregnancy. Raspberry leaf is rich in vitamins and nourishes the uterus in the last 4 weeks. Chamomile is excellent as a calming tea and sleep aid. Dandelion tea aids digestion. Rose hip tea is a good source of vitamin C. Slippery elm tea is an excellent remedy for intestinal problems.

**HIGHLY BENEFICIAL**
Alfalfa                   Hawthorn
Burdock                   Licorice root*
Chamomile                 Parsley*
Echinacea                 Rose hip
Ginger*                   Strawberry leaf
Ginseng*

**NEUTRAL**

Catnip*
Cayenne pepper*
Chickweed
Dandelion*
Dong quai*
Elder
Goldenseal*
Horehound
Mulberry
Peppermint
Raspberry leaf*
Sage
Sarsaparilla
Slippery elm*
Spearmint
St. John's wort*
Thyme
Valerian
Vervain*
White birch
White oak bark
Yarrow*
Yellow dock

**AVOID**

Aloe
Coltsfoot
Corn silk
Fenugreek
Gentian
Hops
Linden
Mullein
Red clover
Rhubarb
Senna
Shepherd's purse
Skullcap

## Miscellaneous Beverages

Start eliminating caffeine and alcohol three to six months before pregnancy and continue until you are no longer breast-feeding. The common caffeine withdrawal symptoms—headache, fatigue, and irritability—won't occur if you wean yourself gradually. Consumption of alcohol during pregnancy can cause miscarriage, lead to birth defects, and cause foetal alcohol syndrome.

---

Food with different values than the standard Type AB diet are indicated with an asterisk (*).

**HIGHLY BENEFICIAL**
Tea, green
Wine, red

**NEUTRAL**

Beer*                              Wine, white*
Soda water*

**AVOID**
Coffee (regular, decaf)            Spirits
Fizzy drinks (all types)           Tea, black (regular, decaf)

## Before You Get Pregnant

The best guarantee for a healthy pregnancy is to be in top condition before you get pregnant. Start getting ready at least six months before you conceive.

## Pre-pregnancy Diet Strategies

Time and again, we have seen compelling evidence that the blood type diet exerts a powerfully positive influence on fertility and pregnancy. The following strategies provide a blueprint for optimal health.

### Get Serious About the Type AB Diet

Begin to increase your compliance to the Type AB diet at least six months prior to attempting to conceive. The most efficient approach is to add to the number of beneficial foods you consume. These beneficial foods exert a powerful medicinal influence on your system, creating the optimal atmosphere for conception. At the same time, make an effort to eliminate those foods that are "avoids" for Type AB. Check the Type AB Chameleon Foods in the table on page 214. Some of these foods show different values for the pre-pregnancy period.

### Control Your Weight

For Type AB, weight control relies on a diet that balances digestable proteins and metabolically useful carbohydrates.

---

Food with different values than the standard Type AB diet are indicated with an asterisk (*).

**TYPE AB HEALTHY WEIGHT-LOSS GUIDELINES**

1. Minimize your consumption of meat—and eat only those meats that are beneficial.
2. Eat plenty of cultured foods, especially cultured dairy and soy.
3. Include sources of essential fatty acids, especially omega-3 oils found in fish.
4. Eat plenty of fresh vegetables and fruit to provide proper natural fibre. This will aid in the eliminative process.
5. Avoid stimulants found in alcohol, caffeine, and refined sugars. Eliminate fizzy drinks, even diet ones.
6. Engage in a combination of meditative exercise and rigorous aerobic exercise several times a week.

## Type AB

| THESE FOODS PROMOTE WEIGHT LOSS | THESE FOODS PROMOTE WEIGHT GAIN |
|---|---|
| Soy foods | Red meat |
| Fish and seafood | Chicken |
| Cultured dairy | Kidney beans |
| Green vegetables | Butter beans |
| Kelp (seaweed) | Corn |
| Pineapple | Wheat |
| | Buckwheat |

## Incorporate Detoxifiers into Your Diet

Toxins are the by-products of bacterial activity on unabsorbed foods that grow in your intestinal tract. Most often these toxins are the result of eating foods that are poorly digested by your blood type—including foods that are overly processed and chemically treated.

**SIGNS OF TOXICITY IN TYPE AB**

- Diminished sex drive
- Circulation problems
- Sensitivity to light
- Bad breath
- Feelings of fullness in lower intestine
- Cystic breasts
- Cold sores

To aid in detoxification before pregnancy, follow this protocol for one week.

## TYPE AB DETOXIFICATION PROTOCOL
(Do not use during pregnancy)

- Burdock root (*Arctium sp.*). As a tea—1 to 3 cups, daily.
- A mixture of fresh red grapes and blueberries. Juice and drink 8 fluid ounces (225 ml) every morning.
- Flaxseeds (*Linum usitatissimum*). Add 1 tablespoon to 8 fluid ounces (225 ml) of water; allow to soak overnight; drink in morning.
- Probiotic supplement (friendly bacteria). Take twice daily (preferably blood type specific).
- Larch arabinogalactan (soluble fibre supplement). Take 1 tablespoon mixed with water or juice, twice daily.
- Dry skin brushing—perform this procedure once a day.

## About Dry Skin Brushing

Dry skin brushing is a method of daily hygiene that has many benefits and has been around for a long time. The skin is a major organ of the body that functions as protection and as a means of elimination. Daily skin brushing will:

- Remove dried, dead cells that block the pores of the skin, allowing the skin to breathe easier and increasing its ability to protect and eliminate the waste products of metabolism.
- Increase circulation of the blood and lymph vessels that are close to the surface just under the skin. The blood, fluid, and its contents are returned to the heart for redistribution and/or elimination.
- Increase the nutrients to the skin. By clearing out stagnant materials, there is an increased oxygen/carbon dioxide exchange, and other nutrients, vitamins, minerals, enzymes, etc., are also brought to the area.
- Remove waste products of cellular metabolism through the blood vessels and sweating.
- Decrease the workload on the rest of the body with regard to circulation and elimination.
- Warm the skin.

### PROCEDURE

Skin brushing should be done with a natural or nylon bristle body brush before the bath or shower. It is suggested the brushing be done toward the heart; start with the lower limbs, arms, and back, and then the front of the body, using a moderate pressure with short strokes upward and inward. If you have a soft complexion brush, the face can be done as well using more circular motions. Strokes should bring a slight pink colour or slight tingling sensation to the skin—never bruising, scraping, bleeding, or pain. One time through for each body area is sufficient.

**AVOID SKIN BRUSHING IF:**

- You have delicate skin.
- You have easily damaged skin.
- You have an open wound.
- You have known malignancies of the skin or lymph system.

Detoxifying foods that are especially effective for Type AB include cultured dairy foods, such as yogurt and kefir, and soy products, such as miso, natto, soy sauce, and tempeh.

## Pre-pregnancy Supplement Guidelines

| VITAMINS | MINERALS | HERBS |
|---|---|---|
| Vitamin C from rose hip or acerola cherry—250 mg daily | Zinc—25 mg daily | Dandelion—250-mg capsule daily; also use fresh in salads or as tea<br><br>Green tea—1 to 3 cups daily *before* pregnancy |

The Type AB diet offers abundant quantities of important nutrients and it's important to get as many of those nutrients as possible from fresh foods. Only use supplements to fill in the minor blanks in your diet. In addition to vitamins, minerals, protein, carbohydrates, and fats, many grains, beans, vegetables, and fruits are excellent sources of fibre, which are necessary for proper digestion. In addition, fresh vegetables are an important source of phytochemicals, the substances in foods that strengthen the immune system and support pregnancy.

VITAMINS

VITAMIN C. Type AB can benefit from an extra dose (250 to 500 milligrams) of vitamin C every day to strengthen your immune system and improve your ability to digest food. Look for food-derived vitamin C preparations, such as those found from rose hip or acerola cherry.

MINERALS

ZINC. A small amount of zinc supplementation can help protect Type AB against infection. However, zinc in high doses can be teratogenic and upset the balance of other minerals, such as copper. Consume less than 25 milligrams per day.

HERBS

GREEN TEA (*Camellia sinensis*). Regular consumption of green tea appears to enhance chances of conception. Green tea does contain small amounts of caffeine, so if you are sensitive, refrain from drinking it after 6 P.M. (Do not drink green tea during pregnancy.)

DANDELION (*Taraxacum officinale*). This is very effective for mild water retention. It can be used in salads or as a tea. It is also a good source of potassium.

## Improve Your Emotional Health

Your emotional well-being—especially your ability to adapt to stress—is every bit as important to your overall health as is your physical well-being. Indeed, the two are inextricably linked. As a Type AB you share Type O's susceptibility to an imbalance of the stress hormones called catecholamines. Yet you have the additional complexity of Type B's rapid clearing of nitrous oxide, which can spark high emotions.

It is crucial that you take steps to regulate your stress levels before you become pregnant, since pregnancy requires optimal health and energy. The key to Type AB stress regulation is the Type AB diet and exercise program.

## Pre-pregnancy Exercise Guidelines

Type AB requires both calming activities and more intense physical exercise. Vary your routine to include a mix of the following—two days calming, three days aerobic.

CALMING

HATHA YOGA. Hatha yoga has become increasingly popular in Western countries as a method for coping with stress, and in my experience it is an excellent form of exercise for Type ABs. Make sure that you spend plenty of time outdoors. The effects of sunlight and fresh air work marvels at tempering the Type AB immune system, in particular the function of the body's natural killer (NK) cells, which can influence conception and fertility.

AEROBIC/WEIGHT-BEARING
Any of the following are useful to round out your fitness regimen.

| EXERCISE | DURATION | FREQUENCY |
|---|---|---|
| Aerobics | 45–60 minutes | 2–3 × week |
| Martial arts | 30–60 minutes | 3 × week |
| Cycling | 45–60 minutes | 3 × week |
| Hiking | 30–60 minutes | 3 × week |
| Weight lifting | 30 minutes | 2 × week |

# Your Pregnancy:
# Type AB Three-Trimester Plan

## Diet Strategies

### First Trimester

## Choose Type AB Beneficial Foods

Continue your compliance with the Type AB diet, paying special attention to the Type AB Chameleon Foods in the table on page 214. These are foods whose normal values are different during pregnancy. If you are new to the Type AB diet, your most important first steps are inclusion of high-quality protein found in soy foods, fish and cultured dairy, and the avoidance of red meat, chicken, wheat, buckwheat, and corn.

The first trimester is such a critical time that you should emphasize your beneficial foods whenever possible. These foods act as medicine for Type AB. While many foods are good choices of important nutrients, your power foods offer an extra benefit. For example:

Choose turkey over lamb.
Choose goat's cheese and kefir over gouda and cheddar.
Choose oat flour over wheat flour.
Choose collard greens and alfalfa sprouts over carrots and leeks.
Choose cherries and figs over melons and peaches.

## Emphasize Pregnancy Power Foods

There are some nutrients that have special importance. These include protein, calcium, iron, and folic acid.

### Blood Type AB Pregnancy Power Foods

| PROTEIN | CALCIUM | IRON | FOLIC ACID |
|---|---|---|---|
| Lean, organic venison | Cultured dairy | Beef liver* | Beef liver* |
| Fish | Soy milk | Eggs | Fish |
| Cultured dairy and soy | Canned sardines (with bones) | | Dark green leafy vegetables |
| | Canned salmon (with bones) | | |
| | Tofu | | |

* Although red meat is discouraged for Type AB, you may have occasional small amounts of beef liver (3 to 5 ounces/75–125 g), which is an excellent source of iron. Avoid chicken liver: It has a deleterious protein (galectin) that can adversely effect your immune function.

## Enhance Digestive Enzymes

Type ABs can have lower levels of stomach acid, pepsin, and gastrin, which may contribute to digestive problems common early in pregnancy. By improving digestive efficiency, you'll experience far less heartburn, nausea, and morning sickness.

- Limit meat, which requires high levels of digestive enzymes, to small portions—3 to 5 ounces (75–125 g).
- If you experience morning sickness, chamomile is a good replacement for ginger. A cup of chamomile tea will soothe your stomach.
- Avoid carbonated beverages, even mineral water. The carbonation can influence gastrin production, which decreases stomach acidity.

## Balance Your Moods

Mood swings are common in the first months of pregnancy, triggered by the many hormonal changes that are occurring, as well as the extra stress that comes with a major life change. Recognize your tendencies and work to avoid stresses that might increase your emotional distress. Here are some suggestions for reducing mood swings:

- Find a support group or friend you can share your anxieties with. Better still, volunteer to help others. Type ABs reduce stress and elevate moods when they are focused outside themselves.
- Keep a journal detailing what you are experiencing.
- Break up your workday with physical activity, especially if your job is sedentary. You'll feel more energized, and exercise serves as a natural mood elevator.
- Plan ahead to have foods on hand for a quick energy snack when you're feeling tired or moody. Mood changes can be triggered by a decrease in blood sugar.
- Type ABs who suffer from mood swings should always supplement with extra folic acid, along with other B-complex vitamins. Folic acid has the additional benefit of being essential for foetal development. (See Supplement Guidelines, page 264).

## Fight Fatigue

It is common for women to feel especially fatigued during the first trimester of pregnancy, as your body adapts to the tremendous changes taking place. You need to get at least 1 to 2 hours of additional sleep every night. Establish a regular sleep schedule and adhere to it as closely as possible. During the day, schedule at least two breaks of 20 minutes each for complete relaxation. Combat sleep disturbances with regular exercise and a relaxing pre-bedtime routine. A light snack before bedtime will help raise your blood sugar levels. Your menu plans offer many suggestions for evening snacks. In addition, a neutral (room temperature) bath before bedtime will help you sleep.

Type ABs may also benefit from the daily consumption of what I call the Membrane Fluidizer Cocktail, which improves the health of your immune and nervous systems:

### MEMBRANE FLUIDIZER COCKTAIL

*1 tablespoon flaxseed oil*
*1 tablespoon high-quality lecithin granules*
*6 to 8 fluid ounces (175–225 ml) fruit juice*

Shake well and drink.

A contributing factor to Type AB fatigue is a susceptibility to iron deficiency anaemia. Ask your doctor about taking an iron supplement and increase your consumption of foods high in folic acid, vitamin C, iron, selenium, and zinc. These include: cold water fish (salmon, mackerel, herring, and sardines), egg, lentils, beets, green vegetables, green beans, spinach, parsley, mustard greens, yams, apricots, blackberries, apples, currants, kelp, lettuce, peaches, molasses, mustard greens, and mulberries.

## Handle Your Cravings and Aversions

If you crave foods that are not beneficial for your blood type, find healthy, blood type–friendly substitutes. For example:

| WHEN YOU CRAVE . . . | EAT . . . |
| --- | --- |
| Sugar | Raisins or a plum; any suitable fruit |
| Salty foods | Nori (seaweed) snack; miso soup |
| Ice cream | Frozen yogurt; soy-based ice cream |
| Fatty foods | Peanuts; walnuts |
| Creamy foods | Vegetable puree—sweet potato, onion, pumpkin, or turnip; yogurt; soy smoothie |

## First Trimester Menu Plans

The following menus offer a guide to healthy eating during the first trimester of your pregnancy. They are designed to offer well-balanced, delicious meals that include the primary values critical for Type AB:

- They emphasize a variety of delicious meat, fish, soy, dairy, beans, fresh fruits, and vegetables.
- They provide an extra boost of calcium and protein with Type AB–specific smoothies and energy bars.
- They provide many foods to help overcome first trimester problems, such as constipation, fatigue, and morning sickness.
- They break the daily diet into six meals/snacks a day—aiding digestion and reducing fatigue by avoiding an empty stomach.

The menus are flexible and can be mixed and reorganized according to your personal needs. I have purposely not included portion sizes for most dishes, since caloric needs vary depending on your height and weight. However, try to eat about 300 calories a day more than normal during the first trimester.

Although beverages are listed with some meals, I suggest you drink them half an hour before or after eating. Liquids consumed with solid foods dilute the digestive juices. Don't forget to keep drinking water throughout the day.

A NOTE ABOUT CERTAIN FOODS

- The Type AB Bar is a specially formulated blood type–specific product. The Super Baby Smoothie also utilizes a blood type–specific protein powder, *Proteus ABO*. They are included only as an option. If you prefer, you can substitute other listed snacks and drinks or a beneficial fruit.

## Menus

### DAY 1

**BREAKFAST**
One-Egg Omelette* with mozzarella
    and broccoli
Sprouted seed toast
Pineapple juice

**MID-MORNING SNACK**
Silken Smoothie*

**LUNCH**
Lentil Soup*
Tossed salad
Crackers

**MID-AFTERNOON SNACK**
Beneficial fruit

**DINNER**
Spicy Stir-Fried Tofu with Apricots
    and Almonds*
Braised shiitake mushrooms
Braised greens with garlic
Raw Enzyme Relish*

**EVENING SNACK**
Super Baby Smoothie*

### DAY 2

**BREAKFAST**
Poached egg
Spelt flakes with raisins and soy milk
Mixed berries

**MID-MORNING SNACK**
Type AB Bar

**LUNCH**
Farmer's Vegetable Soup*
Mesclun Salad*

**MID-AFTERNOON SNACK**
Type AB Trail Mix-2*

**DINNER**
Grilled Salmon Steak*
Wild rice
Braised leeks

**EVENING SNACK**
Super Baby Smoothie*

## DAY 3

**BREAKFAST**
Cottage cheese with fresh pineapple
    and kiwi
Sprouted seed toast with cherry
    preserves
Slippery elm tea

**MID-MORNING SNACK**
High-Energy Protein Shake*

**LUNCH**
Sardine Salad* on rye bread
Apple

**MID-AFTERNOON SNACK**
Toasted Tamari Pumpkin Seeds*
Glass of soy milk

**DINNER**
Roasted Turkey*
Vegetable Fritters*
Green Bean Salad with Walnuts, and
    Goat's Cheese*

**EVENING SNACK**
Super Baby Smoothie*

## DAY 4

**BREAKFAST**
Brown Rice–Spelt Pancakes*
Sautéed Apples*
Cranberry juice
Strawberry leaf tea

**MID-MORNING SNACK**
Type AB Bar

**LUNCH**
Salmon with Wakame Seaweed*
Turkey Soup*

**MID-AFTERNOON SNACK**
Type AB Trail Mix-2*

**DINNER**
Indian Lamb Stew with Spinach*
Sweet Potato Pancakes*
Braised greens with garlic

**EVENING SNACK**
Super Baby Smoothie*

## DAY 5

**BREAKFAST**
Date-Prune Smoothie*
Pumpkin-Almond Bread*
Burdock-rose hip tea

**MID-MORNING SNACK**
Apricot Yogurt Drink*

**LUNCH**
Turkey sandwich on spelt bread, with
    Romaine lettuce and tomato
Grapes

**MID-AFTERNOON SNACK**
Type AB Bar

**DINNER**
Grilled cod
Steamed spinach
Turnip puree

**EVENING SNACK**
Peanut Butter Cookies*
Chamomile tea

## DAY 6

**BREAKFAST**
2 scrambled eggs
½ grapefruit
Manna toast with peanut butter

**MID-MORNING SNACK**
Super Baby Smoothie*

**LUNCH**
Mixed Roots Soup*
Mesclun Salad*

**MID-AFTERNOON SNACK**
Type AB Bar

**DINNER**
Roast Turkey*
Braised greens with garlic
Raw Enzyme Relish*

**EVENING SNACK**
Rice Pudding with Soy Milk*
Chamomile tea

## DAY 7

**BREAKFAST**
Wheat-Free Waffles*
Mixed berries
Vegetable juice
Burdock-rose hip tea

**MID-MORNING SNACK**
High-Energy Protein Shake*

**LUNCH**
Sardine Salad*
Ryvita crackers
Mixed greens

**MID-AFTERNOON SNACK**
Rice cakes with prune butter
Glass of soy milk

**DINNER**
Lasagna with Portabello Mushrooms
   and Pesto*
Tossed salad with lemon vinaigrette

**EVENING SNACK**
Super Baby Smoothie*

## DAY 8

**BREAKFAST**
Vegetable Frittata*
Sprouted seed toast
Mixed berries

**MID-MORNING SNACK**
Pineapple Yogurt Drink*

**LUNCH**
White Bean and Wilted Greens Soup*
Spinach Salad*
Crackers

**MID-AFTERNOON SNACK**
Type AB Bar

**DINNER**
Tofu Vegetable Stir-Fry*
Steamed cauliflower
Wild rice

**EVENING SNACK**
Super Baby Smoothie*

## DAY 9

**BREAKFAST**
Poached egg on toasted sprouted
    seed bread
Pineapple slices
Rose hip tea

**MID-MORNING SNACK**
Type AB Bar

**LUNCH**
Speltberry and Rice Salad*
Carrot and celery sticks
Yogurt

**MID-AFTERNOON SNACK**
Type AB Trail Mix-1*

**DINNER**
Grilled cod
Braised greens
Lentil Salad*

**EVENING SNACK**
Super Baby Smoothie*

## DAY 10

**BREAKFAST**
Oatmeal with raisins and soy milk
Mixed fruit
Rose hip tea

**MID-MORNING SNACK**
Slice of spelt bread with apple butter
Glass of soy-rice milk

**LUNCH**
Griddled Portabello Mushroom* on a
    spelt bun with Romaine
Mixed green salad

**MID-AFTERNOON SNACK**
Raisins and chopped walnuts

**DINNER**
Tempeh Kebabs*
Steamed brown rice
Sesame Broccoli*
Herbal ice tea

**EVENING SNACK**
Super Baby Smoothie*

## DAY 11

**BREAKFAST**
Poached egg
Spelt flakes with fresh berries and soy
   milk
Rose hip tea

**MID-MORNING SNACK**
Apricot Yogurt Drink*

**LUNCH**
Cucumber Yogurt Soup*
Mesclun Salad*

**MID-AFTERNOON SNACK**
Type AB Bar

**DINNER**
Fried Monkfish*
Green beans
Wild rice

**EVENING SNACK**
Super Baby Smoothie*

## DAY 12

**BREAKFAST**
Tropical Salad*
Sprouted seed toast with cherry
   preserves
Slippery elm tea

**MID-MORNING SNACK**
Type AB Bar

**LUNCH**
Miso Soup with Tofu*
Brown rice
Carrot Raisin Salad*

**MID-AFTERNOON SNACK**
Type AB Trail Mix-2*

**DINNER**
Grilled Salmon, Marinated in Tamari
   Dipping Sauce*
2 beneficial vegetables

**EVENING SNACK**
Super Baby Smoothie*

## DAY 13

**BREAKFAST**
Omelette* with fresh spinach and feta
Manna toast with cherry preserves

**MID-MORNING SNACK**
Fresh figs with yogurt

**LUNCH**
Super Broccoli Salad*
Sliced turkey on a bed of Romaine

**MID-AFTERNOON SNACK**
Beneficial fruit

**DINNER**
Steamed Whole Red Snapper*
Glazed Turnips and Onions*
Braised mustard greens with garlic

**EVENING SNACK**
Super Baby Smoothie*

## DAY 14

**BREAKFAST**
Blueberry Muffin*
Mixed fruit
Glass of soy milk
Strawberry leaf tea

**MID-MORNING SNACK**
Rice cakes with apple butter

**LUNCH**
Sliced tomato, fresh mozzarella, and
    basil on spelt bread
Berries with yogurt

**MID-AFTERNOON SNACK**
Type AB Trail Mix-1*

**DINNER**
Grilled Loin of Lamb Chops*
Sautéed greens
Romaine-feta salad

**EVENING SNACK**
Super Baby Smoothie*

## Second Trimester

### Adjust to an Increased Appetite

Foetal growth is rapid during the second trimester, and you may experience a greater appetite, especially if you no longer suffer from the nausea that may have plagued you during the first three months. Use your extra calories to maximum benefit.

---

* You can find recipes for asterisk-marked items in appendix A.

**EMPHASIS FOR EXTRA CALORIES**

- High-quality protein—fish and soy foods
- Calcium-rich foods—cultured dairy, sardines, canned salmon with bones, soy milk, tofu
- Vitamin C–rich foods—dark green leafy vegetables, plums, pineapple

## Keep Your Blood Sugar in Check

For Type AB, blood sugar irregularities are usually the result of carbohydrate intolerance—especially if you're eating too many grains, beans, and potatoes. While some increase in blood sugar is normal during pregnancy, be aware that severely elevated blood sugar leads to a dangerous condition called gestational diabetes, which can cause premature birth and even birth defects. The following symptoms should alert you to blood sugar imbalances:

> Fatigue
> Extreme hunger
> Dry skin
> Anxiety
> Dizziness and light-headedness

To restore a proper balance:

- Increase the protein and decrease the carbohydrates in your diet.
- Eliminate refined sugars and starches.
- Eat fibre-rich foods every day.
- Never skip meals, especially breakfast. Preferably, eat six small meals a day.

## Avoid Urinary Tract Infections

Many women are susceptible to urinary tract infections during the second trimester. As a Type AB, you need to be aware of this tendency, because Type ABs typically have an extremely high risk factor for UTIs. In addition to following the Type AB diet, you can guard against UTIs with the following:

- Eat plenty of cultured dairy foods, such as yogurt and kefir.
- Eat cranberries or blueberries—effective UTI fighters.
- Urinate frequently to avoid buildup of urine in the bladder.
- Continue taking your probiotic supplement. It will help keep the colon flora, vaginal flora, and urinary tract healthy.

## Build Your Immunity

Type AB often struggles with compromised immune function, which can make you more vulnerable to colds and flu. Your overall immune health is critical to your ability to carry a foetus to term, since your immune system is suppressed during pregnancy to accept the foetus. If you have a history of miscarriages, immune health should be your top priority. Many dietary factors have been linked to immune function. Failure to eat breakfast, irregular eating habits, low vegetable intake, inadequate protein, excessive wheat intake, and high-fat diets (especially those with excessive amounts of polyunsaturated fatty acids) have all been associated with lowered immune function.

Deficiencies in a range of nutrients can result in decreased immune function, so keep your nutrient levels high. In particular, selenium, zinc, vitamin C, beta-carotene, vitamin A, vitamin E, and vitamin D deficiencies should be addressed.

Check the nutrient chart below to be sure your diet contains plenty of these nutrient-rich foods.

| SELENIUM | ZINC | VITAMIN C | BETA-CAROTENE |
|---|---|---|---|
| Whole grains | Turkey | Citrus fruit | Dark green |
| Seafood | Dried beans | Strawberries | vegetables |
| | and peas | Brussels sprouts | Carrots |
| | | Dark green | Pumpkin |
| | | vegetables | Peaches |
| **VITAMIN A** | **VITAMIN E** | **VITAMIN D** | |
| Chicken liver | Spinach | Fatty fish | |
| Eggs | Safflower oil | Egg yolk | |

## Eliminate Excess Mucus Production

Type AB has a tendency to suffer from excessive mucus production, which can cause a stuffy nose, respiratory problems, and ear infections. I recommend that all Type ABs begin the day with a glass of room temperature water mixed with the juice of one quarter to one half a lemon. This will reduce mucus.

## Second Trimester Menu Plans

The following menus offer a guide to healthy eating during the second trimester of your pregnancy. They include some adjustments from the first trimester, taking into account the special emphasis on this period in your pregnancy.

- The menu suggestions place an even greater emphasis on meat, soy, fish, grains, and fresh fruits and vegetables—all foods that help regulate Type AB blood sugar.
- They include more calories than the first trimester menus, to accommodate the growing nutritional needs of your foetus.
- They provide an extra boost of calcium and protein with Type AB–specific smoothies and energy bars.
- They provide additional foods that will help to overcome second trimester problems, such as haemorrhoids, varicose veins, and mucus production.

The menus are flexible and can be mixed and reorganized according to your personal needs. I have purposely not included portion sizes for most dishes, since caloric needs vary depending upon your height and weight. However, these menus do offer more foods than the first trimester—and you should try to increase your intake by 100 to 300 calories per day.

Note that although beverages are listed with some meals, I suggest you drink them half an hour before or after eating. Liquids consumed with solid foods dilute the digestive juices. Don't forget to keep drinking water throughout the day.

## Menus

### DAY 1

**BREAKFAST**
Fruit Silken Scramble*
Fresh vegetable juice
Sprouted seed bread

**MID-MORNING SNACK**
Type AB Bar

**LUNCH**
Salmon with Wakame Seaweed*
Rice cakes
Raisins and walnuts with yogurt

**MID-AFTERNOON SNACK**
Type AB Trail Mix-1*

**DINNER**
Peter's Escargot*
Steamed broccoli
Pureed root vegetables
Wild rice

**EVENING SNACK**
Super Baby Smoothie*

## DAY 2

**BREAKFAST**
Omelette* with fresh spinach and feta
Tropical Salad*
Manna toast

**MID-MORNING SNACK**
Pineapple Yogurt Drink*

**LUNCH**
Miso Soup*
Mesclun Salad*
Rye crackers

**MID-AFTERNOON SNACK**
Type AB Bar

**DINNER**
Grilled red snapper
Braised Collards*
Wild and Basmati Rice Pilaf*

**EVENING SNACK**
Rice Pudding*
Chamomile tea

## DAY 3

**BREAKFAST**
Wheat-Free Waffles*
Cherry preserves
Cranberry juice
Rose hip tea

**MID-MORNING SNACK**
Type AB Bar

**LUNCH**
Grilled aubergine and feta on
    sprouted seed bread
Mixed green salad
Grape Ice*

**MID-AFTERNOON SNACK**
Type AB Trail Mix-2*

**DINNER**
Tofu Vegetable Stir-Fry*
Steamed broccoli
Lentil Salad*
Raw Enzyme Relish*

**EVENING SNACK**
Super Baby Smoothie*

## DAY 4

**BREAKFAST**
Scrambled eggs
Poached Fruit*
Manna toast with peanut butter
Strawberry leaf tea

**MID-MORNING SNACK**
Date-Prune Smoothie*

**LUNCH**
Grilled lean ground turkey burger with
    melted goat's cheese, lettuce,
    tomato, and onion
Yogurt with fruit

**MID-AFTERNOON SNACK**
Beneficial fruit

**DINNER**
Grilled Salmon with Lemongrass*
Baked sweet potato
Steamed spinach

**EVENING SNACK**
Super Baby Smoothie*

## DAY 5

**BREAKFAST**
Pineapple Yogurt Drink*
Pumpkin Almond Bread*

**MID-MORNING SNACK**
Type AB Bar

**LUNCH**
Farmer's Vegetable Soup*
Super Broccoli Salad*
Crackers

**MID-AFTERNOON SNACK**
Peanut Butter Cookies*
Soy milk

**DINNER**
Soba Noodles with Pumpkin
    and Tofu*
Broccoli Rabe*
Mixed Roots Puree*

**EVENING SNACK**
Super Baby Smoothie*

## DAY 6

**BREAKFAST**
Poached egg on toasted spelt bread
Fresh pineapple slices
Slippery elm tea

**MID-MORNING SNACK**
Date-Prune Smoothie*

**LUNCH**
Grilled Goat's Cheddar on Sprouted
    Seed Bread*
Miso Soup*

**MID-AFTERNOON SNACK**
Type AB Bar

**DINNER**
Green Leafy Pasta*
Romaine salad with Olive Oil and
    Lemon Dressing*

**EVENING SNACK**
Super Baby Smoothie*

## DAY 7

**BREAKFAST**
Silken Scramble*
Sautéed Pears*
Spelt toast with berry preserves
Strawberry leaf tea

**MID-MORNING SNACK**
Type AB Bar

**LUNCH**
Farmer's Vegetable Soup*
Mesclun Salad*
Crackers

**MID-AFTERNOON SNACK**
Cottage cheese and fresh fruit

**DINNER**
Indian Lamb Stew with Spinach*
Braised greens with garlic
Pureed root vegetables

**EVENING SNACK**
Super Baby Smoothie*

## DAY 8

**BREAKFAST**
Quinoa Almond Muffin*
Stewed plums
Pineapple juice

**MID-MORNING SNACK**
Type AB Bar

**LUNCH**
Sardine Salad*
Rice cakes
Fruit and yogurt

**MID-AFTERNOON SNACK**
Super Baby Smoothie*

**DINNER**
Steamed Whole Red Snapper*
Grilled Sweet Potato Salad*
Steamed broccoli

**EVENING SNACK**
Wild or Basmati Rice Pudding*
Mint-chamomile tea

## DAY 9

**BREAKFAST**
Heidi's Early Morning Shake*
Mixed berries
Strawberry leaf tea

**MID-MORNING SNACK**
Type AB Bar

**LUNCH**
Greek Salad*
Spelt pitta bread
Yogurt

**MID-AFTERNOON SNACK**
Type AB Bar
Bunch of grapes

**DINNER**
Tasty Tofu Pumpkin Stir-Fry*
Basmati rice
Beneficial vegetable

**EVENING SNACK**
Super Baby Smoothie*

## DAY 10

**BREAKFAST**
Poached eggs
Mixed fruit
Vegetable juice
Burdock tea

**MID-MORNING SNACK**
Silken Smoothie*

**LUNCH**
Peanut butter, raisins, and honey on
    spelt toast
Yogurt and fruit

**MID-AFTERNOON SNACK**
Type AB Bar

**DINNER**
Tofu Vegetable Stir-Fry*
Brown rice
Beneficial vegetable

**EVENING SNACK**
Super Baby Smoothie*

## DAY 11

**BREAKFAST**
Wheat-Free Waffles*
Yogurt
Mixed berries
Rose hip tea

**MID-MORNING SNACK**
Super Baby Smoothie*

**LUNCH**
Salmon with Wakame Seaweed*
Rice cakes
Vegetable consommé

**MID-AFTERNOON SNACK**
Papaya-Kiwi Drink*

**DINNER**
Fried Monkfish*
Pureed root vegetables
Braised Collards*

**EVENING SNACK**
Type AB Bar
Chamomile tea

## DAY 12

**BREAKFAST**
Poached egg
Tropical Salad*
Sprouted seed toast with blackberry
    preserves
Type AB Tea

**MID-MORNING SNACK**
Pineapple Yogurt Drink*

**LUNCH**
Sardines on spelt bread with
    horseradish
Spinach Salad*

**MID-AFTERNOON SNACK**
Type AB Bar

**DINNER**
Braised Rabbit*
Braised greens
Grilled Sweet Potato Salad*

**EVENING SNACK**
Super Baby Smoothie*

## DAY 13

**BREAKFAST**
Silken Scramble* with parsley-alfalfa
    sprouts
Sautéed Pears*
Sprouted seed toast

**MID-MORNING SNACK**
High-Energy Protein Shake*

**LUNCH**
White Bean and Wilted Greens Soup*
Mixed green salad with Olive Oil and
    Lemon Dressing*

**MID-AFTERNOON SNACK**
Beneficial fruit

**DINNER**
Tofu Vegetable Stir-Fry*
Faro Pilaf*
Glass of soy milk

**EVENING SNACK**
Super Baby Smoothie*

## DAY 14

**BREAKFAST**
Wheat-Free Pancakes* with blackberry
  preserves
Cranberry juice
Dandelion tea

**MID-MORNING SNACK**
Super Baby Smoothie*

**LUNCH**
Simple Fish Soup*
Green Bean Salad with Walnuts and
  Goat's Cheese*

**MID-AFTERNOON SNACK**
Type AB Bar

**DINNER**
Green Leafy Pasta*
Romaine salad with Olive Oil and
  Lemon Dressing*

**EVENING SNACK**
Peanut Butter Cookies*
Glass of soy-rice milk

## Third Trimester

### Increase Healthy Blood Flow

Pregnancy places extra stress on your blood vessels as your blood volume increases to support your foetus. Type AB has naturally "thicker" blood, making you more susceptible to pulmonary embolisms and clots. To keep your blood flowing efficiently:

- Drink a glass of water with the juice of half a fresh lemon every morning upon rising.
- Get serious about reducing stress. There is good evidence that Type ABs react to stress by increasing the viscosity (thickness) of your blood. Get out into the garden; pull a few weeds! Reduce clutter. Take long walks.
- Continue to take a DHA supplement, 300 milligrams daily.

### Control Your Blood Pressure

Type ABs need to be particularly careful to keep blood pressure under control during pregnancy. Preeclampsia, or pregnancy-induced hypertension, is a very serious condition that afflicts some women in the late stages of pregnancy.

Maintaining your blood type diet is essential.

NATURAL BLOOD PRESSURE REDUCTION TONIC. One excellent method for ensuring healthy blood pressure is to juice several stalks of celery, taking 6 to 8 fluid ounces (200 to 225 ml) as fresh juice daily.

---

* You can find recipes for asterisk-marked items in appendix A.

## Third Trimester Menu Plans

During the third trimester you may feel full after eating very little. Smaller meals, eaten at regular intervals of 3 to 4 hours may be required to get all the nutrients you need. The following menus offer a guide to healthy eating during the third trimester of your pregnancy. They include some adjustments to account for the special emphasis of this period in your pregnancy.

- They place even greater emphasis on soy foods, fish, and fresh fruits and vegetables—all foods that help maintain metabolic balance.
- They provide an extra boost of calcium and protein with Type AB–specific smoothies and energy bars. This will help you prepare for the rigours of labour and delivery.
- Vitamin A– and C–rich foods are abundant, also in preparation for delivery.

The menus are flexible and can be mixed and reorganized according to your personal needs. I have purposely not included portion sizes for most dishes, since caloric needs vary depending upon your height and weight. You may need to divide up the meals and snacks further if you don't think you can finish them at one sitting. However, it's vital that you maintain your overall caloric level.

Note that although beverages are listed with some meals, I suggest you drink them half an hour before or after eating. Liquids consumed with solid foods dilute the digestive juices and fill you up faster. Don't forget to keep drinking water throughout the day.

## Menus

### DAY 1

**BREAKFAST**
Omelette* with fresh spinach and feta
Manna toast with peanut butter
Cranberry juice
Strawberry leaf tea

**MID-MORNING SNACK**
Papaya-Kiwi Drink*

**LUNCH**
Simple Fish Soup*
Carrot Raisin Salad*

**MID-AFTERNOON SNACK**
Type AB Bar

**DINNER**
Pasta with Rappini*
Mixed steamed vegetables

**EVENING SNACK**
Super Baby Smoothie*

## DAY 2

**BREAKFAST**
Spelt flakes with raisins and soy milk
½ grapefruit
Sprouted seed toast

**MID-MORNING SNACK**
Yogurt with sliced kiwi
Strawberry leaf tea

**LUNCH**
Wild Rice Salad*
Sliced tomatoes and cucumbers
Glass of soy milk

**MID-AFTERNOON SNACK**
Type AB Bar
Rose hip tea

**DINNER**
Roast Turkey*
Mashed Plantains*
Steamed broccoli

**EVENING SNACK**
Super Baby Smoothie*

## DAY 3

**BREAKFAST**
Scrambled eggs
Sprouted seed toast with black cherry
    preserves
Mixed fruit salad
Raspberry leaf tea

**MID-MORNING SNACK**
Type AB Bar

**LUNCH**
Turkey Soup*
Super Broccoli Salad*

**MID-AFTERNOON SNACK**
Type AB Trail Mix-2*

**DINNER**
Grilled Salmon with Lemongrass*
Carrots and Parsnips with Garlic and
    Coriander*
Faro Pilaf*

**EVENING SNACK**
Super Baby Smoothie*

## DAY 4

**BREAKFAST**
Poached eggs
2 plums
Glass of goat's milk
Rose hip tea

**MID-MORNING SNACK**
Cherry-Peach Smoothie*

**LUNCH**
Grilled Goat's Cheddar on Sprouted
    Seed Bread or Spelt*
Mesclun Salad*

**MID-AFTERNOON SNACK**
Type AB Bar

**DINNER**
Grilled Salmon Steak* with cherry
    tomatoes
Brown basmati rice
Steamed cauliflower

**EVENING SNACK**
Super Baby Smoothie*

## DAY 5

**BREAKFAST**
Oatmeal with dried cranberries, maple
    syrup and goat's milk
Pineapple slices

**MID-MORNING SNACK**
Type AB Bar

**LUNCH**
Salmon with Wakame Seaweed* on a
    bed of Romaine lettuce
Farmer's Vegetable Soup*

**MID-AFTERNOON SNACK**
Rice cakes with prune butter

**DINNER**
Green Leafy Pasta*
Chicory salad

**EVENING SNACK**
Super Baby Smoothie*

## DAY 6

**BREAKFAST**
Spinach Frittata*
2 plums
Rose hip tea

**MID-MORNING SNACK**
Papaya-Kiwi Drink*

**LUNCH**
Greek Salad*
Yogurt with fruit
Lemon-chamomile tea

**MID-AFTERNOON SNACK**
Sliced apple, raisins, and walnuts
Glass of soy milk

**DINNER**
Grilled Lamb Chops*
Speltberry Salad*
Steamed carrots

**EVENING SNACK**
Super Baby Smoothie*

## DAY 7

**BREAKFAST**
Wheat-Free Waffles* with plum
    preserves
Mixed fruit

**MID-MORNING SNACK**
Type AB Bar

**LUNCH**
Waldorf Salad*
Grilled aubergine and feta on spelt
    bread

**MID-AFTERNOON SNACK**
Rye crackers with prune butter

**DINNER**
Turkey Burger*
Mesclun Salad*

**EVENING SNACK**
Super Baby Smoothie*

## DAY 8

**BREAKFAST**
Puffed rice cereal with dried cherries
    and goat's milk
Sliced honeydew melon
Manna bread with peanut butter
Strawberry leaf tea

**MID-MORNING SNACK**
Type AB Bar

**LUNCH**
White Bean and Wilted Greens Soup*
Mixed Mushroom Salad*
Crackers

**MID-AFTERNOON SNACK**
Rice cakes with peanut butter and
    prune butter

**DINNER**
Steamed Whole Red Snapper* with
    Seaweed Dressing*
Steamed broccoli
Grilled Sweet Potato Salad*

**EVENING SNACK**
Super Baby Smoothie*

## DAY 9

**BREAKFAST**
High-Energy Protein Shake*
Manna bread with plum preserves

**MID-MORNING SNACK**
Type AB Bar

**LUNCH**
Grilled lean ground turkey burger with
    melted goat's cheese and raw
    spinach leaves
Mixed green salad

**MID-AFTERNOON SNACK**
Type AB Trail Mix-1*
Carrot juice

**DINNER**
Tempeh Kebabs*
Brown rice
2 beneficial vegetables

**EVENING SNACK**
Super Baby Smoothie*

## DAY 10

**BREAKFAST**
Poached egg on toasted sprouted
   seed bread
Pineapple slices

**MID-MORNING SNACK**
Cherry-Peach Smoothie*

**LUNCH**
Sardine Salad*
Ryvita crackers
Cream of broccoli soup

**MID-AFTERNOON SNACK**
Type AB Bar

**DINNER**
Fried Monkfish*
Brown rice
Beneficial vegetable
Mixed green salad

**EVENING SNACK**
Super Baby Smoothie*

## DAY 11

**BREAKFAST**
Spelt flakes with raisins and soy milk
Pineapple slices
Sprouted seed toast

**MID-MORNING SNACK**
Apricot Yogurt Drink*

**LUNCH**
Smoked Mackerel Salad*
Mixed green salad
Yogurt with sliced peaches
Rose hip tea

**MID-AFTERNOON SNACK**
Beneficial fruit

**DINNER**
Roast Chicken with Garlic and Herbs*
Broccoli Rabe*
Baked sweet potato

**EVENING SNACK**
Super Baby Smoothie*

## DAY 12

**BREAKFAST**
Scrambled eggs
Sprouted seed toast with plum
   preserves
Beneficial fruit

**MID-MORNING SNACK**
Type AB Bar

**LUNCH**
Turkey Burger*
Mesclun Salad*

**MID-AFTERNOON SNACK**
Type AB Trail Mix-2*

**DINNER**
Tasty Tofu Pumpkin Stir-Fry*
Basmati rice
Beneficial vegetable

**EVENING SNACK**
Super Baby Smoothie*

## DAY 13

**BREAKFAST**
Oatmeal with raisins and soy milk
Beneficial fruit
Raspberry leaf tea

**MID-MORNING SNACK**
Papaya-Kiwi Drink*

**LUNCH**
Griddled portabello mushroom* on a
   spelt bun with Romaine
Mesclun Salad*

**MID-AFTERNOON SNACK**
Type AB Bar

**DINNER**
Aubergine Casserole*
Brown rice
Beneficial vegetable

**EVENING SNACK**
Super Baby Smoothie*

## DAY 14

**BREAKFAST**
Blueberry Muffin*
Glass of soy-rice milk
Mixed fruit
Dandelion tea

**MID-MORNING SNACK**
Tofu Carob Protein Drink*

**LUNCH**
Greek Salad*
Yogurt
Spelt pitta

**MID-AFTERNOON SNACK**
Super Baby Smoothie*

**DINNER**
Steamed Whole Red Snapper*
Brown rice
Braised Collards*

**EVENING SNACK**
Tofu Pumpkin Pudding*
Strawberry leaf tea

## Exercise Guidelines

### First Trimester

#### Maintenance for Healthy Type ABs

If you are healthy, continue to combine moderate aerobic exercise with relaxation and calming exercises on a normal schedule during the first trimester (page 232).

Choose from among the following Type AB exercises for a minimum regimen of 45 minutes, three to four times a week.

| EXERCISE | DURATION |
| --- | --- |
| Tennis | 45–60 minutes |
| Cycling | 25–30 minutes |
| Hiking | 30–60 minutes |
| Treadmill | 30–40 minutes |
| Golf (no cart) | 60 minutes |
| Swimming | 30–45 minutes |

* You can find recipes for asterisk-marked items in appendix A.

CAUTIONS FOR HIGH-RISK PREGNANCIES

Consult with your doctor before continuing your exercise regimen if you are in a high-risk pregnancy. Most doctors will discourage exercise if you:

- Have a history of miscarriages, or have had even one miscarriage, if it is recent.
- Have a history of recurrent pelvic or abdominal infections.
- Have an incompetent cervix. This condition causes the cervix to open early, usually in the second trimester, leading to miscarriage.
- Have had toxaemia in a previous pregnancy.
- Have a history of premature deliveries.
- Have or have had a serious medical condition, such as cancer, heart disease, asthma, or kidney disease.

## Second Trimester

## Adaptations for Advancing Pregnancy

Continue your regular program of exercise during the second trimester, with an additional emphasis on gentle stretching and calming exercises. An ideal second trimester regimen for Type AB includes:

THREE TIMES A WEEK, CHOOSE ONE:

| EXERCISE | DURATION |
|---|---|
| Water aerobics | 40–50 minutes |
| Treadmill | 30 minutes |
| Cycling (recumbent bike) | 30 minutes |
| Swimming | 30 minutes |
| Brisk walking | 45 minutes |

TWO TIMES A WEEK, CHOOSE ONE:

| EXERCISE | DURATION |
|---|---|
| Light yoga | 40–50 minutes |
| T'ai chi | 30 minutes |
| Labour preparation class | 40–50 minutes |

DAILY:

| EXERCISE | DURATION |
|----------|----------|
| Pelvic floor exercises | 2 minutes, 10–20 times |

- Join a yoga class specifically designed for pregnant women.
- Spend more time on your warm-up and cool-down to fully warm and stretch your muscles. This will minimize the muscle cramps that are common as your pregnancy progresses.
- Look for opportunities to incorporate fitness into your daily routine. If feasible, walk to work instead of driving. Take the stairs instead of the elevator.
- Swimming is an excellent exercise for the second and third trimesters. It places minimum stress on your joints and heart rate. A water aerobics class is an ideal substitution for more strenuous aerobics.
- If you haven't already started your pelvic floor exercises (see page 28), do so now.

PREGNANCY-SAFE EXERCISE SUBSTITUTIONS

| INSTEAD OF . . . | TRY . . . |
|------------------|-----------|
| Bicycling | Exercise bike (recumbent) |
| Tennis | Brisk walking/treadmill |
| Aerobics | Water aerobics |

## Third Trimester

### Adaptations for Late Pregnancy

Exercise is essential during the third trimester. It can help keep your blood pressure in check, combat fatigue, regulate your blood sugar, and reduce the effects of stress. It can also keep you limber and reduce some of the aches and pains you're probably experiencing. However, even if you have been exercising vigorously for years, you need to pay close attention to the signs that you may be pushing yourself too hard. If you feel light-headed or crampy during your workout routine, stop exercising. Avoid any exercises that place pressure on your abdominal area.

Sign up for a prenatal yoga class. Also begin your daily perineal massage to tone the vaginal canal (page 31).

An excellent third trimester exercise regimen for Type AB would be the following.

TWO TIMES A WEEK, CHOOSE ONE:

| EXERCISE | DURATION |
|---|---|
| Water aerobics | 40–50 minutes |
| Treadmill | 30 minutes |
| Cycling (recumbent bike) | 30 minutes |
| Swimming | 30 minutes |
| Brisk walking | 45 minutes |

THREE TIMES A WEEK, CHOOSE ONE:

| EXERCISE | DURATION |
|---|---|
| Light yoga | 40–50 minutes |
| Relaxation, stretching | 30 minutes |
| Labour preparation class | 40–50 minutes |

DAILY, PERFORM BOTH:

| EXERCISE | DURATION |
|---|---|
| Pelvic floor exercises | 2 minutes, 10–20 times |
| Perineal massage | 5 minutes, 1–2 times |

## Supplement Guidelines

### First Trimester

## Vitamins/Minerals

Take a standard prenatal vitamin supplement, choosing one made from whole food, not synthetic ingredients. Powder-in-capsule forms dissolve most efficiently. If you would like to use a prenatal supplement specifically formulated for Type AB, see appendix B. The following nutrient breakdown is the optimal formula for Type AB.

| PRENATAL SUPPLEMENT—TYPE AB | |
|---|---|
| Vitamin A<br>(100% as natural beta-carotene from<br>   *Dunaliella salina*) | 3,000 iu |
| Vitamin C<br>(100% from acerola berry, *Malpighia puncifolia*) | 75 mg |
| Vitamin D (cholecalciferol) | 125 iu |
| Vitamin K (phytonadione) | 20 mcg |
| Vitamin E (Natural d,alpha-tocopheryl succinate) | 125 iu |
| Thiamin (from Thiamin HCl) | 20 mg |
| Riboflavin | 10 mg |
| Niacin and niacinamide (vitamin $B_3$) | 15 mg |
| Vitamin $B_6$ (from pyridoxine HCl) | 10 mg |
| Folic acid | 800 mcg |
| Vitamin $B_{12}$ (methylcobalamin) | 15 mcg |
| Biotin | 400 mcg |
| Pantothenic Acid<br>(from D-calcium pantothenate) | 15 mg |
| Calcium (seaweed base, derived from<br>   *Lithothamnium corralliodes* and<br>   *Lithothamnium calcareum*) | 300 mg |
| Iron (ferrous succinate) | 22 mg |
| Iodine (potassium iodide) | 100 mcg |
| Magnesium (citrate and oxide) | 100 mg |
| Zinc (picolinate) | 27 mg |
| Selenium (L-selenomethionine) | 25 mcg |
| Copper (gluconate) | 1 mg |
| Magnesium (citrate) | 1 mg |

## Herbal Remedies

| HERB | FUNCTION | FORM AND DOSAGE |
|---|---|---|
| Chamomile | Calms; relieves heartburn | As tea, 1 to 2 cups daily; or add 2–4 drops of essential oil to bath |
| Horsetail | Contains silica, which supports healthy bones, skin, hair, and nails | 250-mg capsule daily |
| Peppermint | Calms; relieves indigestion | As tea, 2 to 3 cups daily, after meals |
| Slippery elm bark | Relieves heartburn | 250-mg capsule, twice daily; or as tea, 2 cups daily |

| Nutritional Supplements | | |
|---|---|---|
| **NUTRITIONAL SUPPLEMENT** | **FUNCTION** | **FORM AND DOSAGE** |
| Larch arabinogalactan | Relieves constipation | Soluble fibre supplement: 1 tablespoon mixed with water or juice, twice daily |
| Probiotic | For intestinal health | 2 capsules, twice daily* |
| DHA | Provides essential nutrients for foetal development | 300-mg capsule daily |

\* See appendix B for information on blood type–specific probiotics.

## Second Trimester

### Vitamins/Minerals

Continue to take your prenatal supplement, preferably one formulated for Type AB.

| Herbal Remedies | | |
|---|---|---|
| **HERB** | **FUNCTION** | **FORM AND DOSAGE** |
| Bilberry | Relieves haemorrhoids and varicose veins | 25-mg capsule, twice daily |
| Chamomile | Calms; relieves heartburn; relieves haemorrhoids and varicose veins | As tea, 1 to 2 cups daily; or add 2–4 drops of essential oil to bath |
| Horsetail | Contains silica, which supports healthy bones, skin, hair, and nails | 250-mg capsule daily |
| Peppermint | Calms; relieves indigestion | As tea, 2 to 3 cups daily, after meals |
| Rose hips | Treatment for varicose veins, bleeding gums, and allergies | 1 tablespoon concentrate every 30 minutes for allergy attack; as tea, 2 to 3 cups daily |
| Stinging nettle leaf | Allergy relief | As tea, 2 cups daily for symptoms |
| Witch hazel | Treatment for haemorrhoids | Use topically as needed |

## Nutritional Supplements

| NUTRITIONAL SUPPLEMENT | FUNCTION | FORM AND DOSAGE |
|---|---|---|
| Larch arabinogalactan | Relieves constipation | Soluble fibre supplement: 1 tablespoon mixed with water or juice, twice daily |
| Probiotic | For intestinal health; prevention of candida infection | 2 capsules, twice daily* |
| DHA | Provides essential nutrients for foetal development | 300-mg capsule daily |

\* See appendix B for information on blood type–specific probiotics.

## Third Trimester

### Vitamins/Minerals

Continue to take your prenatal supplement, preferably one formulated for Type AB.

## Herbal Remedies

| HERB | FUNCTION | FORM AND DOSAGE |
|---|---|---|
| Astragalus | Prevents oedema; lessens abdominal achiness | 500 mg daily |
| Dandelion leaf/root | Lowers blood pressure; decreases oedema | As tea, 2 cups daily; or 250-mg capsule, twice daily |
| Nettles | Rich in vitamin K, promotes blood clotting | As tea, 2 cups daily; or 250-mg capsule, twice daily |
| Raspberry leaf (last 4 weeks) | Softens the cervix in preparation for birth; stimulates milk production | As tea, 2 cups daily; as tincture, 15–20 drops daily |
| Squaw vine | Prepares uterus for birth | As tincture, 10 drops in warm water, twice daily |

## Nutritional Supplements

| NUTRITIONAL SUPPLEMENT | FUNCTION | FORM AND DOSAGE |
|---|---|---|
| Larch arabinogalactan | Relieves constipation | Soluble fibre supplement: 1 tablespoon mixed with water or juice, twice daily |
| Probiotic | For intestinal health; prevention of candida infection | 2 capsules, twice daily* |
| DHA | Provides essential nutrients for foetal development | 300-mg capsule daily |

\* See appendix B for information on blood type–specific probiotics.

## Labour and Delivery

In addition to the general guidelines for labour and delivery (page 32), you have some specific Type AB needs.

### Type AB Energy Needs

Begin several weeks before your delivery date to prepare yourself for the stress of labour and delivery. Try to get more sleep than usual and eat plenty of nutrient-rich foods.

The first stage of labour can last many hours. Drink plenty of liquids and keep a light protein snack nearby. Stay hydrated. Be sure to discuss in advance with your doctor or midwife what the policy is about eating light foods or drinking liquids during labour.

### Type AB Emotional Needs

Type AB shows major physiological benefits from positive social interaction and support. You might consider engaging a doula to assist in labour, since you feel stronger and more emotionally stable when you are working with others to achieve a common purpose. (See page 32 for a discussion of the role of a doula.)

Anxiety is enhanced by fear of the unknown. Arrange in advance for your doctor, nurse, midwife, and other providers to keep you informed about the process and apprised of any problems or complications.

See page 35 for natural childbirth painkillers.

# The "Fourth" Trimester
# (After the Birth)

THE THREE-MONTH PERIOD following your child's birth is sometimes referred to as the fourth trimester, as all of you—mother, baby, father, and other siblings—begin your new life together. This is an extraordinary period of time in which so many elements must be coordinated and taken into account that the stress factors can threaten to overwhelm all involved.

The fourth trimester is a time of adaptation to the new demands of motherhood, biological repair, and reintegration into the flow of life.

Whatever you may have imagined was going to happen in terms of your thoughts and emotions, give yourself an opportunity to relax and let go now. Don't push yourself to maintain your normal standards. This is a time to "go with the flow". Permit yourself to get plenty of rest. If your home is messier than you'd like, let it be so. Don't force yourself to do more than you may be capable of doing. Concentrate on your baby's needs, and your own needs. Those are the paramount concerns at this time.

## Easing Postpartum Discomfort

Vaginal discharge after birth is called lochia. It is a combination of the sloughed uterine lining and blood. The lochia usually changes from bright red, to pink, to whitish over the course of several weeks.

It is very common for the bleeding to stop and start intermittently as well as to contain clots. Decrease your activity if you notice an increase in the amount of bleeding, as this is a signal for you to slow down and rest more. Special care in cleansing the perineum should be taken as long as postpartum bleeding continues. If you are comfortable, you will be better able to care for your baby during the first days after birth.

Your perineum may be sore and slightly swollen after birth. If you have had an episiotomy, your stitches will be tender. The puffiness decreases in a few days. Any increased pain or swelling should be reported to your health-care provider.

---

### Advice from the Naturopath Midwife Cathy Rogers, N.D.

**SITZ BATHS FOR POSTPARTUM DISCOMFORT**

Fill a tub with water so that it covers the hips and reaches up to mid-abdomen. If possible, immerse the pelvic and abdominal regions in the sitz bath water with your feet immersed in a separate basin with water, which is a few degrees warmer.

When using hot sitz bath, the tub should be filled with water about 110 degrees F. Stay in the bath for 20 to 40 minutes and then take a quick cold shower or bath. For cold sitz bath, fill the tub with ice water and stay in the cold bath for 30 to 60 seconds. Then towel yourself dry.

For alternating hot and cold baths, fill one tub with hot water and a second with ice water. Stay in the hot sitz bath first for 3 to 4 minutes and then shift to the cold sitz bath for 30 to 60 seconds; repeat this three to four times.

---

## Handling Postpartum "Blues" and Depression

Many women I've treated in my clinic suffer from some form of "baby blues" in the weeks following delivery. These mood swings, triggered by hormonal changes, are usually short-lived. The best remedy is to engage in stress-reduction practice, exercise, and get enough rest.

New research indicates that pregnant or nursing women could reduce their chances of developing postpartum depression and improve the neurological development of their babies by increasing the amount of the essential fatty acid DHA they consume. DHA (docosahexaenoic acid) is an omega-3 fatty acid mostly found in eggs and salmon. The standard dosage is 300 milligrams daily.

If fatigue is a factor, and it often is in the early days, the remedy is rest, your blood type diet, and moderate energizing exercise, such as gentle stretching or walking. Refer to your blood type section below.

Postpartum depression is a different matter. Between 10 and 15 percent of new mothers experience a more severe form of depression and need professional help. The symptoms include:

- Anxiety or panic attacks
- Feelings of hopelessness or guilt
- Insomnia
- Lack of interest in your baby
- Thoughts about harming your baby

If your depression is severe and is not eased by stress reduction, exercise, diet, and rest, seek professional help.

## Getting Back into Shape

Most women I've treated are extremely anxious to get back into shape as soon as possible after the birth of their babies. Your blood type guidelines offer strategies for doing this. However, I urge you to take it slow and not rush into a weight-loss program. Place your focus on health and fitness rather than weight loss, and don't use any extreme measures. It is not safe or healthy to lose weight rapidly, especially while nursing. You do not want to risk a reduced milk production or a depletion of your bone and muscle tissue for the sake of getting back to your pre-pregnancy weight. As a general rule, the breast-feeding mother should be carrying an extra 10 pounds (4.5 kg) of weight.

In order to lose weight while nursing, and, in particular, fat weight, a combination of diet and exercise is best. Maintain a calorie level of 1,800 to 2,000 calories a day. While you maintain a relatively high calorie level to provide your baby with the proper nutrients, also increase the intensity of your exercise routine. For example, try running instead of walking, or walk at a brisker pace for a longer time. Also, add weight lifting two times a week to your routine. Muscles burn more calories than fat, plus a muscular body has a higher metabolism. The increase in caloric intake along with the exercise will raise your metabolism and therefore help you to lose weight.

It may take you as long as a year to return to your pre-pregnancy condition. That's okay. Your best approach to the first year is to focus on nurturing your baby—and nurturing yourself.

## The Type O Mother

### Personal Recovery Guidelines

The Type O new mother will benefit enormously from talking about your birth experience—both the positive experience and the painful elements. If you have a doula, she can help you process your experience and provide guidance and support for the early weeks. Also be sure to share your feelings and experiences with your mate. When you meet the new challenges as a team, there will be less stress and anxiety.

Be aware of your own tendencies and work to overcome those that will add to your stress. In particular, be aware of your tendency to exhibit "type A personality" characteristics.

To reduce stress:

- Express yourself in writing. Keep a journal and write down what you are experiencing during the early weeks after the birth of your baby.
- Learn problem-solving techniques. Frustration and anger are most often the result of feeling a loss of control. When you are intent on solving a problem, rather than exploding in a helpless rage, your stress hormones will remain steady.
- Make sure to have a person or persons you can talk to when you're frustrated or angry. The extroverted Type O releases stress by engaging in a supportive conversation. The Internet provides many supportive Web communities that can help you build confidence and security in your parenting.

### TYPE O POSTPARTUM RECOVERY PROTOCOL
Use this protocol for four weeks:

- General multivitamin—preferably Type O specific (see appendix B)
- L-Carnitine—50 mg. Take 1 to 2 capsules, twice daily
- Extra vitamin C, from acerola cherry or rose hip—250 mg, twice daily
- DHA—300-mg capsule, once daily
- L-tyrosine—500 mg, two times a day

## Postpartum Exercise Guidelines

If your delivery was routine, you can begin exercising again soon after your baby's birth, and I encourage you to do so. Exercise is such an essential part of Type O's well-being, both mind and body. Take it slow, though. Your sessions should be shorter and less vigorous than normal, with plenty of attention to stretching. If you're able, sign up for a new mothers' exercise class.

You'll benefit physically and emotionally if you can get away on your own for exercise—even for half an hour. Take a walk or attend a class while someone watches your baby.

## Eight Type O Strategies for Getting Back in Shape

### 1. KNOW YOUR METABOLIC PROFILE

Your body weight alone is not a reliable indicator of your fitness. Your goal is not just to lose pounds but to build muscle and to burn calories efficiently. In addition to weight in pounds, it is important to know your metabolic rate (how efficiently you burn calories) and your body mass index (the ratio of muscle to fat).

BASAL METABOLIC RATE. This is the rate at which you burn calories at rest. That is, how many calories you need to sustain basic functions. You can estimate your average basal metabolic rate by multiplying your weight by 10 calories. If you engage in moderate activity (the level recommended in the average Type O exercise plan), multiply that number by 1.6 to estimate the number of calories you burn in a day.

> *Example:*
> 150 pounds × 10 calories = 1,500 (at rest)
> 1,500 × 1.6 = 2,400
> Total calorie expenditure: 2,400

BODY MASS INDEX. This is a measurement of body fat, based on your height and weight. A body mass index above 25 is considered overweight. To calculate your body mass index, multiply your weight by 704.5. Then multiply your height (in inches) by your height (in inches). Divide the first result by the second.

> *Example:*
> An individual who is 5′5″ and weighs 140 pounds
> 140 pounds × 704.5 = 98,630
> 65 × 65 = 4,225
> 98,630 ÷ 4,225 = 23

### 2. RESOLVE ANY MEDICAL CONDITIONS

Get a thorough checkup to determine whether you have any metabolic impediments to fitness. In particular, thyroid irregularities and insulin resistance syndrome can impede fitness and weight loss.

### 3. CHOOSE FOODS THAT ARE METABOLICALLY EFFICIENT

Many common grain lectins have the effect of inhibiting the breakdown of fats through their effects on insulin. When Type Os adopt low-fat diets rich in metabolically inactivating lectins, you gain weight. Let the Type O diet be your guide. To jump-start your program, adhere to the following plan.

**SEVEN-DAY SUPER O DIET**
- Lean, organic meat—4 to 6 servings weekly
- Fish rich in omega-3 fatty acids—3 to 4 servings weekly
- Eggs—2 to 3 eggs weekly
- Soy milk, tofu—5 to 7 servings weekly (while breast-feeding)
- Olive or flaxseed oil—1 serving daily
- Green vegetables—2 to 3 servings daily
- Other beneficial vegetables—5 to 7 servings weekly
- Fruit—2 to 3 servings daily
- Grains (allowed)—3 to 4 servings weekly

### 4. ELIMINATE ARTIFICIAL STIMULANTS

Many people use stimulants as a weight-loss method, but this approach is counterproductive for Type Os. Often, stimulants contain some form of caffeine. There is strong evidence that even moderate amounts of caffeine can activate the Type O sympathetic nervous system, resulting in a higher adrenaline release. This adrenaline release mimics hypoglycaemia, even when your blood sugar levels are not actually low.

### 5. TRICK YOUR CARBOHYDRATE CRAVING

When you crave carbohydrates, especially sugars, your serotonin levels are low, and your brain is demanding stimulants to raise the levels. As a rule, when you crave sugar, eat some protein.

### 6. GET AEROBIC

Aerobic exercise, at least four times a week, for 30 to 45 minutes, is a necessity for Type Os. In fact, it constitutes 50 percent of your health plan. Watch for signs of boredom or strain and adjust your routine accordingly. Choose from among the following exercises:

| EXERCISE | DURATION | FREQUENCY |
|---|---|---|
| Aerobics | 40–50 minutes | 3–4 × week |
| Running | 40–45 minutes | 3–4 × week |
| Calisthenics | 30–45 minutes | 3 × week |
| Treadmill | 30 minutes | 3 × week |
| Cycling | 30 minutes | 3 × week |
| Swimming | 30 minutes | 2–3 × week |

### 7. LIFT WEIGHTS TO BUILD MUSCLE MASS

Lift weights at least twice a week to build muscle mass. Muscles burn more calories than fat, plus a muscular body has a higher metabolism. The increase in calorie intake along with the exercise will raise your metabolism and therefore help you to lose weight. Lifting weights will also train you to lift and carry your growing child with ease.

### 8. DON'T RUSH IT

Place your focus on health and fitness rather than weight loss, and don't use any extreme measures, especially while you're breast-feeding. It is not safe or healthy to lose weight rapidly, especially while nursing.

## The Type A Mother

## Personal Recovery Guidelines

The new Type A mother faces one of the great stressful moments of her life—and we know that Type As are extremely vulnerable to the effects of stress.

Ease some of your stress by making decisions. This is very important. When a matter remains unresolved, it acts as a chronic stressor. Unresolved issues are like a virus on your computer's hard drive. They eat up all the available memory and make it impossible to run "programs" like good health and peace of mind. Suppressed emotions compromise the quality of your life and your health. They limit mental clarity, productivity, and your ability to adapt to stress. Allow your feelings. Acknowledge that life includes both positive and negative emotions.

### TYPE A POSTPARTUM RECOVERY PROTOCOL

Use this protocol for four weeks:

- General multivitamin
- DHA—300 mg, twice daily

- Liquid chlorophyll supplement—1 teaspoon daily (can be added to a clear glass of spring water and placed by a window for a few minutes; it will absorb light energy and supercharge the molecules)
- Pantothenic acid—250 mg, 1 to 2 capsules daily
- Potassium citrate—100 mg, twice daily
- Extra vitamin C, from acerola cherry or rose hip—250 mg, twice daily
- Chamomile (*Matricaria chamomilla*)—herbal tincture; 25 drops in warm water, two to three times daily
- Holy basil (*Ocinum sanctum*)—leaf extract, take 250-mg capsule, twice daily

## Postpartum Exercise Guidelines

If your delivery was routine, you can begin exercising again soon after your baby's birth, and I encourage you to do so. Take it slow, though. Your sessions should focus on gentle, calming exercises, with plenty of attention to stretching. If you're able, sign up for a new mothers' exercise class.

## Eight Type A Strategies for Getting Back in Shape

### 1. KNOW YOUR METABOLIC PROFILE

Your body weight alone is not a reliable indicator of your fitness. Your goal is not just to lose pounds but to build muscle and to burn calories efficiently. In addition to weight in pounds, it is important to know your metabolic rate (how efficiently you burn calories) and your body mass index (the ratio of muscle to fat).

BASAL METABOLIC RATE. This is the rate at which you burn calories at rest. That is, how many calories you need to sustain basic functions. You can estimate your average basal metabolic rate by multiplying your weight by 10 calories. If you engage in moderate activity (the level recommended in the average Type A exercise plan), multiply that number by 1.6 to estimate the number of calories you burn in a day.

> *Example:*
> 150 pounds × 10 calories = 1,500 (at rest)
> 1,500 × 1.6 = 2,400
> Total calorie expenditure: 2,400

BODY MASS INDEX. This is a measurement of body fat, based on your height and weight. A body mass index above 25 is considered overweight. To calculate your body mass index, multiply your weight by 704.5. Then multiply your height (in inches) by your height (in inches). Divide the first result by the second.

> *Example:*
> An individual who is 5′5″ and weighs 140 pounds
> 140 pounds × 704.5 = 98,630
> 65 × 65 = 4,225
> 98,630 ÷ by 4,225 = 23

## 2. RESOLVE ANY MEDICAL CONDITIONS
Get a thorough checkup to determine whether you have any metabolic impediments to fitness. In particular, make sure that your cardiovascular and digestive systems are all in good working order, so that you can exercise safely and eliminate toxins efficiently.

## 3. CHOOSE FOODS THAT ARE METABOLICALLY EFFICIENT
Let the Type A diet be your guide. To jump-start your program, adhere to the following plan.

### SEVEN-DAY SUPER A DIET
- Soy foods (tofu, tempeh, soy milk, etc.)—1 to 2 servings daily
- Lean, organic poultry—1 to 3 servings weekly
- Fish rich in omega-3 fatty acids—3 to 5 servings weekly
- Eggs—2 to 3 eggs weekly
- Olive or flaxseed oil—1 serving daily
- Beans and legumes
- Grains
- Green vegetables—2 to 3 servings daily
- Other beneficial vegetables—5 to 7 servings weekly
- Fruit—2 to 3 servings daily

## 4. EAT ENOUGH FOOD
Don't undereat or skip meals. Use appropriate blood type snacks between meals if you get hungry. Avoid low-calorie diets. Remember, food deprivation is a huge stress. It raises cortisol levels, lowers metabolism, encourages fat storage, and depletes healthy muscle mass.

## 5. BOOST YOUR METABOLISM

Many meat-eating Type As report feeling fatigued and lacking energy, especially when they engage in aerobic exercise and restrict complex carbohydrates. Another common Type A problem with excessive meat consumption is fluid retention, the result of the inability to properly digest high-protein foods. While Type Os have the capacity to break down the complex proteins in meat, most Type As lack this ability.

## 6. REDUCE STRESS

Type As who struggle with low metabolism and weight gain have another challenge—the effects of high cortisol. Being under constant stress causes weight gain for Type A. That's because high levels of the stress hormone cortisol promote insulin resistance and catabolize (burn) muscle tissue instead of fat. Obesity itself leads to cortisol resistance; it becomes a dangerously vicious circle for Type As. High cortisol is also associated with leptin, a hormone related to the obesity gene, which increases your appetite.

## 7. REGULATE YOUR MEALS

Often, how much you eat is less important than when you eat it. Eat the same amount of calories early in the day and most people lose weight; eat them at night and most people gain weight. Skipping breakfast or eating only a small amount of food for breakfast will have detrimental effects on your slow Type A metabolism. Cortisol and thyroid hormones will both be impacted. The same applies to skipping lunch. If you are serious about losing weight, a critical strategy is to eat a well-balanced breakfast, well-balanced lunch, and an adequate dinner—early in the evening. Resist the late-night munchies.

## 8. EXERCISE FOR YOUR TYPE

The following comprises the ideal exercise regimen for Type A.

THREE TO FOUR TIMES A WEEK, CHOOSE ONE:

| EXERCISE | DURATION |
| --- | --- |
| Hatha yoga | 40–50 minutes |
| T'ai chi | 40–50 minutes |

TWO TO THREE TIMES A WEEK, CHOOSE ONE:

| EXERCISE | DURATION |
| --- | --- |
| Aerobics (low impact) | 40–50 minutes |
| Treadmill | 30 minutes |
| Weight training (5–10 lb free weights) | 15 minutes |
| Cycling (recumbent bike) | 30 minutes |
| Swimming | 30 minutes |
| Brisk walking | 45 minutes |

## The Type B Mother

### Personal Recovery Guidelines

The new Type B mother faces one of the great stressful moments of her life—and we know that Type Bs are vulnerable to the effects of stress when they are overwhelmed or overtired.

Be aware of your own tendencies and work to overcome those that will add to your stress. The collective research that has been done on the Type B personality seems to confirm these neurochemical attributes. When you are in a state of balance, you can be flexible, creative, sensitive, and mentally agile, with a strong intuitive sense. Out of balance, you can suffer from the effects of high stress hormones, such as cortisol, and a susceptibility to viral infections, chronic fatigue, mental fogginess, and autoimmune diseases. Your focus in achieving mind-body integrity needs to be on lowering your cortisol levels and increasing your mental acuity.

According to Japanese pop psychology (and my own clinical experience), individuals with Type B blood tend to exhibit so-called "Type B personality" patterns. People who exhibit these patterns tend to be easygoing. They're able to take upsets in stride, keep their priorities in perspective, and understand their limitations. They are less driven and perhaps less obsessive than other blood types. These qualities can be extremely helpful to a new mother. You'll be happier and healthier (and so will your baby) if you can maintain a balanced perspective and not try to strive for perfection.

TYPE B POSTPARTUM RECOVERY PROTOCOL
Use this protocol for four weeks:

- General multivitamin
- Phosphatidyl choline. Take 1 gram, 2 capsules daily

- Siberian ginseng. Take 200 mg, 1 capsule, twice daily
- Magnesium. Take 350 mg, 1 capsule, twice daily
- Extra vitamin C, from acerola cherry or rose hip. Take 250 mg, twice daily
- DHA. Take 300 mg, twice daily
- Cordyceps (*Cordyceps sinensi*). Take 500 mg, 1 to 2 capsules, twice daily
- Inositol. Take 500 mg, 1 to 2 capsules, twice daily

## Postpartum Exercise Guidelines

If your delivery was routine, you can begin exercising again within a few days. Take it slow. Your sessions should be shorter and less vigorous than normal, with plenty of attention to stretching. If you're able, join an exercise class for new mothers.

## Eight Type B Strategies for Getting Back in Shape

### 1. KNOW YOUR METABOLIC PROFILE
Your body weight alone is not a reliable indicator of your fitness. Your goal is not just to lose pounds but to build muscle and burn calories efficiently. In addition to weight in pounds, it is important to know your metabolic rate (how efficiently you burn calories) and your body mass index (the ratio of muscle to fat).

BASAL METABOLIC RATE. This is the rate at which you burn calories at rest. That is, how many calories you need to sustain basic functions. You can estimate your average basal metabolic rate by multiplying your weight by 10 calories. If you engage in moderate activity (the level recommended in the average Type B exercise plan), multiply that number by 1.6 to estimate the number of calories you burn in a day.

> *Example:*
> 150 pounds × 10 calories = 1,500 (at rest)
> 1,500 × 1.6 = 2,400
> Total calorie expenditure: 2,400

BODY MASS INDEX. This is a measurement of body fat, based on your height and weight. A body mass index above 25 is considered overweight. To calculate your body mass index, multiply your weight by 704.5. Then multiply your height (in inches) by your height (in inches). Divide the first result by the second.

> *Example:*
> An individual who is 5'5" and weighs 140 pounds
> 140 pounds × 704.5 = 98,630
> 65 × 65 = 4,225
> 98,630 ÷ by 4,225 = 23

## 2. RESOLVE ANY MEDICAL CONDITIONS

Get a thorough checkup to determine whether you have any metabolic impediments to fitness. In particular, chronic viral infections and autoimmune conditions, such as chronic fatigue syndrome, can impede fitness and slow weight loss.

## 3. CHOOSE FOODS THAT ARE METABOLICALLY EFFICIENT

### SEVEN-DAY SUPER B DIET
- Lean, organic venison or lamb—4 to 6 servings weekly
- Fish rich in omega-3 fatty acids—3 to 4 servings weekly
- Cultured dairy foods—1 to 2 servings daily
- Noncultured dairy foods—4 to 7 servings weekly
- Eggs—2 to 3 eggs weekly
- Olive or flaxseed oil—1 serving daily
- Green vegetables—2 to 3 servings daily
- Other beneficial vegetables—5 to 7 servings weekly
- Fruit—2 to 3 servings daily
- Grains (allowed)—3 to 4 servings weekly

## 4. REDUCE STRESS

Type Bs who struggle with low metabolism and weight gain have another challenge—the effects of high cortisol. For Type B, being in a condition of stress equals weight gain. That's because the stress hormone cortisol promotes insulin resistance. Obesity itself leads to cortisol resistance; it becomes a dangerously vicious cycle for Type Bs. High cortisol is also associated with leptin, a hormone related to the obesity gene, which increases your appetite.

### 5. REGULATE YOUR MEALS

Often, how much you eat is less important than when you eat it. Eat the same amount of calories early in the day and most people lose weight; eat them at night and most people gain weight. Skipping breakfast or eating only a small amount of food for breakfast will have detrimental effects on your slow Type B metabolism. Cortisol and thyroid hormones will both be impacted. The same applies to skipping lunch. If you are serious about losing weight, a critical strategy is to eat a well-balanced breakfast, well-balanced lunch, and an adequate dinner—early in the evening. Resist the late-night munchies.

### 6. ENGAGE IN MODERATE AEROBIC EXERCISE

Stay active by participating in moderate aerobic exercise at least four times a week, for 30 to 45 minutes each session. Choose from among the following exercises:

| EXERCISE | DURATION | FREQUENCY |
| --- | --- | --- |
| Tennis | 45–60 minutes | 2–3 × week |
| Cycling | 45–60 minutes | 3 × week |
| Hiking | 30–60 minutes | 3 × week |
| Golf (no cart!) | 60–90 minutes | 2 × week |

### 7. BALANCE AEROBIC EXERCISE WITH MENTALLY CHALLENGING DISCIPLINES

For Type Bs, overall fitness is achieved with a balance of moderate aerobic activity and mentally soothing exercise. At least twice a week, participate in a stress-reducing activity, such as T'ai chi or Hatha yoga.

### 8. DON'T RUSH IT

Place your focus on health and fitness rather than weight loss, and don't use any extreme measures, especially while you're breast-feeding. It is not safe or healthy to lose weight rapidly, especially while nursing.

## The Type AB Mother

## Personal Recovery Guidelines

Since many Type ABs have a tendency to internalize their emotions, the new Type AB mother will benefit enormously from resisting that impulse and talking openly about your feelings and experiences. You may want to join a support group for new mothers, where you can not only work on your own emotions but also enjoy the benefits derived from reaching out to others.

Be aware of your own tendencies, and work to overcome those that will add to your stress. Type ABs are extremely sensitive to criticism, so try to be easy on yourself and stay away from people who are overly judgmental. Being a new mother—especially if this is your first time—is full of ups and downs. No one is perfect. In time you'll adjust to your new role.

### TYPE AB POSTPARTUM RECOVERY PROTOCOL

Use this protocol for four weeks:

- General multivitamin—preferably Type AB specific
- DHA—300 mg daily
- Vitamin $B_6$ (pyridoxal phosphate)—25 mg, daily
- Pantothenic acid—250 mg, 1 to 2 capsules, twice daily
- Zinc—25 mg, 1 capsule daily
- Extra vitamin C, from acerola cherry or rose hip—250 mg, twice daily
- Chamomile (*Matricaria chamomilla*)—herbal tincture, 25 drops in warm water, two to three times daily
- Holy basil (*Ocinum sanctum*)—leaf extract, 250-mg capsule, twice daily

## Postpartum Exercise Guidelines

If your delivery was routine, you can begin exercising again soon after your baby's birth, and I encourage you to do so. Take it easy, though. Your sessions should focus on gentle, calming exercises, with plenty of attention to stretching. If you're able, sign up for a new mothers' exercise class.

## Eight Type AB Strategies for Getting Back in Shape

### 1. KNOW YOUR METABOLIC PROFILE

Your body weight alone is not a reliable indicator of your fitness. Your goal is not just to lose pounds but to build muscle and burn calories efficiently. In addition to weight in pounds, it is important to know your metabolic rate (how efficiently you burn calories) and your body mass index (the ratio of muscle to fat).

BASAL METABOLIC RATE. This is the rate at which you burn calories at rest. That is, how many calories you need to sustain basic functions. You can estimate your average basal metabolic rate by multiplying your weight in pounds by 10 calories. If you engage in moderate activity (the level recommended in the average Type AB exercise plan), multiply that number by 1.6 to estimate the number of calories you burn in a day.

*Example:*
150 pounds × 10 calories = 1,500 (at rest)
1,500 × 1.6 = 2,400
Total calorie expenditure: 2,400

BODY MASS INDEX. This is a measurement of body fat, based on your height and weight. A body mass index above 25 is considered overweight. To calculate your body mass index, multiply your weight by 704.5. Then multiply your height (in inches) by your height (in inches). Divide the first result by the second.

*Example:*
An individual who is 5'5" and weighs 140 pounds
140 pounds × 704.5 = 98,630
65 × 65 = 4,225
98,630 ÷ 4,225 = 23

## 2. RESOLVE ANY MEDICAL CONDITIONS

Get a thorough checkup to determine whether you have any metabolic impediments to fitness. In particular, make sure that your cardiovascular and digestive systems are all in good working order, so that you can exercise safely and eliminate toxins efficiently.

## 3. CHOOSE FOODS THAT ARE METABOLICALLY EFFICIENT

Let the Type AB diet be your guide. To jump-start your program, adhere to the following plan.

### SEVEN-DAY SUPER A DIET

- Soy foods (tofu, tempeh, soy milk, etc.)—1 to 2 servings daily
- Lean, organic turkey—1 to 2 servings weekly
- Fish rich in omega-3 fatty acids—5 to 7 servings weekly
- Cultured dairy foods—4 to 5 servings weekly
- Eggs—2 to 3 eggs weekly
- Olive or flaxseed oil—1 serving daily
- Green vegetables—2 to 3 servings daily
- Other beneficial vegetables—5 to 7 servings weekly
- Fruit—2 to 3 servings daily
- Grains (allowed)—3 to 4 servings weekly

## 4. EAT ENOUGH FOOD

Don't undereat or skip meals. Use appropriate blood type snacks between meals if you get hungry. Avoid low-calorie diets. Remember, food deprivation is a huge stress. It raises cortisol levels, lowers metabolism, encourages fat storage, and depletes healthy muscle mass.

## 5. REGULATE YOUR MEALS

Often, how much you eat is less important than when you eat it. Eat the same amount of calories early in the day and most people lose weight; eat them at night and most people gain weight. Skipping breakfast or eating only a small amount of food for breakfast will have detrimental effects on your slow Type AB metabolism. Cortisol and thyroid hormones will both be impacted. The same applies to skipping lunch. If you are serious about losing weight, a critical strategy is to eat a well-balanced breakfast, well-balanced lunch, and an adequate dinner—early in the evening. Resist the late-night munchies.

## 6. ENGAGE IN MODERATE AEROBIC EXERCISE

Stay active by participating in moderate aerobic exercise at least four times a week, for 35 to 45 minutes each session. At least three times a week, engage in one of the following aerobic activities:

| EXERCISE | DURATION | FREQUENCY |
|---|---|---|
| Aerobics | 45–60 minutes | 2–3 × week |
| Martial arts | 30–60 minutes | 3 × week |
| Cycling | 45–60 minutes | 3 × week |
| Hiking | 30–60 minutes | 3 × week |
| Weight lifting | 30 minutes | 2 × week |

## 7. BALANCE AEROBIC EXERCISE WITH CALMING EXERCISES

For Type ABs, overall fitness is achieved with a balance of moderate aerobic activity and calming exercises. At least twice a week, participate in a stress-reducing activity, such as T'ai chi or Hatha yoga.

## 8. DON'T OBSESS

It can take time to get back into the shape that you enjoyed prior to conception and pregnancy. Don't push yourself. Let the changes happen at their own pace. Place your focus on health and fitness rather than weight loss, and don't use any extreme measures. It is not safe or healthy to lose weight rapidly, especially while you're nursing.

# A Healthy Start for Baby

YOUR BABY IS AN INDIVIDUAL from the moment of birth. Most parents say they are immediately aware of their child's unique qualities. Martha and I certainly found this to be true with each of our daughters. It's important to keep this in mind as you begin to develop your infant's patterns and schedules.

A key aspect of your baby's individuality is his or her blood type. It may be the same as yours, or different. Although every newborn has a blood type, infants are not born with functioning antibodies to opposing blood types. However, within two weeks of exposure to the outside world, those antibodies are activated and in play.

## Breast-feeding Diet Strategies

Many parents get especially anxious about feeding schedules—how often, how much. Allow your baby to develop his or her own patterns. Babies will want to feed between eight and eighteen times every day. Some learn the skill of suckling more quickly than others. Be patient, relax, and let your child find his or her own rhythm.

Now, more than ever, you will be focused on eating right for your baby. If you are wondering whether or not to breast-feed, consider the following benefits for you and your baby.

## All Blood Types

BENEFITS OF BREAST-FEEDING FOR YOUR BABY
- The nutrients in breast milk change according to the needs of the baby. For example, if your baby is born prematurely, the nutrient ratio in your milk will increase to aid in accelerating your newborn's neurodevelopment.
- Antibodies are passed through the breast milk, providing a great deal of immunity to your baby during a time when his or her immune system is still developing. This can result in fewer allergies, colds, and ear infections later in the child's life.
- Breast-feeding is particularly protective against some common childhood conditions, including eczema, otitis media, and iron-deficiency anaemia.

BENEFITS OF BREAST-FEEDING FOR MUM
- Nursing contracts your uterus, which helps to prevent postpartum bleeding.
- Breast-feeding appears to provide substantial protection against breast cancer and osteoporosis later in life.
- Breast-feeding creates a deep bond between you and your baby.

GENERAL BREAST-FEEDING TIPS
- Type O, Type A, and Type AB should avoid cow's milk and cheese, which can cause infant colic and other digestive disorders. For Type B, cultured dairy foods, such as yogurt and kefir, are preferable to noncultured dairy. (See blood type breast-feeding power foods later in this chapter.)
- Increase your intake of omega-3 fatty acids (DHA) found in fish oils.
- Continue to abstain from alcohol, which can get into your breast milk. Also be aware that caffeine and chocolate often cause colic in babies.
- Stay away from potential toxins. It's especially important to eat organic foods, clear of pesticides and antibiotics. These can get into your milk supply.
- Be aware that extreme and rapid weight loss can lead to toxicity in your milk supply. When you lose excessive amounts of weight, there is a breakdown of fat tissue. If PCBs are stored in this tissue, they could be released into the bloodstream and contaminate your milk supply.
- Avoid broccoli, cabbage, cauliflower, and Brussels sprouts. They may cause colic in some babies.
- Avoid onions and garlic, as well as hot or sweet peppers, as they also affect the quality of the milk supply and may cause your baby to refuse your breast.
- Drink plenty of fluids. Have a glass of water or juice with every feeding.
- Exercise to increase your fitness and the quality of your milk supply. While extreme weight loss can be hazardous, regular exercise promotes overall fitness and a healthy, gradual weight loss.

- Don't undereat or skip meals. You need to eat 300 to 500 calories a day more than normal while you are breast-feeding. About half the extra calories your baby needs will come from your fat stores and the other half from the food you eat. If you cut back on calories, you're shortchanging your baby's nutritional needs.

---

### Advice from the Naturopath Midwife Cathy Rogers, N.D.

**RELIEVING BREAST-FEEDING ANXIETIES**

It's normal to be a little anxious when you start breast-feeding for the first time. The most common worries are: Is the baby getting enough milk? Will breast-feeding hurt? Will it feel too sensual? (The action of breast-feeding contracts the uterus.) Some mothers feel anxious about the claim a breast-feeding baby places on their body, fearing they'll never be "themselves" again.

Whatever your anxieties, the best way to alleviate them is to press forward into the breast-feeding process and ride out the adjustment period. You and your baby will adjust. And the payoff is enormous. Now your baby, who lived in your womb, has full access to your touch, smell, and heartbeat. Relax and enjoy the intimacy as your baby bonds with you out in the world.

---

### FOUR HERBS THAT IMPROVE MILK PRODUCTION

Each of these herbs can be made into a tea infusion. Drink as often as needed if you are having problems with milk production.

1. Borage (*Borago officinalis*): infusion of flowers and leaves; drink freely to promote nursing.
2. Hops (*Humulus lupulus*): infusions, promote lactation—especially for women whose milk production is impaired by tension or anxiety.
3. Motherwort (*Leonurus cardiaca*): a general women's herb; promotes milk production.
4. Anise (*Pimpinella anisum*): contains phytosterols that promote lactation. Bruise or crush the whole seeds to make a tea.

### GETTING COMFORTABLE WITH BREAST-FEEDING

It's normal to feel some nipple soreness when you start breast-feeding. Give yourself a week or so to get comfortable with the experience. You can alleviate your temporary soreness by trying the following:

- Apply warm black teabags to your nipples between feedings, using a sticking plaster or surgical tape to keep them in place.
- Apply lanolin cream to your nipples after feeding—unless you are allergic to wool. Don't use soap on your nipples for a month or two before giving birth and while you're breast-feeding. It is drying.
- Go braless for periods of time, if you can, to expose your breasts to the air.
- Express a little milk and rub it around your areola and allow to air-dry.
- Apply vitamin E oil directly to your sore nipple.
- When your baby is done feeding, break the suction by gently placing a finger in your baby's mouth before removing him or her from your breast.
- Try holding your baby in a position that will help him or her grasp the areola and nipple, not just the nipple itself. This provides better stimulus for milk production.

---

### 🕊 Advice from the Naturopath Midwife 🕊
### Cathy Rogers, N.D.

**TURN OFF THE PHONE AND CONNECT WITH YOUR BABY**

When you have a new baby in the house, relatives, friends, and neighbours are eager to pay their respects, meet the baby, and shower you with food, gifts, and advice. You in turn feel obligated to be the perfect host. This is *not* a good use of the postpartum period, which should be devoted to bonding with your baby.

Leave a message on your machine and pin a note on your door, politely discouraging visitors. If a relative or friend plans to come and help, ask her to delay her visit for a week.

Make your time all about connecting. Mum, dad, and baby should snuggle together and get to know each other.

Your privacy is paramount. And it's so important for a mother to learn to trust her own instincts, without feeling pressured to fulfill others' expectations.

---

If you experience clogged ducts or mastitis, continue nursing on the affected breast. Cessation of nursing can impair milk flow, increase discomfort, and even endanger your milk supply. Nurse frequently, but just enough to empty your breast of milk. To relieve discomfort:

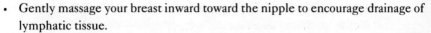

- Gently massage your breast inward toward the nipple to encourage drainage of lymphatic tissue.
- Use a castor oil pack: soak a washcloth in castor oil and apply it to your breast. Cover the cloth with cling film, then hot wet towels, and leave it on for 20 minutes. Wash the oil off with baking soda and water.

## WHAT TO DO IF YOU CAN'T BREAST-FEED

There will be some mothers who are unable to nurse their babies for a variety of reasons, or will not be able to produce enough milk to meet their baby's needs. If the issue is related to feeding (latch-on problems, prematurity, etc.) and not to milk production, you can still pump your breast milk to give your baby the benefits. If you need to use a commercial formula, there are many available in the following categories:

1. Dairy-based
2. Soy-based
3. Predigested protein

Talk to your paediatrician about the best formula for your baby. Increasingly, the soy formulas are gaining in popularity, since so many infants develop colic and digestive problems from cow's milk.

If you are bottle-feeding, you need not give up the special bonding with your baby. Hold him close as you feed him, establish skin-to-skin contact, and look into his eyes, establishing the connection that is so vital in early life.

## EAT RIGHT FOR *YOUR* TYPE, NOT YOUR BABY'S

New mothers always ask me: Should they eat for their own blood type or their baby's blood type when they're breast-feeding? The answer is that you eat what's right for *your* blood type, which constitutes the healthiest formula for your baby. If you and your baby have different blood types, there's no reason to be concerned about your breast milk. Breast milk is, to a degree, immunologically privileged. Human breast milk is inordinately high in the sugar fucose, which is the staple sugar of the O antigen. This is not normally a problem, as the O factor is considered universal. None of the other blood types will react negatively to it.

## Type O Mother—Breast-feeding Power Foods

| PROTEIN | CALCIUM | IRON | ZINC |
|---|---|---|---|
| • Lean, organic meats, especially beef, beef liver, and venison<br>• Fish and seafood | • Canned sardines with bone<br>• Canned salmon with bone<br>• Soy milk<br>• Tofu | • Lean, organic meat<br>• Calf's liver, heart, sweetbreads<br>• Dried apricots<br>• Dark green leafy vegetables | • Oysters<br>• Black-eyed peas<br>• Butter beans |
| **VITAMIN B$_6$** | **VITAMIN C** | **VITAMIN D** | **VITAMIN K** |
| • Chicken<br>• Fish<br>• Bananas<br>• Black-eyed peas | • Strawberries<br>• Grapefruit<br>• Pineapple | • Fortified juice and soy milk<br>• Fatty fish | • Calf's liver<br>• Egg yolks<br>• Green, leafy vegetables |

## Type A Mother—Breast-feeding Power Foods

| PROTEIN | CALCIUM | IRON | ZINC |
|---|---|---|---|
| • Soy foods, fish, organic poultry, beans | • Canned sardines with bone<br>• Canned salmon with bone<br>• Soy milk<br>• Tofu<br>• Cultured dairy<br>• Seaweed<br>• Spinach | • Molasses<br>• Egg yolks<br>• Dried apricots<br>• Dark green leafy vegetables | • Snails<br>• Black-eyed peas<br>• Aduki beans |
| **VITAMIN B$_6$** | **VITAMIN C** | **VITAMIN D** | **VITAMIN K** |
| • Chicken<br>• Fish<br>• Apricots, figs<br>• Black-eyed peas | • Cherries<br>• Grapefruit<br>• Pineapple | • Fortified juice and soy milk<br>• Fatty fish | • Fatty fish<br>• Egg yolks<br>• Green, leafy vegetables |

## Type B Mother—Breast-feeding Power Foods

| PROTEIN | CALCIUM | IRON | ZINC |
|---|---|---|---|
| • Lean, organic meats, especially lamb, mutton, liver, and venison<br>• Fish and seafood | • Cow's milk<br>• Goat's milk<br>• Yogurt<br>• Canned sardines with bone<br>• Seaweed | • Lean, organic meat<br>• Calf's liver, heart, sweetbreads<br>• Dried apricots<br>• Dark green leafy vegetables | • Black-eyed peas<br>• Butter beans |
| **VITAMIN B$_6$** | **VITAMIN C** | **VITAMIN D** | **VITAMIN K** |
| • Turkey<br>• Fish<br>• Bananas<br>• Black-eyed peas | • Strawberries<br>• Watermelon<br>• Pineapple | • Fortified juice and milk<br>• Fatty fish | • Egg yolks<br>• Green, leafy vegetables |

## Type AB Mother—Breast-feeding Power Foods

| PROTEIN | CALCIUM | IRON | ZINC |
|---|---|---|---|
| • Fish and seafood<br>• Soy foods<br>• Cultured dairy<br>• Small amounts of lean, organic venison | • Cow's milk<br>• Soy milk<br>• Tofu<br>• Canned sardines with bone<br>• Canned salmon with bone | • Lean, organic calf's liver<br>• Dried apricots<br>• Dark green leafy vegetables | • Oysters<br>• Black-eyed peas<br>• Butter beans |
| **VITAMIN B$_6$** | **VITAMIN C** | **VITAMIN D** | **VITAMIN K** |
| • Turkey<br>• Fish<br>• Black-eyed peas | • Strawberries<br>• Grapefruit<br>• Pineapple | • Fortified cow's milk<br>• Fortified juice and soy milk<br>• Fatty fish | • Calf's liver<br>• Egg yolks<br>• Green, leafy vegetables |

## Starting Solids—All Blood Types

Your breast milk is the best food for your baby. Don't rush the introduction of solid foods. Begin to introduce solids between four and six months, depending on your baby's readiness. Before four months, your baby lacks the digestive enzymes necessary to handle solid foods. Furthermore, the swallowing and tongue reflexes are not yet developed. However, don't delay the introduction of solid foods beyond six months. (See appendix A for recipes.)

When you do begin to introduce strained or pureed foods, go very slowly, beginning with a rice cereal of a semiliquid consistency. If you have a food processor, blender, or grinder, you can make your own strained fruits and vegetables, selected from organic whole foods. Introduce meat last—between nine months and a year. Your baby is already receiving its best protein source from your milk.

Even when you do introduce solids, continue breast-feeding for at least nine months to a year, if possible. Don't be too rigid, though. Infants really do have minds of their own when it comes to eating. Our first daughter, Claudia, was comfortable breast-feeding for a year. Emily, however, was eager to get off the breast after six months and eat like her big sister, a response that is probably more common when there are older children in the house.

### Just Say No to Commercial Baby Foods

In spite of the hype, commercial baby foods are not a healthy choice for your child. Most of them include fillers, such as tapioca, rice flour, and modified cornflour. Many contain sugar, salt, and corn syrup. Look for organic baby foods in your market or health-food stores, or, better still, make your own baby food. It doesn't have to be a big production. Once your baby has been introduced to foods beyond breast milk, you can even puree your own organic food, and your baby can eat what you're eating. There are some helpful recipes for homemade baby food in appendix A.

### Safety Rules for Homemade Baby Food

1. Wash your hands thoroughly before you begin preparing food.
2. Wash utensils and cutting board between preparing different foods, and use different cutting boards for raw and cooked foods.
3. Only store prepared foods in the refrigerator or freezer for the recommended times: Refrigerate pureed meats and eggs for one day; refrigerate pureed fruit and vegetables for three days; freeze prepared foods in airtight containers for up to two months.
4. Refrigerate or freeze unused foods immediately.

5. Wash fresh fruits and vegetables thoroughly to remove any chemical residue. Use an organic vegetable wash, available in health-food markets.

## Avoid These Foods in the First Year

- Honey is dangerous to children underage one because of the possible contraction of botulism.
- Nuts, raisins, popcorn, raw vegetables, and peanut butter can cause choking.
- Salt, sugar, or strong spices should not be added to homemade baby food.
- Canned vegetables are usually loaded with sodium and additives.
- Highly acidic fruits, such as oranges, tangerines, and pineapples, are not suitable for an immature digestive system.
- Egg whites can cause allergic reactions (yolks are okay).

## Your Baby's First Blood Type Diet

Babies are marvellous creatures, full of curiosity about themselves and the vast world that surrounds them. As your infant begins to explore the world of food beyond your breast milk, it's your job to respect his individuality. That means beginning to introduce him to the foods that are right for his blood type. Begin with the basics of the blood type diet. Choose as many highly beneficial foods and juices as you possibly can and make them the centrepiece of your child's diet. There are plenty of wonderful choices for all of the blood types, and they ensure optimum health and vitality for your growing child.

The following chapters provide individual guidelines for your baby's first year, according to blood type.

# The Type O Baby

## Type O Baby Health Issues

AS YOUR BABY GROWS, his or her blood type will provide protection against some health conditions and increase susceptibility to others. In particular, watch for:

- A tendency to develop colic or gastric problems.
- A susceptibility to food and environmental allergies.
- Bacterial infections—in particular, those causing digestive distress and ulcerative conditions (such as infection with *H. pylori*).
- Skin rashes, including nappy rash.
- Restlessness, inability to be comforted.

## Type O Remedies for Common Conditions

### FOOD ALLERGIES
Almost all food allergies your Type O baby experiences will be related to the introduction of wheat or dairy into the diet. Avoid these foods altogether. If you are breast-feeding during the first year, your baby is getting plenty of nutrients. Otherwise, you can substitute soy or rice milk and choose from the allowable grains on your baby's Type O diet (below).

### GASTRIC DISTRESS
Type Os have high levels of stomach acid, which can sometimes contribute to acid reflux and gastric distress. I believe digestive discomfort is the most common cause of colic. Prevent gastric distress this way:

- While you are breast-feeding, avoid milk, sugars, coffee, hot and spicy foods, onions, and garlic.
- While you are breast-feeding, drink fennel, lemon, ginger, and chamomile teas. Choose those you prefer and drink 1 cup, two to three times a day.
- Rub a calming mixture of 3 drops of lavender oil and 3 drops of almond oil over your baby's abdomen.

### Advice from the Naturopath Midwife Cathy Rogers, N.D.

#### SOOTHING CHAMOMILE TREATMENTS FOR THE COLICKY BABY

- Make chamomile tea, using 1 tablespoon tea to 1½ pints or 900 ml water. Steep 5 to 10 minutes. Cool. Using a teaspoon, dribble the liquid into your baby's mouth.
- Add 3 to 4 drops of chamomile oil to baby's bath.
- Warm 1 tablespoon olive oil and mix with 2 drops of chamomile oil. Gently massage oil over baby's belly.

### DIARRHOEA

Type O children often experience mild to moderate diarrhoea in reaction to eating dairy products. If your baby is eating some solids and drinking liquids, avoid giving him or her fruit juice. Instead, replenish fluids with vegetable or meat broths.

### Advice from the Naturopath Midwife Cathy Rogers, N.D.

#### A GENTLE REMEDY FOR MILD INFANT DIARRHOEA

Occasional mild diarrhoea is normal. If the diarrhoea is severe or continues, see your doctor immediately to rule out a bacterial infection.

To prevent dehydration, try the following with a very small infant. Cook carrots (well washed and peeled) in boiling water for 20 minutes or longer, until the water has become a carrot broth. Cool the broth and dribble a teaspoon into your baby's mouth several times a day.

If your child is eating solids, limit fruit. Too much fruit can stimulate diarrhoea. Rice cereal is binding.

## EAR INFECTIONS

Although Type O babies are less susceptible to ear infections than others, I've found that any child can contract chronic ear infections if she eats foods that react poorly in her system. My personal feeling is that ear infections can be prevented in Type O children simply by breast-feeding instead of bottle-feeding. Breast-feeding for a period of a year or so allows a child's immune system and digestive tract time to develop. When your child begins to eat solid foods, avoid wheat and dairy.

## NAPPY RASH

Type O babies are more susceptible to inflammations and rashes. If your baby has nappy rash, try the following remedies:

- Avoid rubber pants and change your baby's nappy often. Leave the nappy off whenever possible.
- Use cloth nappies and change them often.
- Treat the area with goldenseal (*Hydrastis canadensis*) powder and marigold (*Calendula off.*) cream.

---

### ⚜ Advice from the Naturopath Midwife ⚜
### Cathy Rogers, N.D.

**AN EASY REMEDY FOR NAPPY RASH**

At the changing table, mix 1 tablespoon baking soda with 4 fluid ounces (100 ml) spring water and rub on rash, then pat dry. Gently rub area with a small amount of calendula cream.

---

## RESTLESSNESS/HYPERACTIVITY

Research shows that many hyperactive children also suffer from hypersensitivity and allergies. Typically, I find that Type Os with allergies are eating wheat-based foods. Do not give your baby wheat—be it cream of wheat cereal, teething biscuits, or prepared foods with wheat-starch fillers. See the diet below for alternatives.

## The Type O Baby Diet

When you begin to introduce solid foods and liquids other than breast milk, follow these guidelines for your Type O baby:

- Limit sugars and artificial sweeteners. This will help your baby avoid infections and strengthen his immune system.
- Avoid any wheat-based foods or wheat-based fillers in seemingly innocuous foods. Wheat flour and wheat gluten are in a wide variety of

foods, so read the ingredient labels before allowing your child to eat an unfamiliar food product.

- Avoid foods made with cow's milk.
- Avoid acidic fruits, such as oranges and kiwi.
- Choose organic foods only.
- Pay attention to the recommended "start date" for different foods (see below).

## Type O Beneficial Baby Foods—First Year

NOTE: Most foods in the first year are strained, mashed, or pureed.

### CEREALS
Cream of rice—6 months
Kasha—9 to 12 months

### VEGETABLES
Beets—12 months
Broccoli—12 months
Carrots—6 months
Collard greens—12 months
Pumpkin—6 months
Spinach—12 months
Squash—6 months
Sweet potato—6 months

### FRUITS
Apple—7 to 9 months
Apricot—6 months
Banana—6 months
Blueberries—6 months
Grapes—9 to 12 months
Mango—9 to 12 months
Papaya—12 months
Pear—6 months
Pineapple—12 months
Plum—7 to 9 months
Strawberries—12 months

**BEANS/LEGUMES**
Black-eyed peas—9 to 12 months
Butter beans—7 to 9 months
Green beans and peas—6 months
Miso—7 to 9 months
Soy milk—6 to 9 months
Tofu—9 to 12 months

**GRAINS/RICE/PASTA**
Quinoa pasta—12 months
Rice—12 months
Rice cakes—9 to 12 months
Rice milk—12 months
Rolled oats—6 to 9 months
Soba noodles—12 months

**MEAT**
Beef—9 to 12 months
Chicken—9 to 12 months
Turkey—9 to 12 months

## Type O Avoid Baby Foods—First Year

**CEREALS**
Cornflakes
Cream of wheat
Oatmeal
Wheat flakes

**VEGETABLES**
Corn
Potato

**FRUITS**
Avocado
Kiwi
Orange
Tangerine

**BEANS/LEGUMES**
Butter beans
Haricot beans
Kidney beans

**GRAINS/RICE/PASTA**
Semolina pasta
All wheat-based grains

**DAIRY**
Cheese
Cottage cheese
Cow's milk
Yogurt

**MEAT**
All pork-based foods

See appendix A for nutritious, delicious recipes for Type O homemade baby food.

# 10

# The Type A Baby

## Type A Baby Health Issues

AS YOUR BABY GROWS, his or her blood type will provide protection against some health conditions and increase susceptibility to others. In particular, watch for:

- Overproduction of mucus.
- Throat and respiratory problems.
- Eczema-like skin rashes.
- Increased ear infections.
- Frequent colds and viruses.
- Restlessness and sleep problems.

## Type A Remedies for Common Conditions

### EAR INFECTIONS/OVERPRODUCTION OF MUCUS
Avoid dairy foods and sugar. In addition to diet, treating Type A children with ear infections almost always involves enhancing their immunity. The simplest way to enhance the immunity of any child is to cut down on his or her intake of sugar. Also note that longer breast-feeding (nine months to one year) is associated with stronger immune system protection.

### COLDS AND CONGESTION
The Type A immune system is highly sensitive, and your baby may be more prone to colds and respiratory infections. While you are breast-feeding, keep your

own immune system in healthy shape and take extra precautions with hygiene around the baby.

## ECZEMA-LIKE SKIN RASHES

Type A children often have scaly, itchy skin patches on the legs, stomach, and arms. If your child displays these symptoms, it is a sure sign that he or she is consuming too much dairy or that the diet is deficient in essential fatty acids. If you're still breast-feeding, you may want to increase your own intake of fatty acids either by taking a black currant seed oil supplement or by increasing your intake of olive oil. If your child is on solids already, try to wiggle a little of these products into his or her diet. For example, black currant seed oil capsules can be opened and added to fruit purees.

## COLIC

I believe digestive discomfort is the most common cause of colic. Prevent gastric distress this way:

- While you are breast-feeding, avoid milk, sugars, coffee, hot and spicy foods, onions, and garlic.
- While you are breast-feeding, drink these teas: fennel, dill, lemon balm, chamomile, and ginger. Choose those you prefer and drink 1 cup, two to three times a day.
- Rub a calming mixture of 3 drops of lavender oil and 3 drops of almond oil over your baby's abdomen.

See box on page 298 for naturopath Cathy Rogers' Soothing Chamomile Treatments for the Colicky Baby.

## DIARRHOEA

Type A children often experience mild to moderate diarrhoea in reaction to eating dairy products. If your baby is eating some solids and drinking liquids, avoid giving him or her fruit juice. Instead, replenish fluids with vegetable or meat broths. Also, see box on page 298 for naturopath Cathy Rogers' Gentle Remedy for Mild Infant Diarrhoea.

## NAPPY RASH

Any baby can develop nappy rash, but diarrhoea and infections can make your Type A baby more vulnerable. To prevent nappy rash:

- Avoid rubber pants and change your baby's nappy often. Leave the nappy off whenever possible.
- Use cloth nappies and change them often.

- Treat the area with goldenseal (*Hydrastis canadensis*) powder and marigold (*Calendula off.*) cream.

See the box on page 299 for naturopath Cathy Rogers' Easy Remedy for Nappy Rash.

### RESTLESSNESS/SLEEP PROBLEMS
Type A babies show special sensitivity to their environments, so don't rule out environmental factors if your infant is restless or has trouble sleeping. Keep baby's sleep area away from the noise of the household. Dim the lights, play soft music, or sing softly.

## The Type A Baby Diet

When you begin to introduce solid foods and liquids other than breast milk, follow these guidelines for your Type A baby:

- Limit sugars and artificial sweeteners. This will help your baby avoid infections and strengthen his or her immune system.
- When your baby begins to eat more complex solid foods (after nine months), avoid beef and favour soy foods such as tofu over chicken and turkey.
- Avoid noncultured dairy foods. Small amounts of cultured dairy, such as yogurt and kefir, are allowed.
- Choose organic foods only.
- Pay attention to the recommended "start date" for different foods (see below).

## Type A Beneficial Baby Foods—First Year

NOTE: Most foods in the first year are strained, mashed, or pureed.

### CEREALS
Cream of rice—6 months
Oatmeal—9 to 12 months

### VEGETABLES
Beets—12 months
Broccoli—12 months
Carrots—6 months

Collard greens—12 months
Corn—9 to 12 months
Pumpkin—6 months
Spinach—7 to 9 months
Squash—6 months

**FRUITS**
Apple—7 to 9 months
Apricot—6 months
Avocado—7 to 9 months
Blueberries—6 months
Kiwi—9 to 12 months
Pear—6 months
Plum—7 to 9 months
Strawberries—12 months

**BEANS/LEGUMES**
Black-eyed peas—9 to 12 months
Green beans and peas—6 months
Lentil beans—9 to 12 months
Miso—9 months
Soy milk—6 to 9 months
Tofu—9 months

**GRAINS/RICE/PASTA**
Cornbread—12 months
Quinoa pasta—12 months
Rice—12 months
Rice cake—12 months
Rice milk—12 months
Rolled oats—6 to 9 months
Soba noodles—12 months

**DAIRY**
Goat's cheese—9 to 12 months
Goat's milk—9 to 12 months
Yogurt—7 to 9 months

**MEAT**
Chicken—9 to 12 months
Turkey—9 to 12 months

## Type A Avoid Baby Foods—First Year

**CEREALS**
Cream of wheat
Farina

**VEGETABLES**
Cabbage
Potato
Sweet potato
Tomato

**FRUITS**
Banana
Orange
Papaya
Tangerine

**BEANS/LEGUMES**
Butter beans
Chickpeas
Haricot beans
Kidney beans

**GRAINS/RICE/PASTA**
Wheat bran
Wheat germ

**DAIRY**
Cheese
Cottage cheese
Cow's milk

**MEAT**
Beef
Pork and pork-based foods

See appendix A for nutritious, delicious recipes for Type A homemade baby food.

11

# The Type B Baby

## Type B Baby Health Issues

AS YOUR BABY GROWS, his or her blood type will provide protection against some health conditions and increase susceptibility to others. In particular, you may observe:

- A tendency to develop strep infections.
- A tendency to develop chronic ear infections.
- A tendency to develop respiratory problems, which may become chronic.
- A susceptibility to food allergies.

## Type B Remedies for Common Conditions

### RESPIRATORY/EAR INFECTIONS

In Type B children, ear infections are usually the result of an underlying infection with a bacteria called *Haemophilus*, to which Type B is unusually susceptible. The dietary fix involves restricting tomatoes, corn, and chicken. The lectins in these foods react with the surface of the digestive tract, causing swelling and mucus secretion, which usually carry over to the ears and throat.

Here's an interesting note for Type B babies who may have asthmatic tendencies. Studies show that babies who are breast-fed at least nine months to one year have fewer incidences of asthma, thanks to the immune system protection of mother's milk.

FOOD ALLERGIES

Type B children are extremely sensitive to foods containing reactive lectins. While you are breast-feeding, the foods you eat can cause allergic reactions in your baby. These reactions can include a rash or cramping, nausea, vomiting, or diarrhoea. Other common symptoms are hives, wheezing, sneezing, runny nose, unusual crying, and shortness of breath. In extreme cases, a child may develop a life-threatening condition called anaphylactic shock. Severe symptoms or reactions to any allergen require immediate medical attention.

Foods a mother eats that are the most likely to cause an allergy for a Type B infant are wheat, shellfish, peanuts, corn, buckwheat, and chicken.

DIARRHOEA

Type B children will contract diarrhoea if they overindulge in wheat products, or in reaction to eating chicken and corn. If the diarrhoea is caused by a food-related intolerance or allergy, your child will often exhibit other symptoms, such as dark, puffy circles under the eyes, rash, or wheezy breathing. Also, see box on page 298 for naturopath Cathy Rogers' Gentle Remedy for Mild Infant Diarrhoea.

NAPPY RASH

Allergies and diarrhoea can be factors in skin inflammation and nappy rash. In particular, food allergies are known to cause eczema. If you infant has nappy rash, see the box on page 299 for naturopath Cathy Rogers' Easy Remedy for Nappy Rash.

RESTLESSNESS/HYPERACTIVITY

Research shows that many hyperactive children also suffer from hypersensitivity and allergies. Typically, I find that Type Bs with allergies are eating foods with reactive lectins, the worst offenders being corn, buckwheat, lentils, peanuts, and tomatoes. See the diet below for the appropriate foods to give your Type B baby when he or she starts eating solids.

## The Type B Baby Diet

When you begin to introduce solid foods and liquids other than breast milk, follow these guidelines for your Type B baby:

- Limit sugars and artificial sweeteners. This will help prevent infections and strengthen your baby's immune system.
- When your baby begins to eat more complex solid foods (after nine months), avoid chicken, which causes allergic reactions.
- Gradually introduce dairy foods, starting with cultured dairy such as sugar-free yogurt made from organic milk.

- Choose organic foods only.
- Pay attention to the recommended "start date" for different foods listed below.

## Type B Beneficial Baby Foods—First Year

NOTE: Most foods in the first year are strained, mashed, or pureed.

**CEREALS**
    Cream of rice—6 months
    Oatmeal—9 months

**VEGETABLES**
    Beets—12 months
    Broccoli—12 months
    Cabbage—12 months
    Carrots—6 months
    Potato—9 months
    Seaweed—9 to 12 months
    Spinach—12 months
    Squash—6 months
    Sweet potato—6 months

**FRUITS**
    Apple—7 to 9 months
    Apricot—6 months
    Banana—6 months
    Blueberries—6 months
    Papaya—12 months
    Pear—6 months
    Pineapple—12 months
    Plum—7 to 9 months
    Strawberries—12 months

**BEANS/LEGUMES**
    Butter beans—9 to 12 months
    Green beans and peas—6 months
    Haricot beans—9 to 12 months
    Kidney beans—9 to 12 months

**GRAINS/RICE/PASTA**

Rice—9 to 12 months

Rice cake—9 to 12 months

Rice milk—9 to 12 months

Rolled oats—6 to 9 months

Spelt flour—9 to 12 months

**DAIRY**

Butter—12 months

Cottage cheese—9 to 12 months

Goat's cheese—12 months

Kefir—9 to 12 months

Ricotta—12 months

Yogurt—7 to 9 months

**MEAT**

Beef—9 to 12 months

Lamb—9 to 12 months

Turkey—9 to 12 months

Venison—12 months

## Type B Avoid Baby Foods—First Year

**CEREALS**

Cream of wheat

Kasha

**VEGETABLES**

Corn

Pumpkin

Tomato

**FRUITS**

Avocado

Star fruit (carambola)

**BEANS/LEGUMES**

Black-eyed peas

Chickpeas

Lentils

Miso
Pinto beans
Soy milk
Tofu

**GRAINS/RICE/PASTA**
Buckwheat
Cornmeal
Soba noodles
Wheat bran
Wheat germ

**DAIRY**
Hard cheese
Ice cream

**MEAT**
Chicken
Pork and pork-based foods

See appendix A for nutritious, delicious recipes for Type B homemade baby food.

# 12

# The Type AB Baby

## Type AB Baby Health Issues

AS YOUR BABY GROWS, his or her blood type will provide protection against some health conditions and increase susceptibility to others. In particular, watch for:

- Overproduction of mucus.
- Throat and respiratory problems.
- Increased risk of ear infections.
- Susceptibility to frequent colds and viruses.

## Type AB Remedies for Common Conditions

### EAR INFECTIONS/OVERPRODUCTION OF MUCUS

Avoid dairy foods and sugar. In addition to diet, treating Type AB children with ear infections almost always involves enhancing their immunity. The simplest way to enhance the immunity of any child is to cut down on his or her intake of sugar, so keep that in mind when your baby begins eating solid foods. Many commercial brands contain sugar. Also note that longer breast-feeding (nine months to one year) is associated with stronger immune system protection.

### COLDS AND CONGESTION

The Type AB immune system is highly sensitive, and your baby may be more prone to colds and respiratory infections. While you are breast-feeding, keep your own immune system in healthy shape and take extra precautions with hygiene around the baby.

DIARRHOEA

Type AB children can suffer from digestive upset if they overindulge in wheat products or in reaction to eating chicken and corn. If the diarrhoea is caused by a food-related intolerance or allergy, your child will often exhibit other symptoms, such as puffy circles under the eyes, rashes, and wheezy breathing. Also, see box on page 298 for naturopath Cathy Rogers' Gentle Remedy for Mild Infant Diarrhoea.

NAPPY RASH

Any baby can develop nappy rash, but diarrhoea and infections can make your Type AB baby more vulnerable. To prevent nappy rash:

- Avoid rubber pants and change your baby's nappy often. Leave the nappy off whenever possible.
- Use cloth nappies and change them often.
- Treat the area with goldenseal (*Hydrastis canadensis*) powder and marigold (*Calendula off.*) cream.

See box on page 299 for naturopath Cathy Rogers' Easy Remedy for Nappy Rash.

## The Type AB Baby Diet

When you begin to introduce solid foods and liquids other than breast milk, follow these guidelines for your Type AB baby:

- Limit sugars and artificial sweeteners. Type AB babies are highly sensitive to the effects.
- When your baby begins to eat more complex solid foods (after nine months), avoid chicken, which causes allergic reactions.
- Go easy on meats, such as turkey and lamb. Start with very small quantities—two to three spoonfuls.
- Choose organic foods only.
- Pay attention to the recommended "start date" for different foods listed below.

## Type AB Beneficial Baby Foods—First Year

NOTE: Most foods in the first year are strained, mashed, or pureed.

CEREALS
Cream of rice—6 months
Oatmeal—9 to 12 months

**VEGETABLES**
Beets—12 months
Broccoli—12 months
Cabbage—12 months
Carrots—6 months
Collard greens—9 to 12 months
Potato—9 months
Pumpkin—6 months
Spinach—9 to 12 months
Sweet potato—6 months
Tomato—12 months

**FRUITS**
Apple—7 to 9 months
Apricot—6 months
Blueberries—6 months
Cranberries—7 to 9 months
Grapes—9 to 12 months
Kiwi—9 to 12 months
Pineapple—12 months
Plum—9 to 12 months
Strawberries—9 to 12 months

**BEANS/LEGUMES**
Green beans and peas—6 months
Lentils—7 to 9 months
Miso—7 to 9 months
Pinto beans—9 to 12 months
Soy milk—7 to 9 months
Tofu—9 to 12 months

**GRAINS/RICE/PASTA**
Rice—9 to 12 months
Rice cake—9 to 12 months
Rice milk—9 to 12 months
Rolled oats—6 to 9 months
Spelt flour—9 to 12 months

**DAIRY**
Cottage cheese—9 to 12 months
Goat's cheese—12 months

Kefir—9 to 12 months
Ricotta—12 months
Yogurt—6 months

**MEAT**
Lamb—9 to 12 months
Turkey—9 to 12 months
Venison—12 months

## Type AB Avoid Baby Foods—First Year

**CEREALS**
Kasha

**VEGETABLES**
Artichoke
Corn
Sprouts

**FRUITS**
Avocado
Banana
Mango
Orange

**BEANS/LEGUMES**
Black-eyed peas
Butter beans
Kidney beans

**GRAINS/RICE/PASTA**
Buckwheat
Cornbread
Soba noodles

**DAIRY**
Hard cheese
Cow's milk
Ice cream

**MEAT**
> Beef
> Chicken
> All pork products

See appendix A for nutritious, delicious recipes for Type AB homemade baby food.

Appendix **A**

# Blood Type Friendly Recipes
# for Mum and Baby

THE FOLLOWING RECIPES provide a wide variety of healthy choices for every blood type. They are adapted from *Cook Right for Your Type* and from the personal recipes of visitors to Dr. D'Adamo's blood type website. Use them according to the suggested meal plans in your blood type sections or create your own menus. Just be sure to include a variety of nutritious foods that provide the necessary nutrients—and stay with those foods that are approved for your blood type.

There is also a section of homemade baby foods, according to blood type. Try them when your baby starts on solid foods.

See appendix B for more information about cooking for your blood type, including where to find blood type–specific recipes and how to order *Cook Right 4 (for) Your Type*.

## For Mum

## Contents

Meat and Poultry
Seafood
Tofu and Tempeh
Pasta and Noodles
Legumes and Grains
Soups and Stews

Salads
Vegetables
Sandwiches, Eggs, Tarts, and Frittatas
Breads, Muffins, Pancakes, and Batters
Snacks
Desserts
Beverages
Dressings and Relishes

## Meat and Poultry

### BRAISED RABBIT

#### (O, B, AB)

*2 tablespoons olive oil*
*1 rabbit, cut into about 12 pieces*
*2 tablespoons butter*
*1 large carrot, diced*
*4 cloves garlic, chopped*
*1 stalk celery, finely sliced*
*1 medium onion, diced*
*8 fluid ounces/225 ml water*

Heat the oil in heavy frying pan and add the rabbit, cooking over a low flame until nicely browned. Remove the rabbit to a platter, add the butter to the pan. When melted, add the carrot, garlic, celery, and onion, turning until golden. Pushing aside the vegetables, put the rabbit back into pan, spoon the vegetables over the rabbit pieces and add the water, or enough to braise the rabbit. Bring to a boil, cover, reduce heat, and take care that there is always enough braising liquid in the pan. Cook the rabbit 1½ hours, or until very tender. Spoon the "sauce" over rice. *Serves 3 to 4.*

### SESAME CHICKEN

#### (O, A)

*8 chicken pieces or breasts on bone*
*2 tablespoons soy sauce or tamari*
*3 to 5 cloves garlic, crushed*
*4 tablespoons black sesame seeds*

Preheat the oven to 190°C/gas 5. Put the chicken pieces in a baking dish. Sprinkle each piece with the soy sauce. Rub with the crushed garlic. Sprinkle the black sesame seeds over the top and bake for 50 minutes or until done. *Serves 4 to 8.*

## GRILLED LAMB CHOPS

### (O, B, AB)

*Allow 2 to 3 rib lamb chops per person*
*1 large clove garlic, peeled and cut*
*1 tablespoon dry rub of salt and pepper*
*Olive oil*

Preheat the grill and adjust the shelf so that chops are 3 to 4 inches from the heat. Remove excess fat from the chops and place in a flame-proof pan. Rub the meat with the cut garlic clove, then the salt and pepper rub. Pour a few teaspoons of olive oil over the chops and turn them once to coat both sides with oil. Place under the grill and cook 5 to 7 minutes, or until the meat is well browned. Turn the chops and replace under grill, browning other side as well. Serve with mashed sweet potatoes and braised greens.

## PEANUT CHICKEN

### (A)

*2 pounds/900 g boneless chicken breasts*
*10 ounces/250 g peanuts*

Poach, cool, and drain the chicken breasts. Cut into finger-length pieces. Toast the nuts by placing in a frying pan and flipping them around for a few minutes. Watch carefully so they do not scorch. When cooled, place them in the bowl of a food processor or into a blender and pulse until the nuts are finely chopped. Dip the chicken in the Chutney-Yogurt Sauce (recipe below), then roll each piece in the nuts. Carefully arrange on a serving tray or on a bed of lettuce.

### CHUTNEY-YOGURT SAUCE

*12 ounces/300 g pineapple chutney*
*2 tablespoons plain yogurt*
*2 tablespoons Egg-Free Mayonnaise (page 406)*

In the bowl of a food processor, blend all ingredients.

## TURKEY BURGERS

### (O, A, B, AB)

*1 pound/450 g minced turkey*
*2 slices spelt or sprouted seed bread*
*1 tablespoon olive oil*
*1 medium onion, finely chopped*
*2 eggs*
*Handful of tarragon, chopped*
*Pinch salt*
*Olive oil for frying*

Place the minced turkey in a large bowl and shred the bread over the meat. In a frying pan, heat the oil and sauté the onion over medium heat until soft and golden. Add to the bowl. Beat the eggs in a small bowl, then combine with other ingredients. Add the chopped tarragon and salt. With your hands, mix the ingredients gently but completely, using a very light touch. Do not condense the mixture; keep it fluffy. When the ingredients are well mixed, shape them into 5 or 6 burgers and fry in olive oil over medium heat until brown. Turn and continue to fry. Cover the pan after a few minutes, reduce heat, and let them "steam" just a little until the juices run clear. This also keeps them moist.

## GRILLED LOIN OF LAMB CHOPS

### (O, B, AB)

*6 to 8 double loin chops or 1 leg of lamb*
*Tamari-Mustard Marinade (see below)*

Marinate the lamb in the marinade for 1 to 2 hours. Grill under medium heat 15 minutes on each side for chops or 30 to 35 minutes on each side for boneless leg. Let sit for 10 minutes before serving.

### TAMARI-MUSTARD MARINADE

*4 tablespoons tamari*
*2 tablespoons Dijon or dry mustard*
*1 tablespoon honey*
*2 cloves garlic, minced*
*1 lemon, zest and juice*
*1 tablespoon ground ginger*

*1 tablespoon ground cumin*
*2 tablespoons sesame oil*

Mix all the ingredients together and store in the refrigerator. *Makes 6 fluid ounces/150 ml.*

## OLD-FASHIONED YANKEE POT ROAST

### (O, B)

*4 tablespoons olive oil*
*3 to 4 pounds/1.35 to 1.8 kg chuck roast*
*1½ pints/850 ml Vegetable Stock (page 354)*
*4 tablespoons chopped sweet basil*
*1 bay leaf*
*2 large carrots*
*2 stalks of celery*
*1 large onion*
*1 sweet potato*
*Salt to taste*

In a large pot, heat the oil and brown the meat on both sides. Add the stock and herbs, bring to a boil, reduce heat to simmer, and cook 1½ hours. Add all the vegetables and cook another 45 to 60 minutes. Check the meat for tenderness. If it is not easy to pierce with a fork, then continue to cook another 20 to 30 minutes, or until done.

## GRIDDLED CURRIED LEG OF LAMB

### (O, B, AB)

*2 tablespoons curry powder*
*2 tablespoons ground cumin*
*1 tablespoon iodized salt*
*2 tablespoons kelp powder*
*1 tablespoon 5-spice powder*
*1 leg of lamb, boned and butterflied*

Combine spices and dry rub each side of the leg of lamb. Let sit for 1 hour. Griddle 20 minutes on each side for medium; 25 minutes for well done. Remove lamb from the griddle, and let stand for 10 minutes, then slice thin. *Serves 4.*

## GREAT MEATLOAF

### (O)

*1 egg*
*8 fluid ounces/225 ml rice, soy, or almond milk, or Chicken Stock (page 353)*
*3 slices stale bread (sprouted seed, spelt, or rice/almond)*
*1 pound/450 g minced organic beef*
*1 pound/450 g free-range turkey, minced*
*2 tablespoons kelp powder*
*1 tablespoon ground cumin*
*2 tablespoons tamari*
*3 tablespoons ketchup or tomato paste*

In a large bowl, beat the egg and mix in the milk or chicken stock. Cut the stale bread into cubes and soak in egg and milk mixture until soggy. Mix the rest of the ingredients together in the bowl. Preheat the oven to 190°C/gas 5. Form meat into a 10- by 5- by 5-inch (25×13×13 cm) loaf and bake on a baking sheet for 1 hour and 15 minutes or until juices run clear. Let sit for 10 minutes before serving.

## TURKEY CUTLETS

### (O, A, B, AB)

*2 tablespoons vegetable or olive oil*
*about 1 pound/450 g turkey cutlets*
*4 tablespoons spelt breadcrumbs*
*Squeeze of lemon*
*Salt to taste*

In a large frying pan, heat oil until very hot, but not smoking. Roll each cutlet in breadcrumbs and slip into pan, being careful not to overcrowd. Make two batches if necessary. Cook each side for 4 to 5 minutes or until nicely browned. Turn once only. Serve with a squeeze of lemon and add salt to taste. *Serves 2.*

## PAN-FRIED LIVER AND ONIONS

### (O, B, AB)

*2 tablespoons olive oil*
*1 large onion, peeled and sliced thin*
*2 oz/50 g butter or light olive oil*
*1 pound/450 g sliced calves or beef liver*

*4 ounces/100 g spelt flour (2 white and 2 whole is fine)*
*Salt to taste*

In a medium frying pan, heat the olive oil and cook onions until wilted and slightly browned. In a large frying pan, heat the butter or oil until almost smoking. Dredge the liver in the flour one piece at a time, shake off any excess flour, and cook each side for 4 to 5 minutes. Be careful not to overcrowd the pan. Turn once only. Salt to taste. Serve the liver smothered with onions. *Serves 4 to 5.*

## FLANK STEAK

### (O, B)

*2 tablespoons minced garlic*
*2 tablespoons ground cumin*
*1 tablespoon ground chilli powder*
*1 tablespoon ground coriander*
*½ teaspoon ground cloves*
*½ teaspoon red pepper flakes*
*1 tablespoon salt*
*1 1-pound/450-g flank steak*

Mix the garlic and spices together and rub generously over the flank steak. Grill under medium heat for 8 to 10 minutes per side. Allow to rest 5 minutes before slicing. Serve with Fresh Mint Sauce (page 408) as a refreshing contrast to the spicy rub.

## ROAST TURKEY

### (O, A, B, AB)

*1 8- to 10-pound/3.5- to 4.5-kg turkey or turkey breast*
*Mixed herbs*
*1 tablespoon salt*

There are no secrets to roasting a great turkey. The rule is 15 to 18 minutes per pound or until the juices run clear if poked in the thigh. A 10-pound (4.5 kg) turkey will roast for a good 2½ hours. Always allow it to rest 10 minutes before carving.

Preheat the oven to 190°C/gas 5. Remove all giblets from the turkey, front and back. Save them for future stock by freezing. Rinse the cavity and rub the bird with the herbs and salt. If that is unappealing to you, then stick the herbs in the cavity and sprinkle with salt. Roast until done. If the bird is large, you can make a tent out of foil to cover the breast for the first 1½ hours, but don't forget to remove for the last hour of cooking. Crispy skin is part of the whole appeal. When done, please be careful removing the hot roasting pan from the oven. Make sure the surface on which you place the turkey is close-by.

## ROAST CHICKEN WITH GARLIC AND HERBS

### (O, A)

*1 large chicken*
*10 cloves garlic, peeled and smashed*
*2 tablespoons Herbes de Provence*
*1 teaspoon salt*

Preheat the oven to 190°C/gas 5. Prepare the chicken for baking and rub well with a little of the garlic. Put the rest of the cloves in the cavity and season the chicken with the Herbes de Provence and salt. Bake 1 hour and 15 minutes or until the juices run clear. Allow to rest 5 minutes before carving.

## Seafood

## GRILLED SALMON WITH LEMONGRASS

### (O, A, B, AB)

*3 stalks of lemongrass, bottom ⅓ only, chopped fine*
*3 tablespoons soy sauce*
*2 plum tomatoes (Types A and B omit)*
*2 tablespoons finely chopped fresh coriander*
*Juice of one lemon*
*2 spring onions, sliced fine*
*1 small side of salmon, 1 to 1½ pounds/450 to 675 g, filleted*

Combine all the ingredients except the salmon. Put the salmon on a large platter and pour the marinade over the whole fillet. Let marinate for approximately 2 hours. Remove the salmon from the marinade and grill 15 minutes for medium, 20 minutes for well done. *Serves 4.*

## PETER'S ESCARGOT

### (A, AB)

*4 tablespoons olive oil*
*2 tablespoons chopped and pressed garlic*
*12 escargots*
*A handful of chopped parsley*

Preheat the grill. Combine the oil and garlic in a small bowl and mash into a paste using the back of a spoon. Arrange the escargots on a baking sheet and brush them with the garlic paste. Grill about 10 minutes. Serve garnished with chopped parsley. *Serves 2.*

## GRILLED SALMON STEAKS

### (O, A, B, AB)

*4 salmon steaks*
*1 tablespoon Garlic-Shallot Mixture (page 409)*
*2 tablespoons olive oil*
*1 lemon*
*3 tablespoons chopped fresh dill*
*Salt to taste*

Rub the steaks with the Garlic-Shallot Mixture, oil, and lemon. Preheat the grill and cook the fish as close to the heat as possible, about 4 minutes on each side. Test for doneness by poking with a finger and seeing if the flesh separates. Serve hot or cold with chopped fresh dill, salt, and an additional squeeze of lemon.

## FRIED MONKFISH

### (O, A, B, AB)

*1 pound/450 g monkfish*
*1 teaspoon dried basil*
*Brown rice or spelt flour*
*1 to 2 eggs*
*2 tablespoons olive oil*

*Salt*
*Pepper*

Cut the monkfish into 1-inch (2.5-cm) cubes. Add the basil to the flour. Beat the eggs well and dip the monkfish in, a few pieces at a time. Heat the olive oil in a heavy frying pan. Roll the pieces of monkfish in the seasoned flour. Put the floured fish into the pan, but do not overcrowd it. Fry gently, several minutes on each side, until the batter is crisp and the fish is done. Season with salt and pepper. *Serves 4.*

## PRAWN KEBABS

### (O)

*1 lemon, juiced*
*4 tablespoons olive oil*
*3 cloves garlic, peeled and smashed*
*2 tablespoons chopped sweet basil*
*1 stalk lemongrass, bottom third removed, peeled and chopped*
*1-inch/2.5-cm piece of ginger, peeled and chopped or grated*
*1 pound/450 g large prawns, cleaned and deveined*

Combine the lemon juice, olive oil, garlic, sweet basil, lemongrass, and ginger. Place the prawns in the marinade and marinate for at least 4 hours. The longer marinating time the better. Overnight is just about right. Skewer 4 to 6 on each kebab stick and grill under high heat 3 minutes on a side. *Serves 2.*

## STEAMED WHOLE RED SNAPPER

### (O, A, B, AB)

Any small, whole, white-fleshed fish can be steamed by this method. Varying the sauce permits you a wide range of delicious possibilities (see Dressings and Relishes on page 405). Steam the fish on a heavy, restaurant-style platter that fits inside the top of a steaming utensil. A large wok, bamboo steamer, or a traditional fish poacher with removable "tray" modified to lift fish above the boiling water are all suitable. It is worth working out some kind of system for this recipe because not only is it easy, it is a way to serve mixed blood types the same meal using personalized sauces.

*1½ pounds/675 g red snapper, head and tail on; washed, cleaned, scaled, and trimmed*
*3 tablespoons olive oil*
*3 cloves garlic, peeled and smashed*
*5 spring onions, sliced small*

*2 tablespoons tamari*
*1 to 2 tablespoons sesame oil (Type O only)*
*1 spring onion, slivered lengthwise*
*Handful coriander, chopped*

Steam the fish for 10 to 15 minutes. To prepare the sauce, heat the oil in a heavy pan and gently sauté garlic and spring onions until just soft but not brown. Remove from the heat and add the tamari. Type O can add 1 to 2 teaspoons sesame oil. When the fish is done, drain accumulated juices and pour the sauce over fish. Garnish with slivered spring onion and coriander. *Serves 3 to 4.*

## Tofu and Tempeh

### TOFU VEGETABLE STIR-FRY

#### (O, A, AB)

*2 to 3 tablespoons olive oil*
*1 medium onion, diced*
*1 head broccoli, cut into flowers, stems sliced*
*1 small bunch bok choy, sliced into 1-inch/2.5-cm pieces*
*6 cloves garlic, crushed*
*4 fluid ounces/110 ml Vegetable Stock (page 354) or water*
*½ pound/225 g mangetouts*
*1 cake tofu, cut into ½-inch/1-cm cubes*
*1 tablespoon tamari*
*1¼ teaspoons arrowroot (optional)*

In a wok or large heavy frying pan, heat the olive oil and add the onion, stirring constantly over a fairly high heat. Add the broccoli, stirring a moment or two. Add the bok choy, stirring again. Add the garlic. Add the vegetable stock or water, let it come to a boil, and then cover, steaming vegetables for several minutes until the broccoli is tender but still crisp. Add the mangetouts, and a minute or two later, the tofu. Reduce the heat and let it steam a few more minutes. Add tamari, stir well, and serve. If you prefer a thick sauce, push the vegetables to one side, add 1¼ teaspoons arrowroot, stirring until thickened. Remix the contents of the wok before serving. *Serves 4 to 6.*

## RICE STICKS AND TOFU WITH VEGETABLES

### (O, A, AB)

These rice sticks are not the same as the rice spaghetti you find in the stores. They are, instead, similar in texture to bean threads.

*4 fluid ounces/110 ml tamari sauce*
*4 tablespoons water*
*1 tablespoon sugar*
*5 cloves garlic, peeled and mashed or put through a press*
*5 spring onions, sliced thin*
*1-inch/2.5-cm piece of ginger, grated*
*2 tablespoons vegetable oil*
*2 packs firm tofu, drained*
*1 pack rice sticks*
*1 bag fresh spinach, washed and stems removed*
*1 pound/450 g green beans or sugar snap peas, washed, stems removed*
*2 tablespoons chopped fresh coriander*

Combine the tamari, water, sugar, garlic, spring onions, ginger, and vegetable oil. Marinate the tofu in this mixture for at least 1 hour. Grill the tofu for 5 minutes on each side. Set aside.

Cook the noodles according to the instructions. Drain and rinse again in warm water; drain well. Remove to a platter. Steam the vegetables and arrange around the noodles. Slice the tofu and place on top of the noodles. Pour the marinade over the tofu and top with chopped coriander. *Serves 4.*

## TEMPEH KEBABS

### (O, A, AB)

*1 pack tempeh, any flavour*
*6 ounces/150 g plum jam*
*2 fluid ounces/50 ml pineapple juice (from the pineapple)*
*3 tablespoons tamari sauce*
*2 cloves garlic, through a press*
*2 spring onions, sliced thin*
*1 large onion, quartered and separated into layers, two layers per piece*
*2 portabello mushrooms, cut into 1- by 1-inch (2.5×2.5 cm) pieces*

*2 medium courgettes, cut into 1-inch/2.5-cm slices*
*1 pound/450 g pineapple chunks, about 1- by 1-inch (2.5×2.5 cm) pieces*

Steam the tempeh for 10 to 15 minutes. Meanwhile, combine the plum jam, pineapple juice, tamari, garlic, and spring onions to make the barbecue sauce. When the tempeh is cool enough to handle, slice into same-sized pieces as the vegetables. Skewer the pieces by alternating vegetables with the tempeh and pineapple. Brush with the marinade and grill under medium heat until nicely browned. Note: When skewering the courgettes, do so through the green, since the inside is pulpy and will not hold on well. Serve on a bed of rice. *Serves 4.*

## BUTTERNUT SQUASH AND TOFU WITH MIXED VEGETABLES

### (A, AB)

*1 butternut squash*
*1 pack of tofu (fresh and soft is best)*
*4 fluid ounces/110 ml of soy or other nut milk*
*6 fluid ounces/160 ml low-salt soy sauce*
*4 fluid ounces/110 ml raw honey*
*2 tablespoons ground mace*
*2 tablespoons ground ginger*
*1 teaspoon ground nutmeg*
*1 pressed clove of garlic*
*Pinch of curry powder (optional)*
*1 head of organic broccoli*
*½ head of organic cauliflower*
*1 pound/450 g green beans*
*6 large carrots, julienned*
*Garnish: shelled sunflower or pumpkin seeds, and fresh coriander*

Remove the seeds and clean the centre of the squash. Slice lengthwise and steam for 15 to 20 minutes or until soft. Remove the skin and cut into small pieces. Add the squash and all of the other ingredients (except vegetables) to a large mixing bowl. Whip with an electric mixer until smooth and fluffy. Transfer to a large frying pan and simmer on low for 15 to 20 minutes. Steam the broccoli, cauliflower, beans, and carrots until al dente, about 10 to 15 minutes, or until brightly coloured and moist. To serve, place 2 ladles of mashed squash in the centre of a dinner plate. Arrange the steamed veggies around the squash. Garnish with nuts or seeds and coriander. *Serves 6.*

## TOFU AND BLACK BEAN CHILLI

### (O, A)

*4 tablespoons vegetable oil*
*2 onions, diced*
*1 red pepper, diced (Type O only)*
*½ tablespoon ground chilli*
*½ tablespoon ground cumin*
*1 tablespoon ground coriander*
*1 tablespoon chopped fresh thyme*
*1 teaspoon ground cloves*
*2 tablespoons spelt flour*
*2 cans black beans, drained and rinsed or 8 ounces/225 g dry black beans,*
*soaked overnight and cooked al dente*
*8 to 12 fluid ounces/225–335 ml Chicken Stock (page 353)*
*1 bay leaf*
*6 cloves garlic, peeled and chopped*
*1 pack firm tofu, drained and cubed*

In a large pot heat the oil and add the onions and red pepper. Cook 2 minutes, until wilted, and add all of the spices, stirring and toasting well to release the
flavours. Add the flour and cook 2 more minutes. Be sure this spice paste does not
burn. Add the black beans, stirring well to coat with the spices. Add most of the
chicken stock, bay leaf, and garlic. Stir to incorporate and simmer for 30 minutes,
adding additional chicken stock as needed. For the last 10 minutes of cooking,
add the tofu. Since tofu can be rather fragile, handle it gently, using a wooden
spoon. Be sure to remove the bay leaf before serving. Serve with rice or homemade tortillas. *Serves 4 to 6.*

## KUNG PAO TOFU AND CHICKEN

### (A)

*½ pound/225 g extra-firm tofu, cubed*
*4 tablespoons water*
*1 tablespoon cornflour*
*4 tablespoons soy sauce*
*1 teaspoon sugar*
*Vegetable oil for frying*

*2 to 10 dried red chillies (the ones that look like trumpets)*
*2 ounces/50 g unskinned, unsalted peanuts*
*½ pound/225 g boneless, skinless chicken breast, cubed*
*1 bunch spring onions, cut into 1-inch/2.5-cm pieces (white and green parts)*

Put a medium pot of salted water to boil; place the tofu into the rapidly boiling salted water. Let the tofu remain in the water until it returns to a boil and the tofu cubes rise to the top. Drain.

To make the sauce: In a bowl, mix the cornflour into the water. Add the soy sauce and sugar. Stir to blend.

To cook the dish: (A non-stick frying pan works well; keep the flame/temperature on medium high throughout the approximately 10 minutes it takes to complete the dish.) Heat the pan and pour enough oil to coat the bottom. Fry chillies until they begin to turn brown. Remove with a slotted spoon to a plate. In the same oil, fry the peanuts until they begin to turn brown and remove them with a slotted spoon to a plate. In same oil, fry the tofu and chicken cubes. Let the chicken and tofu cook until brown (the tofu will be crispy-looking), turning to brown all sides, about 5 to 7 minutes. Pour the sauce over all. The sauce will thicken very quickly—30 to 60 seconds. (This is not a runny-sauce dish.) Add the spring onions and cook together less than a minute. Add the chillies and peanuts back to re-warm for a few seconds and serve! Serve with a nice Asian rice.

## TOFU-SESAME FRY

### (O, A, AB)

*2 tablespoons olive oil*
*1 cake tofu*
*1 to 2 tablespoons white sesame seeds*
*1 to 2 tablespoons black sesame seeds*
*Salt*
*Lemon juice*
*3 to 4 tablespoons tahini*
*Juice of ½ lemon*
*1 teaspoon tamari*

Heat olive oil in a heavy frying pan. Slice tofu about ½ inch (1 cm) thick. Coat half the slices with the white seeds, the other half with the black. Carefully fry in the oil, a few minutes on each side. Serve with a sprinkle of salt and a squeeze of lemon. Or drizzle a little tahini, thinned with a little lemon juice and 1 teaspoon tamari, over the tofu. *Allow 2 slices per serving.*

## SILKEN SCRAMBLE

### (O, A, AB)

Silken is the softest tofu available and makes a wonderful substitute for eggs, ricotta, or yogurt.

*1 tablespoon olive oil*
*1 teaspoon Garlic-Shallot Mixture (page 409)*
*1 small carrot, grated*
*1 small courgette, grated*
*5 ounces/125 g silken tofu*
*Salt to taste*
*1 tablespoon chopped fresh basil*

In a small frying pan, heat the oil and sauté the Shallot-Garlic Mixture on low for 2 minutes. Add the grated carrot and cook another 3 to 4 minutes. Add the courgette and silken tofu. With a spoon, chop the silken tofu as it warms and stir the whole mix until warmed. Season with salt and basil.

## FRUIT SILKEN SCRAMBLE

### (O, A, B, AB)

| TYPE O | TYPES A, B, AB |
|---|---|
| *2 tablespoons unsalted butter* | *2 tablespoons margarine* |
| *1 banana, sliced* | *1 peach, sliced with pit removed* |
| *6 ounces/150 g blueberries* | *6 ounces/150 g blueberries* |
| *8 ounces/225 g silken tofu, drained* | *8 ounces/225 g silken tofu, drained* |
| *Salt to taste* | *Salt to taste* |

In a medium frying pan, melt the shortening and gently cook the fruit for 2 to 3 minutes. Bananas are always extra delicious if they can caramelize a bit. Push the fruit to one side and add the silken to the other side, chopping and warming it. The fruit and silken tofu are kept separate so that the silken doesn't get too discoloured by the berries. At the final minute of cooking, toss together, add the salt, and serve in a fruit bowl.

## GRILLED WILD RICE TEMPEH

### (O, A, AB )

*1 pack wild rice tempeh*
*3 tablespoons olive oil*
*2 tablespoons tamari*
*2 tablespoons Garlic-Shallot Mixture (page 409)*
*2 tablespoons chopped fresh coriander*
*2 tablespoons lemon juice*

Remove the tempeh from the wrapper and place in a shallow bowl. In a small bowl, mix together the remaining ingredients and pour this marinade over the tempeh, turning once. Refrigerate for several hours. For a quick marinade, first steam tempeh for 20 minutes then marinate for 1 hour. Grill under medium flame, turning and basting with the marinade until nicely browned, about 15 minutes. Let it sit a few minutes before slicing. Serve with brown rice pilaf and a crisp romaine salad for a delightfully light but satisfying meal. *Serves 4.*

## SPICY STIR-FRIED TOFU WITH APRICOTS AND ALMONDS

### (O, A, AB)

### SPICY CURRY MARINADE

*2 tablespoons tamari*
*1 tablespoon fresh lemon or lime juice (about ½ lemon)*
*1 tablespoon chopped coriander*
*1 tablespoon chopped chives*
*1 tablespoon sugar*
*2 teaspoons curry powder*
*1 teaspoon chilli powder*
*1 teaspoon black sesame seeds*
*1 cake firm tofu, drained and cut into cubes*

Combine the tamari, lemon or lime juice, coriander, chives, sugar, curry powder, chilli powder, and black sesame seeds to make the marinade. Add the tofu cubes, tossing lightly once to cover. Let marinate for 1 hour or longer. Prepare the rest of the stir-fry.

*3 tablespoons olive oil*
*1 small onion or 3 spring onions, sliced*

*3 carrots, sliced on an angle*
*2 cloves garlic, crushed*
*6 ounces/150 g sliced apricots (dried or fresh)*
*3 ounces/75 g sliced almonds*

Heat the oil in a wok or large frying pan. Quickly cook the onion or spring onions, add the carrots and the garlic, and cook 2 minutes on a medium-high flame, watching that the garlic doesn't burn. Add the tofu all at once and reserve whatever marinade is left over, adding 2 tablespoons of water. Set the diluted marinade aside. Cook the tofu until heated through, and then add the apricots and almonds. Cook 3 more minutes and serve over white basmati rice with the remainder of the marinade.

## TASTY TOFU-PUMPKIN STIR-FRY

### (A, AB)

*One small pumpkin, diced (raw)*
*One pack of honey-sesame flavoured (or other flavour) baked tofu, diced*
*2 tablespoons vegetable oil*
*½ teaspoon mace*
*⅛ teaspoon cloves*
*Salt to taste*

Stir-fry the diced pumpkin in oil. When the pumpkin begins to soften, add spices and toss for a minute or two. Add diced tofu and stir-fry until tofu is heated through. Serve the stir-fried mixture over steamed rice (optional) and add salt to taste, if desired. *Makes 2 to 3 servings.*

## TERIYAKI TOFU STEAK

### (A, AB)

*1 pound/450 g extra-firm tofu, well drained*
*2 medium cloves garlic, crushed*
*2 spring onions, chopped*
*2 tablespoons honey*
*6 tablespoons soy sauce*
*4 tablespoons olive oil*
*1 tablespoon arrowroot powder*

Cut the tofu into six equal ½-inch (1-cm) strips. Marinate the tofu in garlic, spring onions, honey, soy sauce, and 2 tablespoons oil for 20 minutes. Heat the remaining oil in wok over medium heat. Cook the tofu in the wok until brown on both sides. Place on a serving platter. Bring the leftover marinade sauce to a boil and simmer for 2 minutes. Thicken the sauce with the arrowroot. Pour over the tofu before serving. *Makes 5 servings.*

## Pasta and Noodles

### SOBA NOODLES WITH PUMPKIN AND TOFU

**(O, A, AB)**

*2 tablespoons olive oil*
*6 cloves garlic, crushed*
*1 medium leek, thinly sliced (Type O use onion)*
*Small fresh pumpkin*
*1 pound/450 g tofu*
*1 pound/450 g soba noodles*

Put a pot of water on to boil. In a large, heavy frying pan, heat the olive oil and add the crushed garlic and the leek, stirring for a few moments. Add 4 fluid ounces (100 ml) of water, cover, and let steam over low heat until the leeks are tender, 10 to 15 minutes. Add more water if necessary. Meanwhile, cut the pumpkin in half, remove the seeds (save for toasting later) and carefully peel. Cut into manageable pieces for eating (½ to 1 inch/1–2.5 cm) and add to the pan with the garlic and leek. Add another 4 fluid ounces of water again and steam the pumpkin until tender, about 10 to 15 minutes. The water for the soba should be boiling. Add the noodles and cook according to the package directions. When all the vegetables are done, cut the tofu into ½-inch (1-cm) pieces, add to the pan, and heat thoroughly. Put the pumpkin mixture on top of the hot soba noodles. *Serves 4 to 6.*

### STUFFED CANNELLONI SHELLS WITH PESTO

**(B, AB)**

*1 pound/450 g cannelloni shells (either spelt, semolina, or rice flour)*
*1 pound/450 g ricotta cheese*
*½ pound/225 g mozzarella cheese*
*8 fluid ounces/225 ml Vegetable Stock (page 354)*
*Pesto (page 409)*

Boil the pasta until done, undercooking by a minute or two. In a bowl, combine the ricotta and mozzarella. Put about 1 tablespoon inside each shell, then place them into a buttered glass baking dish, lining them up in neat little rows. When all the shells are filled, pour in the vegetable stock, cover dish with aluminum foil, and bake at 150°C/gas 2 for about 20 minutes. Remove from oven and serve, spooning pesto over the top. *Serves 4.*

## GREEN LEAFY PASTA

### (A, B, AB)

*1 pound/450 g spinach pasta (Types B and AB) or 1 pound artichoke pasta (Type A)*
*4 tablespoons olive oil*
*2 leeks, washed and sliced*
*3 cloves garlic, chopped*
*1 bunch spinach, washed and rinsed*
*1 bunch Swiss chard, washed and trimmed*
*Salt and pepper to taste*
*Romano cheese to taste*

Bring a large pot of water to a boil, cook the pasta, drain, and dress with a little oil. Keep covered. Meanwhile, in a large frying pan, heat the olive oil and add the leeks, turning to coat with the oil. Over a medium heat, cook them gently for several minutes, until they begin to soften and wilt. Add the garlic and stir, and a few moments later add the spinach and Swiss chard and turn to coat with oil and garlic. The greens will begin to wilt. Steam, uncovered, so the water evaporates for several more minutes, or until the greens are fully cooked. Mix with pasta, season to taste and grate on some Romano. *Serves 4.*

## LASAGNE WITH PORTABELLO MUSHROOMS AND PESTO

### (AB)

*One box of lasagne sheets*
*1 2-pound/900-g pack low-fat ricotta*
*2½ pints/1.4 l organic tomato sauce*
*4 firm portabello mushrooms, sliced ¼-inch/½-cm thick*
*½ pound/225 g low-fat mozzarella*
*8 tablespoons Pesto (page 409)*

Preheat oven to 190°C/gas 5. In an 8-by-13-inch (20×33 cm) lasagne dish, assemble the ingredients as follows:

A quarter of the tomato sauce on the bottom
A third of the uncooked lasagne to cover the sauce
Half the ricotta, spread evenly
Paint on half of the pesto
Half of the sliced portabelli over the pesto
Another quarter of the tomato sauce
Another third of the lasagne
The rest of the ricotta
The rest of the pesto
The rest of the portabelli
The last of the lasagne
The rest of the tomato sauce (about half)
All the mozzarella

Bake 1 hour and 15 minutes, remove from oven, and let sit 15 minutes.

## CELLOPHANE NOODLES WITH GRILLED SIRLOIN AND GREEN VEGETABLES

### (O, B)

#### MARINADE

*5 tablespoons tamari (wheat-free—check the labels)*
*4 tablespoons water*
*5 cloves garlic, minced or through a press*
*1 tablespoon sugar*
*2 spring onions, sliced thin*
*2 tablespoons vegetable oil*
*2 pounds lean sirloin steak*

Combine the tamari, water, garlic, sugar, spring onions, and vegetable oil and pour over the steak, turning at least once. Marinate for at least 1 hour, but the longer the better.

#### NOODLES

*Cellophane noodles (made from beans)*
*2 cloves garlic, peeled*
*1 pound/450 g sugar snap peas or haricots vert or delicate string beans, stems removed*
*1 bag fresh spinach*
*2 tablespoons chopped fresh coriander*

After marinating the steak, grill it to medium rare and set aside. Bring a pot of water to a boil for the noodles and a small pot of water to a boil to steam the vegetables. Soften the noodles in hot water and then boil according to directions, or until tender. Rinse in warm water and drain thoroughly. Pile high on a platter. Quickly steam the garlic and peas for a minute or so, then add the spinach on top, and steam for 2 more minutes. Arrange the vegetables around the noodles. Slice the steak, place it on top of noodles, and drizzle with the dipping sauce. Top with fresh coriander. *Serves 4.*

### TAMARI DIPPING SAUCE

*4 tablespoons tamari*
*1 lime, juiced*
*1 tablespoon olive oil*
*2 tablespoons chopped coriander*
*1 tablespoon sugar*
*2 tablespoons brown rice vinegar*
*1 clove garlic, mashed*

Combine all ingredients.

## FETTUCCINE WITH GRILLED LAMB SAUSAGES AND VEGETABLES

### (O, B, AB)

*2 red peppers*
*2 yellow peppers*
*2 portabello mushrooms*
*2 cloves mashed garlic (for rubbing vegetables and to toss with pasta)*
*4 tablespoons olive oil (for brushing on vegetables and on pasta)*
*1 pound/450 g lamb sausages*
*1 pound/450 g rice fettuccine (any shape rice pasta is fine)*
*Salt to taste*
*2 tablespoons chopped fresh basil*
*Romano cheese*

Prepare a medium-hot grill. Prepare the vegetables by slicing the peppers in half lengthwise and removing the seeds and stems. Remove the stems from the mushrooms so they lie flat on the grill. Rub all vegetables with garlic and brush with oil. Grill sausages until nicely browned and juices run clear. Hold the sausages on the side of the grill to keep them warm while the vegetables are cooking. Meanwhile, cook the pasta in plenty of boiling water, drain, and rinse with warm water when done. Pour remaining olive oil over pasta and season with salt. When all the vegetables are nicely grilled (they should be soft but not burned), slice into long strips and toss with garlic. Serve atop the fettuccine along with a couple of sausages. Sprinkle with fresh basil and grated Romano cheese. *Serves 4.*

## COLD BUCKWHEAT NOODLES WITH PEANUT SAUCE

### (A)

*1 pack buckwheat (soba) noodles*
*4 ounces/100 g shredded Romaine, washed and dried*
*5 ounces/125 g grated carrots*
*2 spring onions, sliced thin*
*chopped fresh coriander*

Cook the noodles in plenty of water, according to the package. Drain and rinse in tepid water. Toss with the Peanut Sauce. On a platter or 2 serving plates spread the lettuce and then the grated carrots and roll the noodles on top. Sprinkle with chopped spring onions and fresh coriander and serve. *Serves 2.*

### PEANUT SAUCE

*1 clove garlic, peeled and crushed*
*2 spring onions*
*4 tablespoons fresh coriander, washed and coarsely chopped*
*8 tablespoons peanut butter*
*4 tablespoons tamari*
*1 tablespoon brown rice vinegar*
*4 fluid ounces/100 ml water*
*Juice of 1 lemon*

In a food processor, chop the garlic, spring onions, and coriander on high speed. Add peanut butter, tamari, lemon juice, and vinegar. The mixture will be very thick. Slowly add water until the sauce reaches the desired consistency.

## PASTA (RICE OR SPELT) WITH RAPPINI (BROCCOLI RABE)

### (O, A, B, AB)

*1 bag pasta of choice*
*2 tablespoons olive oil*
*2 tablespoons Garlic-Shallot Mixture (page 409)*

*1 bunch rappini (broccoli rabe), washed and trimmed*
*2 to 3 tablespoons water*
*2 tablespoons tamari*
*1 tablespoon olive oil*
*Salt to taste*
*Freshly shaved Pecorino Romano*

Prepare to cook the pasta by bringing a pot to boil with plenty of water. Heat the oil in a large frying pan. Add the Garlic-Shallot Mixture and cook for 1 minute. Meanwhile, cut the tip off the stems of the broccoli rabe and discard. Cut the remaining greens into thirds. Put in the pan and cook a few minutes, turn once, add 2 tablespoons water, cover, and cook another few minutes. "Throw" the pasta in boiling water and stir well, return to a boil, and stir again. The pasta will cook in about 5 to 7 minutes. At this point, check the broccoli rabe. If it is tender, remove from the pan and dress with 2 tablespoons tamari and set aside. Drain the pasta and toss with a tablespoon of oil and salt to taste. Serve pasta topped with the rabe and freshly shaved Pecorino Romano cheese. *Serves 4.*

## QUINOA FLOUR TORTILLAS WITH PUREED PINTO BEANS

### (O, A, AB)

### TORTILLAS

*10 ounces/250 g quinoa flour*
*6 ounces/150 g white spelt flour*
*1 teaspoon salt*
*1½ teaspoons baking powder*
*4 tablespoons vegetable oil (for Type B, substitute olive oil)*
*12 fluid ounces/340 ml warm water*

In a large mixing bowl, stir together the dry ingredients. Add the oil and water. Using a wooden spoon, mix until the dough forms a ball. Turn onto a well-floured surface and knead for 10 minutes. Cover loosely with plastic wrap and let the dough "rest" for another 10 minutes. Divide the dough into 14 pieces and form into balls. With a rolling pin, flatten each ball into a 10-inch (25-cm) tortilla. In a 12-inch (30-cm) pan or griddle, cook 1 minute on each side. Be sure not to overcook or the tortillas will become too brittle. As you remove them from the pan, wrap them in a large clean dish towel. *Yields 14 tortillas.*

## PUREED PINTO BEANS

*2 tablespoons olive oil*
*1 medium onion, diced*
*6 cloves garlic, crushed*
*1 can pinto beans, drained and rinsed, or 6 ounces/150 g dry beans, soaked and cooked*
*1 teaspoon powdered cumin*
*A generous pinch salt*
*A handful chopped coriander*

In a frying pan, heat 2 tablespoons olive oil and add the diced onion. Cook 10 minutes over very low heat, stirring frequently, until onion is golden brown. Add the crushed garlic and sauté a few more minutes. Add the beans and spices and cook another few minutes. Put in the blender and puree until very smooth. You might have to scrape down the blender once or twice. Sprinkle with coriander and serve. *Serves 4.*

## Legumes and Grains

### BUTTER BEANS WITH GOAT'S CHEESE AND SPRING ONIONS

#### (O, B)

*6 ounces/150 g dried or 12 ounces/300 g fresh butter beans*
*1 tablespoon olive oil*
*2 spring onions, finely sliced*
*2 cloves garlic, crushed*
*2 to 3 tablespoons dressing of choice*
*4 ounces/100 g goat's cheese*

Prepare the beans and place them into a serving bowl. In a frying pan, heat the oil and sauté the spring onions for a minute or two until fragrant. Add the crushed garlic, turning briefly until it just begins to colour. Add spring onions and garlic to beans. Pour 2 to 3 tablespoons of the chosen dressing over the beans and toss gently. Crumble the goat's cheese over the top. Serve at room temperature. *Serves 4.*

### BLACK-EYED PEAS, OKRA, AND LEEK MELANGE

#### (A)

*½ small yellow onion*
*1 leek*

*⅛ teaspoon turmeric*
*½ teaspoon ground coriander*
*14 ounces/400 g frozen okra*
*16-ounce/450-g can of black-eyed peas*
*3 tablespoons wheat-free tamari*

Chop the onion and sauté for 2 minutes. Add well-washed and sliced leek and dried spices. Immediately add the frozen okra. Cook on high until okra is warm and soft (about 5 minutes). Add the black-eyed peas and tamari and reduce the heat to medium. Cook until the peas are warm—about 5 minutes. Serve over rice.

## BLACK-EYED PEAS WITH LEEKS

### (O, A)

If you use canned beans, or if you think ahead to soak some the night before, this is an easy, delicious dish, served either hot or cold.

*12 ounces/300 g cooked black-eyed peas*
*1 tablespoon olive oil*
*1 small leek, thinly sliced*
*1 clove garlic, crushed*
*Pinch of salt*
*½ handful coriander to garnish*

Put the beans in a pot. In a frying pan, heat the oil and add the leeks and garlic, turning well to coat with oil. Add 4 tablespoons of water, cover, and braise the leeks over low heat until soft. Add more water as needed, a tablespoon at a time. When the leeks are tender, add them to the beans and heat thoroughly.

## LENTIL SALAD

### (A, AB)

Bean salads taste great and are excellent backdrops to other, interesting ingredients. This is a slightly "sweet" salad that is perfect for lunch.

*12 ounces/300 g lentils*
*Plenty of water*
*3 ounces/75 g dried cherries*
*3 ounces/75 g raisins*
*2 ounces/50 g broken walnuts*
*2 tablespoons olive oil*

*Juice of ½ lemon*
*Pinch of salt*

Cook the lentils in the water until done, 30 to 40 minutes. Start checking at 30 minutes because lentils can get overcooked very quickly. Drain and let cool. Add the cherries, raisins, and walnuts. Whisk together the olive oil, lemon, and salt and pour over the salad, mixing gently and thoroughly. *Serves 4 to 6.*

## PUREED PINTO BEANS WITH GARLIC

### (O, A, AB)

*2 tablespoons olive oil*
*1 medium onion, diced*
*6 cloves garlic, crushed*
*1 can pinto beans, drained and rinsed, or 6 ounces/150 g dry beans, soaked and cooked*
*1 teaspoon powdered cumin (or more to taste)*
*Generous pinch salt*
*Handful chopped coriander (garnish)*

In a frying pan, heat the olive oil and add the diced onion. Cook 10 minutes over very low heat, stirring frequently, until onion is golden brown. Add the crushed garlic and sauté a few more minutes. Add the beans and spices and cook another few minutes. Put in the blender and puree until very smooth. You might have to scrape down the blender once or twice. Serve sprinkled with the coriander. *Serves 4.*

## FARO PILAF

### (O, A, B, AB)

Faro, the Italian word for "spelt", makes a delectable change from rice in this pilaf.

*5 ounces/125 g faro*
*16 fluid ounces/450 ml water*
*2 tablespoons olive oil*
*3 cloves garlic, crushed*
*2 small courgettes, cut into small dice*
*Salt*
*Pecorino Romano cheese*

Place the faro and water in saucepan. Bring to a boil, reduce heat, cover, and steam until all the water is absorbed, about 20 minutes. Meanwhile, add olive oil to a heavy frying pan. Heat the oil and add the garlic. Sauté a few moments over low-medium heat, then add the courgettes. Continue to stir until coated with oil. Cover and steam until soft, about 5 minutes. Remove from the heat and toss in the bowl with the faro. Add salt to taste. Grate on a little Pecorino Romano if you'd like. *Serves 3 to 4.*

## WILD AND BASMATI RICE PILAF

### (O, A, AB)

*7 ounces/175 g wild rice, cooked in 16 to 24 fluid ounces/450–675 ml water*
*6 ounces/150 g basmati rice, cooked in 16 fluid ounces/450 ml water*
*3 spring onions, sliced*
*4 tablespoons olive oil*
*2 teaspoons salt*

In two separate saucepans, cook the rices. When done, combine the two rices, toss with the spring onions and olive oil, and season with salt.

## MILLET TABBOULEH

### (O, A, B, AB)

*16 fluid ounces/450 ml water (Vegetable Stock makes for more flavour; see page 354)*
*6 ounces/150 g millet (lightly toasted in pan, no oil please)*
*3 spring onions, sliced thinly*
*1 cucumber, peeled and seeded, small dice (Type O omit cucumber)*
*3 plum tomatoes, chopped (optional)*
*2 tablespoons chopped fresh mint*
*2 tablespoons olive oil*
*Juice of 1 lemon*
*Salt to taste*

Bring the water to a boil, add the millet, stir, return to boil, reduce heat, and simmer 15 to 20 minutes, or until all the water is absorbed. Let sit off heat for 10 minutes. Remove to a bowl and let cool slightly. Add the spring onions, cucumber, tomatoes, and mint. Mix well and dress with oil and lemon and add salt to taste.

## MILLET COUSCOUS

### (O, A, B, AB)

*6 ounces/150 g millet (lightly toasted, no oil, please)*
*1¼ pints/650 ml water or Vegetable Stock (page 354)*
*2 carrots, small dice*
*1 small red onion, small dice*
*4 tablespoons raisins, plumped (by soaking in hot water)*
*3 tablespoons sunflower seeds (Types O and A)*
*or 3 tablespoons chopped walnuts (Types O, B, and AB)*
*2 tablespoons olive oil*
*1 lemon, juiced*
*Salt to taste*

Cook the millet (as directed in the Millet Tabbouleh recipe, page 348) and remove to a bowl. Add the carrots, red onion, raisins, and sunflower seeds or walnuts. In a small bowl, whisk together the olive oil and lemon juice and pour over
the millet. Add salt to taste. This is also delicious topped with silken tofu.


## SPELTBERRY AND BASMATI RICE PILAF

### (O, A, B, AB)

*4 ounces/100 g cooked speltberries*
*7 ounces/175 g cooked basmati rice (more rice works well, too)*
*2 spring onions, diced*
*2 tablespoons olive oil*
*Salt to taste*

Combine all of the ingredients and let sit for at least 15 minutes. Serve at room
temperature.


## SPELTBERRY AND RICE SALAD

### (O, B, AB)

*4 ounces/100 g cooked speltberries*
*7 to 10 ounces/175–250 g cooked rice (any kind)*
*1 yellow pepper, diced small*

*3 tablespoons chopped sweet basil*
*1 tablespoon finely diced jalapeños (not for Type AB)*
*3 tablespoons olive oil*
*Salt to taste*

Combine all of the ingredients and serve at room temperature. This salad can be refrigerated for up to four days.

## QUINOA RISOTTO

### (O, A, B, AB)

*2 tablespoons olive oil*
*1 onion, diced*
*2 cloves garlic, minced*
*1 red pepper, very small dice (optional)*
*3 tablespoons chopped sweet basil*
*12 ounces/300 g quinoa*
*1½ pints/800 ml Vegetable Stock (page 354)*
*Salt and pepper to taste*

Heat the oil in a medium saucepan and add the onion and garlic. Cook a few minutes on medium heat, being careful not to burn the garlic. Add the red pepper and chopped sweet basil and continue cooking for another minute. Rinse the quinoa before adding. Cook the quinoa for a few moments, then add the vegetable stock (water will do, although vegetable broth is so sweet and delicious). Bring to a boil, reduce to a simmer, and cover for 15 minutes. Season with salt and pepper. Serve immediately. This recipe is also delicious cold the following day for lunch. *Serves 4.*

## BROWN RICE PILAF

### (O, A, B, AB)

*7 ounces/175 g brown rice*
*16 fluid ounces/450 ml water for cooking rice*
*2 tablespoons olive oil*
*4 cloves garlic, crushed*
*1 large carrot, diced*
*8 tablespoons water*

*½ handful chopped coriander*
*Salt to taste*

Place rice and water in a saucepan. Bring to a boil, reduce heat, cover, and steam for 40 minutes, or until all water has been absorbed. Always check your rice toward the end of the cooking time. Rices are particular and vary slightly. While the rice is cooking, heat 2 tablespoons of olive oil in a heavy frying pan, add the crushed garlic cloves, and sauté gently for a few moments. Add the carrot, stir to coat with oil, and add the smaller quantity of water. Reduce the heat, cover the pan, and simmer until the carrot is tender but not soft. Check carefully that there is always sufficient water to braise the carrot, adding water in small quantities if necessary. Add the chopped coriander for the last moments, letting it steam. When the rice is done, place the carrot and rice in a bowl and mix gently. Add salt to taste. *Serves 4.*

## WILD RICE SALAD

### (O, A, AB)

*2¼ pints/1.2 l water*
*7 ounces/175 g wild rice*
*4 ounces/100 g walnuts*
*5 ounces/125 g dried cherries*
*6 ounces/150 g dried diced apricots*
*4 tablespoons olive oil*
*Juice of 1 lemon*
*1 tablespoon maple syrup*
*Salt*

Boil the water and add the wild rice. Cover, reduce heat, and simmer for about 45 minutes, or until tender. Drain any remaining water and reserve for stock. Toss the rice lightly with a fork. Plump unsulphured apricots over boiling water until soft. When the rice has cooled somewhat, add walnuts, cherries, and apricots, mixing well. Whisk together olive oil, lemon juice, maple syrup, and pinch of salt. Pour the dressing over the salad, turning well. Taste for seasoning. *Serves 3 to 4.*

## SPELTBERRY SALAD

### (O, A, B, AB)

*3 pints/1.6 l water*
*4 ounces/100 g speltberries*

*1 cucumber, peeled, if not organic, and diced*
*2 spring onions, sliced finely*
*4 ounces/100 g finely chopped red onion*
*½ handful coriander, chopped*
*2 tablespoons olive oil*
*Juice of 1 lemon*
*Salt to taste*
*Goat's cheese*

Cook spelt in 4 cups of water until tender and chewy, not mushy, about 45 minutes. Add the cucumber, spring onions, red onion, and coriander and mix gently to combine. Dress with olive oil, juice of 1 lemon, and salt to taste. Sprinkle with goat's cheese. *Serves 4.*

## BLACK-EYED PEAS AND BARLEY SALAD

### (O, A)

*4 ounces/100 g cooked black-eyed peas (if canned, then rinse and drain)*
*7 ounces/175 g cooked barley*
*½ red onion, diced small*
*2 tablespoons chopped coriander*
*1 tablespoon salt*
*2 tablespoons olive oil*
*1 tablespoon diced jalapeño pepper (Type O)*
*2 ounces/50 g cooked sweetcorn (Type A)*

Combine all ingredients and let flavours mingle for at least 15 minutes before serving.

## BARLEY BLACK BEAN SALAD

### (O, A)

*3 ounces/75 g black beans*
*1 tablespoon ground cumin*
*3 ounces/75 g barley*
*3 ears fresh sweetcorn (Type O omit)*
*Handful chopped coriander*
*½ red onion, diced small*
*4 tablespoons olive oil*
*Lemon juice to taste*

*Salt*
*1 jalapeño, diced (optional)*

Soak the black beans overnight in water to cover. Drain. Cover with fresh water, add the cumin, and cook on low heat until tender, about 40 minutes. Drain, rinse well, and reserve in a bowl. Boil the barley until done, about 15 to 20 minutes. Drain, rinse, and add to the black beans in the bowl. Cut the corn off the cob, steam until tender, and add to the beans and barley. Mix in the coriander and red onion and cool all ingredients. Whisk the olive oil, lemon juice, and salt to taste and pour over the salad. Add the jalapeño if desired. Gently turn all ingredients to mix. This can be eaten at room temperature or cool. *Serves 4.*

## ADUKI BEAN AND SWEET BROWN RICE

### (O, A)

*12 ounces/300 g cooked aduki beans (leftover or canned is fine)*
*14 ounces/350 g sweet brown rice*
*3 pints/1.6 l water or Vegetable Stock (page 354)*
*2 teaspoons salt*
*1 small red onion, diced small*
*4 tablespoons chopped fresh coriander (always wash first)*
*2 ounces/50 g crumbled goat's cheese*

If the beans have not been cooked, then cook according to the directions on package. Aduki are small and delicate and really do not have to be soaked overnight. If you start soaking them in the morning, they will be ready to cook by that afternoon.

Cook the rice by placing the rice, stock or water, and salt in a 2-quart saucepan. Bring to a boil, turn down the heat, and simmer, covered, until done (about 35 to 40 minutes).

Heat the beans if canned (rinse first) or leftover. In a large serving bowl, combine the hot rice, beans, onion, and coriander. Mix well, but gently. Top with crumbled cheese and serve. *Serves 4 to 6.*

## Soups and Stews

### BASIC STOCK (CHICKEN OR TURKEY)

#### (O, A, B, AB)

It's always a good idea to have stocks on hand. They are basic to any sauce, soup, or stew. Making a stock really takes very little effort, but there are a couple of ways to approach it. The first is to roast a chicken or a turkey and use the carcass and neck and other organs packed inside the bird. The second is to buy necks and backs from the butcher and go from there. Either way is great, and since you are going through the effort, make a lot! Since turkey is neutral for Types O, A, B and highly beneficial for Type AB, it makes sense to make a stock from the ends of a roasted turkey.

The ingredients for stock should always be fresh. A stock can be enriched by the stems of mushrooms and herbs, the peels of onions, tops of leek, or leaves of celery. Everything should be washed well and free of dirt and grit. Do not add the sulphur vegetables like broccoli, cauliflower, or Brussels sprouts. They add a distinct and not so pleasant odour to the basic stock. This is the time to clean out your vegetable rack.

> *1 medium turkey carcass, picked fairly clean (reserve any meat for soup)*
> *2 onions, roots removed, skins on, cut in quarters*
> *3 large carrots, cut into chunks*
> *3 sticks of celery, washed and cut into large pieces*
> *¼ bunch fresh parsley, washed with stems*
> *Fresh herbs like basil, bay leaf, mint, or tarragon*

Fill a very large stock or lobster pot ¾ full with water. Add all the ingredients, bring to a boil, reduce heat, and simmer at least 2½ hours. The stock should reduce by ⅓. Let the stock cool to room temperature and skim any obvious scum or fat from the surface. It's not that critical to get all the fat because once strained and cold the fat will harden on the top. At the same time, the scum sinks to the bottom. Strain out the vegetables. Stock made with bones will gel when cold. The stock can be frozen.

## VEGETABLE STOCK

### (O, A, B, AB)

> *1 large yellow onion, cut into quarters*
> *2 carrots, washed, with ends removed, cut into large pieces*
> *2 celery sticks, washed and cut*
> *Parsley stems*
> *Garlic skins*
> *Apple skins and cores*
> *Mushroom stems*
> *Parsnips*
> *Leeks*

Bring a large pot of water to a boil and add all the ingredients. Simmer for 40 minutes. Cool and strain. Refrigerate or freeze.

## TURKEY SOUP

### (O, A, B, AB)

*4 pints/2 l Turkey Stock (page 353)*
*2 carrots, diced small*
*2 sticks of celery, diced small*
*1 spring onion, sliced (optional)*
*6 ounces/150 g turkey meat, torn into small pieces*
*4 ounces/100 g noodles (rice or spelt)*
*1 tablespoon salt*

In a large saucepan, bring the stock to a boil. Add the carrots and celery and simmer for about 20 minutes, or until the vegetables are done. Add the spring onion, turkey, and noodles and cook another 10 minutes, or until the noodles are done. *Serves 4.*

## BEEF STEW WITH GREEN BEANS AND CARROTS

### (O, B)

*2 pounds/900 g stew beef*
*4 tablespoons spelt flour (or less, for dredging meat)*
*3 tablespoons vegetable oil*
*1 teaspoon salt*
*1 tablespoon ground cumin*
*½ tablespoon ground kelp*
*1 tablespoon chilli powder*
*Water*
*2 pints/1 l stock (chicken or vegetable) (page 353–354)*
*1 tablespoon Garlic-Shallot Mixture (page 409)*
*or 1 medium onion plus 2 cloves garlic (optional)*
*4 skinny carrots, peeled and sliced on the diagonal*
*1 pound/450 g green beans*

Cut away any fat from the meat and cube into bite-sized pieces. Roll lightly in the flour and shake off any excess. Heat oil in a large pot and brown the beef in two batches. After the second one is almost done, replace the first batch of meat and add all the spices. Cook with the meat for 5 minutes on a low heat, then add water to deglaze. Add 1½ pints/850 ml of the stock and stir in the shallot mixture. If you are using onions and garlic add them at this point. Simmer, covered for 1 hour. Check to see if more liquid is needed and add it at this time. Add the carrots and cover again for another 30 minutes. Check for tenderness. Add the green beans and cook another 10 to 15 minutes.

## MIXED ROOTS SOUP

### (O, A, B, AB)

*2 tablespoons olive oil*
*4 ounces/100 g diced leeks or 5½ ounces/140 g diced onions (Type O use onion)*
*6 cloves garlic, crushed*
*4 ounces/100 g diced turnips and/or 4 ounces/100 g swede*
*4 ounces/100 g diced carrots*
*4 ounces/100 g diced parsnips*
*Boiling water to cover, about 3 pints/1.6 l*
*Salt*
*Bay leaf*
*Handful of basil, chopped*

Cut all vegetables into a roughly uniform dice so that they will cook at the same rate. Heat olive oil in a heavy casserole dish. Add your chosen onion and the garlic. Sauté in oil until fragrant, about 5 minutes. Add hardest vegetables first (turnips and swede) and turn in oil a few minutes. Add carrots and parsnips, turning for several minutes more. Pour enough boiling water over all these vegetables to cover by an inch, add the salt and bay leaf, and simmer for 45 minutes, or until vegetables are tender. The soup can be coarsely mashed in its cooking pot using a potato masher or you may put it through a blender, food processor, or food mill. Garnish with chopped basil. *Serves 10 to 12.*

## FRESH CHERRIES AND YOGURT SOUP

### (A, B, AB)

*1 pound/450 g pitted cherries*
*3 tablespoons sugar*
*3 2-inch/5-cm slivers of orange peel*
*2 cloves*
*1¼ pints/700 ml water*

*16 fluid ounces/450 ml yogurt*
*Mint leaves*

Combine the cherries, sugar, orange peel, and cloves with water in a pot and poach gently until fruit is tender, 8 to 10 minutes. Remove the cloves and coarsely mash the cherries in their own liquid. Let cool. Add yogurt, mix well, and garnish with mint leaves. *Serves 8.*

## LENTIL SOUP

### (A, AB)

*2½ pints/1.4 l water*
*1 pack dried lentils*
*1 carrot, chopped*
*1 celery stalk, chopped*
*2 to 3 portabello mushrooms, chopped*
*½ onion, chopped*
*1 teaspoon sweet basil*
*2 vegetable bouillon cubes*
*1 tablespoon salt*

In a large pot, combine all the ingredients. Bring to a boil, then turn down heat and simmer for about 1 hour.

## CARROT-TOFU SOUP WITH DILL

### (O, A, AB)

*16 fluid ounces/450 ml water*
*1½ pounds/675 g carrots, peeled and sliced*
*1 small onion*
*1 teaspoon salt*
*16 fluid ounces/450 ml vegetable broth*
*12 ounces/300 g soft silken tofu, regular or low-fat*
*1 tablespoon dill*
*1 teaspoon red miso, or to taste*
*White pepper (optional)*

In a medium saucepan, combine carrots, onion, salt, and vegetable broth, and cook over medium heat until carrots are tender, about 15 minutes. Scoop carrots and onion out of cooking water; place in a blender or food processor. Add tofu, dill, miso, white pepper, and a small amount of the cooking water; puree. Return the puree to the cooking water, mix well and serve immediately. *Makes 4 to 6 servings.*

## CREAM OF BUTTER BEAN SOUP

### (B)

*1 small onion, minced*
*1 tablespoon butter*
*16 fluid ounces/450 ml low-fat milk*
*6 ounces/150 g fresh, or 1 large can thoroughly drained butter beans*
*Salt*
*Parsley, chopped*

Sauté the onion in butter until soft. Add the milk and beans, bring to a boil, reduce heat, and simmer gently until beans are tender. If using frozen, 5 to 7 minutes. If fresh, about the same, but please check often, since they will vary in size. When the beans are done, puree the milk and beans in a blender until smooth. Season with salt. Garnish with chopped parsley. *Serves 4 to 6.*

## FARMER'S VEGETABLE SOUP

### (O, A, B, AB)

*3 medium leeks, trimmed and cut into 1-inch/2.5-cm cubes (Type O use onion)*
*1 medium swede, peeled and cut into 1-inch/2.5-cm cubes*
*1 medium turnip, peeled and cut into 1-inch/2.5-cm cubes*
*1 small parsnip, peeled and cut into 1-inch/2.5-cm cubes*
*1 large carrot, peeled and sliced*
*1 large stalk of celery with leaves, sliced*
*A generous handful or more of baby spinach leaves*
*2 5-inch/12.5-cm sprigs rosemary*
*Salt to taste*
*Hot pepper sauce (optional)*
*2½ pints/1.4 l water*
*3 pints/1.6 l beef or chicken broth*

In a casserole dish add the vegetables and seasonings to the water, plus the beef or chicken broth. Bring to a boil. Reduce the heat and simmer with the lid on for about 30 to 45 minutes. Note: Many different root vegetables will work in this versatile, homey soup. Fennel can be used in place of or in addition to one of the other root vegetables, for example. For a heartier meal, add diced cooked chicken or cooked rice to the bottom of the soup bowl before ladling soup into the bowl.

## MISO SOUP

### (O, A, AB)

*1 piece (about 8 to 10 inches/20 to 25 cm) of giant kelp, wiped quickly with a damp cloth*
*1½ pints/1 l water*
*4 tablespoons miso*
*½ cake tofu, cut into ½-inch/1-cm cubes*
*Additional vegetables according to taste (spring onions, thinly sliced mushrooms,*
*delicate celery leaves, tender dandelion leaves, light-green spinach leaves)*

Place the kelp and water in a large bowl and let it stand overnight. In the morning, discard the kelp and pour the water into a pot. Bring the kelp stock to a simmer. Put the miso in a bowl and add a few tablespoons of kelp stock, stirring to soften and "melt" the miso. Add the softened miso to the pot and bring back to a low simmer. Add the tofu and any vegetables you would like. Let this simmer briefly and serve for breakfast with rice. A quicker, although more temperamental, version of the stock preparation follows: Place kelp and water in a pot and bring just to a boil, slowly. Do not let the water boil or the stock will be ruined. Pull out the kelp and if it is soft, the stock is ready. If the kelp is still too firm, return it to the pot and cook another minute or two. Again, do not boil, adding a few tablespoons of cold water over the brief cooking time. Proceed with the recipe as above.

## JERUSALEM ARTICHOKE SOUP

### (O, A)

*1 pound/450 g Jerusalem artichokes*
*Juice from ½ lemon*
*4 tablespoons butter (or oil)*
*2 leeks, the white part, sliced*
*2 carrots, sliced*
*1¼ pints/700 ml Chicken Stock (page 353)*
*Salt*
*1 pound/450 g soft tofu*

Scrub the Jerusalem artichokes well. (You don't need to peel them if they are well scrubbed.) Slice and toss with lemon juice. Melt the butter in a pan. Add the leeks, carrots, and Jerusalem artichokes. Cover and cook over low heat 20 to 25 minutes. Add 1 pint/550 ml stock and a pinch of salt, cover, and cook 30 minutes longer. Puree with the rest of the stock and the tofu. *Makes 4 servings.*

## CUCUMBER-YOGURT SOUP

### (A, B, AB)

*1 cucumber*
*8 fluid ounces/225 ml yogurt*
*Handful fresh dill*
*Squeeze of lemon*
*Pinch of salt*
*Dill leaves (garnish)*

If the cucumber skin is not too tough, leave it on. Dice the cucumber and put it in the blender with the yogurt, dill, lemon, and salt. Blend until smooth. Pour into a bowl and garnish with some dill leaves.

## ADUKI BEAN AND PUMPKIN OR WINTER SQUASH SOUP

### (A)

*2 tablespoons olive oil*
*2 medium leeks, washed well and sliced thin*
*6 large cloves garlic, chopped*
*Water for cooking*
*1 small pumpkin, 6 to 8 inches across, or*
*1 acorn or butternut squash, peeled and cut into ½-inch pieces*
*2½ pints/1.4 l water*
*1 can aduki beans, drained and rinsed well*
*Salt to taste*

In a heavy pot, heat the oil and add the leeks and garlic. Turn to coat with oil and cook for a few minutes, until they begin to colour. Add enough water to cover the vegetables, bring to a boil, reduce heat, and let simmer 10 minutes. Add the squash to the pot and cover vegetables with the water. Bring to a boil, reduce heat, and simmer 15 to 20 minutes, depending on squash, or until tender. Add drained beans, let them heat through. Salt to taste. *Serves 4 to 6.*

## WHITE BEAN AND WILTED GREENS SOUP

### (O, A, B, AB)

*1 can cooked cannellini beans, drained and rinsed*
*1 clove garlic, peeled and end trimmed*
*12 to 16 fluid ounces/350–450 ml stock (according to type and preference);*
*water will also do, but the flavour of the soup will not be so deep*
*2 handfuls Swiss chard, chopped*
*½ teaspoon salt*
*Black pepper to taste (optional)*

In a 3-pint/1.6-l saucepan, bring the beans, garlic, and stock to a boil. Reduce the heat and simmer for 10 to 15 minutes. Carefully, with a slotted spoon, scoop out the beans with 8 tablespoons liquid into the bowl of a food processor or blender. Or, if you own a handheld processor, leave the soup in the saucepan. (This piece of kitchen equipment is invaluable for just this.) Puree until smooth and return to the saucepan, stirring into the remaining stock. Add the greens, season with salt, and cook another 5 minutes. *Serves 2.*

## MUSHROOM BARLEY SOUP WITH SPINACH

### (A, B)

*1 tablespoon olive oil*
*1 small onion, diced*
*3 ounces/75 g barley (uncooked)*
*1 tablespoon water*
*1 portabello mushroom, halved then sliced*
*3 pints/1.6 l liquid, either Chicken, Turkey, or Vegetable*
*Stock, according to type (pages 353–354);*
*water is acceptable but the flavour will be less deep*
*1 tablespoon salt*
*1 large handful of fresh spinach, washed; stems cut or chopped*

In a 5-pint/2.75-l saucepan, heat the oil and add the onion. Cook 2 minutes or until the onion is wilted. Add the uncooked barley, stirring well into the onion. Cook 2 minutes, and add the water and the mushroom, stirring again. Cover for 2 minutes and reduce heat. When the mushroom is softer, add the stock and bring to a boil. Reduce heat and simmer for 45 to 50 minutes. Season with salt and add the chopped spinach; it will "cook" in a few moments. *Serves 4.*

## CUBAN BLACK BEAN SOUP

### (O, A)

*½ pound/225 g dried black beans*
*1 onion, peeled and chopped*
*4 cloves garlic, peeled and smashed*
*1½ to 2 pints/850 ml to 1 l Chicken or Vegetable Stock (pages 353–354)*
*4 tablespoons fresh lemon juice*
*2 teaspoons salt (or to taste)*
*Lemon for garnish*
*Dollop plain yogurt (Type A only)*

Wash and soak beans in three times the water to cover and refrigerate overnight or for at least 8 hours. Drain and rinse. Put the beans, onion, and garlic in a pot with the stock. Cook the beans slowly on a low heat until very tender, about 1 hour. Let cool slightly, then transfer to the bowl of a food processor and puree in batches, adding liquid from cooking to desired consistency. Stir in lemon juice and salt. Serve immediately with a slice of lemon on top, or chill and serve with a dollop of plain yogurt (Type A only).

## INDIAN LAMB STEW WITH SPINACH

### (B, AB)

*3 tablespoons olive oil*
*1 large onion*
*2 tablespoons ground mustard seed*
*2 tablespoons ground cumin*
*2 tablespoons ground coriander*
*1 tablespoon ground chilli powder*
*4 pound/1.8 kg leg of lamb, cubed small*
*8 fluid ounces/225 ml plain low-fat yogurt*
*Water as needed*
*4 to 5 cloves fresh garlic, peeled and diced*
*2 pounds/900 g fresh spinach, cleaned and chopped*
*Salt to taste*

In a large stew pot or saucepan, heat the oil and add the onion. Cook several minutes until translucent. Add all the spices and cook 2 to 3 minutes to release the flavours. Add the lamb, mixing well into the spices. Bit by bit, stir in the yogurt and add enough water to cover. Stir in the garlic. Simmer the meat, covered, until tender, about 1 hour and 15 minutes. Remove cover and simmer another 15 minutes, if necessary, to reduce liquid. Add the spinach in batches, stirring it down to incorporate it into the stew. It will cook in just a few minutes. Season with salt to taste.

## SIMPLE FISH SOUP

### (O, A, B, AB)

*1 tablespoon olive oil*
*1 carrot, diced small*
*2 small sticks of celery, diced small*
*½ onion, diced small*
*1½ pints/850 ml water*
*¾ pound/300 g sole or monkfish, cut into 1-inch/2.5-cm pieces*
*Salt and pepper to taste*

Heat the olive oil and sauté the carrot, celery, and onion for several minutes. Add water and cook until the vegetables are soft, about 10 minutes. Add the sole or monkfish and cook a few minutes longer, until the fish is thoroughly done. Season with salt and pepper. *Serves 2.*

## Salads

## COLE SLAW

### (B, AB)

*White cabbage, ½ head*
*Red cabbage, ¼ head*
*Chinese cabbage, ½ head*
*2 carrots, grated*
*1 red onion, chopped*
*6 to 8 fluid ounces/175–225 ml Egg-Free Mayonnaise (page 406)*
*2 tablespoons grated horseradish*
*½ teaspoon celery salt*
*1 teaspoon caraway seeds*
*3 to 4 ounces/75–100 g broken walnuts*

The leaves of all 3 cabbages should be finely shredded. Mix in the grated carrots and chopped onion. Combine mayonnaise, horseradish, celery salt, and caraway seeds in a small bowl and pour over the cabbage leaves. Mix well and let marinate in refrigerator several hours to develop flavours. This can be served at room temperature. Add the walnuts just before serving. *Serves 6 to 8.*

## MESCLUN SALAD

### (A, B, AB)

*Walnut Vinaigrette to taste (page 409)*
*1 pound/450 g fresh Mesclun lettuce*
*2 medium tomatoes, sliced (Types O, AB)*
*1 cucumber, sliced (Types A, B, AB)*
*4 tablespoons crumbled Roquefort (sheep's milk)*
*Fresh pepper to taste (optional)*

In a large bowl, spoon in 2 tablespoons of the dressing. Add the lettuce and toss with another tablespoon of the dressing so there is a light coating on the greens. Top with sliced tomato and/or cucumber (according to blood type) and crumbled cheese. Add fresh pepper to taste.

## SUPER BROCCOLI SALAD

### (O, A, B, AB)

*6 to 8 tablespoons mayonnaise*
*2 tablespoons sugar*
*2 tablespoons lemon juice*
*2 large heads of broccoli, broken up into small pieces*
*3–6 ounces/75–150 g raisins*
*4 to 8 tablespoons imitation soy-based bacon bits (Types O, A, AB only)*
*or diced turkey bacon (all types)*
*3 ounces/75 g sunflower seeds or almond slices*

Combine the mayonnaise, sugar, and lemon juice, and allow it to sit. Combine the broccoli, raisins, and soy-based bacon bits or diced turkey bacon. Pour the dressing over the broccoli, raisins, and imitation bacon bits or diced turkey bacon. Stir to distribute dressing and let it sit overnight refrigerated. Dressing melds well as it sits. Just before serving, sprinkle with the seeds or nuts and toss. *Serves 4 to 6.*

## "WATCHDOG SALAD"

### (O)

*Romaine lettuce, thinly sliced*
*A handful of bean sprouts, rinsed*
*2 ounces/50 g broken walnuts*
*1 spring onion, sliced*
*1 grated carrot*
*2 tablespoons raisins*
*4 to 8 ounces/100–200 g cooked roast beef, sliced thinly and cut*
*into matchstick-sized pieces*

Combine the lettuce, sprouts, walnuts, onion, carrot, raisins, and roast beef in a salad bowl. Serve with Honey Mustard Dressing.

## HONEY MUSTARD DRESSING

*8 tablespoons mayonnaise*
*1 tablespoon dry mustard*
*1 teaspoon minced onion*
*4 tablespoons honey*
*1 tablespoon minced sweet basil*

In a small bowl, combine the mayonnaise, mustard, onion, honey, and sweet basil, and mix thoroughly. Pour the honey mustard dressing over the salad.

## SPINACH SALAD

### (O, A, B, AB)

*1 pound/450 g fresh spinach*
*Olive Oil and Lemon Dressing (page 407)*
*1 hard-boiled egg, chopped*
*2 slices organic turkey bacon, cooked and chopped*
*2 tablespoons grated Romano cheese*
*Salt and pepper to taste*

Wash the spinach several times to clean it of dirt and grit and then dry. Place it in a large salad bowl. Heat the dressing and pour it over the spinach. Toss well to mix. If not wilted enough, then put spinach and dressing into a pan for 1 minute only. Top with chopped egg, turkey bacon, and Romano cheese. Add salt and pepper to taste. *Serves 2.*

## SARDINE SALAD

### (O, A, B, AB)

*2 tins water-packed (if possible) sardines*
*3 to 4 cloves garlic, minced*
*2 tablespoons tahini*
*½ teaspoon salt*
*1 teaspoon ground cumin*
*2 medium onions, diced*
*1 pepper, diced*
*1 tablespoon olive oil (less, if the sardines are packed in oil)*
*Juice of ½ lemon*

Drain and mash the sardines well in a mixing bowl. Add the next four ingredients. In a 7-inch frying pan, sauté the onions and pepper in oil until lightly browned. Add the sautéed mixture to the sardines while still hot. Mix well and add freshly squeezed lemon juice. Chill and serve.

## GREEK SALAD

### (A, B, AB)

*1 head crisp Romaine, washed, dried, and torn into bite-sized pieces*
*8 tablespoons Olive Oil and Lemon Dressing (see page 407)*
*2 cucumbers, washed, peeled, and sliced*
*1 green pepper, halved, seeded, and cut into bite-sized pieces (Types A and AB omit)*
*1 small red onion, sliced*
*4 tablespoons crumbled feta*
*Greek olives (for Type AB only)*
*1 teaspoon dried tarragon*

In a large salad bowl, toss the Romaine with the dressing. Top with all other ingredients and mix well. *Serves 2 to 4.*

## SALMON WITH WAKAME SEAWEED

### (O, A, B, AB)

*6-ounce/150-g can salmon with bones*
*1 organic yellow onion*

*6 ounces/150 g wakame seaweed from your favourite health-food store*
*2 tablespoons cold-pressed olive oil*
*Garlic (as much as you like)*
*Salt*

Drain the salmon. Mince or chop the onion. Soak the wakame seaweed for 5 minutes in a separate bowl, then drain. Combine the salmon, onion, and wakame in a bowl. Add the olive oil and garlic. Salt to taste.

## MIXED MUSHROOM SALAD

### (O, A, B, AB)

*10 to 12 ounces/250–300 g mushrooms:*
*TYPE A enoki and oyster*
*TYPE O enoki, oyster, and abalone*
*TYPES B and AB closed cap, oyster, and enoki*
*8 ounces vinaigrette*
*2 tablespoons chopped parsley*
*2 tablespoons chopped chives*
*6 ounces/150 g shredded lettuce*

Choose a salad dressing appropriate to your blood type. For most, the Sweet Onion Vinaigrette (page 407) or Olive Oil and Lemon Dressing (page 407) works nicely. Marinate the mushrooms in 1 cup of the dressing for 1 to 2 hours. Mix in the fresh herbs. Using a slotted spoon, serve on a bed of lettuce. *Serves 4.*

## CARROT RAISIN SALAD

### (O, A, B, AB)

*2 pounds/900 g carrots, washed, ends removed, and grated*
*3 ounces/75 g raisins, plumped in hot water*
*3 tablespoons Egg-Free Mayonnaise (see recipe on page 406)*
*3 tablespoons chopped coriander*
*1 spring onion, sliced thin, or 1 tablespoon chopped chives*

Place the carrots in a serving bowl. Drain the raisins and add them to the carrots. Mix in the rest of the ingredients and toss well. *Serves 4.*

# CAESAR SALAD

### (O, A, B, AB)

### THE SALAD

*1 head Romaine lettuce, washed and dried*
*4 anchovy fillets*

Tear or cut the lettuce, place in a bowl, and set aside.

### THE DRESSING

*1 egg*
*2 lemons, juiced*
*8 fluid ounces/225 ml extra virgin olive oil*
*2-ounce/50-g can anchovy fillets or 2 tablespoons kelp powder*
*5 large cloves garlic*
*4 tablespoons grated Pecorino Romano cheese*

Place the egg, lemon juice, and olive oil in a pestle and mortar and blend thoroughly. Remove the mayonnaise to a mixing bowl. Without washing the pestle and mortar, blend the anchovy, garlic, and cheese into a paste. If it gets lumpy and needs thinning, add 2 tablespoons of the mayonnaise and blend until smooth. Combine the two mixtures by hand for a truly pungent dressing.

### THE CROUTONS

*4 tablespoons olive or vegetable oil, or 2 tablespoons each of olive oil and vegetable oil*
*2 cloves garlic, through a press*
*1 tablespoon salt*
*6 ounces/150 g cubed stale bread made from spelt flour (or cubed bread of any sort that is*
*appropriate to your blood type; large cubes make a nice change from the tiny packaged*
*ones we've all grown up with; it's also a lot easier to make)*

Preheat the oven to 220°C/gas 7. Whisk together the oil, garlic, and salt. Coat the cubed bread with the mixture and place on a baking sheet with plenty of room between them for toasting. Bake 5 minutes, check, turn, and bake another 2 minutes or until golden brown. Remove from the oven and cool thoroughly. Croutons can be stored in an airtight container for several days.

TO ASSEMBLE THE SALAD

Toss the lettuce with the dressing. Top with the croutons and the anchovy fillets.
Serve chilled.

## GRILLED SWEET POTATO SALAD

### (O, B, AB)

*2 pounds/900 g sweet potatoes cooked, sliced and grilled*
*3 tablespoons olive oil*
*1 spring onion, sliced*
*2 tablespoons chopped coriander*
*1 lime, juiced*
*Salt and pepper to taste*

Cube the sweet potatoes after they've cooled. Add the remaining ingredients,
toss well, and serve. *Serves 4 to 6.*

## SMOKED MACKEREL SALAD

### (O, A, B, AB)

*4 smoked mackerel fillets, skinned and boned*
*½ red onion, diced small*
*6 to 8 tablespoons Egg-Free Mayonnaise (see recipe, page 406)*
*Juice of 1 lemon*

Chop fillets by hand, add onion, mayonnaise, and lemon juice. Mix well and serve
with crackers. *Yields approximately 2 cups.*

## GRILLED CHICKEN SALAD

### (O, A)

*8 to 16 ounces/225–450 g grilled, diced chicken*
*3 tablespoons homemade mayonnaise*
*1 lime, juiced*
*3 tablespoons chopped coriander*
*2 spring onions, sliced thin*
*1 red pepper, either roasted or grilled, with the skin removed, or fresh,*
*cut in half, then sliced (Type O only)*
*Salt and pepper to taste*

Put the chicken in a bowl. Thin the mayonnaise with the lime juice and add that to the chicken. Add all other ingredients, toss well, and serve with crackers, on sprouted seed bread, or rolled in a Romaine lettuce leaf. *Serves 2 to 4.*

## GREEN BEAN SALAD WITH WALNUTS AND GOAT'S CHEESE

### (O, A, B, AB)

*2 pounds/900 g green beans, stems removed*
*2 ounces/50 g walnut pieces and halves*
*2 tablespoons crumbled goat's cheese*
*2 tablespoons extra virgin olive oil*
*Salt and pepper to taste*
*Squeeze of lemon*

Quickly blanch the green beans by throwing them in a pot of boiling water, counting to 30, then removing them to an ice bath. Drain well and dry. On a serving plate, layer the beans, walnuts, and crumbled goat's cheese. Dress with good olive oil, salt and pepper to taste, and a squeeze of the lemon. *Serves 4 to 6.*

## Vegetables

## GLAZED TURNIPS AND ONIONS

### (O, A, B, AB)

*2 tablespoons butter*
*2 tablespoons olive oil*
*1 yellow onion, quartered*
*4 turnips, cut into wedges*
*4 cloves garlic, crushed*
*6 to 8 fluid ounces/175–225 ml Chicken Stock (page 353) or water*
*Salt*
*½ handful parsley, chopped*

In a heavy frying pan, melt the butter in the oil over low heat and add the onion, turning to coat with butter and oil. Cook gently over very low heat until soft and very golden, about 20 minutes. Add the turnips and garlic, turning well. Add the chicken stock or water and a little salt, bring to a boil, reduce heat, and cover. Simmer until done, about 20 minutes. Check to be sure there is always liquid in the pan. Add a few tablespoons at a time as needed. There should be very little liquid left. Take the lid off and allow the last of the liquid to evaporate. Continue to turn the vegetables. Serve at once, spooning the "syrup" over them. Salt to taste and sprinkle with parsley. *Serves 4.*

## AUBERGINE CASSEROLE

### (B, AB)

*1 medium to large aubergine, sliced thin*
*4 courgettes, sliced*
*8 ounces/225 g sliced mushrooms*
*4 ounces/100 g Pesto (page 409)*
*4 ounces/100 g shredded mozzarella cheese*
*Sea salt to taste*

Divide all ingredients in half. Layer everything in a large baking dish. Start with half the aubergine slices, then half the courgettes and mushrooms, dot with half the Pesto, and then sprinkle half the mozzarella. Salt to taste. Repeat all layers. Cover with foil and bake at 300 degrees for 1 hour and 20 minutes.

## CARROTS AND PARSNIPS WITH GARLIC AND CORIANDER

### (O, A, B, AB)

*2 carrots*
*2 parsnips*
*1 to 2 tablespoons olive oil*
*6 cloves garlic, peeled and crushed*
*4 fluid ounces/100 ml water (or more if needed)*
*½ handful coriander, chopped*
*Salt to taste*

Slice carrots and parsnips on the diagonal. Heat 1 to 2 tablespoons of olive oil in a heavy frying pan, add sliced vegetables, and turn in oil a few moments until coated. Add garlic, stirring in oil another moment. Add the water, bring to boil, reduce heat, cover, and braise 15 to 20 minutes or until carrots and parsnips are tender. Be sure that there is always a little water in the pan, adding a tablespoon or two as needed. By the end of the cooking time, the water should be absorbed. For the last moments of cooking, add the chopped coriander and salt.

## GRIDDLED PEPPER MEDLEY

### (O, B)

*3 peppers, mixed (sweet red, green, yellow, or orange)*
*1 large onion*
*2 cloves garlic*
*2 tablespoons olive oil*
*Salt*

Core and seed the peppers, then slice thinly. Chop the onion into small pieces. Crush the garlic. Heat the oil in a heavy griddle pan over medium heat. Add the garlic and onions and sauté gently until translucent. Add the peppers and toss to coat with the oil. Sauté the mixture until peppers are soft. Add salt to taste. *Serves 4.*

## SWEET POTATO PANCAKES

### (O, B, AB)

*1 large sweet potato, grated*
*¼ red onion, grated*
*2 tablespoons chopped fresh coriander*
*1 large egg*
*1 ounce/25 g spelt flour*
*¼ teaspoon salt*
*4 tablespoons vegetable oil for cooking*

Wash and rinse the sweet potato. Do not peel. Grate over a large plate. Add the onion and coriander. Mix in the egg and flour until all is well incorporated and add the salt. The mixture will be loose, yet easy to form patties, which will spread out in the pan. Heat oil and carefully pan-fry each pancake 4 to 5 minutes on each side. At this point, the pancakes can be held in the oven for an hour or so. *Yields 6 large dinner-sized pancakes or 15 appetizer-sized pancakes.*

## CAULIFLOWER WITH GARLIC AND PARSLEY

### (A, B, AB)

*1 head cauliflower*
*2 tablespoons olive oil*
*4 to 6 cloves garlic, crushed*

*About 8 fluid ounces/225 ml water*
*Salt to taste*

Cut the cauliflower into reasonably uniform "florets". In a large, heavy frying pan, heat 2 tablespoons olive oil and add garlic, sautéing until fragrant. Add the florets and turn in oil. Then add the water, bring to a low boil, and cover. The cauliflower will steam in this. When the cauliflower is soft but firm, the water should be almost absorbed. If not, remove the lid and allow the rest to boil away, leaving a rich garlic/oil residue. With the back of a wooden spoon, roughly mash the cauliflower and add the salt. This is a delicious pasta sauce or serve as a vegetable with pan-roasted chicken. *Serves 4 to 6.*

## MASHED PLANTAINS

### (B, AB)

*2 ripe plantains*
*Water*
*2 to 3 tablespoons butter*
*Salt*

Peel the plantains. They do not peel as bananas do; you will probably have to cut them into smaller pieces first. Once peeled, cut them into 1- to 2-inch (2.5- to 5-cm) lengths and place them in a pot. Cover completely with water, bring to a boil, and cook until they are fully tender, 20 to 30 minutes, but check because riper ones will cook more quickly. Do not overcook. Drain, reserving a little of the broth. Mash well and add 2 to 3 tablespoons of butter and salt to taste. You may also use the cooking water, a tablespoon at a time, in the mashing process.

## VEGETABLE FRITTERS

### (O, A, B, AB)

*12 ounces/300 g grated vegetables (choose vegetables such as peppers, mushrooms, cauliflower, broccoli, aubergine, and courgette)*
*1 tablespoon finely minced onion*
*2 eggs*
*Olive oil*
*Salt to taste*

Mix the grated vegetables, used either alone or in combination, with the onion and eggs. In a large, heavy frying pan, heat the olive oil. Lightly shape a handful of the batter for each fritter and gently drop into the oil, being careful not to splatter yourself. Flatten with a spatula. Let them fry over medium heat until the bottoms begin to colour. Carefully turn over and fry several more minutes. Drain on paper towels, sprinkle with salt, and serve.

## STEAMED ARTICHOKE

### (O, A)

*1 stalk of lemongrass, peeled and cut into pieces (large is okay)*
*1 teaspoon olive oil*
*4 cloves garlic, peeled and smashed*
*1 artichoke per person*
*Squeeze of lemon*

Place all ingredients in the steamer. With or without trimming, the stem long or short, the bottoms up or tips down, an artichoke usually takes between 45 and 55 minutes to cook. Keep plenty of water in the bottom of the pan, and the pot mostly covered. Serve with a squeeze of lemon. *Allow one artichoke per person.*

## SWISS CHARD WITH SARDINES

### (O, A, B, AB)

*2 pounds/900 g Swiss chard*
*2 tablespoons olive oil*
*3 cloves garlic, minced*
*1 small onion, sliced thin*
*6 canned sardines, chopped*
*1 tomato (Types O and AB only)*
*Salt to taste*

Wash the chard well, slice into 1-inch (2.5-cm) strips, and quickly steam. Remove them from the pan and set aside. In a large frying pan, heat the oil and add the garlic and onion and cook until slightly browned and soft. Add the sardines and tomato (Types O and AB only). Salt to taste. Add the greens and toss lightly. *Serves 4.*

## SESAME BROCCOLI

### (O, A, B, AB)

*8 fluid ounces/225 ml water*
*1 head of broccoli, cut into bite-sized florets; reserve stems for another purpose*
*Juice of ½ lemon*
*1 teaspoon black sesame seeds*

Bring the water to a boil (you can use your kettle). Put all the broccoli in a steamer or a large frying pan. Make sure there is a top to cover. When the water is boiling, pour evenly over the broccoli, cover, and put heat on high. Cook for only 3 to 4 minutes. Remove to a plate, squeeze the lemon generously, and sprinkle on the seeds. *Serves 4.*

## BRAISED COLLARDS

### (O, A, B, AB)

*3 tablespoons of olive oil*
*1 large sweet onion, peeled and sliced thin*
*1 bunch of fresh collard greens, washed well and tips of stems removed*
*(the stems themselves are quite delicious)*
*2 tablespoons tamari*

Heat the oil in a very large frying pan or saucepan. Cook the onion for 5 minutes. Meanwhile, slice the collards by rolling them in one large bunch and cutting across the leaves in 1-inch (2.5-cm) intervals. Add all the collards at once and cover. Turn the heat down and, after 5 minutes, with a pair of tongs, turn the collards so the wilted greens are on top. Add the tamari sauce and cover again. From time to time, over 40 minutes, turn the collards so as to cook them evenly. Unlike other greens, these are much more tasty if they are allowed to cook longer. *Serves 4.*

## GRIDDLED PORTABELLO MUSHROOMS

### (O, A, B, AB)

*4 large portabello mushrooms, stems removed and saved for soups or stews*
*4 teaspoons Garlic-Shallot Mixture (page 409)*

*Salt to taste*
*Chopped parsley or basil*

Brush the mushrooms with plenty of the Garlic-Shallot Mixture. Griddle over medium heat for 5 to 8 minutes. Turn over. If making cheeseburgers, place cheese on top. Whether you use cheese or not, cook another 5 to 8 minutes. Season with salt and serve on a bun, or plate together with griddled meats or tempeh. Top with parsley or basil.

## Sandwiches, Eggs, Tarts, and Frittata

### Sandwiches

Try these sandwich fillings on bread that is right for your type:

| | |
|---|---|
| Griddled peppers (yellow, red, green, orange), goat's cheese | (O, B) |
| Grilled aubergine, feta | (B, AB) |
| Sliced tomatoes, fresh mozzarella, and basil | (O, AB) |
| Braised red peppers and onions with feta | (O, B) |
| Grilled aubergine, braised shiitake mushrooms, goat's cheese | (B) |
| Almond butter and sliced bananas | (O, B) |
| Ricotta, chopped walnuts, raisins, honey drizzle | (O, A, B, AB) |
| Peanut butter, raisins, honey | (A, AB) |
| Tofu, avocado, Lemon Vinaigrette | (A) |
| Tofu, sliced tomato, chopped Spanish olives, Lemon Vinaigrette | (AB) |
| Mashed sardines, minced clove garlic | (O, A, B, AB) |
| Soft goat's cheese and your best preserves | (O, A, B, AB) |
| Sunflower butter and plum preserves | (O, A) |
| Sliced lamb with homemade mango (O, B) or peach (AB) chutney | (O, B, AB) |
| Fresh mozzarella, sautéed courgette, and garlic | (O, A, B, AB) |

## GRILLED OR ROASTED PEPPERS ON RYE CRACKERS WITH CHÈVRE

### (O, B)

*2 red or yellow peppers, grilled or roasted with some olive oil*
*4 rye crackers*
*2 ounces/50 g crumbled goat's cheese*

Slice the peppers to the size and shape of the crackers. Crumble goat's cheese on top. This makes a great snack or light lunch.

## GRILLED GOAT'S CHEDDAR ON SPROUTED SEED OR SPELT BREAD

### (O, A, B, AB)

*2 slices sprouted seed or spelt bread*
*3 to 4 slices goat's cheddar*
*2 tablespoons butter or margarine*

Mix all ingredients together and serve on bread or rice crackers.

## CURRIED EGG SALAD

### (O)

*4 eggs, hard-boiled, peeled, and mashed*
*2 tablespoons mayonnaise*
*1 tablespoon salt, or to taste*
*1 teaspoon good curry powder*

Mix all ingredients together and serve on sprouted seed bread or rice crackers.

## Eggs

## ONE-EGG OMELETTE

### (O, A)

*1 tablespoon plus 1 teaspoon olive oil*
*1 small green courgette, washed and grated*
*1 large organic egg*
*1 tablespoon water*
*2 basil leaves*

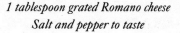
*1 tablespoon grated Romano cheese*
*Salt and pepper to taste*

In a medium frying pan, heat 1 tablespoon of olive oil and quickly cook the courgette for 2 to 3 minutes, then set aside on plate. Briskly beat the egg, add 1 tablespoon of water, and beat again. The idea is to get the egg as fluffy as possible. Add 1 teaspoon of olive oil to grease the pan and pour in the egg. Let the egg run around the whole bottom of the pan. Since there's only one egg, it's bound to be thin. Quickly add the courgette, basil, and Romano cheese. With a spatula, lift the edges of the omelette and carefully fold over the filling to make a half moon. "Roll" onto plate. Add salt and pepper to taste.

### OTHER FILLINGS

*Any leftover vegetables from last night's dinner*
*Braised collards*
*Steamed carrots*
*Freshly grated carrot with crumbled goat's cheese and fresh dill*
*Tomato and basil*
*Tofu and spring onion with hoisin sauce*
*Wild rice tempeh with basmati*
*Fresh spinach and feta*
*Feta cheese and chopped parsley*
*Mozzarella cheese and broccoli*
*Courgette and grated carrots with crumbled goat's cheese*

Make sure to warm any leftovers before filling the omelette.

## Tarts

## ARTICHOKE AND SWEET ONION TART

### (A)

*6 ounces/150 g white spelt flour*
*2 ounces/50 g whole spelt flour*
*½ teaspoon salt*
*4 ounces/100 g unsalted butter, cold, cut into small pieces (Type A substitute*
*3 tablespoons soy oil margarine)*
*4 to 5 tablespoons cold water*

In a large mixing bowl, combine both flours and the salt. Cut in the cold butter or margarine. Work the flour into the butter using your fingertips. When mix resembles coarse meal, add water 1 tablespoon at a time; it may not take all the water. The dough should be formed into a ball, but not be too wet. Wrap in plastic and chill in the refrigerator for at least 2 hours. At this point, it will last for 5 days.

When ready to use, remove the dough from the refrigerator and let sit for 45 minutes. Slice into two pieces and roll out on a floured board. Roll to ⅛-inch (3-mm) thick, cut in a circle shape, and brush with olive oil. Pierce with fork at intervals over the surface.

Bake on a baking sheet at 180°C/gas 4 for 5 to 8 minutes. Let cool. At this point, you can store the baked crust in an airtight container in the refrigerator for a couple of days.

### FILLING

*1 sweet onion, sliced thin*
*1 tablespoon olive oil*
*2 cooked artichoke hearts, sliced*
*2 tablespoons crumbled goat's cheese*
*Salt and pepper to taste*

Sauté the onion in the oil until lightly caramelized. Cool. Top the crust with onion, artichoke, and goat's cheese. Add salt and pepper to taste.

## Frittatas

## COURGETTE AND MUSHROOM FRITTATA

### (O, A, B, AB)

*3 tablespoons olive oil*
*2 shallots or ½ small onion, chopped*
*2 medium courgettes, cut lengthwise, then on the diagonal*
*1 portabello mushroom, sliced*
*5 eggs*
*1 tablespoon water*
*4 tablespoons grated Romano cheese*
*Salt to taste*

Preheat the oven to 350 degrees. In a large, heavy frying pan, heat 1 tablespoon of oil and gently cook the shallots. Add the courgettes and sliced mushroom and cook until soft. Meanwhile, beat the eggs with a tablespoon of water. Add the cheese and the vegetables to the egg mixture. Mix well. Add 2 more tablespoons of oil to the pan. When the oil is hot, add the egg mixture. Cook on low heat until halfway done, then finish in the oven. The frittata will puff up nicely. Salt to taste.

## SPINACH FRITTATA

### (O, A, B, AB)

*5 eggs*
*1 teaspoon water*
*1 pack spinach, washed, dried, and chopped fine*
*2 tablespoons olive oil*
*1 tablespoon Garlic-Shallot Mixture (page 409)*
*4 tablespoons grated Pecorino Romano cheese*
*Salt and pepper to taste*

Preheat the grill. Beat the eggs with a teaspoon of water and add the spinach. In a large frying pan, heat the oil and cook the Garlic-Shallot Mixture for 2 minutes. Add the spinach-egg mixture all at once and cook on medium heat until almost done. While the top is still a bit runny, sprinkle with cheese and run under the grill until done, about 2 minutes. Season with salt and pepper and serve.

## Breads, Muffins, Pancakes, and Batters

### Breads

Type O can use all spelt flour.

## BANANA PLUM BREAD

### (O, B)

*4 ounces/100 g spelt flour*
*3 ounces/75 g oat flour*
*2½ teaspoons baking powder*
*½ teaspoon salt*
*5 tablespoons softened butter*
*4 ounces/100 g sugar*
*1 to 2 teaspoons lemon rind*
*1 to 2 eggs, beaten*
*2 mashed bananas*

*3 ripe plums, diced*
*2 to 4 ounces/50–100 g broken walnuts*

Preheat oven to 180°G/gas 4. Sift flours, baking powder, and salt. Blend the butter, sugar, and lemon rind until creamy. Beat in the eggs and mashed banana. Add dry ingredients to butter mixture in 3 parts, beating well after each addition. Fold in plums and walnuts. Pour into 2 small, well-buttered loaf pans. Bake about 40 minutes or until a straw comes out clean. Cool.

## PUMPKIN-ALMOND BREAD

### (O, A, AB)

*4 ounces/100 g white spelt flour*
*2 ounces/50 g ground almonds*
*½ teaspoon baking powder*
*1 teaspoon baking soda*
*½ teaspoon salt*
*⅛ teaspoon cloves*
*¼ teaspoon mace*
*7 ounces/175 g sugar*
*2 ounces/50 g butter, at room temperature*
*2 eggs*
*½ small pumpkin, finely diced*
*5 fluid ounces/150 ml soy milk*
*8 tablespoons raisins or chopped figs*
*Butter or oil for pan*

Preheat oven to 180°/gas 4. Prepare a 9- by 13-inch (23×33 cm) glass pan. In a large bowl, mix thoroughly the flour, ground almonds, baking powder, baking soda, salt, cloves, and mace. In a separate bowl, beat the sugar, butter, and eggs until very light. Add the pumpkin and beat again. Swiftly add the dry ingredients alternately with the soy milk in two additions. Stir in the raisins or figs. Pour into pan and bake about 30 minutes or until a straw comes out clean.

## SPELT BREAD

### (for Bread Machine)

### (O, A, B, AB)

*12 fluid ounces/340 g water*
*1½ teaspoons yeast*
*2 tablespoons soy powder*

*2 tablespoons vegetable oil (Type B substitute light olive oil)*
*2 tablespoons honey*
*2 tablespoons molasses*
*1½ teaspoons salt*
*1 pound 4 ounces/500 g whole spelt flour*

Measure the ingredients in the baking pan in the order listed. Insert into the baking chamber and close the lid. Select a whole-grain setting, and bake according to the machine. Let cool before slicing. For a lighter loaf, substitute 4 ounces (100 g) white spelt for 4 ounces (100 g) whole-grain spelt.

## Muffins

### QUINOA ALMOND MUFFINS

#### (O, A, B, AB)

*4 ounces/100 g quinoa flour*
*4 ounces/100 g white spelt flour*
*2 ounces/50 g raw cane sugar*
*2½ teaspoons baking powder*
*¼ teaspoon salt*
*1 egg*
*8 fluid ounces/225 ml almond milk*
*8 tablespoons vegetable oil (Type B use butter)*

Preheat oven to 200°C/gas 6 and prepare muffin tins using butter, oil, or paper liners. Combine all dry ingredients. Beat egg. Add almond milk and oil. Fold quickly into dry ingredients. Fill tins to almost full. Add water to remaining empty tins and bake 15 to 20 minutes.

### BANANA WALNUT BREAD OR MUFFINS

#### (O, B)

*Butter for pans*
*8 ounces/200 g white spelt flour*
*1 teaspoon salt*
*2 teaspoons baking soda*
*6 fluid ounces/170 ml vegetable oil (Type B use butter)*
*6 ounces/150 g raw cane sugar*
*2 large bananas, ripe and cut into chunks*

*3 eggs, beaten*
*2 ounces/50 g chopped walnuts*

Preheat the oven to 180°C/gas 4. Prepare pans: If nonstick, they do not need buttering; otherwise butter and flour the pan(s), or if you're making muffins, you can use paper liners. Mix the flour, baking soda, and oil in one bowl and all the sugar, bananas, and eggs in another. Blend together and add the walnuts for the last few turns with the spoon. Be careful not to overmix the batter. Fill the pans ¾ full, and bake 25 to 30 minutes for muffins and 30 to 35 minutes for breads, or until a cake tester comes out clean. Let cool on a rack. For whole-wheat banana bread, substitute 4 ounces (100 g) whole spelt flour for 4 ounces (100 g) white spelt flour.

## BLUEBERRY BUCKWHEAT MUFFINS

### (A, AB)

*4 ounces/100 g buckwheat flour*
*4 ounces/100 g white spelt flour*
*2½ teaspoons baking powder*
*½ teaspoon salt*
*3 ounces/75 g sugar*
*2 tablespoons honey*
*8 fluid ounces/225 ml soy milk*
*4 tablespoons vegetable oil*
*1 egg, beaten*
*2 ounces/50 g blueberries*
*Oil or margarine for tins*

Preheat the oven to 180°C/gas 4. In a large bowl, mix the dry ingredients together. In another bowl, stir together the honey, soy milk, oil, and egg. Lightly combine the dry and wet ingredients. Fold in the blueberries. Grease the muffin tins or use paper liners and fill each muffin cup to the top. Bake for 20 minutes or until a toothpick comes out clean.

## CORNBREAD

### (A)

*3 ounces/75 g white spelt flour*
*3 ounces/75 g stone-ground cornmeal*
*2 ounces/50 g buckwheat flour*
*2 tablespoons brown sugar*
*2½ teaspoons baking powder*
*Pinch salt*
*2 eggs*

*4 tablespoons melted butter*
*8 fluid ounces/225 ml soy milk*

Butter a 9-inch (23-cm) square pan or cast iron skillet and preheat it at 220°C/gas 7. Mix together the spelt flour, cornmeal, buckwheat flour, brown sugar, baking powder, and salt. In another bowl, beat the eggs very well and add the melted butter and soy milk. Add the liquid ingredients to the dry, stirring quickly until just thoroughly mixed. Do not overbeat. Pour into the hot pan or skillet and bake for 20 to 25 minutes. Serve hot.

## BANANA SPELT BREAD OR MUFFINS

### (O)

This recipe can make either 12 large muffins or 3 small loaves.

*Butter for pans*
*8 ounces/200 g white spelt flour*
*1 teaspoon salt*
*2 teaspoons baking soda*
*6 fluid ounces/175 ml vegetable oil (Type B use butter)*
*6 ounces/150 g raw cane sugar*
*2 large bananas, ripe and cut into chunks*
*3 eggs, beaten*
*2 ounces/50 g chopped walnuts*

Preheat oven to 180°/gas 4. Prepare pans: If nonstick, they do not need buttering; otherwise butter and flour the pan(s), or if you're making muffins, you can use paper liners. Mix all dry ingredients in one bowl and all wet ingredients in another. Blend together and add walnuts for the last few turns with the spoon. Be careful not to overmix the batter. Fill pans ¾ full, and bake 25 to 30 minutes for muffins and 30 to 35 minutes for breads, or until a cake tester comes out clean. Let cool on rack.

## Pancakes and Batters

### BARLEY-SPELT PANCAKES

### (O, A)

*4 ounces/100 g barley flour*
*4 ounces/100 g spelt flour*

*2 teaspoons baking powder*
*Pinch salt*
*2 eggs*
*12 fluid ounces/340 ml soy milk*
*Water as needed*
*Butter, margarine, or oil for pan*

Combine the two flours, the baking powder, and the salt in a large bowl. In a separate bowl, beat the eggs very well and stir in the soy milk. Pour the liquid into the dry ingredients and stir until blended. The addition of water here depends on whether you prefer thick or thin pancakes. Heat butter, margarine, or oil in a heavy frying pan and when hot, ladle in the batter. Cook on low heat until bubbles fully cover the surface of the pancakes. Turn once and cook until beautifully coloured. Serve with maple syrup, honey, or your favourite preserve. *Makes 15 to 20 pancakes.*

## MILLET-SPELT-SOY PANCAKES

### (O, A, AB)

*4 ounces/100 g millet flour*
*2 ounces/50 g spelt flour*
*2 ounces/50 g soy flour*
*1 tablespoon baking powder*
*Pinch salt*
*2 eggs*
*12 fluid ounces/340 ml soy milk*
*Water as needed*
*Butter, margarine, or oil for pan*

Combine flours, baking powder, and salt and stir well. In a separate bowl, beat eggs and add soy milk, mixing well. Pour liquid into dry ingredients and blend thoroughly. Melt butter, margarine, or oil in a heavy frying pan and when hot ladle in the batter. Cook over low heat until bubbles cover the surface of the pancakes. Flip over and cook until lightly coloured on the underside. Serve with maple syrup, honey, or your favourite preserve. *Makes 15 to 20 pancakes.*

## AMARANTH PANCAKES

### (O, A, AB)

*4 ounces/100 g amaranth flour*
*4 ounces/100 g white spelt flour*

*1 teaspoon sugar*
*½ teaspoon salt*
*1 teaspoon baking powder*
*2 eggs, beaten*
*6 ounces/150 g ricotta cheese*
*8 fluid ounces/225 ml filtered water*
*½ teaspoon almond extract*
*Butter, margarine, or oil for pan*

In a medium bowl, mix together both flours, sugar, salt, and baking powder. In another bowl, blend the eggs, ricotta, water, and almond extract. Combine the two mixtures without overmixing. The batter may seem a bit thin, but after sitting 5 minutes it thickens. Melt butter, margarine, or oil in a heavy frying pan. Spoon the batter into the pan and cook until bubbles form on the surface. Turn over, and cook until lightly coloured. *Makes 15 to 20 pancakes.*

## BROWN RICE–SPELT PANCAKES

### (O, A, B, AB)

*4 ounces/100 g brown rice flour*
*4 ounces/100 g whole spelt flour*
*1 teaspoon baking powder*
*2 eggs*
*12 fluid ounces/340 ml rice milk*
*Butter, margarine, or oil for pan*

Combine the two flours and the baking powder, mixing well. Beat in the eggs and the rice milk and stir thoroughly. Melt the butter in a hot frying pan, ladle in the batter, and flip over when bubbles appear on the surface. Serve with maple syrup. *Makes 15 to 20 pancakes.*

## WHEAT-FREE WAFFLE BATTER

### (O, A, B, AB)

*4 ounces/100 g brown rice flour*
*4 ounces/100 g millet flour*
*1 tablespoon rice bran*
*½ teaspoon salt*
*1½ teaspoons corn-free baking powder*
*1 egg*

*12 fluid ounces/340 ml low-fat soy milk (Type B use 1% cow's milk)*
*4 tablespoons vegetable oil*

Mix all the ingredients to the proper consistency. You may need a little more flour or milk. Bake in a waffle iron 3 minutes or according to the directions of your waffle maker. Serve with sugar-free applesauce or banana slices. The batter keeps in the refrigerator for at least a week.

## Snacks

### TRAIL MIX OR GORP

Combine all ingredients and store in a glass container.

**TYPE O**
*5 ounces/125 g broken walnuts*
*2 ounces/50 g halved hazelnuts*
*3 ounces/75 g quartered dried apricots*
*3 ounces/75 g dried cherries*
*2 ounces/50 g chocolate or carob chips*
or
*4 ounces/100 g pumpkin seeds*
*2 ounces/50 g sunflower seeds*
*2 ounces/50 g chopped dried pears*
*2 ounces/50 g chopped dried pineapple*

**TYPE A**
*5 ounces/125 g peanuts*
*3 ounces/75 g quartered dried apricots*
*3 ounces/75 g raisins*
or
*4 ounces/100 g pumpkin seeds*
*2 ounces/50 g sunflower seeds*
*2 ounces/50 g broken walnuts*
*4 ounces/100 g chopped dried pineapple*

**TYPE B**
*4 ounces/100 g chopped Brazil nuts*
*2 ounces/50 g sliced dried bananas*

*3 ounces/75 g quartered dried apricots*

or

*4 ounces/100 g halved macadamia nuts*
*4 ounces/100 g chopped dried pineapple*
*4 ounces/100 g dried cranberries*

TYPE AB

*7 ounces/175 g peanuts*
*4 ounces/100 g walnuts*
*3 ounces/75 g raisins*
*3 ounces/75 g quartered dried apricots*

or

*2 ounces/50 g cashews*
*2 ounces/50 g pine nuts*
*2 ounces/50 g dried cranberries*

## RAISIN PEANUT BALLS

### (A, AB)

*5 ounces/125 g shelled peanuts*
*6 ounces/150 g raisins*
*Molasses or honey*
*Finely chopped peanuts*

Put peanuts and raisins into a food processor or mill and grind. Moisten slightly with molasses or honey to hold together. Make into little balls and roll in finely chopped peanuts.

## TAMARI TOASTED SUNFLOWER SEEDS

### (O, A)

*4 ounces/100 g raw shelled sunflower seeds*
*1 tablespoon tamari sauce*
*Handful of raisins*

In a large frying pan, heat seeds until almost popping. Flip around to toast evenly, then add the tamari. Toss only for a few more seconds so they are well coated but the tamari doesn't burn. Mix with raisins for a sweet and savoury snack.

## TOASTED TAMARI PUMPKIN SEEDS

### (O, A, B, AB)

*4 ounces/100 g raw pumpkin seeds*
*1 tablespoon tamari sauce*

In a large pan, heat the pumpkin seeds until almost popping. They behave a lot like popcorn. Shake the pan so the bottom seeds don't burn. Toss over a few times and add the tamari. Toss again and let cook a few more seconds. Remove from the pan and cool.

## Desserts

## WALNUT COOKIES

### (O, A, B)

*4 ounces/100 g butter, room temperature*
*2 ounces/50 g sugar*
*4 ounces/100 g walnuts*
*4 ounces/100 g spelt flour*

Preheat the oven to 180°C/gas 4. Cream the butter and sugar. Finely chop the walnuts with a heavy kitchen knife. Add the nuts and flour to the butter/sugar mixture. Drop teaspoonful-sized mounds on to buttered baking sheets, about 2 inches (5 cm) apart. Bake about 25 minutes, watching carefully that the cookies do not get darker than golden. Remove at once from pans and cool on a wire rack. Sprinkle lightly with sugar. *Makes 20 to 30 cookies.*

## CARROT RAISIN CAKE

### (O, A, AB)

*Butter, margarine, or oil for pans*
*8 ounces/200 g whole spelt flour*
*2 teaspoons baking soda*
*2 teaspoons baking powder*
*1 teaspoon salt*
*10 fluid ounces/285 ml vegetable oil*
*9 ounces/225 g light brown sugar*
*4 eggs, slightly beaten*

*12 ounces/300 g grated carrots*
*3 ounces/75 g raisins*
*4 ounces/100 g chopped walnuts*

Preheat the oven to 160°C/gas 3, and grease and flour two 8-inch (20-cm) round cake pans. Mix together the flour, baking soda, baking powder, and salt. In a separate bowl combine the oil, sugar, eggs, and carrots. Add them to the dry ingredients with a minimum of strokes, then stir in the raisins and walnuts. Do not overmix. Fill the pans almost to the top. Bake 55 minutes, or until a cake tester comes out clean. Let cool and remove from pan.

## WILD OR BASMATI RICE PUDDING

### (B, AB)

*8 eggs*
*1¼ pints/700 ml milk*
*10 tablespoons sugar*
*4 tablespoons melted butter*
*2 teaspoons vanilla*
*Pinch salt*
*Grated rind of 1 orange*
*2 tablespoons orange juice*
*4 handfuls of raisins*
*10 ounces/250 g cooked wild or Basmati rice*

Preheat the oven to 160°C/gas 3. Beat the eggs with a whisk until light. Add milk, sugar, melted butter, vanilla, and salt. Beat again until well combined. Add grated orange rind and orange juice. Add raisins to the rice and blend well. Place rice and raisins in a buttered 9- by 13- by 2-inch (23×33×5 cm) glass baking dish. Pour in the milk and egg mixture and stir lightly. Bake for 45 minutes or until set. Delicious hot or cold. *Serves 6 to 8.*

## CRANBERRY BISCOTTI

### (O, A, B, AB)

*3 eggs*
*2 ounces/50 g sugar*
*3 tablespoons butter or margarine, melted and cooled*
*1 teaspoon vanilla*
*1 tablespoon pineapple or orange juice*

*Zest of 1 lemon or orange*
*7 ounces/175 g spelt flour*
*1 teaspoon baking powder*
*¼ teaspoon salt*
*¼ teaspoon mace*
*2 ounces/50 g chopped fresh cranberries*

Preheat the oven to 180°C/gas 4. In a mixer, beat the eggs until foamy, then slowly add the sugar and, on high speed, beat until light. Add butter, vanilla, pineapple or orange juice, and the zest. In a separate bowl, mix the flour, baking powder, salt, and mace. On low speed, add the dry ingredients to the egg mixture and blend well. Stir in the cranberries. The dough will be soft. Divide the dough in half and, on a greased cookie sheet, mould each half into a long thin loaf (about 8 by 3 inches/20×8 cm). Bake for 25 minutes. Remove from the oven, and reduce heat to 160°C/gas 3. Let the loaves cool for 10 minutes. Put the loaves on a cutting board and slice on the diagonal into ½-inch (1-cm) pieces. Return the cookies to the baking sheet and toast on one side for 5 minutes, then turn each cookie and toast on the other side for another 10 minutes. Remove from oven when golden brown. Cool completely. *Makes about 30 biscotti.*

## RICE CRISPY CAKES

### (O, A, B, AB)

*2 tablespoons butter or vegetable margarine (depending on type)*
*4 tablespoons honey, maple syrup, or brown rice syrup*
*2 tablespoons brown sugar*
*¼ teaspoon salt*
*6 ounces/150 g crispy rice cereal (brown rice is always preferable)*

In a 5-pint/2.5-l saucepan, melt the butter or margarine, then add the honey (or other liquid sweetener), sugar, and salt. Add the rice cereal all at once. Stir to incorporate thoroughly. Immediately press into a flat, rectangular plastic or glass container. A 5- by 8-inch (13×20 cm) dish works well. The cakes should be about 1-inch (2.5-cm) high by 2-inches (5-cm) square. Unlike the ones made with marshmallows, these must be refrigerated to hold together. *Makes 8 to 10 cakes.*

## OATMEAL COOKIES

### (A, B, AB)

*10 ounces/250 g butter (Types A and AB use margarine)*
*2 ounces/50 g brown sugar*
*2 ounces/50 g raw sugar*
*1 egg*
*1 teaspoon vanilla*
*6 ounces/150 g white spelt flour*
*1 teaspoon baking soda*
*1 teaspoon salt*
*9 ounces/227 g rolled oats*
*1 tablespoon water (for moistening hands)*

In a mixing bowl or with electric beater, cream together the butter (or margarine), the two sugars, the egg, and vanilla. In a separate bowl, mix the dry ingredients. Slowly add the dry ingredients to the wet ingredients and combine well. Chill the dough for at least half an hour. Preheat oven to 190°C/gas 5 and grease a couple of cookie sheets. Remove the dough from the refrigerator and scoop out a tablespoon at a time and place on a cookie sheet. Flatten each scoop a bit with the palm of your hand. If the dough is too sticky, moisten your hand with water. Bake for 15 minutes. Note: Cookies can be made either small or large. If large, bake 2 extra minutes.

## PEANUT BUTTER COOKIES

### (A, AB)

*4 ounces/100 g butter*
*2 ounces/50 g brown sugar*
*1 ounce/25 g white sugar*
*2 eggs*
*6 ounces/150 g chunky, unsalted peanut butter*
*1 teaspoon vanilla*
*½ teaspoon baking soda*
*Generous pinch of salt*
*4 ounces/100 g spelt flour*
*2 ounces/50 g oat flour*

Preheat the oven to 180°C/gas 4. Beat the butter until soft, then add the sugars, beating until creamy. Beat in the eggs, peanut butter, vanilla, baking soda, and salt, fully incorporating all the peanut butter. Stir in both flours and mix well.

Roll between your palms into 1-inch (2.5-cm) balls and place on buttered cookie sheet or unbuttered parchment paper. Flatten to about ¼ inch (7 mm) with the tines of a fork. Bake for about 7 to 10 minutes, or until the cookies are beginning to colour. Cool on wire racks. *Makes about 40 cookies.*

## RICE PUDDING WITH SOY MILK

### (O, A, B, AB)

*Butter for baking dish*
*12 ounces/250 g Basmati rice, cooked*
*4 eggs*
*16 fluid ounces/450 ml soy milk*
*2 ounces/50 g sugar*
*2 tablespoons melted butter*
*Grated rind of 1 lemon*
*Juice of ½ lemon*
*3 ounces/75 g raisins*

Preheat the oven to 180°C/gas 4. Butter a baking dish and add the rice. In a large mixing bowl, beat the eggs with a whisk until frothy. Add the rest of ingredients and mix thoroughly. Pour these ingredients over the rice, combining well with a fork. Bake the pudding until set, about 40 to 50 minutes. *Serves 6 to 8.*

## TOFU BANANA PUDDING

### (O, B)

*1 cake tofu*
*2 ripe bananas*

Place both ingredients in a blender and puree for a few moments. Pour into individual little bowls and chill. *Serves 2 to 4.*

## TOFU PUMPKIN PUDDING

### (O, A, AB)

*1 cake tofu*
*8 ounces/200 g pumpkin, diced and well cooked*
*Honey as needed (start with 1 to 2 tablespoons)*

Puree the ingredients in a blender, pour into bowls, and chill. *Serves 6 to 8.*

## SAUTÉED PEARS OR APPLES

### (O, A, B, AB)

*2 pears or apples*
*2 tablespoons butter (Types A and AB can use soy or vegetable margarine)*

Peel and thinly slice the pears or apples. Melt the butter in a heavy frying pan and add the fruit, turning gently to coat with butter. Turn heat very low and cover the pan, stewing the fruit in the butter and whatever water the fruit expresses. If there doesn't seem to be enough liquid, add 1 tablespoon of water at a time. Cook 7 to 10 minutes or until the fruit is soft. There should be a little syrup. Types A and AB can sprinkle the fruit with cinnamon or nutmeg. Type B can sprinkle nutmeg. *Serves 2 to 4.*

## SAUTÉED BANANAS

### (O, B)

*2 ripe bananas*
*2 tablespoons butter*
*1 tablespoon lemon juice, optional*
*1 grated lemon rind*

Cut bananas in half, then slice them lengthwise. The bananas should be quartered. Melt the butter in a heavy frying pan, lower the heat, and add the bananas, turning carefully in the butter. They will brown and get softer. They will be done in just a few minutes. Sprinkle on the lemon juice and rind and serve. *Serves 2.*

## FRESH FIG SALAD

### (O, A, B, AB)

*Fresh figs*
*Goat's cheese*

Slice figs lengthwise. Fan out on a plate and top with bits of broken goat's cheese.

## RICOTTA ORANGE CREAM

### (B)

*6 ounces/150 g ricotta*
*1 tablespoon orange blossom water*
*1 grated orange rind*

Whip ingredients in blender and refrigerate.

## CITRUS SALAD

### (O, A, B, AB)

Grapefruit, orange, and tangerine make sparkling salads either on their own or mixed together for interesting combinations. Serve topped with a little of the Ricotta Orange Cream (Type B) or any other dressing of your type. One grapefruit, two oranges, and two tangerines. *Serves 4.*

*Grapefruit (O, A, B, AB)*
*Orange (B)*
*Tangerine (B, AB)*
*Whole mint leaves*

Peel and section fruits over the serving bowl in order to catch the juices. Cut grapefruit wedges into halves or thirds and halve the orange and tangerine wedges. Toss to mix well (if using more than one fruit) and pour dressing over the top of the fruits. Garnish with some small, whole mint leaves.

## TROPICAL SALAD

### (O, A, B, AB)

Combine these lovely, fragrant fruits according to your taste and type. A generous squeeze of lemon or lime keeps the colours intact and is dressing enough for many people. If you prefer, swirl Ricotta Orange Cream (see recipe above) over the top of each portion for a richer version.

*Papaya (O, B, AB)*
*Mango (O, B)*
*Kiwi (O, A, B, AB)*
*Pineapple (O, A, B, AB)*
*Carambola (star fruit) (O, A)*
*Banana (O, B)*

*Guava (O, A, B)*
*Juice of 1 lemon*
*Juice of 1 lime*

Peel, seed, and cut the papaya and mango, so that they are of uniform size. Peel the kiwi and either cut into slices or wedges. Cut the pineapple into small chunks. Slice the carambola so that each piece is a little star. Slice the banana. Peel and slice the guava. This salad can be layered in a glass bowl, each individual fruit in its own layer, or very gently turned to mix the fruits. Sprinkle each layer with lemon or lime juice or pour the squeezed juice over the salad before turning.

## POACHED FRUIT

### (O, A, B, AB)

*8 fluid ounces/225 ml water*
*3 ounces/75 g sugar*
*1 lemon, juiced, rind peeled and cut into strips*
*3 cloves*
*Apples*
*Pears*
*Peaches*
*Plums*
*Apricots*
*Grapes*
*Nectarines*
*Cherries*
*Handful torn mint leaves*

Make a poaching syrup: Bring to a boil the water, sugar, lemon juice, strips of lemon rind, and cloves. Prepare the fruits: If you prefer, you do not have to peel them. In general, just remove all seeds and pits, slice larger fruits, and halve the smaller ones like apricots and plums. If you have a cherry pitter, leave the cherries whole; if not, halve them, too. Leave the grapes whole. Add any combination of fruits to the boiling syrup, allowing one large and several smaller fruits per person. Poach, uncovered, for about 10 to 15 minutes. Lift the fruit carefully from the syrup with a slotted spoon and place it in a serving bowl. Reduce the syrup another 8 to 10 minutes, remove the cloves, and pour over the fruits. Cool in the refrigerator. Sprinkle with mint leaves if desired.

## BAKED APPLES

### (O, A, B, AB)

*4 cooking apples*
*2 ounces/50 g chopped walnuts*
*3 ounces/75 g mixed dried figs and apricots*
*½ lemon, juiced*
*Grated rind of ½ lemon*
*2 tablespoons maple syrup*
*Pat of butter*
*8 fluid ounces/225 ml boiling water*

Core the apples, being careful not to pierce the bottoms. Mix the walnuts, dried fruit, lemon juice, and rind together. Pour enough maple syrup over this to moisten well, about 2 tablespoons. Fill the apples with this, but don't pack the filling in too tightly. If the filling mounds at the top of the apple, that's okay. Put a generous pat of butter on top of the filling, place apples in a glass baking dish, and pour 8 fluid ounces/225 ml boiling water into the dish, around the apples. Bake at 180°C/gas 4 for 20 to 30 minutes, or until the apples are tender. During the baking time, you can baste the apples with the pan juices. When the apples are done, remove to a serving dish, transfer the liquid to a small pan, and reduce. Spoon over the apples before serving. *One apple per serving.*

## Beverages

### Super Baby Smoothies

These blood type–specific protein smoothies provide an excellent nutritional boost. For the protein base use either *Proteus ABO,* our specially formulated product, or a commercial protein powder suitable for your blood type.

## SUPER BABY SMOOTHIE—TYPE O

*2 tablespoons Proteus ABO protein powder for Type O*
*or egg albumin–based commercial protein powder*
*5 ounces/125 g blueberries*
*1 banana*
*4 fluid ounces/115 ml pineapple juice*

Blend well and serve.

## SUPER BABY SMOOTHIE—TYPE A

*2 tablespoons Proteus ABO protein powder for Type A
or soy-based commercial protein powder
5 ounces/125 g blueberries
3 ounces/75 g blackberries
4 fluid ounces/115 ml pineapple juice*

Blend well and serve.

## SUPER BABY SMOOTHIE—TYPE B

*2 tablespoons Proteus ABO protein powder for Type B
or whey–based commercial protein powder
1 banana
1 papaya, peeled and sliced
4 fluid ounces/115 ml pineapple juice*

Blend well and serve.

## SUPER BABY SMOOTHIE—TYPE AB

*2 tablespoons Proteus ABO protein powder for Type AB
or whey–based commercial protein powder
1 kiwi, peeled and sliced
3 ounces/75 g pitted cherries
4 fluid ounces/115 ml pineapple juice*

Blend well and serve.

## Yogurt Drinks

### PINEAPPLE

**(A, B, AB)**

*8 fluid ounces/225 ml yogurt
5 ounces/125 g chopped pineapple
4 fluid ounces/115 ml pineapple juice
Mint leaves*

Put the yogurt, pineapple, and pineapple juice in a blender and blend well. Pour into a tall glass and garnish with mint leaves. *Serves 1 or 2.*

## APRICOT

### (A, B, AB)

*8 fluid ounces/225 ml yogurt*
*6 ounces/150 g fresh apricots*
*4 fluid ounces/115 ml apricot juice*

Put the ingredients into a blender and blend well. *Serves 1 or 2.*

## BANANA

### (O, B)

*8 fluid ounces/225 ml yogurt*
*1 large, ripe banana*
*4 fluid ounces/115 ml pineapple juice*

Put ingredients into a blender and blend well. *Serves 1 or 2.*

## MINT

### (A, B, AB)

*8 fluid ounces/225 ml yogurt*
*½ handful fresh mint leaves*
*8 fluid ounces/225 ml water*
*½ teaspoon ground, roasted cumin seeds*
*Sprinkle of salt*

Puree all ingredients in a blender. Drink ice cold. *Serves 1.*

## ROSE WATER LASSI

### (A, B, AB)

Types A and AB can use low-fat yogurt.

*8 fluid ounces/225 ml whole milk yogurt*
*2 teaspoons rose water*
*3 tablespoons sugar*

Blend all ingredients. *Serves 1.*

## STRAWBERRY-BANANA SMOOTHIE

### (B)

*8 fluid ounces/225 ml low-fat vanilla yogurt*
*8 fluid ounces/225 ml low-fat milk*
*5 ounces/125 g frozen unsweetened strawberries*
*2 ripe bananas*
*1 teaspoon honey*

Place all ingredients in a blender and mix for about 1 minute. *Make 2 servings.*

## Soy Drinks

## TOFU CAROB PROTEIN DRINK

### (O, A, AB)

*8 ounces/225 g extra-soft tofu*
*1 large can creamed rice*
*¼ teaspoon honey*
*1 tablespoon carob powder*

Blend and chill.

## PINEAPPLE PROTEIN SHAKE

### (A)

*3 ounces/75 g egg substitute*
*6 fluid ounces/160 ml vanilla soy milk*
*6 fluid ounces/160 ml pineapple juice*
*4 ice cubes*

Combine ingredients in blender. Mix on high for 30 seconds.

## SASSY SMOOTHIE

### (O, A)

*8 fluid ounces/225 ml 100% pineapple or black cherry juice*
*3 to 4 tablespoons of 100% almond butter*
*2 medium-sized ripe bananas*
*5 ounces/125 g frozen blueberries or cherries*

Blend all ingredients until smooth and creamy. *Serves 1 or 2.*

## MANGO-LIME SMOOTHIE

### (O, B)

*8 fluid ounces/225 ml soy milk*
*1 ripe mango, peeled, pitted, and cut into chunks*
*4 fluid ounces/115 ml pineapple juice*
*Juice of ½ lime*

Blend all ingredients until smooth and serve very cold. *Serves 1 or 2.*

## PAPAYA-KIWI DRINK

### (O, B, AB)

*8 fluid ounces/225 ml soy milk*
*½ small papaya, peeled, seeded, cut into chunks*
*1 kiwi, peeled, cut into chunks*
*4 fluid ounces/115 ml papaya juice*

Blend all ingredients until smooth and serve very cold. *Serves 1.*

## CHERRY-PEACH SMOOTHIE

### (O, A, B, AB)

*8 fluid ounces/225 ml soy milk*
*3 ounces/75 g pitted black cherries*
*2 ripe peaches, pitted and cut into chunks*
*8 fluid ounces/225 ml cherry juice*

Blend well and serve ice cold. *Serves 2.*

## BANANA-PAPAYA SMOOTHIE

### (O, B)

*8 fluid ounces/225 ml soy milk*
*1 ripe banana*
*½ ripe papaya*
*4 fluid ounces/115 ml pineapple juice*

Blend well and drink well chilled. *Serves 2.*

## DATE-PRUNE SMOOTHIE

### (O, A, B, AB)

*8 fluid ounces/225 ml soy milk*
*4 pitted prunes*
*2 to 3 pitted dates*
*8 fluid ounces/225 ml prune juice*

Blend very well and enjoy ice cold. *Serves 2.*

## GRAPE-PEACH SMOOTHIE

### (O, A, B, AB)

*4 fluid ounces/115 ml soy milk*
*4 fluid ounces/115 ml apple juice*
*1 small peach, pitted*
*Handful of seedless grapes (green or red)*
*½ lime, juiced*

Blend thoroughly. *Serves 1.*

## PINEAPPLE-APRICOT SILKEN SMOOTHIE

### (O, A, AB)

Instead of using soy milk, this recipe calls for the softest tofu: silken.

*5 ounces/125 g fresh pineapple chunks*
*3 ounces/75 g silken tofu*
*4 fluid ounces/115 ml pineapple juice*

*1 fresh apricot*
*4 ice cubes*

Combine all ingredients in a blender and mix for 2 minutes or until smooth. Drink immediately.

## HEIDI'S EARLY MORNING SHAKE

### (O, A, AB)

*8 fluid ounces/225 ml soy milk or carob soy milk or 2 to 3 tablespoons carob powder*
*(if not using carob soy milk)*
*1 teaspoon raw honey*
*1½ frozen bananas or 5 ounces/125 g frozen blueberries*
*1 teaspoon flaxseeds*

In a blender, combine the milk and honey. Add all other ingredients and blend.

## Rice/Almond Milk

## HIGH-ENERGY PROTEIN SHAKE

### (O, A, B, AB)

*8 to 12 fluid ounces/225–300 ml almond milk (rice milk or soy can be used)*
*3 heaped tablespoons rice protein powder (health-food store)*
*½ cut-up banana (or desired fruit)*
*1 tablespoon flaxseed oil (must be kept refrigerated)*
*½ tablespoon honey*
*(Note: For a lower carbohydrate/sugar shake, use half almond milk, half water.)*

Combine all ingredients and blend until smooth.

## CARROT-CUCUMBER-APPLE SMOOTHIE

### (O, A, B)

*4 carrots*
*1 cucumber*
*1 apple*
*4 fluid ounces/115 ml of rice milk*

*Honey to taste*
*2 ice cube trays or use crushed ice*

Cut ends off carrots. Peel the cucumber. Cut the apple, removing the seeds and keeping the skin. Place in a blender with rice milk. Add honey and ice. Blend.

## Fruit and Vegetable Juices

### CARROT-CELERY

**(O, A, B, AB)**

*4 carrots, ends removed*
*2 stalks celery, leaves on*

Combine ingredients in a juicer and juice until smooth.

### CARROT-ROMAINE-BROCCOLI

**(O, A, B, AB)**

*4 carrots*
*2 Romaine leaves, or more*
*1 stalk of broccoli, peeled*

Combine ingredients in a juicer and juice until smooth.

### CARROT-CUCUMBER

**(A, B, AB)**

*4 carrots*
*1 cucumber, peeled if not organic*

Combine ingredients in a juicer and juice until smooth.

## CARROT-APPLE

### (O, A, B, AB)

*4 carrots*
*1 apple, peeled if not organic*

Place ingredients in a juicer and juice until smooth.

## APPLE-GRAPE

### (O, A, B, AB)

*3 apples*
*1 cluster of grapes*

Place ingredients in a juicer and juice until smooth.

## Dressings and Relishes

### TAHINI DRESSING

#### (O, A)

*8 tablespoons tahini*
*1 tablespoon honey*
*1 to 2 tablespoons water (or more as needed)*

Combine well in small bowl and drizzle over fruit.

### TOFU MISO DRESSING

#### (O, A, AB)

*½ cake tofu*
*1 tablespoon miso*
*2 to 3 tablespoons Vegetable Stock (page 354)*
*2 tablespoons sesame seeds*

Place all ingredients in a blender and puree until smooth.

## EGG-FREE MAYONNAISE

### (O, A, B, AB)

Pour into blender:

> *1 ounce/25 g egg substitute*
> *½ teaspoon dry mustard*
> *½ teaspoon salt*
> *1½ tablespoons lemon juice*

Blend on low, and pour in slowly:

> *8 tablespoons cold-pressed, extra virgin olive oil*
> *2 teaspoons very hot water to emulsify the mayonnaise*

Then, pouring in slowly again:

> *8 tablespoons of olive oil*

Follow with:

> *1 teaspoon of very hot water*

This mayonnaise may be stored in the refrigerator for three weeks.

## LEMON-HONEY DRESSING

### (O, A, B, AB)

> *2 lemons, juiced*
> *4 tablespoons olive oil*
> *1 to 2 tablespoons honey*
> *1 to 2 teaspoons tamari sauce*

Put all the ingredients into a jar and shake well.

## SEAWEED DRESSING

### (O, A, B, AB)

> *4 ounces/100 g dulse flakes, wakame, or nori*
> *8 tablespoons olive oil*
> *1 ounce/25 g sesame seeds*

*1 tablespoon sesame oil*
*1 teaspoon rice vinegar*
*1 teaspoon soy sauce*
*4 tablespoons water (approximately)*

Place all ingredients in a blender to mix. Thin with water to desired consistency.

## OLIVE OIL AND LEMON DRESSING

### (O, A, B, AB)

*8 tablespoons extra virgin olive oil*
*2 lemons, juiced*
*½ teaspoon dry mustard*
*½ teaspoon salt*
*¼ teaspoon honey*

Whisk all the ingredients together and serve on any salad.

## SWEET ONION VINAIGRETTE

### (O, A, B, AB)

*½ small sweet onion*
*Juice of 2 lemons*
*1 tablespoon chopped basil*
*1 teaspoon salt*
*½ teaspoon sugar*
*12 fluid ounces/300 ml olive oil*

Grate or finely chop the onion. Add all the other ingredients except the oil and allow to marinate for 1 hour. Drizzle the oil on to the onion-lemon mixture and whisk briskly. When the vinaigrette separates, shake or whisk again.

## BALSAMIC MUSTARD VINAIGRETTE

### (B)

*2 tablespoons honey*
*2 tablespoons Dijon mustard*

*8 tablespoons balsamic vinegar*
*8 fluid ounces/225 ml olive oil*

In the bowl of a food processor, mix the first three ingredients. Slowly drizzle the oil, so it incorporates completely. This can last in the refrigerator indefinitely.

## CUCUMBER YOGURT SAUCE

### (A, AB)

*16 fluid ounces/450 ml plain yogurt*
*½ red onion, diced small*
*1 tablespoon chopped fresh mint*
*1 tablespoon chopped coriander*
*1 small cucumber*
*2 teaspoons ground cumin*
*Squeeze of lemon*

Combine all the ingredients in a blender until smooth.

## FRESH MINT SAUCE

### (O, A, B, AB)

*2 ounces/50 g fresh mint leaves, cleaned and dried*
*1½-inch (3-cm) piece fresh ginger, peeled and cut into quarters*
*1 spring onion*
*3 stalks lemongrass, bottom quarter cut and peeled to the soft layer;*
*reserve tough outer leaves for broth*
*1 tablespoon brown rice vinegar*
*Juice of 1 lime*
*½ teaspoon sugar*
*4 tablespoons olive oil*

In a blender or food processor, puree the first seven ingredients. Slowly drizzle the oil into the bowl of the machine and blend 10 more seconds. Chill and serve.

## GARLIC-SHALLOT MIXTURE

### (O, A, B, AB)

*10 cloves garlic, peeled*
*10 shallots, peeled*
*Olive oil to cover*

In a food processor or blender, finely chop the garlic and shallots by pulsing the blade and scraping down the sides. Put the mixture in an airtight container and cover with oil. This mixture will last refrigerated for 10 days or so.

## CHUTNEY YOGURT MAYONNAISE

### (A)

*8 tablespoons plain yogurt*
*5 tablespoons homemade vegetable or olive oil mayonnaise*
*3 tablespoons mango-ginger or pineapple chutney*
*1 teaspoon ground cumin*

Stir all the ingredients together.

## WALNUT VINAIGRETTE

### (O, A, B, AB)

*8 tablespoons olive oil*
*4 tablespoons walnut oil*
*2 tablespoons fresh lemon juice*
*½ teaspoon dry mustard*
*¼ teaspoon salt*
*1 ounce/25 g broken walnuts*
*2 tablespoons chopped basil*

Combine all the ingredients in a blender and mix for 1 to 2 minutes.

## PESTO

### (O, A, B, AB)

*1 teaspoon coarse salt*
*2 handfuls basil*

*½ handful parsley*
*2 to 3 cloves garlic*
*2 ounces/50 g broken walnuts*
*Olive oil*

Place the salt in a mortar and begin adding basil and parsley leaves while crushing with a pestle. Add some garlic, continuing to work in each new addition. Add broken nuts, more leaves, then garlic, until mixture is well ground but not necessarily smooth. Add the oil slowly, stirring until desired consistency is achieved.

## PLUM BARBECUE SAUCE

### (O, A, B, AB)

*6 ounces/150 g plum jam*
*2 fluid ounces/50 ml pineapple juice*
*3 tablespoons tamari sauce*
*2 cloves garlic, through a press*
*2 spring onions, sliced thin*

Combine all the ingredients and brush lightly over any fish, especially tuna. It also works very well for chicken.

## APPLE ONION CONFIT

### (O, A, B, AB)

*4 ounces/100 g butter (Types O, B) or margarine (Types A, AB)*
*1 very large yellow onion*
*6 apples*

Melt the butter or margarine in a heavy, lidded pot. Peel and halve the onion, slice it very thin, and add to melted butter, turning well. Peel and core the apples; slice into thin wedges and add to pot, incorporating into the onion. Let simmer over very low heat until tender. The apples will "melt" and the onion will be in long, thin pieces. Serve warm or at room temperature.

## RAW ENZYME RELISH

### (A, B, AB)

*1 pound/450 g fresh (cleaned/spun dry) cranberries*
*8 ounces/200 g raw pumpkin seeds*

*1 large Fuji apple (tart/crisp)*
*3 ounces/75 g diced raw pineapple*
*3 ounces/75 g thinly sliced celery*
*4 tablespoons plain yogurt*
*4 tablespoons blackstrap molasses (or maple syrup)*
*2 ounces/50 g raw cane sugar*
*3 tablespoons lemon juice*
*Poppy seeds*
*Allspice*
*Salt*

In a food processor, coarsely chop cranberries and pumpkin seeds. In a large bowl, combine cranberry/seed mixture with Fuji apple, raw pineapple, celery, yogurt, blackstrap molasses, raw cane sugar, and lemon juice. Sprinkle with poppy seeds, allspice, and a pinch of salt.

## For Baby

## Contents

Vegetables
Fruits
Biscuits and Cereals
Rice
Meats

## Vegetables

### VEGETABLE PUREES

#### (O, A, B, AB)

Cut washed vegetables (according to blood type) into small pieces and steam them in a vegetable steamer over 1 or 2 inches (2.5–5 cm) of water in a tightly covered pot. Use this water as a thinner when pureeing vegetables. The approximate ratio of vegetables to liquid is 10 ounces (250 g) of fresh vegetables to between 5 to 8 tablespoons of liquid. Place steamed vegetables and a little of the steaming water in a food processor or baby-food grinder and puree to a soft consistency. To add flavour and protein, try adding an equal amount of baked or steamed potato to the steamed vegetables and puree together. Thin the mixture with infant formula or breast milk to desired consistency. Freeze unused portions immediately.

## PUREED BLACK-EYED PEAS

### (O, A)

Carefully rinse and pick over 6 ounces (150 g) of black-eyed peas. Soak in water overnight or bring to a boil for 2 minutes, cover, and then allow to sit for 2 hours. Drain off the soaking water or the cooking water, then add 1¼ pints (700 ml) fresh water and bring the beans to a boil. Reduce the heat and simmer, covered, until the beans are tender. Skim the surface often as beans are simmering. Puree with 6 fluid ounces (160 ml) soy or breast milk.

## BAKED SWEET POTATOES

### (O, B, AB)

Scrub the sweet potatoes thoroughly and prick several times with a fork. Bake at 180°C/gas 4 until soft and tender. Scoop the meat of the sweet potato out of the skin and mash it with a fork. Cool to warm and serve.

## PUREED GREEN BEANS

### (O, A, B, AB)

*3 ounces/75 g green beans*
*2 tablespoons water or breast milk*

Steam the beans until tender. Add water or breast milk and puree to a smooth texture.

## CRUSTLESS SWEET POTATO AND CARROT PIE

### (B, AB)

*1 sweet potato*
*1 carrot, finely grated*
*4 tablespoons plain yogurt*
*1 egg*

In a microwave oven, cook the sweet potato at 100 percent for 5 minutes, or longer if it is very big. Prick the skin before cooking. Carefully remove the meat of the potato. In a bowl, mix in the carrot and yogurt, then the egg; blend until smooth. If the mixture appears dry, add another tablespoon of yogurt. Cook at 100 percent, uncovered, for 2 minutes. Stir, cook 1½ minutes more. Let rest 2 to 3 minutes. This tastes best if served as soon as it cools. Serve with a dollop of cold yogurt. *Yield: 2 cups.*

## Fruits

### BLUEBERRY BANANA YOGURT

**(B, AB)**

*4 ounces/100 g blueberries*
*1 whole banana*
*8 fluid ounces/225 ml plain yogurt*

Microwave the blueberries just until the juices start to run, about 30 seconds. Place the banana, yogurt, and blueberries in a blender and puree until smooth.

### STRAWBERRIES AND BANANA

**(O)**

Mash ½ a banana and mix with 1 tablespoon of pureed strawberries. Serve immediately.

### STRAWBERRY YOGURT

**(A, B)**

Mix 4 tablespoons of plain whole yogurt with 1 tablespoon pureed strawberries and serve.

### STRAWBERRY-TOFU PARFAIT

**(O, A)**

Puree 3 tablespoons of silken tofu until real smooth and add 1 tablespoon of pureed strawberries. Blend well.

### APPLESAUCE

**(O, A, B, AB)**

Wash, quarter, and core 5 apples just before cooking. Place apple quarters in a steamer basket in a pot filled with a low level of boiling water. Cover the pot tightly and steam the apples for 10 minutes or until they are tender. You may have to add more water. The apples should pierce easily when they're ready. Cool the apples, then strain them in a food mill or food processor. Add 1 tablespoon of the cooking liquid per apple to the puree.

## BABY'S FIRST PEARS

### (O, A, B, AB)

Peel, core, and slice pears thickly. Steam 5 to 10 minutes, until tender. Blend or puree to a smooth consistency. Cool and serve.

## PLUMS

### (O, A, B, AB)

Simmer 2 pounds (900 g) of plums in a covered saucepan with 4 tablespoons of water for 10 minutes, until tender. *Two pounds yields 3 cups.*

## Biscuits and Cereals

## Biscuits

## TEETHING BISCUIT NO. 1

### (O, A, B, AB)

*1 egg*
*2 tablespoons honey*
*¼ teaspoon salt*
*1 tablespoon soy flour*
*4 ounces/100 g spelt flour*
*1 tablespoon breast milk or formula*

Preheat the oven to 180°C/gas 4. Beat the egg in a mixing bowl, add the honey, and mix well. Add the remaining ingredients and mix thoroughly. Roll onto a flour-dusted surface until about 1 inch (2.5 cm) thick and cut into the size you want. (Use cookie cutters, if you prefer.) Place on a greased baking sheet and cook for 7 minutes. Flip over and cook for 4 minutes.

## TEETHING BISCUIT NO. 2

### (B, AB)

*3 ounces/75 g brown rice flour*
*3 ounces/75 g whole barley flour*
*½ teaspoon blackstrap molasses*
*Water for consistency*

Combine the flours and molasses and stir in water until the dough is a pasty consistency. Place approximately ¼-inch-thick (6-mm) rounds on a cookie sheet. Bake at 120°C/gas 1 for 90 minutes.

## Cereals

### BABY CEREAL

### (A, B, AB)

*1 tablespoon rolled oats*
*2 tablespoons organic plain yogurt*
*4 tablespoons breast milk or formula*

Mix together the oats and yogurt. Bring the milk to a boil and pour over the oat-yogurt mix, stirring constantly. Cool to taste and serve.

## Rice

### RICE-VEGETABLE PUREE

### (O, A, B, AB)

*2 tablespoons brown rice*
*4 carrots, chopped into small pieces*
*10 fluid ounces/250 ml water*

Place the rice and carrots in a saucepan with water. Cover and simmer until the water is absorbed—about 30 minutes. Cool to warm temperature and blend in the food processor until smooth.

## RICE WITH MUSHROOMS

### (O, A, B, AB)

*2 tablespoons long-grain rice*
*6 to 8 small mushrooms, cleaned and chopped*
*1 tablespoon breast milk or formula*
*Water*

Place rice, mushrooms, and milk in a pan and cover with water. Bring to a boil and simmer for 15 minutes or until rice is tender. Drain and puree. Add the milk as needed for consistency.

## Meats

### PUREED MEATS

### (O, A, B, AB)

Cut meat (according to blood type) into ½-inch (1-cm) cubes. Trim off all fat. Add 8 fluid ounces (225 ml) of stock (either meat or vegetable) to 8 ounces (225 g) of meat. Simmer until meat is tender—45 minutes to an hour. Drain stock, reserving the liquid. When you puree, use 4 fluid ounces (115 ml) of cooking liquid for each cup of meat. Freeze extra portions immediately.

# Resources and Products

## General

### www.dadamo.com

The World Wide Web has proven to be a valuable venue for exploring and applying the tenets of the blood type diet and lifestyle. Since January 1997, hundreds of thousands have visited the site to participate in the ABO chat groups, to peruse the scientific archives, to share experiences and recipes, and to learn more about the science of blood type.

### Blood Type Specialty Products and Supplements

Stacktheme Ltd is the official European distributor of Blood Type Specialty Products. The product line includes supplements, books, tapes, teas, meal-replacement bars, and support material that make eating and living right for your type easier.

> Stacktheme Ltd
> 59 Bridge Street
> Dollar
> Clackmannanshire
> Scotland FK14 7DQ
> Tel: 01259 743200
> www.stacktheme.dial.pipex.com

## Home Blood Typing Kits

Stacktheme Ltd is the official distributor of Home Blood Type Testing Kits. Each kit is a single-use disposable educational device capable of determining an individual's ABO and rhesus blood type. Results are obtained in about 4 to 5 minutes. If you have several friends or family members who need to learn their blood types, you will need to order a separate home blood typing kit for each individual.

## The Blood Type Library

The following books are available.

*Eat Right 4 Your Type: The Individualized Diet Solution to Staying Healthy, Living Longer, and Achieving Your Ideal Weight*
By Dr. Peter J. D'Adamo, with Catherine Whitney
Century, 1998
    The original blood type diet book.

*Cook Right 4 Your Type: The Practical Kitchen Companion to Eat Right 4 Your Type*
By Dr. Peter J. D'Adamo, with Catherine Whitney
Century, 2001
    Includes more than two hundred original recipes, thirty-day meal plans, and guidelines for each blood type.

*Live Right 4 Your Type: The Individualized Prescription for Maximizing Health, Metabolism, and Vitality in Every Stage of Your Life*
By Dr. Peter J. D'Adamo, with Catherine Whitney
Penguin, 2002

*Eat Right 4 Your Type Complete Blood Type Encyclopedia*
By Dr. Peter J. D'Adamo, with Catherine Whitney
Michael Joseph, 2002
    The A to Z reference guide for the blood type connection to symptoms, diseases, conditions, medications, vitamins, supplements, herbs, and food.

*4 Your Type Pocket Guides: Blood Type, Food, Drink, and Supplement Lists*
By Peter J. D'Adamo, with Catherine Whitney
Penguin, 2003
    The Eat Right 4 Your Type Portable and Personal Blood Type Guides are pocket-sized and user-friendly. They serve as a handy reference tool while shop-

ping, cooking, and eating out. Each book contains the food, beverage, and supplement list for each blood type, plus handy tips and ideas for incorporating the blood type diet into your daily life.

## Babies' Health Problems

Association for Spina Bifida and Hydrocephalus (ASBAH)
42 Park Road
Peterborough PE1 2UQ
01733 555 988
postmaster@asbah.org; www.asbah.org

ASBAH aims to improve services for people with spina bifida and/ or hydrocephalus, to work with them to extend their choices, and maximise opportunities for independence and achievement.

The Down's Syndrome Association
155 Mitcham Road
London SW17 9PG
020 8682 4001
infor@downs-syndrome.org.uk; www.dsa-uk.com

Supports people with Down's Syndrome, their family and carers, as well as providing information for those with a professional interest.

The Fetal Echo Charity
Trafalgar Chambers
Royal Brompton NHS Trust
Sydney Street
London SW3 6NP
echocharity@yahoo.co.uk; www.echocharity.org.uk

A charity that aims to improve the early detection, care and treatment of congenital heart disease, working with parents and health professionals.

## Birth

Active Birth Centre
25 Bickerton Road
London N19 5JT
020 7281 6760
info@activebirthcentre.com; www.activebirthcentre.com
   Offers advice to help you make informed choices regarding your pregnancy, birth and early parenting.

The Birth Centre
34 Elm Quay Court
Nine Elms Lane
London SW8 5DE
020 7498 2322
midwifecf@aol.com; www.birthcentre.com
   Helps you with your choice of childbirth: home birth, birth centre birth, hospital birth, epidural birth, waterbirth, active birth, gentle birth or natural birth.

BirthWorks
58 Shalmsford Street
Chartham
Canterbury
Kent CT4 7RH
General enquiries: 01227 730 081
www.birthworks.co.uk
   Have a good range of products for birthing at home, hospital births, and also Baptismal Pools for churches. Also offer workshops for parents-to-be and study days for midwives.

Home Birth
www.homebirth.org.uk
   A website that provides birth stories, pain-relief options, recommended books and videos, articles, and what to do if your GP opposes home birth.

## Breastfeeding

Association of Breastfeeding Mothers
PO Box 207
Bridgewater
Somerset TA6 7YT
24-hour helpline: 020 7813 1481
abm@clara.net; http://home.clara.net/abm
A charity run by mothers for mothers, offering support and supplying information to all women wishing to breastfeed.

Jane's Breastfeeding and Childbirth Resources
www.breastfeeding.co.uk
A website providing research and advice regarding breastfeeding. Also has links to other useful sites and a helpful Frequently Asked Questions section with good advice on breastfeeding technique and weaning.

La Leche League
PO Box 29
West Bridgford
Nottingham NG2 7NP
24-hour helpline: 020 7242 1278
lllgb@wsds.co.uk; www.laleche.org.uk
Provides breastfeeding information, help and support through a network of trained counsellors.

The National Childbirth Trust
Alexandra House
Oldham Terrace
Acton
London W3 6NH
Enquiry line: 0870 444 8708
Breastfeeding line: 0870 444 8708
www.nctpregnancyandbabycare.com
Offers advice on breastfeeding, as well as on pregnancy, childbirth and early parenthood.

## Complementary Health

British Acupuncture Council
63 Jeddo Road
London W12 9HQ
020 8735 0400
info@acupuncture.org.uk; www.acupuncture.org.uk
    The UK's main regulatory body for the practice of acupuncture. Can provide a nationwide listing of qualified acupuncturists.

British Chiropractic Association
Blagrave House
17 Blagrave Street
Reading
Berkshire RG1 1QB
0118 950 5950
enquiries@chiropractic-uk.co.uk; www.chiropractic-uk.co.uk
    The largest and longest-established association for chiropractors in the UK and can provide a nationwide listing of qualified practitioners.

British Homeopathic Association
15 Clerkenwell Close
London EC1R 0AA
020 7566 7800
info@trusthomeopathy.org; www.trusthomeopathy.org
    Provides free public information about homeopathy and publishes lists of homeopathic doctors and other homeopathic practitioners for the public.

The British Wheel of Yoga
25 Jermyn Street
Sleaford
Lincs NG34 7RU
01529 306 851
office@bwy.org.uk; www.bwy.org.uk
    A registered charity providing information about yoga and classes around the UK.

General Osteopathic Council
Osteopathy House
176 Tower Bridge Road
London SE1 3OU
020 7357 6655
info@osteopathy.org.uk; www.osteopathy.org.uk
Provides useful information on osteopathy, including a section on Frequently Asked Questions, and will help you find a registered osteopath in your area. Also offers information for practitioners.

Institute for Complementary Medicine (ICM)
PO Box 194
London SE16 7QZ
020 7237 5165
icm@icmedicine.co.uk; www.icmedicine.co.uk
A charity providing information on complementary medicine and referrals to qualified practitioners or helpful organisations.

## Crying

CRY-SIS
Helpline: 020 7404 5011
Provides emotional support and practical advice to parents of babies who cry incessantly and have sleep problems. They also offer information about the causes of such behaviour.

## Doulas

Doula UK
PO Box 26678
London N14 4WB
info@doula.org.uk; www.doula.org.uk
A network of doulas run voluntarily by doulas.

Millennia Doulas
82 Lawn Road
London NW3 2XB
020 7586 1028
infor@millenniadoulas.com; www.millenniadoulas.com
Train women from all over the country and also place families with suitable doulas.

## Exercise

The Guild of Postnatal Exercise Teachers
megwalker@pnex.freeserve.co.uk; www.postnatalexercise.co.uk
    Trains teachers and has a list of qualified teachers across the UK.

## Fertility

British Infertility Counselling Association
69 Division Street
Sheffield S1 4GE
01342 843 880
info@bica.net; www.bica.net
    Specialist infertility counsellors who can provide the specific practical info you need.

Foresight (Association for the Promotion of Pre-conceptual Care)
28 The Paddock
Godalming
Surrey GU7 1XD
01483 427 839
www.foresight-preconception.org.uk
    Helps prepare you for pregnancy by optimising nutrition.

The National Infertility Support Group
Charter House
43 St Leonards Rd
Bexhill on Sea
East Sussex TN40 1JA
01424 732 361
office@child.org.uk; www.child.org.uk
    The network has a number of factsheets and also has a stock of recent and helpful books for sale.

## Grief and Loss

The Child Bereavement Trust
Aston House
West Wycombe
High Wycombe
Bucks HP14 3AG
01494 446 648
enquiries@childbereavement.org.uk; www.childbereavement.org.uk
Support offered by professionals to grieving families.

FSID (Foundation for the Study of Infant Deaths)
Artillery House
11–19 Artillery Row
London SW1P 1RT
Helpline: 0870 787 0554
fsid@sids.org.uk; www.sids.org.uk/fsid
Aims to prevent unexpected infant death, promotes baby health and provides support to families whose babies have died suddenly and unexectedly.

Miscarriage Association
c/o: Clayton Hospital
Northgate
Wakefield
West Yorkshire WF1 3JS
Helpline: 01924 200 799
infor@miscarriageassociation.org.uk; www.miscarriageassociation.org.uk
Support for those who have suffered the loss of a baby in pregnancy.

SANDS (Stillbirth and Neonatal Death Society)
28 Portland Place
London W1B 1LY
Helpline: 020 7436 5881
support@uk-sands.org; www.uk-sands.org
Provides support for parents and families whose baby is stillborn or dies soon after birth.

## Immunisation

NHS Immunisation Information
NHS Response line: 08701 555 455 (for leaflets and materials);
or write to:
The Department of Health
PO Box 777
London SE1 6XH
doh@prolog.uk.com; www.immunisation.nhs.uk;
www.mmrthefacts.nhs.uk

This UK government-funded site has extensive information on childhood, pre-school and school immunisations.

Institute of Vaccine Safety
www.vaccinesafety.edu/cc-mmr.htm

A US institute based at Johns Hopkins University that has an informative website with well-presented news, articles and research.

## Midwives

IMA (Independent Midwives Association)
1 The Great Quarry
Guildford
Surrey GU1 3XN
01483 821 104
info@independentmidwives.org.uk; www.independentmidwives.org.uk

Fully qualified midwives who work outside the NHS in a self-employed capacity.

ARM (Association of Radical Midwives)
62 Greetby Hill
Ormskirk
Lancashire L39 2DT
01695 572776
Midwifery Helpline: 01243 671 673
arm@radmid.demon.co.uk; midwifery.org.uk

Primarily a support group for people having difficulty either getting or giving sympathethic midwifery.

BirthChoiceUK

www.birthchoiceuk.com

A website that helps you choose where to have your baby and who to look after you in labour.

## Organic Baby Foods

Baby Organix

Freepost BH1 336

Mill Road

Christchurch

Dorset BH23 2ZZ

Freephone: 0800 393 511

lizzie.vann@organixbrands.com; www.babyorganix.org.uk

A range of organic baby food that avoids the use of chemical pesticides, artificial colourings and flavourings and never adds processed sugars, salt, thickeners, processing aids and unnecessary fillers.

Truuuly Scrumptious

Unit 2, Charmborough Farm

Charleton Road

Holcombe

Radstock

Somerset BA3 5EX

01761 239 300

sales@bathorganicbabyfood.co.uk; www.bathorganicbabyfood.co.uk

Freshly-made meals for babies and toddlers of 4 months and upwards. The entire range is Soil Association Certified and is made from 100 per cent organic ingredients of the finest quality. List of distributors on website.

## Parenting

35-Plus

www.mothers35plus.co.uk

A website for older mothers with information and stories from mothers, and links to other sites.

Baby Centre

www.babycentre.co.uk

A website providing a hands-on guide to pregnancy, birth and babies.

Disability, Pregnancy and Parenthood International (DPPI)
National Centre for Disabled Parents
Unit F9, 89/93 Fonthill Road
London N4 3JH
Freephone: 0800 018 4730
Textphone: 0800 018 9949
info@dppi.org.uk; www.dppi.org.uk
   Promotes better awareness and support for disabled people during
pregnancy and as parents.

Disabled Parents Network
National Centre for Disabled Parents
Unit F9, 89/93 Fonthill Road
London N4 3JH
Helpline: 0870 241 0450
information@DisabledParentsNetwork.org.uk;
www.disabledparentsnetwork.org.uk
   A network for disabled parents offering support in pregnancy, child-
birth and parenting.

Families Online
www.familiesonline.co.uk
   A useful website covering babies, children and children-related
issues like health, schools, childcare, plus topical news items and a
monthly What's On section.

Fathers Direct
www.fathersdirect.com
   A website that aims to promote close relationships between men
and their children from Day One.

Gingerbread
1st floor, 7 Sovereign Close
Sovereign Court
London E1W 3HW
Advice Line: 0800 018 4318
office@gingerbread.org.uk; www.gingerbread.org.uk
   Offers support, advice and friendship to lone parents and lone
parents-to-be.

The National Childbirth Trust
Alexandra House
Oldham Terrace
Acton
London W3 6NH
Enquiry line: 0870 444 8707
Breastfeeding line: 0870 444 8708
www.nctpregnancyandbabycare.com
    Offers support in pregnancy, childbirth and early parenthood.

Natural Parenting UK
www.natural-parenting.com
    A website providing information and resources covering all areas of natural and alternative parenting from pregnancy to education.

Parentline Plus
Helpline: 0808 800 2222
Textphone: 0800 783 6783
www.parentlineplus.org.uk
    A UK-registered charity that offers support to anyone parenting a child.

Realparents.co.uk
www.realparents.co.uk
    A web-based parenting magazine that offers support and advice to all parents and carers.

## Postnatal Depression

Association for Post Natal Illness
145 Dawes Road
Fulham
London SW6 7EB
Helpline: 020 7386 0868
info@apni.org; www.apni.org
    One-to-one support for women suffering from postnatal illness. To receive an information pack send a stamped, self-addressed envelope to the address above.

## Premature Babies

Bliss (Premature Baby Charity)
68 South Lambeth Road
London SW8 1RL
Helpline: 0500 618 140
information@bliss.org.uk; www.bliss.org.uk
Provides advice, support and information for families whose babies need special care or neonatal intensive care.

## Screening and Blood Tests

ARC (Antenatal Results and Choices)
73–75 Charlotte Street
London W1T 4PN
Helpline: 020 7631 0285
arcsatfa@aol.com; ww.arc-uk.org
Self-help charity offering support by parents who have had similiar experiences.

Sickle Cell Society
54 Station Road
Harlesden
London NW10 4UA
020 8961 7795/4006
info@sicklecellsociety.org; www.sicklecellsociety.org
Advice and support line for parents affected by this blood disorder.

UK Thalassaemia Society
19 The Broadway
Southgate Circus
London N14 6PH
020 882 0011
office@ukts.org; www.ukts.org
Advice for parents and families affected by thalassaemia.

## Twins and Multiple Births

MBF (Multiple Births Foundation)
Hammersmith House
Level 4
Queen Charlotte's & Chelsea Hospital
Du Cane Road
London W12 0HS
020 8383 3519
info@multiplebirths.org.uk; www.multiplebirths.org.uk
   Support for families with twins and higher multiple births.

TAMBA (Twins and Multiple Births Association)
2 The Willows
Gardner Road
Guildford
Surrey GU1 4PG
Enquiries: 0870 770 3305
Twinline: 01732 868 000 (Mon–Fri 7pm–11pm, Sat/Sun 10am–11pm)
enquiries@tamba.org.uk; www.tamba.org.uk
   Provides information and mutual support networks for families of
twins, triplets and more.

# Products

Some of the foodstuffs recommended in this book are not widely available, but
you should be able to purchase or order many of them from good health-food
shops. If this proves difficult, the following addresses may be of help.

Allergyfree Direct
(part of Oxford Wholefoods Ltd)
Unit 5, Centre Mead
Osney Mead
Oxford OX2 0ES
Tel: 01865 722003
Fax: 01865 244134
www.allergyfreedirect.co.uk
   Supplies a range of savoury and sweet sprouted wheat breads,
wheatfree rice pastas, soba noodles, quinoa flakes, etc. Delivers across
the UK. Order by internet or by phone.

GoodnessDirect
South March
Daventry
Northants NN1 4PH
Tel: 0871 871 6611
Fax: 01327 301135
www.goodnessdirect.co.uk
    This company supplies a wide range of organic foods, from many reputable producers, and delivers throughout the UK. Products include various flours, rice cakes, crackers, quinoa, miso, gluten-free pastas, breads, noodles, rice, etc. Also provides a search facility for specific products. Order over internet, or phone for a catalogue.

GranoVita UK Ltd
5 Stanton Close
Wellingborough
Northamptonshire NN8 4HN
Tel: 01933 273717
www.granovita.co.uk
    Mail-order supplier of amaranth, bulgar, quinoa and spelt products.

Simply Organic Food Company Ltd
Horsley Road
Kingsthorpe Hollow
Northampton NN2 6LJ
Tel: 01604 791911
www.simplyorganic.net
    Supplies a variety of organic produce including flour, quinoa flakes, seeds, cereals, pasta and bread throughout the UK. Order over internet or by phone.

Sunnyfields Organic
Jacobs Gutter Lane
Totton
Southamptonshire SO40 9FX
Tel: 0238 0871408
Fax: 0238 0871146
www.sunnyfields.co.uk
    A shop with a home delivery service across much of Hampshire and Central London. Stocks a wide variety of products, including amaranth, buckwheat, millet, quinoa, spelt and sprouted seeds.

If you should find that you are unable to locate a supplier of manna bread, the following website provides some very interesting recipes. You will find manna bread listed as essene bread. There are other sprouted seed bread recipes under the name of ezekiel bread.

www.allrecipes.com

INDEX